All This Time

Walking with Love, Compassion, and Grace

Written by

Rene K. Gutierrez

ALL THIS TIME: WALKING WITH LOVE, COMPASSION, AND GRACE
Copyright © 2023 Rene K. Gutierrez.

Authorunit
17130 Van Buren Blvd., Ste. 238,
Riverside, CA 92504
877-826-5888
www.authorunit.com

ISBN 978-1-960075-62-8 (Paperback)
ISBN 978-1-960075-63-5 (Ebook)

Printed in the United States of America

Contents

Introduction

*A*s I begin to embark on this journey that God has entrusted me to do, I have this need to mention a little about myself and how I came to write this book, all for the glory of my Heavenly Father. You see, I am not by far a writer or even a person of many speaking words. I am mostly well comfortable staying at home and doing puzzles, coloring those big coloring posters and coloring books (it's the little child in me that never grew up), and doing word searches (all in my spare time, of course). However, God has this plan for me, and He says that He wants me to do this, and when God speaks, I listen. He told me not to worry about what to write; He will supply all that I need to write. Therefore, I went to my room and got on my knees and prayed, asking for the wisdom and knowledge I needed to fulfill my Father's request. Just as I got on my knees and whispered the words, "Please help me, Jesus," a river of His words came flowing into my brain. I knew that the words were from God, because He spoke them to me, before in a dream. I was, what people say, convicted by His Spirit. I have not been the same or even think the same ever since I opened the door to my Lord and Savior.

This book is about bringing all that I go through in this fallen world, of how I endured it all with the help of Jesus Christ, my Lord and Savior, putting peace and comfort into my mind and soul. This is a lifelong journey that I chose, that leads me straight to the finish line, where my Heavenly Father is waiting with open arms.

I did not go to school for writing, but God told me that I need not be afraid, for Jesus is with me every step of this journey. The Word of God (the

Bible) tells me: *"God chose the foolish things of the world to shame the wise; God chose the weak things of the world to shame the strong". (1Corinthians1:27).* Therefore, I took the step out of the boat (my comfort zone) and told God that I am ready to do whatever He wants me to do. I know that I was stepping onto a rocky path that I was not familiar with, being full of obstacles, along the way. Nevertheless, Jesus was there holding out His hand that I could grab onto, if I felt like slipping. I am never letting go, no matter what I go through. Jesus will always be there to help me handle every kind of situation. Jesus is the friend I never had (when I was growing up). At one time, I thought that I would not have anyone to comfort and protect me or even to be there for me. The friend I have in Jesus is always going to be with me, wherever I go. I need not be afraid. My Heavenly Father will never leave me alone, to walk this journey alone; He loves me too much. This is why He gave His Son to us, because He loves us.

The plan God has for me is to share what I observe with all who need to know the comforting love that Jesus gave me, when I was alone and scared. I know now that I had (and always will have) Jesus right at my side, watching over me and helping me endure all I go through. I never have to feel sad, depressed, or scared. Jesus will never leave me or forsake me. I just have to enjoy all that my God is (and of course), love Him, and obey His commands.

God sees all that is happening in our lives. We just have to take the time and lift our eyes to acknowledge the One who loves and helps us. Loving God and listening to Him, we will be able to walk with the confidence that His Son Jesus possesses. Open your eyes wide and see what God will do in your life. Open your ears and listen to His instructions on what to say and do for Him. God loves us no matter who we are. God made us to love and live in His presence, where we are free to go whenever we need comfort. The Word of God says this: *"Lift your eyes and look to the Heavens: Who created all these? He brings out the starry hosts one by one, and calls them each by name. He gives strength to the weary and increases the power of the weak. Even youths grow tired and weary, and young men stumble and fall; but those who hope in the Lord will renew their strength. They will soar on wings like eagles; they will run and not grow weary, they walk and not faint". (Isaiah 40:26, 29-31).*

"For I know what I have planned for you, says the Lord. I have plans to prosper you, not to harm you. I have plans to give you a future filled with hope"". *(Jeremiah 29:11).*

So just find a quiet place, sit back, and get comfortable, and let God's Words be your strength and comfort to face all those destructive arrows that Satan is flinging at you. As you will see in the pages that follow, God's love and comfort never failed me. God will never fail you. Just remember that you are a child of the One, True God. In your weakness, God is strong. Always!

Read these Scripture verses that describe who God is and why we should love and know God: *"Whoever does not love does not know God, because God is Love". (1 John 4:8).*

"Love is patient, Love is kind. Love does not envy, Love does not boast, Love is not proud. Love does not dishonor others. Love is not self-seeking, Love is not easily angered, and Love keeps no record of wrongs. Love does not delight in evil, but rejoices with the truth. Love always protects, always trusts, always hopes, and always perseveres. Love never fails. And now these three remain: Faith, Hope and Love. But the greatest of these is Love". (1 Corinthians 13:4-8, 13).

Now, replace the word Love with God, and you will know who God is. This world may have many changes, but God will never change. God will always stay the same. Since God is love and God never changes, then the love that God has for us will never change. Nothing can separate us from God's unfailing love. Nothing.

I started writing this book feeling inadequate; I know that this feeling was from Satan who is always trying to turn me away from obeying my Heavenly Father. However, I know that I am doing this for my Lord who died for me so that I could love and live in His presence. Then God said to me, "Do not worry, for I will be with you, teaching you and giving you the words you need to write." Right then, I started preparing myself and writing down all that God was revealing to me.

You will also read in this book how I depend on my Star Team—a team that consists of my Father God, His Son Jesus, and the Holy Spirit. I will go into more detail in how my Star Team accepts me and lets me sit in on their conversation of the problems of this corrupt world that we live in, in addition, all the comfort they supplied to me, when I needed it the most (which was all the time). I pray you enjoy this book, are encouraged to open your Bible, and seek to read further the words of wisdom, knowledge, peace, comfort, and most of all love that only God can supply. God bless you all.

All This Time: Walking with Jesus (Comfort) and Overcoming the Ways of This World

----

As I start recalling my journey back through the times of how I struggled through this world and thinking that I was alone through this walk, I realized that I was not alone all this time. The times that I felt weak—God gave me strength. God would provide just enough for that moment, enough to walk through the pain that was making me weak. I know now that Jesus was with me all this time, placing me on His shoulders and walking me through the pain and keeping me from getting hurt. I owe Him my life. This is why I am here, going through my memory bank, to fulfill my Heavenly Father's request to write down how His Son Jesus and I overcame the struggles of this world's ways. Jesus is still walking by my side. As Jesus says in the Bible:

*"**Never will I leave you, nor will I forsake you**". (Hebrews13:5b).*

A Touch of Comfort: My heart filled with love and comfort at that first touch of my Lord.

It all started when I was five years old—the first time that fear entered my life. It was when I was watching my mom in the kitchen cooking, and I was coloring in my coloring book—at the kitchen table, as I always did. I always sat there when my mom was in the kitchen cooking. When my mom asked me to get a kitchen towel from our dog, Spot, who grabbed it and went under the table where I was sitting, I went under the table to try to get the towel. When I was about to take away the towel, Spot snapped at me, sending me running and jumping onto the couch. Mind you, when I jumped on the couch, I mean all the way on top of the back of the couch. My mom heard me crying and jumping on the couch and told me to get down and sit right on the couch. I was shaking so bad I could not get any words out to tell my mom what was wrong. I just sat there on the couch shaking, not knowing what to do. When I felt a sudden touch of comfort and assurance come over me, I somehow knew (even though I was only five) that it was God putting His gentle arms around me and giving me the love and comfort that He so readily gives to His children in need. This comfort was just what I needed. I should have gotten it from my mom, but she was distracted with cooking supper for the rest of the family. When I did not get comfort from her, I got it from my Lord. From that moment on, I was afraid of all kinds of dogs, even really, really, small ones—for a long time.

Going through this trial of fear, I always wondered what I needed to learn from it. I kept asking God, but He kept telling me to be patient and wait and watch Him work the things out that gets me so anxious. That is what I did—I put my trust in my Heavenly Father to work out all that was making me anxious.

This also was the beginning of a long battle I had with Satan—who was starting a process to separate me from my family, emotionally and physically.

Witnessing can be confusing, but with Jesus at my side, nothing is impossible. It is written:

*"**With man this is impossible, but with God, all things are possible**"*. *(Matthew 19:26).*

Reliving this childhood fear, I realized that the moment my heart cries out for help, Jesus hears it and comes to lift me up into His arms and comforts you until my hurt subsides. I also realized that this was when Jesus started knocking at my heart's door. In addition, when I finally opened the door of my heart to Him, He took total control of my life. Ten years later, I now know that I (we) are to live out and obey God's every word—just like Jesus did when He was walking this earth. Scripture says: *"To this you were called, because Christ suffered for you, leaving you an example that you should follow in His steps". (1 Peter 2:21).*

"Therefore, be imitators of God, as beloved children; and walk in love, just as Christ also loved you and gave Himself up for us, and offering a sacrifice to God

as a fragrant aroma". (Ephesians 5:1-2).

"If anyone obeys His word, love for God is truly made complete in them. This is how we know we are in Him: Whoever claims to live in Him must live as Jesus did" (1 John 2:5-6).

"Dear brothers and sisters, let us not love with words or speech but with actions and in Truth. This is how we know that we belong to the Truth and how we set our hearts at rest in His Presence". (1 John 3:18-19).

As God teaches me His Word, I am confident knowing that Jesus is also walking by my side, making sure that I walk in the way of His Father's, giving me that sense of security that surpasses all fear, so I could move forward and live that life that He desires of me to live. In my youth, I did not know I had Jesus always with me, walking right beside me, helping me cope with the trails I endured. You see, I had no one to go to, talk over all that I was feeling and experiencing. However, Jesus was always there, picking me up when I was feeling down, speaking to me when there was no one to talk to. Jesus was and is all that I have to hold on to. He entered my life and opened my eyes to His love and compassion. All the events that happen here on this earth are just shadows against the Light of Jesus.

After fifty years, God is having me write down all I have learned (and still learning) of how Jesus was with me all this time. Thinking back then, I never thought I would be writing a book. However, when God tells you to do something, you obey Him and trust Him all the way through the assignment. For Jesus is—and always will be—the one to talk to and walk with always.

Here are some Scriptures that help me dissolve my fears:

"*Have I not commanded you? Be strong and courageous. Do not be frightened, and do not be dismayed, for the Lord your God is with you wherever you go'".* (Joshua 1:9).

"Even though I walk through the valley of the shadow of death, I will fear no evil, for you are with me; your rod and your staff, they comfort me". (Psalm 23:4).

"The Lord is my light and my salvation; whom shall I fear? The Lord is the stronghold of my life; of whom shall I be afraid?—Wait for the Lord; be strong, and let your heart take courage; wait for the Lord!". (Psalm 27:1, 14).

"When I am afraid, I put my trust in You". (Psalm 56:3). "He who dwells in the shelter of the Most High will abide in the shadow of the Almighty". (Psalm 91:1). "He is not afraid of bad news; his heart is firm, trusting in the Lord". (Psalms 112:7).

"The fear of man lays a snare, but whoever trusts in the Lord is safe". (Proverbs 26:25).

"Fear not for I am with you; be not dismayed, for I am your God; I will strengthen you, I will help you, I will uphold you with my righteous right hand". *(Isaiah 41:10).*

"For I, the Lord your God, hold your right hand; it is I who says to you, 'Fear not, I am the one who helps you'. *(Isaiah 41:13).*

"But now thus says the Lord, He who created you, O Jacob, He who formed you, O Israel: ***'Fear not, for I have called you by name, you are mine. When you pass through the waters, I will be with you; and through the rivers they shall not overwhelm you; when you walk through the fire you shall not be burned, and the flame shall not consume you'"*** *(Isaiah 43:1-2).*

"For God gave us a spirit not of fear but of power and love and self-control". (2 Timothy 1:7).

"There is no fear in love, but perfect love casts out fear. For fear has to do with punishment, and whoever fears has not been perfected in love". (1 John 4:18).

"'Do not fear what you are about to suffer. Behold, the devil is about to throw some of you into prison, that you may be tested, and for ten days you will have tribulation. Be faithful unto death, and I will give you the Crown of Life'". *(Revelation 2:10).*

As I read these verses they dissolve any fears I may be having and send them flying away; bringing strength and wisdom to my soul. Sometimes I sit in silence and listen to God's Voice speaking to me. His Words are so comforting. Being silent before Him is the only way that you can hear God speaking to you—In the quiet of His presence—listening only to His gentle voice. I trusted that silence many times in my youth—I did not have anyone to sit and listen and learn from. And still today, I go straight to my Bible when I start feeling that I need someone to talk to—the Voice of Truth—who is my companion. Just hold on to these Scriptures and you too will have the strength of God. God never changes and neither does His promises.

The Strength of God

Here are some to start you off:

"He gives strength to the weary and increases the power of the weak. Even youths grow tired and weary, and young men stumble and fall; but those who hope in the Lord will renew their strength. They will renew their strength. They will soar on wings like eagles; they will run and not grow weary, they will walk and not be faint". (Isaiah 40:29-31).

"I can do everything through Him who gives me strength". (Philippians 4:13).

"My soul is weary with sorrow; strengthen me according to your word". (Psalm 119:28).

"Serve wholeheartedly, as if you were serving the Lord, not people, because you know that the Lord will reward each one for whatever good they do, whether they are slave or free". (Ephesians 6:7-8).

"Be strong in the Lord and in His mighty power. Put on the full armor of God so that you can take your stand against the devil's schemes". (Ephesians 6:10-11).

"Stand firm then, with the belt of truth buckled around your waist; with the breastplate of righteousness in place and with your feet fitted with the readiness that comes from the gospel of peace. In addition to all this, take up the shield of faith, with which you can extinguish all the flaming arrows of the evil one. Take the helmet of salvation and the sword of the Spirit, which is the word of God. In addition, pray in the Spirit on all occasions with all kinds of prayers and requests. With this in mind, be alert and always keep on praying for all the saints". (Ephesians 6:14-18).

*"Therefore, in order to keep me from becoming conceited, I was given a thorn in my flesh, a messenger of Satan, to torment me. Three times, I pleaded with the Lord to take it away from me. However, He said to me; **'My grace is sufficient for you, for My power is made perfect in weakness'**. Therefore,*

I will boast all the more gladly about my weaknesses, so that Christ's power may rest on me. That is why, for Christ's sake, I delight in weaknesses, in insults, in hardships, in persecutions, in difficulties. For when I am weak, then I am strong". (2 Corinthians 12:7b).

"God is our refuge and strength, an ever-present help in trouble. Therefore, we will not fear, though the earth gives way and the mountains fall into the heart of the sea, though the waters roar and foam and the mountains quake with their surging. Selah". (Psalm 46:1-3).

"Be still and know I am God. I will be exalted among the nations. I will be exalted in the earth'". *(Psalm 46:10).*

"You, O Lord, be not far off, O my strength, come quickly to help me. Deliver my life from the sword, my precious life, from the power of the dogs. Rescue me from the mouth of the lions; save me from the horns of the wild oxen. I will declare your name to my brothers; in the congregation I will praise you". (Psalm 22:19-22).

"The Lord is my strength and my shield; my heart trusts in Him, and I am helped. My heart leaps for joy and I will give thanks to Him in song. The Lord is the strength of His people, a fortress of salvation for His anointed one". (Psalm 28:7-8).

"I was pushed back and about to fall, but the Lord helped me. The Lord is my strength and my song; He has become my salvation". (Psalm 118:13-14).

"Surely God is my salvation; I will trust and not be afraid. The Lord, the Lord Himself, is my strength and my defense; He has become my salvation". (Isaiah 12:2).

"O Lord, be gracious to us; we long for you. Be our strength every morning, our salvation in time of distress". (Isaiah 33:2).

"The Sovereign Lord is my strength; He makes my feet like the feet of a deer, He enables me to go on the heights. For the director of music. On my stringed instruments". (Habakkuk 3:19).

"I pray that out of His glorious riches He may strengthen you with power through His Spirit in your inner being so that Christ may dwell in your hearts

through faith. And I pray that you, being rooted and established in love, may have power, together with all the saints, to grasp how wide and long and high and deep is the love of Christ, and to know this love that surpasses knowledge— that you may be filled to the measure of all the fullness of God". (Ephesians 3:16-19).

These Scriptures of God's strength are an assurance of His presence in my life and yours. No matter what I am going through, I could always count on Him to be right by my side, giving me the strength that I would need in every situation I am to endure. Always having awareness of God—His strength and His works—is what brings peace into your life no matter what is going on around you. Acknowledge always that Jesus is right beside you, helping you in every step. Do not let unexpected events throw you off course. Remember always to respond calmly and confidently and always remember that Jesus is with you, every step of the way. For Jesus has overcome all that you are going through, and He knows just how to make the arrows of Satan never touch you, sending them right back to him and not hurting you. Doing this is the way to stay on the path of peace.

Here are some verses from the Bible that calm you and assure you of His Presence:

"Lord, you will establish peace for us—for You have also done all our work for us". (Isaiah 26:12).

"You will keep him in perfect peace—whose mind stays on You—because he trusts in You". (Isaiah 26:3).

"And let the peace of God rule in your hearts, to which also you were called in one body; and be thankful". (Colossians 3:15). "I will both lie down in peace and sleep, for you alone, O Lord, make me dwell in safety". (Psalm 4:8).

"The Lord will give strength to His people. The Lord will bless His people with peace". (Psalm 29:11).

"Peace I leave with you—My peace I give to you; not as the world gives—do I give to you. Let not your heart be troubled, neither let it be afraid"'. (John 14:27).

"He will have no fear of bad news; his heart is steadfast, trusting in the Lord". (Psalm 112:7).

And the Lord says: *"**So, do not fear, for I am with you; do not be dismayed—for I am your God. I will strengthen you and help you. I will uphold you with My righteous right hand. All who rage against you will surely be ashamed and disgraced. Those who oppose you will be nothing and perish'". (Isaiah 41:10-11).***

Trusting God Always in Everything

----

*T*rusting Jesus is a moment-by-moment choice and a day-by-day choice. Worrying about what tomorrow brings will only bring you pain and heartache and get you stuck dwelling in the past. When you are stuck in the past, you begin to grumble. Grumbling (complaining) takes you outside of God's presence, for He does not like grumbling. Grumbling shows God that you do not trust in Him. When things go wrong (and they will) and you start complaining how things are going wrong, it will slow down the response time of what God is working on in your situation, making you rebel and turn away from Him and right onto the path of destruction and darkness—where Satan is waiting. The next time you want to complain, pick up your Bible and listen to what God is speaking to you (through His Word) of the situation. Stay on the path of life with Jesus (who is the way to life) and dwell in His presence of love, trust, and hope—instead of dwelling in your past and circumstances. Nothing is more calming than the presence of God. In Him, you will find the peace that calms the storm.

Here is what God's Word says:

"Lord, save us! Lord, grant us success! Blessed is he who comes in the name of the Lord. From the house of the Lord, we bless you. The Lord is God, and He has made His light shine on us. With boughs in hand, join in the festival procession up to the horns of the altar. You are my God, and I will praise you; you are my God, and I will exalt you. Give thanks to the Lord, for He is good; His love endures forever". (Psalm 118:25-29).

"In you, Lord, I have taken refuge; let me never be put to shame; deliver me in your righteousness. Turn your ear to me, come quickly to my rescue; be my rock of refuge, a strong fortress to save me. Since you are my rock and my fortress, for the sake of your name lead and guide me. Keep me free from the trap that

is set for me, for you are my refuge. Into your hands I commit my spirit; deliver me, Lord, my faithful God". (Psalm 31:1-5).

"Be merciful to me, Lord, for I am in distress; my eyes grow weak with sorrow, my soul and body with grief. My life is consumed by groaning; my strength fails because of my affliction, and my bones grow weak" (Psalm 31:9-10).

"But I trust in You, Lord; I say, 'You are my God'. My times are in your hands; deliver me from the hands of my enemies, from those who pursue me. Let your face shine on your servant; save me in your unfailing love. Let me not be put to shame, Lord, for I have cried out to you; but let the wicked be put to shame and be silent in the realm of the dead. Let their lying lips be silenced, for with pride and contempt they speak arrogantly against the righteous. How abundant are the good things that you have stored up for those who fear you that you bestow in the sight of all, on those who take refuge in you. In the shelter of your presence you hide them from all human intrigues; you keep them safe in your dwelling from accusing tongues". (Psalm 31:14-20).

Thankfulness in the Quiet times

----

*B*eing thankful in the quiet times that God gives you is the most important thing you can ever do. For in those quiet times, you can spend quality time seeking to get to know God better. This quietness speaks volume to your heart and opens your eyes to see exactly who God is in your life and what He is doing in your life. Moreover, the quietness guides you to where God wants you to be and who God wants you to be. You are richly blessed when you trustingly walk with Jesus through your daily life. The Bible explains it best: *"Whatever you do, work at it with all your heart, as working for the Lord, not for human masters, since you know that you will receive an inheritance from the Lord as a reward (It is the Lord Christ you are serving). Anyone who does wrong will be repaid for their wrongs, and there is no favoritism". (Colossians 3:23-25).* The Lord tells us: *"**Remain in Me, as I also remain in you. No branch can bear fruit by itself; it must remain in the vine. Neither can you bear fruit unless you remain in Me. I am the vine; you are the branches. If you remain in Me and I in you, you will bear much fruit; apart from Me, you can do nothing. If you do not remain in Me, you are like a branch that is thrown away and withers; such branches are picked up, thrown into the fire and burned. If you remain in Me and My words remain in you, ask whatever you wish, and it will be done for you. This is to My Father's glory, that you bear much fruit, showing yourselves to be My disciples. As the Father has loved Me, so have I loved you. Now remain in My love. If you keep My commands, you will remain in My love, just as I have kept My Father's Commands and remain in His love'".* (John 15:4-10).*

God is calling us to come to Him, to trust in Him, to obey Him, and be in awe of Him. Also, to take refuge in the shelter of His wings, just like a baby bird does in his mother's wings. This world can be very scary, but we need not be afraid—Jesus overcame this world. God's shelter is so secure that anything in this world cannot break-in and shake us from its foundation of love, hope, peace, and comfort. Just read these verses from God's Word: *"On that day you will say: 'I will praise you, Lord. Although you were angry with me, your anger has turned away and you have comforted me. Surely, God is my salvation; I will trust and not be afraid. The Lord—the Lord Himself—is my strength and my defense; He has become my salvation. With joy you will draw water from the wells of Salvation'"*. (Isaiah 12:1-3).

"Hear my cry, O God; listen to my prayer. From the ends of the earth I call to you, I call, as my heart grows faint; lead me to the rock that is higher than I. for you have been my refuge, a strong tower against the foe. I long to dwell in your tent forever and take refuge in the shelter of your wings. For you, God, have heard my vows; you have given me the heritage of those who fear your name". (Psalm 61:2-5). *"Therefore, since we have such a hope, we are very bold. We are not like Moses, who would put a veil over his face to prevent the Israelites from seeing the end of what was passing away. However, their minds were made dull, for to this day the same veil remains when the old covenant is read. It has not been removed, because only in Christ is it taken away. Even to this day when Moses is read, a veil covers their hearts. However, whenever anyone turns to the Lord, the veil is taken away. Now the Lord is the Spirit, and where the Spirit of the Lord is, there is freedom. And we all, who with unveiled faces contemplate the Lord's glory, are being transformed into His image with ever-increasing glory, which comes from the Lord, who is the Spirit"* (2 Corinthians 3:12-18).

Living by faith and not by sight leads you through the darkness of this world. Instead of complaining about the wrongs of this world, just bring the wrongs to God (in prayer) and trust Him that He will work His solutions to the wrongs and let glory shine. Just the fact that you acknowledge God in your circumstances is enough to start His work in your life.

Here is what the Bible says: *"I saw the Lord, high and exalted, seated on a throne; and the train of His robe filled the temple. Above Him were seraphim, each with six wings: With two wings, they covered their faces, with two, they covered their feet, and with two, they were flying. And they were calling to one another: 'Holy, holy, holy is the Lord Almighty; the whole earth is full of His glory.' At the sound of their voices, the doorposts and thresholds shook and the temple was filled with smoke. 'Woe to me!' I cried. 'I am ruined! For I am a man of unclean lips, and I live among a people of unclean lips, and my eyes have seen the King, the Lord Almighty.' Then one of the Seraphim flew to me with a live coal in his hand, which he had taken with tongs from the altar. With it he touched my mouth and said, 'See, this has touched your lips; your guilt is taken away and your sin atoned for'. Then I heard the voice of the Lord saying, 'Whom shall I send? And who will go for us?' and I said, 'Here am I. Send me!'". (Isaiah 6:1-8).*

"Acknowledge those who work hard among you, who care for you in the Lord and who admonish you. Hold them in the highest regard in love because of their work. Live in peace with each other. And we urge you, brothers and sisters, warn those who are idle and disruptive, encourage the disheartened, help the weak, and be patient with everyone. Make sure that nobody pays back wrong for wrong, but always strive to do what is good for each other and for everyone else. Rejoice always, pray continually; give thanks in all circumstances, for this is God's will for you in Christ Jesus. Do not quench the Spirit; hold on to what is good, reject every kind of evil. May God, Himself, the God of peace; sanctify you through and through. May your whole spirit, soul and body be kept blameless at the coming of our Lord Jesus Christ—The One who calls you, is Faithful; and He will do it". (1 Thessalonians 5:12-19, 21b-24).

"For we live by faith, not by sight. We are confident, I say, and would prefer to be away from the body and at home with the Lord. Therefore, we make it our goal to please Him, whether we are at home in the body or away from it. For we must all appear before the judgment seat of Christ, so that each of us may receive what is due us for the things done while in the body, whether good or bad". (2 Corinthians 5:7-10).

The Meaning of the Power of Prayer

----

*T*he power of prayer is in God's reaction—in His responses to the petitions of the righteous, releasing His healing power toward the object of concern. A prayer-less person is a powerless person. God's power is released when we pray with a strong desire for God to intercede, filled with faith, hope, and love. This will crush every barrier that Satan erects, stopping him from hurting you. This will happen through your relationship with Jesus giving you the opportunity to speak to His Father, one on one—in His glorious presence. When you are in prayer, you can talk to Him about all that is on your mind and what you see is wrong in this world. Praying made me understand all that God was doing in my life.

Here is how I overcame anxiety (nervousness), discouragement, and loneliness. All with the help of my Lord and Savior Jesus Christ. There is no place that I could have gone to get the help that I got from my Lord Jesus Christ. There is no person on this earth that will comfort me like my Lord Jesus Christ.

Anxiety

What is anxiety? It is a fear or nervousness about what might happen and a feeling of wanting to do something very much. Throughout my life, I have endured many times of nervousness. Many times, I did not have anyone to tell me how to ease (comfort) my nervousness until I found my Lord Jesus and He walked me through it.

All through the Bible, you can find help with dealing with your anxiety (nervousness) and worry. I am continually in my Bible seeking ways to deal and avoid my nervousness from my life. This part of my journey is never ending. I spend a lot of time reading my Bible, and what I found out is that when I worry or I'm nervous, it prevents the word of God to take root in my life, and worry also can make you sin, if you are not aware of the signs of anxiety that creep in oh so sneakily. Because when you are anxious, you tend not to think of the consequences of rushing in before the appropriate time.

These Scriptures from the Bible (God's Word) that really helped me with easing my mind:

"Since then, you have been raised with Christ, set your hearts on things above, where Christ is, seated at the right hand of God. Set your minds on things above, not on earthly things. For your death, and your life is now hidden with Christ in God. When Christ, who is your life, appears, then you also will appear with Him in glory". (Colossians 3:1-4).

"Moses told the people 'Don't be afraid. Stand firm and you will see the deliverance the Lord will bring you today'". (Exodus 14:13a).

"The Lord will fight for you; you need only to be still". (Exodus 14:14).

"Rejoice in the Lord always. I will say it again: Rejoice! Let your gentleness be evident to all. The Lord is near. Do not be anxious about anything, but in every situation, by prayer and petition, with thanksgiving, present your requests to God. In addition, the peace of God, which transcends all understanding, will guard your hearts and your minds in Christ Jesus. Finally, brothers and sisters, whatever is true, whatever is noble, whatever is right, whatever is pure, whatever is lovely, whatever is admirable—if anything is excellent or praiseworthy—think about such things. Whatever you have learned or received or heard from me, or seen in me—put it into practice. And the God of peace will be with you". (Philippians 4:4-8).

"Truly my soul finds rest in God; my salvation comes from Him. Truly He is my rock and my salvation; He is my fortress, I will never be shaken". (Psalm 62:1-2).

"Yes, my soul, find rest in God; my hope comes from Him. Truly, He is my rock and my salvation; He is my fortress; I will not be shaken. My salvation and my honor depend on God; He is my mighty rock, my refuge. Trust in Him at all times, you people; pour out your hearts to

Him, for God is our refuge" (Psalm 62:5-8). "Therefore, I tell you, do not worry about your life, what you will eat or drink; or about your body, what you will wear. Is not life more than food and the body more than clothes?" (Matthew 6:25).

"Can any one of you by worrying add a single hour to your life?". (Matthew 6:27).

"Humble yourselves, therefore, under God's mighty hand, that He may lift you up in due time. Cast all your anxiety on Him because He cares for you. Be alert and of a sober mind. Your enemy, the devil prowls around like a roaring lion looking for someone to devour. Resist him, standing firm in the faith, because you know that the family of believers throughout the world is undergoing the same kind of suffering. And the God of all grace, who called you to His eternal glory in Christ, after you have suffered a little while, will Himself restore you and make you strong, firm and steadfast. To Him be the power forever and ever. Amen". (1 Peter 5:6-11).

"Set your minds on things above, not on earthly things. For you died, and your life is now hidden with Christ in God. When Christ, who is your life, appears, then you also will appear with Him in glory". (Colossians 3:2-4).

"As for me, I call to God, and the Lord saves me. Evening, morning and noon I cry out in distress, and He hears my voice. He rescues me unharmed from the battle waged against me, even though many oppose me. God, who is enthroned from of old, who does not change—He will hear them and humble them, because they have no fear of God". (Psalm 55:16-19).

I learned from these Scriptures to worry less, to remember to trust in God's promises more and place all my worries on Jesus's shoulders and let Him carry me right through the worries. I sure was encouraged, strengthened, and assured that it was Jesus that was comforting me on that couch (when I was shaking with fear). In addition, Jesus protected me from my classmates' mean insults. And Jesus was the one that kept me from hitting my head on that huge boulder that was inches away when I fell with my bike. Having Jesus by my side is the only way for me to live a life of peace (which is in God's presence and His Word). There is no other place I would rather be than in the presence of my Heavenly Father and His Son Jesus Christ.

Discouragement

What is discouragement? It is the act of making something less likely to happen or making people less likely to do something. Discouragement entered my life in second grade when my teachers and classmates were saying that something must be wrong with me and even proclaiming that I may be "retarded," feeding the fire for my classmates to start making insults (bullying) about me, names that I cannot even repeat. The names were so degrading and hurtful that when I recall those times, I feel the hurt all over again. They insulted me all because I talked funny (when I did talk) and did not raise my hand to ask or answer any questions in class. No one wanted to have anything to do with me or even be around me. This continued all through my school years and beyond, leaving me feeling alone. My family seemed to be too busy for me, but somehow I felt that I was being comforted; just like when I was five. I know now, that I am (and always will be) carried and comforted by my Lord Jesus. He is always by my side ready to comfort and lift me up onto His shoulders and carry me through the hurts of this world. Therefore, when bouts of discouragement come my way, I go straight to the Bible for the comfort, encouragement, strength, and love I so need to walk this journey. Here then are some of the Scripture verses that my Heavenly Father has revealed to me—all in order for me to hold on to—resulting in giving me courage to face the trials and temptations of this world:

"These things I have spoken to you, so that in Me you may have peace. In the world you will have tribulation, but take courage; I have overcome the world". (John 16:33). "No one will be able to stand against you all the days of your life. As I was with Moses, so I will be with you, I will never leave you nor forsake you. Be strong and courageous, because you will lead these people to inherit the land I swore to their ancestors to give them. Be strong and very courageous! Be careful to obey all my servant Moses gave you; do not turn from it to the right or to the left, that you may be successful wherever you go. Keep this Book of the Law always on your lips; meditate on it day and night, so that you may be careful to do everything written in it. Then you will be prosperous and successful.

Have I not commanded? Be strong and courageous. Do not be afraid; do not be discouraged, for the Lord your God will be with you wherever you go'" (Joshua 1:5-9). *"Therefore let us draw near with confidence to the throne of grace, so that we receive mercy and find grace to help in time of need".* (Hebrews 4:16). *"Peace I leave with you; my peace I give to you; not as the world gives do I give to you. Do not let your heart be troubled, nor let it be fearful'"* (John 14:27).

"I write these things to you who believe in the name of the Son of God so that you may know that you have Eternal Life. This is the confidence we have in approaching God; that if we ask anything according to His will, he hears us. And if we know that He hears us—whatever we ask—we know that we have what we asked of Him" (1 John 5:14).

"Wait for the Lord; be strong and take heart and wait for the Lord". (Psalm 27:14).

"Arise, for it is your task, and we are with you; be strong and do it". (Ezra 10:4).

Loneliness

What is loneliness? Loneliness causes sad feelings that come from being apart from other people. The many times I felt lonely, I filled those lonely times with finding ways to occupy my mind.

I took a walk to the park; watching the ducks swim on the pond. These ducks got so used to me coming and watching them they became my company in my lonely times (when no one seemed to want my company). On rainy days when I couldn't go to the park, I would color in my coloring books/velvet posters and do word searches. I did things that I could do by myself. Somehow, when I did all this stuff, I felt I was not alone. I knew it was my Lord Jesus who was with me. He has been my friend all those "lonely" times. These Scriptures are not only about loneliness; they are the comfort that never fails to comfort:

"Do not let your hearts be troubled'" (John 14:1a). *"I will not leave you as orphans; I will come to you'"* (John 14:18).

"On that day you will realize that I am in My Father, and you are in

Me, and I am in you. Whoever has My commands and keeps them is the one who loves Me. The one who loves Me will be loved by My Father, and I too will love them and show Myself to them" (John 14:20-21).

"Be strong and courageous. Do not be afraid or terrified because of them, for it is the Lord your God who goes with you. He will not leave you nor forsake you" (Deuteronomy 31:6).

"The Lord Himself goes before you and will be with you; He will never leave you nor forsake you. Do not be afraid; do not be discouraged". (Deuteronomy 31:8).

"Turn to me and be gracious to me, for I am lonely and afflicted. The troubles of my heart are enlarged; bring me out of my distress". (Psalm 25:16-17).

"For my father and my mother have forsaken me, the Lord will receive me. Teach me your way, Lord; lead me in a straight path because of my oppressors" (Psalm 27:10-11).

"I remain confident of this: I will see the goodness of the Lord in the land of the living. Wait for the Lord; be strong and take heart and wait for the Lord" (Psalm 27:13-14).

"God is our refuge and strength, an ever-present help in trouble. Therefore, we will not fear, though the earth gives way and the mountains fall into the heart of the sea, though its waters roar and foam and the mountains quake with their surging" (Psalm 46:1-3).

"So do not fear, for I am with you; do not be dismayed, for I am your God; I will strengthen you and help you; I will uphold you with My righteous right hand" (Isaiah 41:10).

"Have I not commanded you? Be strong and courageous. Do not be afraid; do not be discouraged, for the Lord your God will be with you wherever you go" (Joshua 1:9).

"For the sake of His great name the Lord will not reject His people, because the Lord was pleased to make you His own" (1 Samuel 12:22). *"Can a mother forget the baby at her breast and have no compassion for the child she has borne? Though she may forget, I will not forget you!".* (Isaiah 49:15).

"The Lord is my Light and my Salvation—whom shall I fear? The Lord is the stronghold of my life—of whom shall I be afraid?" (Psalm 27:1).

"Teach me your way, Lord; lead me in a straight path, because of my oppressors" (Psalm 27:11).

*"**When you pass through the waters, I will be with you; and when you pass through the rivers, they will not sweep over you. When you walk through the fire, you will not be burned; the flames will not set you ablaze. For I am the Lord your God, the Holy One of Israel, your Savior**". (Isaiah 43:2, 3a).*

"Who shall separate us from the love of Christ? Shall trouble or hardship or persecution or famine or nakedness or danger or sword? As it is written: 'For your sake we face death all day long; we are considered as sheep to be slaughtered.' No, in all these things we are more than conquerors through Him who loved us. For I am convinced that neither death nor life, neither angels nor demons, neither the present nor the future, nor any powers, neither height nor depth, nor anything else in all creation, will be able to separate us from the love of God that is in Christ Jesus our Lord" (Romans 8:35-38). "Surely the arm of the Lord is not too short to save, nor His ear too dull to hear" (Isaiah 59:1).

*"Keep your lives free from the love of money and be content with what you have, because God has said; '**Never will I leave you; never will I forsake you**'. So we say with confidence; 'The Lord is my helper; I will not be afraid. What can mere mortals do to me?'". (Hebrews 13:5-6).*

"One who has unreliable friends soon comes to ruin, but there is a friend who sticks closer than a brother". (Proverbs 18:24).

"He [the Lord] heals the brokenhearted and binds up their wounds". (Psalm 147:3).

"'I will cleanse them from all the sin they have committed against Me and will forgive all their sins of rebellion against Me'". (Jeremiah 33:8).

From these Scriptures, we learn that our Lord Jesus knows what it is like to be deserted and lonely. We can also learn that with every act of faithfulness, it is a comfort to God's heart. Remember, learn, and understand: That it is not until man has failed, that he learns true humility. Only the humble can inherit the earth. As the Bible says: *"**Blessed are the meek, for they will inherit the earth**". (Matthew 5:5). "The meek will inherit the land and enjoy peace and prosperity". (Psalm 37:11). "God gives us more Grace. That is why the*

Scriptures say: 'God opposes the proud, but shows favor to the humble'. Submit yourselves, then, to God. Resist the devil, and he will flee from you. Come near to God and He will come near to you. Wash your hands, you sinners, and purify your hearts, you double-minded". (James 4:6-8). "Therefore, humble yourselves before the Lord, and He will lift you up". (James 4:10). "He has shown you, O mortal, what is good. And does the Lord require of you? To act justly and to love mercy and to walk humbly with your God". (Micah 6:8).

"When pride comes, then comes disgrace. But with humility comes Wisdom". (Proverbs 11:2).

The time that humbled me most was when I had my bicycle accident—where I cracked my head open, getting fourteen stitches. I do not remember much of the accident because I kept blacking out. I do remember people telling me I missed a really big boulder by just inches and how the nurses kept asking if a truck hit me. The way I felt, something as big as a truck must have hit me. In all my pain, I felt that there was someone holding my hand and wiping my tears away (even when no one was in the room). That someone was once again my Lord Jesus. Just like before, when I was five, He was comforting me (cradling me in the shelter of His wings), helping me deal with the pain, so I did not feel alone and scared. My loving, compassionate, and awesome Heavenly Father heard my heartfelt cry, came rushing in to rescue, and healed His hurting and lonely child—who was in need of His healing and protection and love.

Our cry for help goes right to God's ears the moment we cry out to Him. However, we fail to hear God responding, which then, we tend to start making ourselves feel bitter, angry, and go to places that we think is the cure for our hurt. Perfect harmony does not happen that way. It starts out with us calling out to Him, He hears, and then He responds. We do our part (cry out in prayer), and God does His part (respond with compassionate love). It is like these examples: In football, the coach calls the plays, and then the players respond. In baseball, the catcher gives a sign for a pitch; then, the pitcher responds. They call this pattern—teamwork. God works the same way with us—God calls the plays (His commandments) and then we respond. What we need to do in times of prayer is to "be silent and listen" to God speaking His instructions to us. Instead of giving God lipwork, give Him your ears. God always listens to us. Let us just try to listen to Him. God is always speaking to us. Open your Bible and listen to His Words that He speaks. God is never far away to reach out His hand and help us out of our slums. As the Bible says: *"And God says:* **'Be still and know that I AM God. I will be exalted among the nations. I will be exalted among the earth'"** *(Psalm 46:10).*

"Even a fool, when he keeps silent, is considered wise; when he closes his lips, he is considered prudent" (Proverb 17:28).

"Let him sit alone and be silent, since He has laid it on him". (Lamentations 3:28).

"My dear brothers and sisters, take note of this: Everyone should be quick to listen, slow to speak and slow to become angry, because human anger does not produce the righteousness that God desires". (James 1:19-20).

These four Scriptures are just the first steps in seeking to know who God is and how He works. I urge you to continue to build an unshakeable faith by furnishing a quiet place in your soul—where you can talk to God about all that concerns you. Now is the time to do so. For we do not know when our Savior will return to bring us home to His Father. When our Lord arrives, He wants to find us seeking and living out His Father's ways. There is no other way to live than our loving, compassionate, and peaceful Heavenly Father's ways.

God's love is priceless and always forthcoming. God's Word renews the heart and mind to keep us walking steady and upright, giving us the assurance that Jesus will walk at your side—right through the darkness of this world. Always listen, trust, obey, and live abundantly in the presence of your Heavenly Father and Lord Jesus Christ. The Bible explains this better. Meditate on these verses of Scripture, and start living the life that your Heavenly Father created in you to live: *"This is what the Lord says:* **'The people who survive the sword will find favor in the wilderness; I will come to give rest to Israel'.** *The Lord appeared to us in the past saying:* **'I have loved you with an everlasting love; I have drawn you with**

23

unfailing kindness. I will build you up again, and you, Virgin Israel will be rebuilt. Again you will take up your timbrels and go out to dance with the joyful. Again, you will plant vineyards on the hills of Samaria; the farmers will plant them and enjoy their fruit. There will be a day when watchmen cry out on the hills of Ephraim, 'Come, let us go up to Zion, to the Lord our God'" (Jeremiah 31:2-6).

"I delight in the Lord; my soul rejoices in my God. For He has clothed me with garments of salvation and arrayed me in a robe of His righteousness, as a bridegroom adorns his head like a priest, and as a bride adorns herself with her jewels. For as the soil makes the sprout come up, and a garden causes seeds to grow, so the Sovereign Lord will make righteousness and praise spring up before all nations". (Isaiah 61:10-11).

"My times are in your hands; deliver me from the hands of my enemies, from those who pursue me. Let your face shine on your servant; save me in your unfailing love. Let me not be put to shame, Lord, for I have cried out to You; but let the wicked be put to shame and be silent in the realm of the dead. Let their lying lips be silenced, for with pride and contempt they speak arrogantly against the righteous" (Psalm 31:15-18).

"Then they cried out to the Lord in their trouble, and He delivered them from their trouble, and He delivered them from their distress. He led them by a straight path to a city where they could settle. Let them give thanks to the Lord for His unfailing love and His wonderful deeds for mankind, for He satisfies the thirsty and fills the hungry with good things". (Psalm 107:6-9).

"Yet, I am always with you; You hold me by my right hand. You guide me with Your counsel, and afterward You will take me into glory. Whom have I in Heaven but you? And earth has nothing I desire besides You. My flesh and my heart may fail, but God is the strength of my heart and my portion forever. Those who are far from You will perish; You destroy all who are unfaithful to You. But as for me, it is good to be near God. I have made the Sovereign Lord my refuge; I will tell of all Your deeds" (Psalm 73:23-28).

*"He says: **'Be still and know that I am God; I will be exalted among the nations; I will be exalted in the earth'".** (Psalm 46:10).*

"Many are the plans in a person's heart, but it is the Lord's purpose that prevails" (Proverbs 19:21).

"The fear of the Lord leads to life; then one rests content, untouched by trouble". (Proverbs 19:23). "So if the Son sets you free, you will be free indeed". (John 8:36).

"My sheep listen to My voice; I know them, and they follow Me'". *(John 10:27).*

God Is Always Looking for People That Are Willing to Be Filled

----

*H*armony and wisdom. Beauty and endurance. Faith and hope. Love and peace. Patience and self-control. All these are found in the Book of Galatians. Where the Apostle Paul explains the fruits of the Spirit, which are God's character—the characters that we are to obtain with the help of our Lord and Savior Jesus Christ. Having these characters, we are living like our Lord Jesus who frees us from any burdens we might be holding. When we hold on to our burdens, we slow down any blessings that our Heavenly Father has for us. I walk through the fruits of Spirit later in the book.

We must be ready, willing, and trusting all the time and all the way to the last hour. For at that last moment is when you will receive the reward for living God's way. The final (and biggest) test is walking by faith and relying on God alone.

Remember: Believe, trust, and fear not. You then will receive the reward that our Lord has promised. We are not going through this journey alone. We belong to the best team: the Star Team (God's team). To be on the Star Team, you have to consistently expose all rebellious tendencies that you might have toward God. Because when we do this, we are letting God know we really want to live His ways. By listening to Him, we show our obedience to Him.

I saw how my listening and obedience to God worked for me. I saw courage work in my life.

The year was 1991 at the age of thirty-one when I got the call to pack up my things and drive out to California. Yes, I drove out to California. This sure took a lot of courage to do. One of my biggest challenges that I ever took was driving across nine states. I—the driver—was with my mom and my three-year-old son. My brother and sisters were against it and wanted us to take a plane. They thought it was too "hard" and "dangerous" for me being the only driver and a woman. They did not think I was able to handle it. Therefore, I continually asked my Heavenly Father about this challenge, and He told me to not be afraid—He will be with me and protect me all the way. Just trust Him. I took the challenge and trusted that my Lord would be my co-pilot to drive across the country. If we had taken a plane, I would not have proof that God was with me through the whole trip.

We were on our way to California. Why California? Well, the doctors told my mom (who had been in an accident) to avoid hip replacement, she needed to move away from the Ohio's weather, to either Florida or California. My mom decided to go to California. If it were my choice, I would have chosen Florida. Yet God had a different plan for me (it is not what I want, it is what He wants). We were off to California.

You know, I was confident I had God with me all the way across the country. I was not driving alone. I remember one incident where God showed me His presence and protection. It was right before I made my first stop for rest. I was just reaching the five hundred miles goal that I had set for myself, and I started looking for a hotel so I could rest for the night when all of a sudden I saw very dark, black clouds approaching the town we were going through. I quietly whispered a prayer to God to help me get to Des Moines, Iowa, before the storm hit. A hundred miles later, I arrived safely in Des Moines. The next morning, turning on the television, for the weather and traffic report to see how the day was going to be, I saw the news reported that three tornadoes touched down right in the town where we were and two people died. That one simple whispered prayer showed me that God heard my cry for help and came to my rescue. God was not done with me yet—He had a plan. I felt blessed and very courageous—able to finish the trip. I was so courageous that I finished the trip in four days. I even passed the moving truck that was carrying our things. The truck arrived three days later.

Later that year, I met my husband, Franklin. It was at a job I replied to—a warehouse job, a job I never worked before. My husband started in January and I in August. The meeting was only something that God planned. On my first day, they introduced me to everyone (as all jobs do on the first day); they were telling me who everyone was. When it came to introducing my husband, they said; "You see that guy on the forklift, that's Frank. He's not very nice [they used another word that is not very nice, and I will not mention]. Stay away from him." At the time, I said nothing and just did my work (I kept my distance from him). However, little by little, God started bringing us together. He gave me courage to say hello to him. When I finally got that courage, I was able to talk to him, and he asked me out. It has been twenty-three years, and we are still together. All the glory goes to my Heavenly Father.

God has been teaching me His ways ever since, which brings me to why I am writing this book. It takes a lot of courage to write a book, because in doing so, it stirs up a lot of hurtful memories that I have endured along the way and let go since I opened my heart's door to Jesus and gave Him total control over my life. God has been calling me to help others who feel that they are walking this journey alone. He tells me that He knows all my strengths and weaknesses, and He will provide for me all that I need to get me through my trials and through writing this book. As the Bible says: *"'With God all things are possible'"*. *(Matthew 19:25)*. This promise will always get me through all the hurtful memories and all of Satan's negative comments. As long as I stay in God's Word and trust Him with total control, I will overcome this world. For my Lord overcame this world first, and He is right at my side. I cannot go wrong.

As you can see that all through my life—so far—God was and still is with me. He speaks to me all through my daily walk on this earth. Yes, I run into roadblocks, but the armor and shield (His Grace) that God provides for me is enough to fight off those arrows of destruction that Satan is throwing at me. Like the Lord said earlier, *"'With God all things are possible'"*. Another promise God always speaks to me is: *"Have I not commanded you? Be strong and courageous. Do not be afraid; do not be discouraged, for the Lord your God will be with you wherever you go'"*. *(Joshua 1:9)*.

A Comfort (Jesus) in Disguise

Well, as you can see, God hears my silent cries and gives me comfort (Jesus) to walk through it all. God will also hear and see when we are hurting. This is why He gave us His Son to comfort. My Lord Jesus is always around; I can feel safe and secure in every moment that I need His comfort. God's comfort comes when you least expect it to. Just when you think no one cares—bam! Jesus comes and wraps you in His loving and compassionate embrace. He never lets me get hurt, and He never lets me down. I could always depend on Him. Many times, I wanted to give up, but Jesus kept encouraging me to keep going and walk with Him.

Here is what I found when I searched the Bible for some comforting Scriptures that confirms how Jesus helps me (and you too). Read them and be comforted.

Jesus helps me to always walk in His Light: *"For you were once darkness, but now you are light in the Lord. Love as children of light (for the fruit of the Light consists in all goodness, righteousness and truth)". (Ephesians 5:8-9).*

Jesus helps me walk in His Spirit: *"Those who belong to Christ Jesus have crucified the flesh with its passions and desires. Since we live by the Spirit, let us keep in step with the Spirit. Let us not become conceited, provoking and envying each other". (Galatians 5:24-26).*

Jesus helps me walk in His love: *"Follow God's example, therefore, as dearly loved children and walk in the way of love, just as Christ loved us and gave Himself up for us as a fragrant offering and sacrifice to God". (Ephesians 5:1-2).*

Jesus helps me walk in His truth: *"I have no greater joy than to hear that my children are walking in the truth…We ought therefore to show hospitality to such people so that we may work together for the truth". (3 John 1:4, 8).*

Jesus helps me walk in Him: *"So, then, just as you received Christ Jesus as Lord, continue to live your lives in Him, rooted and built up in Him, strengthened in the faith, as you were taught and overflowing with thankfulness. See to it that no one takes you captive through hollow and deceptive philosophy, which depends on human tradition and the elemental spiritual forces of this world rather than on Christ". (Colossians 2:6-8).*

When you read these Scriptures (and there are more), you have no excuse that you have no one to help you through your trials. In God's Word (the Bible), we learn more and more about God and His Ways. As the Bible says: *"This is what the Lord says;* **'Stand at the crossroads and look; ask for the ancient paths; ask where the good way is, and walk in it, and you will find rest for your souls'".** *(Jeremiah 6:16).*

I did not know early in my life about God. But now that I read my Bible daily, God speaks to me and teaches me how to live out His Will and His Way and who He is. I am a better and stronger woman.

"Listen to my words, Lord, consider my lament. Hear my cry for help, my King and my God, for to you I pray. In the morning, Lord, you hear my voice; in the morning I lay my requests before you and wait expectantly. For you are not a God who is pleased with wickedness; with you, evil people are not welcome. The arrogant cannot stand in your presence. You hate all who do wrong; you destroy those who tell lies. The bloodthirsty and deceitful you, Lord, detest. But I, by your great love, can come into your house; in reverence I bow down toward your holy temple. Lead me, Lord, in your righteousness because of my enemies—make your way straight before me". (Psalm 5:1-8).

After I read these verses, God spoke these words to me, once again: **"'Have I not commanded you? Be strong and courageous. Do not be afraid; do not be discouraged, for the Lord your God will be with you wherever you go'".** *(Joshua 1:9).* The words that God speaks to me, I am convinced that He will be with me through it all. Now, my contentment is only in the Lord my God—who is my refuge forever.

I have another moment of a "Jesus in disguise" that showed me His comfort and power. When I spent a weekend at my aunt and uncle's house, their dog got rid of my fear of dogs. My cousin and I were playing with her dog outside until a loud thunder rumbled through and scared the dog (she was scared of thunder). I grabbed the dog (without thinking of my fear) and brought her into the house and stayed with her to comfort her. It ended up that she had comforted me. As I was staying with the dog until she stopped shaking, it gave me the courage to help her and forget my fear. I looked down at her, and it seemed like she had a big smile on her face. I felt so comfortable helping her with her fear, and I came out of the whole situation unharmed. When they took me home (at the end of the week), I asked if I could walk the dog to the door so that my family could see that I was not afraid of dogs anymore. It turned out that they were not that impressed as I was; they just said, "That's nice," and went on with what they were doing. My heart just broke, and I went into my room. In my room, I was feeling lonely and abandoned. I just wanted to crawl in a hole and never come out. However, God saw everything, and He shined down His compassionate love and told me He loves me. At that moment, I was in His presence, and He covered me with His wings until I was feeling better. There was no one else in the room, by the way. My Lord noticed and comforted me. I now know that the only one that will be with me is my Lord Jesus. Jesus will always be with me to comfort me so I could in turn comfort other people who are in need. With Jesus by my side, I can conquer anything that this world throws at me. I tell you, you must not let anything (or anyone) get in the way of following Jesus. There will be times when you need a friend to talk over your problems and no one is around for you. Just whisper, "Jesus, I need to talk," and He will be that friend. As Jesus says in the Bible: *"I no longer call you servants...I have called you friend"*. *(John 15:15)*. This comes when you trust and obey God's instructions. I will continually thank my Lord Jesus and praise Him for all the times He was with me when I thought I had no one.

Being in the Shadow

---

*B*e all heard that evil lurks in the shadows. That is why we all do not like walking in the shadows alone. Remember we can take refuge in the good shadow of God's wings; so we shall not be afraid. That is why when a evil shadow makes an appearance in your life, do not be afraid. Just say three simple words "Jesus is Lord," and the evil shadow turns from dark to Light—where Jesus is always standing, ready to intervene, when needed. The quiet gray days we face are made for us to trust the great I AM—who is with us and will never leave us. For me, when I feel the quiet gray days come upon me, I open up my Bible and start reading until the Light of Jesus chases away the gray clouds and I feel His sunshine of joy once again.

Our Heavenly Father wants to be with us and wants us to know all about Him. He wants us to live a life of freedom and peace (His Peace). He wants to give us good things so much that He wrote His laws in our hearts and minds so that we would never be without Him. We just need to acknowledge Him at all times, even on those gray days that seem to drag us down. Did you ever hear of the song 'You are my sunshine'? Well, when I sing it I sing it this way as a praise song to my Star Team. Here goes: 'You are my Son-shine, my only Son-shine. You make me happy when skies are gray. You'll always know Father how much I love You. Please don't take Your Son-shine away'. How's that?

Now let us meditate on some Scriptures that fill us with encouragement and be filled with the Father's Glorious Son-shine:

"Ah, Sovereign Lord, you have made the Heavens and the earth by Your Great Power and outstretched arms. Nothing is too hard for you. You show love to thousands but bring the punishment for the parents' sins into the laps of their children after them. Great and mighty God, whose name is the Lord Almighty,

great are your purposes and mighty are Your Deeds, Your eyes are open to the ways of all mankind; You reward each person according to their conduct and as their deeds deserve". (Jeremiah 32:17-19).

*"Then the word of the Lord came to Jeremiah: '**I am the Lord, the God of all mankind. Is anything too hard for Me?**'" (Jeremiah 32:26-27).*

Trust then on the Star Team (the Father, the Son and the Holy Spirit) to handle any problem you face. When you come to Him in your difficult situation, He will lead you to victory. It may not be as quick as you would like, but you need to wait and trust Him that He will fulfill His promises. His Son Jesus is proof of His love for us. God's Love never fails. When times seem to come crashing down around you, just turn to Jesus. He will turn your problems into dust.

A Spiritual Journey

What is a spiritual journey? It is a call to walk in the Light of Jesus, to walk with the strength of Jesus, to walk with the courage of Jesus, to overcome the ways of this world like Jesus. When God called Joshua, He told him: *"**No one will be able to stand up against you all the days of your life. As I was with Moses, so I will be with you. I will never leave you nor forsake you**". (Joshua 1:5).* The Lord then told Joshua, *"**Be strong and very courageous. Be careful to obey all the laws, my servant Moses gave you; DO NOT turn from it; to the right or to the left that you may be successful wherever you go. Keep this Book of the Law always on your lips; meditate on it day and night, so that you may be careful to do everything written in it. Then you will be prosperous and successful. Have I not commanded you? BE STRONG and COURAGEOUS. DO NOT be afraid; DO NOT be discouraged, for the Lord your God will be with you wherever you go**". (Joshua 1:7-9).*

These words are the best encouraging words anyone can hear for they are from God's mouth. Our spiritual journey is a call to continually fight the evil giants of this world and take our families back. Back from where you ask. Back from the wicked hands of Satan (the evil giant). The battle that we have with Satan—of how he wants to break up the family—is one that our Lord Jesus knows all too well. That is why He is the only One that can defeat Satan and repair the family home. Satan cannot stand when we yell into his face, "Jesus is the Lord of my life!" This is the best defense to fight for our families. This is why we must wait on God to do His work. While we are waiting, take this time as a process that will lead to victory, all for the glory of our Heavenly Father. Always remain faithful to Him and know He is always by your side, walking with us.

To help me to stay faithful to my Star Team,
I put together this simple little thought poem:
God goes before me.
He stands behind me, never to let me fall.
God is right beside me.
Walking with me through it all.
I will always walk by Faith, not by sight.
To believe in the One who holds me tight.

I say this simple little poem every time I am faced with these evil shadows that keep trying to turn from living the Life of Love, Compassion and Grace.

Facing and Understanding Ungodly Fear

What is ungodly fear? It is worldly, and it is disobedient to God. Ungodly fear is sinful, and it leads to death. This death is not only physical (which we all are familiar with). This death is a death that is caused from anger, bitterness, selfishness, pride, haughty eyes, a lying tongue, murder, and jealousy and fornicating. All these are sinful, and they are all detestable to God. Therefore, you must make every effort to not harvest any of these sinful things; they just block any kind of Blessing that God has for you. This is what the Word of God (the Bible) tells us:

"*A troublemaker and a villain, who goes about with a corrupt mouth, who winks maliciously with his eye, signals with his feet and motions with his fingers, who plots evil with deceit in his heart and he always stirs up conflicts. Therefore, disaster will overtake him in an instant; he will suddenly be destroyed, without remedy. There are six things the Lord hates, seven that are detestable to Him: haughty eyes, a lying tongue, hands that shed innocent blood, a heart that devises wicked schemes, feet that are quick to rush into evil, a false witness who pours out lies and a person who stirs up conflict in the community*". (Proverbs 6:12-19).

"***Truly, truly, I say to you; if anyone keeps My word, he will never see death***". (*John 8:51*).

Therefore, you must:"*Refrain from anger, and forsake wrath! Fret not yourself; it tends only to evil*". (Psalm 37:8).

"*Wrath is cruel, anger is overwhelming, but who can stand before jealousy?*". (Proverbs 27:4).

"*Know this, my beloved brothers: let every person be quick to hear, slow to speak, slow to anger; for the anger of man does not produce the righteousness of God*". (James 1:19-20).

"*Do not say, 'I will repay evil'; wait for the Lord, and He will deliver you*". (Proverbs 20:22).

"*Make every effort to live in peace with everyone and to be holy; without holiness no one will see the Lord. See to it that no one falls short of the grace of God and that no bitter root grows up to cause trouble and defile many*" (Hebrews 12:14-15). "*But if you harbor bitter envy and selfish ambition in your hearts, do not boast about it or deny the truth. Such 'wisdom' does not come down from heaven but is earthly, unspiritual, and demonic. For where you have envy and selfish ambition, there you find disorder and every evil practice. But the wisdom that comes from heaven is first of all pure; then peace-loving, considerate, submissive, full of mercy and good fruit, impartial and sincere. Peacemakers who sow in peace reap a harvest of righteousness*". (James 3:14-18). "*Anyone who claims to be in the light but hates a brother or sister is still in the darkness. Anyone who loves their brother and sister lives in the light, and there is nothing in them to make them stumble. But anyone who hates a brother or sister is in the darkness and walks around in the darkness. They do not know where they are going, because the darkness has blinded them*" (1 John 2:9-11).

Ungodly (worldly) fear is a feeling of uneasiness, and uneasiness is sinful and wicked. It shows that you do not believe and trust in God—who is always there to comfort you and is in total control of all that goes on in your life. When you get that uneasy feeling, you need to examine that feeling further. Start with these three things to remember:

*The presence of God will be with you to keep you from ungodly (worldly) fear:

"Though, I walk through the valley of the shadow of death, I will fear no evil; for you are with me; your rod and your staff they comfort me". (Psalm 23:4).

*The promises of God will empower you to reject ungodly (worldly) fear:

"Fear not, for I am with you; be not dismayed, for I am your God. I will strengthen you, yes, I will help you, I will uphold you with my righteous right hand". (Isaiah 41:10).

*The love of God will take ungodly (worldly) fear away:

"There is no fear in love; but perfect love casts out fear, because fear involves torment. But he who fears has not been made perfect in love". (1 John 4:18).

The Fear of God:

We are called to fear the Lord. Like it says in Proverbs 1:7, *"The fear of the Lord is the beginning of knowledge, but fools despise wisdom and instruction".* The call to fear the Lord is a call of:

1.) Submission—a condition of being submissive, humble, or complaint.

2.) Devotion—the act of devoting the object of one's devotion.

3.) Awe—a wonder that is inspired by authority.

4.) Adoration—strong feelings of love or admiration.

5.) Worship—the act of showing excessive admiration for someone.

6.) Overwhelmed—to cover over completely, submerge.

To fear the Lord is to reject ungodly (worldly) fear and evil, which are always in negative forms. An example of ungodly (worldly) fear is when we spend most of our lives dreading the things that will not happen: like (1) to not get cancer, (2) to be betrayed, and (3) to die early. These worldly fears are what "the fear of the Lord" drives out. Here is what Scripture says:

"Moses said to the people; 'Do not fear, for God has come to test you that the fear of Him may be before you that you may not sin'". (Exodus 20:20).

"There is no fear in Love, but perfect love casts out fear". (1 John 4:18).

When the fear of God is rooted, in our hearts ungodly fear goes from dread to delight.

"Then you will look and be radiant, your heart will throb and swell with joy; the wealth on the seas will be brought to you, to you the riches of the nations will come". (Isaiah 60:5).

"Who will not fear you, O Lord, and bring glory to your name? For you alone are holy. All nations will come and worship before you, for your righteous acts have been revealed". (Revelation 15:4).

"We live by faith, not by sight. Since then, we know what it is to fear the Lord. Whatever we do, it is because Christ's love controls us" (2 Corinthians 5:7, 11a, 14a).

Weigh your options, and choose this day whom you will fear—the Lord your God (and feeling at peace) or fear dread (which Satan uses to confuse you). The choice is yours. As for me, I choose and will always choose to fear God who keeps me in His loving embrace.

Reasons to fear God:

The Word of God (the Bible) makes it very clear for us to fear the Lord. It says: *"The fear of the Lord is the beginning of knowledge". (Proverb 1:7).*

What does this mean, to fear the Lord, and gain knowledge? It means once you work these following reasons into your life, you will gain the knowledge of our Lord God and live a prosperous life that He has designed for you. Therefore, you must:

Keep your heart from entertaining destructive behavior (shun evil).

Steer clear from any foolish thoughts, actions, or words (encourage others with kindness).

Cause your life to work the way God intended it to (focus on things of truth and love).

When the spirit of fear creeps in on you, the only way to break its hold is to stand on God's Word and proclaim the Truth, knowing that God does not give us the spirit of fear. God gives us love and His power so we could have a sound mind to live freely in His presence. We can reject the spirit of fear with one name. Lord Jesus is that name who surpasses all that is evil.

Prayer:

Father, I am so in awe of you. Enable me (and my fellow believers) to absorb all your instructions. *"Teach me your ways, O Lord; I will walk in your truth; unite my heart to fear your name. I will praise you, O Lord, my God, with all my heart and I will glorify your name forevermore". (Psalm 86:11-12).*

I will place all my fears at your feet so you can take them from me and replace them with your love and strength. You are *"my light and my salvation"* and *"the strength of my life. Of whom shall I be afraid?". (Psalm 29:11).*

Help me to make praise my first reaction to fear whenever it comes upon me. I can trust your Word and your power to protect me. *"Though an army may encamp against me, my heart shall not fear (Psalm 27:3). "I sought the Lord, and He answered me; He delivered me from all my fears". (Psalm 34:4).* You bring life and keep me away from the pit that leads to death. Enable me to have godly fear in my heart always. Thank you for always protecting me (and my family). I am in love with you. I will always speak your Words of Truth, Hope, and most of all Love. In the name of Jesus, I pray. Amen.

Word Power to the Fear of the Lord to Gain Wisdom and Knowledge:

"Whoever fears the Lord has a secure Fortress, and for their children it will be a Refuge. The fear of the Lord is a fountain of Life, to turn one away from the snares of death". (Proverbs 14:26-27).

"Though an army may encamp against me, my heart shall not fear; though war may rise against me, in this I will be confident. One thing I ask from the Lord, this only do I seek: that I may dwell in the House of the Lord all the days of my life". (Psalm 27:3-4).

"By humility and the fear of the Lord are riches and honor and life". (Proverbs 22:4).

"As a father has compassion on his children, so the Lord has compassion on those who fear Him" (Psalm 103:13). "But from everlasting to everlasting the Lord's love is with those who fear Him, and His righteousness with their children's children—with those who keep His covenant and remember to obey His precepts". (Psalm 103:17-18).

"For gaining wisdom and instruction; for understanding words of insight; for receiving instruction in prudent behavior, doing what is right and just and fair; for giving prudence to those who are simple, knowledge and discretion to the young—let the wise listen and add to their learning, and let the discerning get guidance—for understanding proverbs and parables, the sayings and riddles of the wise". (Proverbs 1:2-6).

"My son, do not forget My teaching, but keep My commands in your heart, for they will prolong your life many years and bring you peace and prosperity. Let love and faithfulness never leave you; bind them around your neck, write them on the tablet of your heart. Then you will win favor and a good name in the sight of God and man. Trust in the Lord with all your heart and lean not on your own understanding; in all your ways submit to Him, and He will make your paths straight. Do not be wise in your own eyes; fear the Lord and shun evil. This will bring health to your body and nourishment to your bones". (Proverbs 3:1-8).

"I sought the Lord, and He answered me; He delivered me from all my fears. Those who look to Him are radiant; their faces are never covered with shame". (Psalm 34:4-5).

"The angel of the Lord encamps around those who fear Him, and He delivers them. Taste and see that the Lord is good; blessed is the one who takes refuge in Him. Fear the Lord, you His holy people, for those who fear Him lack nothing.

The lions may grow weak and hungry, but those who seek the Lord lack no good thing. Come, My children, listen to Me; I will teach you the fear of the Lord. Whoever of you loves life and desires to see many good days, keep your tongue from evil and your lips from telling lies. Turn from evil and do good; seek peace and pursue it". (Psalm 34:7-14).

These are just some of the Scriptures that will remind you to fear the Lord. Take the time to open your Bible and start walking in the Light of Life, right on through the dark valleys. For it is the Word of God that brings Light into the evil shadow of this world; to fade it away.

Walking through the Dark Valleys

This life on this earth is full of dark valleys. If you are not paying attention to God's Words of warning, you could be walking in the dark valleys for a long, long time. The ruler of this world—Satan—is always tormenting us. Here are some examples that you should be looking out for: sudden change in your health and finances, an unexpected loss of a loved one, the abandonment of family and relatives, your friend suddenly stops calling or hanging around you.

These (and many more) are just some of Satan's ways to keep us in the dark valleys. I know, because I have been there many, many, many times until my Star Team gave me a good talking. Now, I walk in the Light of Life with my Lord Jesus.

When you endure a dark season, it is for a good reason. All lessons from God are tests of Faith and Trust—to see how long we will walk, on our own (through the darkness) without going to Him for help. Being held in the Arms of the Father is the only reward worth living for.

These lessons of Faith and Trust are all for us to stand strong when faced with adversity. The one key to walking through the dark valleys is to embrace and believe in our Lord Jesus. With our Lord Jesus with us, who can come against you? Like the Bible says: *"If God is for us who can be against us?" (Romans 8:31b).*

No matter what the circumstances, the sufferings, or even the losses, we are never alone. Nothing can separate us from God's love and presence. Jesus said it Himself:

"Therefore go and make disciples of all nations, baptizing them in the name of the Father and of the Son and of the Holy Spirit, and teaching them to obey everything I have commanded you. And surely I am with you always, to the very end of the age'". (Matthew 28:19-20).

Plant this promise in your hearts, and nothing will shake you whenever Satan, our enemy (that is prowling around looking for someone to devour), places hard times at your feet.

Receiving Blessings—In the Midst of Trials.

Even in the midst of the dark valleys (trials), God will carry out His plan to bless you and your family. For God to accomplish His plan, you must learn His words, His way of living, and develop leadership skills to mature spiritually. Once you learn these, God's plan will be fulfilled. Even Jesus, His One and only Son, had accomplished what His Father wanted Him to do, and now He sits on His Father's right side.

All this can be overwhelming—all that we have to absorb and learn. Yet you have the most powerful resource right in your hand (and I do not mean the Internet)—it is your Bible. There are sixty-six books in the Bible that can answer any question that you may have. God knows that we get weak when the trials of this world come our way and God provided His Word (the Bible) to help us understand our trials (and how to endure them) like Jesus told His disciples: *"I have told you these things, so that in Me, you may have peace. In this world you will have trouble—But take heart! I have overcome the world'". (John 16:33).*

Here are four lessons that I have learned and hold on to tight:

First—Jesus overcame this world, and He is faithful to walk with me all through the journey I am on, never leaving my side.

Second—To be patient and wait for God to accomplish His purpose.

Third—Trusting that God knows what is going on in this world and He is in control.

<u>Fourth</u>—Just to believe in God's Timing that He will always be by my side, no matter the situation.

When you believe and trust in the one true God, you breathe the life given to you through His Son, our Lord Jesus Christ. The Bible says, *"For those who are led by the Spirit of God are the children of God. The Spirit you received does not make you slaves, so that you live in fear again; rather, the Spirit you received brought about your adoption to sonship. In addition, by Him we cry; 'Abba, Father.' The Spirit Himself testifies with our spirit that we are God's children. Now, if we are children, then we are heirs—heirs of God and co-heirs with Christ, if indeed we share in His sufferings in order that we may also share in His glory". (Romans 8:14-17).*

When we are walking through the dark valleys, it can be painful. However, with Jesus by our side, there is always victory. This is God's plan for you and me. Here are two little poems I wrote that reminds me of God's plan:

<u>Carrying Us Through</u>

This world is full of wondrous things, from big to very small.

We live our lives so fast; we hardly see them at all.

Most of the things we miss are right before our eyes and lips.

Like sunsets, raindrops, rainbows, stars that shine, or even a smile that grows like a vine.

On the days when we are feeling blue, just remember God loves you.

In addition to His Love, He will always carry us through, no matter what the world shows you.

<u>Believe!</u>

When all odds are against you—Believe!

When the world is not for you—Believe!

When the mountains you face are too big for you to move through your eyes—Believe!

When they say that you will never amount to anything—Believe!

When your family and friends turn against you—Believe!

When they say it will not be long until you fall, again—Believe!

When they tell you that you are crazy for believing in a God that you cannot see—Believe!

When all you see are dark clouds—Believe!

When there seems to be no way out of your situation—Believe!

When people tell you that you are worthless—Believe!

When your children have been making the wrong choices and not listening to you—Believe!

When you have lost your way and no one is around for guidance and advice—Believe!

When you just think you cannot go one more day—Believe!

When you have lost everything repeatedly—Believe!

When discouragement shows its ugly head—Believe!

When you are facing the giants of this world that seem to be taunting you repeatedly—Believe!

When you are afraid to take that step of faith out on the rough waters of this world—Believe!

When all things seem impossible—Believe!

"With God nothing is impossible". (Matthew 19:26).

So, take the Step of Faith and Believe in the God of Possible.

Jesus overcame everything in this world, and He lights the way to break through the chains of darkness. For Jesus is the light that never goes out: *"Your Word is a lamp for my feet, a light on my path". (Psalm 119:105).*

Jesus is my helper:
"My help comes from the Lord, the Maker of heaven and earth". (Psalm 121:2).
Jesus is my healer:

43

"Bless the Lord, O my soul, and all that is within me, bless His holy name! Bless the Lord, O my soul, and forget not all His benefits, who forgives all your iniquity, who heals all your diseases". (Psalm 103:1-3).

<u>Jesus is my friend</u>:

"Greater love has no one than this that one lay down His life for His friends". (John 15:13).

<u>Jesus is my rescuer</u>: Always there to pull me out of that pit of weakness and despair.

"For God did not send His Son into the world to condemn the world, but to save the world through Him". (John 3:17).

My Lord Jesus will always lift me up and place me on His shoulders when I am too weak to take another step. Also, Jesus shows me how much He cares. My Star Team makes my crooked paths straight and places hope in my heart. My Star Team blesses me every moment I live for Him and Him alone. I will always believe in God's unfailing love, and I trust in His plan for my life. As God's peace is always with me, so is His Son Jesus (holding my hand all the way through this journey). This is what keeps me moving forward to fulfill God's purpose for me.

I tell you, do not stop believing and praying. God hears. God sees. God cares. God knows. God loves. God protects. Most of all God will never leave us alone.

"Jesus answered, 'I am the Way and the Truth and the Life. No one comes to the Father except through me'". (John 14:6).

"Jesus answered, 'The work of God is this: to believe in the One He has sent'". (John 6:29).

"No longer do I call you slaves, for the slave does not know what his master is doing; but I have called you friends, for all things that I have heard from My Father I have made known to you'". (John 15:15).

"Draw near to God and He will draw near to you. Cleanse your hands, you sinners; and purify your hearts, you double-minded". (James 4:8). "Above all, keep fervent in your love for one another, because love covers a multitude of sins". (1 Peter 4:8).

Learning from Our Failures:

Obedience to God is a process, which is something we need to learn and remember. Failures happen when we do not listen to God's instruction and direction for our lives. Through our failures, we can start the process of learning, which we receive from God and His Son Jesus Christ. Failures are part of our development—to humble us to yield to the temptations of sin. Sin is everything that pulls you away from the path that leads to life. Failure is an excellent tool, and through trial and error, we discover that we should always fix our eyes on Jesus and follow His ways of living a peaceful life—all for the glory of His Father in Heaven.

The only way that we can learn from our failures is to focus on our Lord and Savior Jesus. He will teach us and lead us through all we go through. Learn how to take courage and not be afraid, from these Scripture verses. All to stand against the ways of this world.

This first set of Scripture verses are to <u>teach</u> us what happens when we take our eyes off Jesus and sink into the world:

*"Immediately, Jesus made the disciples into the boat and went on ahead of Him to the other side, while He dismissed the crowd. After He had dismissed them, He went up on a mountainside by Himself to pray. Later that night, He was there alone, and the boat was already a considerable distance from land, buffeted by the waves because the wind was against it. Shortly before dawn, Jesus went out to them, walking on the lake. When the disciples saw Him walking on the lake, they were terrified. 'It's a ghost', they said, and cried out in fear. However, Jesus immediately said to them; **'Take courage! It is I. Do not be afraid'** 'Lord, if it is you', Peter replied, 'Tell me to come to you on the water'. **'Come'**, He said. Then Peter got down out of the boat, walked on the water and came toward Jesus. However, when he saw the wind, he was afraid and, beginning to sink, cried out: 'Lord, save me!' Immediately, Jesus reached out His hand and caught him. **'You of little faith'**, He said, **'why did you doubt'**? And when they climbed into the boat, the wind died down. Then those who were in the boat worshiped Him, saying, 'Truly, You are the Son of God'".* (Matthew 14:22-33).

The second set of Scripture verses are to <u>remind</u> us of what happens

45

when we dwell in the presence of God Almighty. For when I take refuge in His shelter, all pain leaves me and all that is left is the Love of God. For I know *"God is Love". (1 John 4:8).*

"He who dwells in the shelter of the Most High; will rest in the shadow of the Almighty. I will say of the Lord, 'He is my refuge and my fortress, my God, in whom I trust'". (Psalm 91:1-2).

"Love is patient, love is kind. It does not envy, it does not boast, it is not proud. It does not dishonor others, it is not self-seeking, it is not easily angered, and it keeps no record of wrongs. Love does not delight in evil but rejoices with the truth. It always protects, always trusts, always hopes, and always perseveres. Love never fails". (1 Corinthians 13:4-8a).

The third set of Scripture verses once again are to <u>teach</u> us that our plans are nothing without Jesus in them. *"All a person's ways seem pure to them, but motives are weighed by the Lord. Commit to the Lord whatever you do, and He will establish your plans. The Lord works out everything to its proper end—even the wicked for a day of disaster. The Lord detests all the proud of heart. Be sure of this; they will not go unpunished. Through love and faithfulness, sin is atoned for. Through the fear of the Lord, evil is avoided. When the Lord takes pleasure in anyone's way, He causes their enemies to make peace with them. Better a little with righteousness than much gain with injustice. In their hearts humans plan their course, but the Lord establishes their steps". (Proverbs 16:2-9).*

Therefore, keep your eyes and minds on Jesus, and all the confusion will clear up. And then, the Light of God will clear the fog of destruction of this life on this earth.

<u>When you look in the mirror, who do you see?</u>

Before I invited Jesus into my heart (ten years ago), I was always looking in the mirror and wondering why I seemed to have a dull and dim appearance to my face. My eyes had no twinkle or showed any kind of life to them. My face had no pinkish color to my cheeks. I even started to put make-up on, thinking that would make me feel better (made me feel fake). Now, since I gave my Lord total control over my life, when I look in the mirror, I see the brightness in my face, the twinkle in my eye returned, and the rosiness in my cheeks showed up. I felt alive!

The Light that shines brighter than the sun, shines the faith, trust, hope, grace, and love that is found in our Lord Jesus Christ. The light and love of Jesus overcomes all darkness and struggles. The light never goes out as long as you walk the path that Jesus walked (the path of Righteousness and Humility). This is what God's Plan is for us, to walk in the Light of His Son—Christ Jesus. Walking in the Light shows that we believe in His Son—who is *the Way, the Truth, and the Life* (see *John 14:6*). Through this journey, Jesus's Light will lead us right into the Gates of Heaven. As we walk the Righteous and Humble Path of our Lord Jesus, we are confident that the Love of God will always be with us.

Read these Scripture verses and rest in Grace, Compassion, and Love of our Heavenly Father. You will feel His Light strengthening and Protecting: *"He has brought down rulers from thrones, but has lifted up the humble. He has filled the hungry with good things, but has sent the rich away empty. He has helped His servant Israel, remembering to be merciful". (Luke 1:52-54).*

"Therefore, as God's chosen people, holy and dearly loved, clothe yourselves with compassion, kindness, humility, gentleness and patience. Bear with each other and forgive one another if any of you has a grievance against someone. Forgive as the Lord forgave you. And over all these virtues, put on Love, which binds them all together in perfect unity". (Colossians 3:12-14).

"Humble yourselves in the presence of the Lord and He will lift you up". (James 4:10).

"For the eyes of the Lord are on the righteous and His ears are attentive to their prayer, but the face of the Lord is against those who do evil". (1 Peter 3:12).

"Be completely humble and gentle; be patient, bearing with one another in love. Make every effort to keep the unity of the Spirit through the bond of peace. There is one body and one Spirit, just as you were called to one hope when you were called; one Lord, one faith, one baptism; one God and Father of all, who is over all and through all and in all. But to each one of us grace has been given as Christ apportioned it". (Ephesians 4:2-7).

"Who among you is wise and understanding? Let them show it by their good life, by deeds done in the humility that comes from wisdom. But if you harbor bitter envy and selfish ambition in your hearts, do not boast about it or deny the truth. Such "wisdom" does not come down from heaven but is earthly, unspiritual, and demonic. For where you have envy and selfish ambition, there you find disorder and every evil practice". (James 3:13-16)

"You younger men, likewise, be subject to your elders; and all of you clothes yourselves with humility toward one another. For—GOD OPPOSES TO THE PROUD, BUT GIVES GRACE TO THE HUMBLE. Therefore, humble yourselves under the mighty hand of God that He may exalt you at the proper time. Cast all your anxiety on Him because He cares for you". (1 Peter 5:5-7).

"He guides the humble in what is right and teaches them His way". (Psalm 25:9).

"He mocks proud mockers, but shows favor to the humble and oppressed. The wise inherit honor, but fools get only shame". (Proverbs 3:34-35).

"Wisdom's instruction is to fear the Lord, and humility comes before honor" (Proverbs 15:33).

"Humility is the fear of the Lord; its wages are riches and honor and life" (Proverbs 22:4).

"A gift opens the way and ushers the giver into the presence of the Great" (Proverbs 18:16).

"Trust in the Lord with all your heart and lean not on your own understanding; in all your ways submit to Him, and He will make your paths straight. Do not be wise in your own eyes; fear the Lord and shun evil. This will bring health to your body and nourishment to your bones". (Proverbs 3:5-8).

Each of these verses are lessons for you to take to heart and grow stronger in your Faith, putting Romans 8:28 into action: *"And we know that in all things God works for the good of those who love Him, who have been called according to His purpose". (Romans 8:28).*

Learning from our failures makes us eager to mature spiritually and serve God wholeheartedly. God does not reward rebellion or wrongdoings. By His grace, He blesses those who turn from their sin. Choosing repentance and walking in step with His Son Jesus who teaches us that it is wise to obey

His Father. The grace of God is a gift that we cannot get from no one else but through His Son Jesus. Meditate on these Scriptures of truth and from the heart of our awesome Creator: *"Set your minds on things above, not on earthly things". (Colossians 3:2).*

"You will keep in perfect peace those whose minds are steadfast, because they trust in You". (Isaiah 26:3-4).

"Fixing our eyes on Jesus, the pioneer and perfecter of faith. For the joy set before Him He endured the cross, scorning its shame, and sat down at the right hand of the throne of God. Consider Him who endured such opposition from sinners, so that you will not grow weary and lose heart". (Hebrews 12:2-3).

*"Thomas said to Him, 'Lord, we do not know where you are going, so how can we know the way?' Jesus answered, '**I am the way and the truth and the life. No one comes to the Father except through Me. If you really know Me, you will know My Father as well. From now on, you do know Him and have seen Him'**". (John 14:5-7).*

"Surely the arm of the Lord is not too short to save, nor His ear too dull to hear". (Isaiah 59:1).

*"'**If anyone does attack you, it will not be My doing; whoever attacks you will surrender to you. See, it is I, who created the blacksmith, who fans the coals into flame and forges a weapon fit for its work. And, it is I who have created the destroyer to wreak havoc; no weapon forged against you will prevail, and you will refute every tongue that accuses you. This is the heritage of the servants of the Lord, and this is their vindication from Me'**, declares the Lord". (Isaiah 54:15-17).*

*"'**I am sending you out like sheep among wolves. Therefore, be as shrewd as snakes and as innocent as doves. Be on your guard'**" (Matthew 10:16-17a).*

This is a reminder: It is the Control of God, who helps us to stay walking the Righteous Path of Life that He so desires for us to walk. It is God who is Greater in us and that is for us, than the one (Satan) that is against us.

The Heart of God is the Heart of Love

When you give your heart to God, you receive His heart of Love. Receiving our Lord Jesus into our life is receiving His Father's Heart of Love and Compassion. This is why Jesus went to the cross—so we can receive His Father's Love. We seek to know more of our Heavenly Father, finding that His love is everywhere.

Before I received God's heart of love, I had to have my heart cleaned out of all the dirt of this world. The dirt of this world is what made me feel dirty. The sweep-clean that God did on my heart took away any shame that I was harvesting, which had dragged me into a deep, dark slimy pit. In that pit, I was not that much into reading my Bible. I was a "part-time reader." I did have the sense when I was in distress that I needed to pray, asking God to help me. I admitted all my mistakes (the dirt of this world). God then instructed me to read more of my Bible. Which helped me to sweep-clean the dirt of this world. I was on my way to a pure and loving Heart of God.

With God's Heart, my heart has become:

Filled with Obedience –

"Do not merely listen to the word, and deceive yourselves. Do what it says". (James 1:22).

"Walk in obedience to all I command you that it may go well for you". (Jeremiah 7:23b).

"Walk in obedience to all that the Lord your God has commanded you, so that you may live and prosper and prolong your days in the land that you will possess". (Deuteronomy 5:33).

*"Jesus replied, **'Anyone who loves Me will obey My teaching. My Father will love them, and we will come to them and make our home with them'**".*

(John 14:23).

"Keep this Book of the Law always on your lips; meditate on it day and night, so that you may be careful to do everything written in it. Then you will be prosperous and successful". *(Joshua 1:8).*

"Do not conform to the pattern of this world, but be transformed by the renewing of your mind. Then you will be able to test and approve what God's will is—His good, pleasing and perfect will". (Romans 12:2).

Be Filled with Integrity –

"For the Lord gives wisdom; from His mouth come knowledge and understanding; He holds success in store for the upright, He is a shield to those whose walk is blameless, for He guards the course of just and protects the way of His faithful ones". (Proverbs 2:6-8).

"The righteousness of the blameless makes their paths straight, but the wicked are brought down by their own wickedness. The righteousness of the upright delivers them, but the unfaithful are trapped by evil desires". (Proverb 11:5-6).

Be Filled with Honesty –

"An honest witness tells the truth, but a false witness tells lies. The words of the reckless pierce like swords, but the tongue of the wise brings healing. Truthful lips endure forever, but a lying tongue lasts only a moment". (Proverbs 12:17-19).

"My sacrifice, O God, is a broken spirit; a broken and contrite heart, you God, will not despise". (Psalm 51:17).

Filled with Purity –

"Cleanse me with hyssop, and I will be clean; wash me, and I will be whiter than snow". (Psalm 51:7).

"Create in me a pure heart, O God, and renew a steadfast spirit within me". (Psalm 51:10).

"Teach me Your Way, Lord, that I may rely on Your Faithfulness; give me an undivided heart, that I may fear your name. I will praise you, Lord my God, with all my heart; I will glorify your name forever. For great is your love toward

me; you have delivered me from the depths, from the realm of the dead". (Psalm 86:11-13).

"Blessed are the pure in heart, for they will see God". (Matthew 5:8).

Filled with Humility –

"When pride comes, then comes disgrace, but with humility comes wisdom". (Proverb 11:2).

"Before a downfall the heart is haughty, but humility comes before honor" (Proverb 18:12).

"You save the humble, but bring low those whose eyes are haughty. You, Lord, keep my lamp burning; my God turns my darkness into light. With your help I can advance against a troop; with my God I can scale a wall. As for God, His way is perfect: The Lord's word is flawless; He shields all who take refuge in Him". (Psalm 18:27-30).

"Good and upright is the Lord; therefore, He instructs sinners in His ways. He guides the humble in what is right and teaches them His way. All the ways of the Lord are loving and faithful toward those who keep the demands of His covenant". (Psalm 25:8-10).

Filled with His Grace –

"Blessed are those whose strength is in You, whose hearts are set on pilgrimage". (Psalm 84:4-5).

"Better is one day in Your courts than a thousand elsewhere; I would rather be a doorkeeper in the house of my God, than dwell in the tents of the wicked. For the Lord God is a sun and shield; the Lord bestows favor and honor; no good thing does He withhold from those whose walk is blameless. Lord Almighty, blessed is the one who trusts in You". (Psalm 84:10-12).

"Your righteousness is like the highest mountains, your justice like the great deep. You, Lord, preserve both people and animals. How priceless is your unfailing love, O God! People take refuge in the shadow of your wings. They feast on the abundance of your river of delights. For with You is the fountain of life; in your light we see light". (Psalm 36:6-9).

"Surely, Lord, you bless the righteous; You surround them with your favor as

with a shield". (Psalm 5:12).

"It is written: 'I believed; therefore, I have spoken.' Since we have that same spirit of faith, we also believe and therefore speak, because we know that the one who raised the Lord Jesus from the dead will also raise us with Jesus and present us with you to Himself. All this is for your benefit, so that the grace that is reaching more and more people may cause thanksgiving to overflow to the glory of God". (2 Corinthians 4:13-15).

Filled with Eternal Faith –

"Therefore, we do not lose heart. Though outwardly, we are wasting away, yet, inwardly, we are being renewed day by day. For our light and momentary troubles are achieving an Eternal Glory that far outweighs them all. So we fix our eyes not on what is seen, but on what is unseen, since what is seen is temporary, but what is unseen is eternal". (2 Corinthians 4:16-18).

"So in Christ Jesus, you are all children of God through faith, for all you who were baptized into Christ have clothed yourselves with Christ". (Galatians 3:26-27).

"I pray that out of His glorious riches he may strengthen you with power through His Spirit in your inner being, so that Christ may dwell in your hearts through faith. And I pray that you, Being rooted and established in love, may have power, together with all the Lord's holy people, to grasp how wide and long and high and deep is that love of Christ, and to know this love that surpasses knowledge—that you may be filled to the measure of all the fullness of God". (Ephesians 3:16-19)

"Therefore, I tell you, whatever you ask for in prayer, believe that you have received it, and it will be yours'. (Mark 11:24).

"You need to persevere so that when you have done the will of God, you will receive what He has promised". (Hebrews 10:36).

"May the God of hope fill you with all joy and peace as you trust in Him, so that you may overflow with hope by the power of the Holy Spirit". (Romans 15:13).

"If any of you lacks wisdom, you should ask God, who gives generously to all without finding fault, and it will be given to you. However, when you ask, you

must believe and not doubt, because the one who doubts is like a wave of the sea, blown and tossed by the wind. That person should not expect to receive anything from the Lord; such a person is double-minded and unstable in all they do". (James 1:5-7).

"Consider it pure joy, my brothers and sisters, whenever you face trials of many kinds, because you know that the testing of your faith produces perseverance". (James 1:2-3).

"Blessed is the one who perseveres under trial, because having stood the test that person will receive the crown of life that the Lord has promised to those who love Him" (James 1:12).

"For we live by faith, not by sight. We are confident, I say, and would prefer to be away from the body and at home with the Lord. Therefore, we make it our goal to please Him, whether we are at home in the body or away from it. For we must all appear before the judgment seat of Christ, so that each of us may receive what is due us for the things done while in the body, whether good or bad". (2 Corinthians 5:7-9).

"Whoever believes and is baptized will be saved, but whoever does not believe will be condemned". (Mark 16:16).

"For God so loved the world that He gave His one and only Son, that whoever believes in Him shall perish but have eternal life". (John 3:16).

"I write these things to you who believe in the name of the Son of God so that you may know that you have eternal life. This is the confidence we have in approaching God: that if we ask anything according to His will, He hears us. And if we know that He hears us—whatever we ask—we know that we have what we asked of Him". (1 John 5:13-15).

My God has cleaned my heart and has mended all my wounds, back to where He originally designed me to be. God has turned my heart to match up with His, making me feel strong and loved, so I am able to show others the proof of His love and companionship to live how He wants us to live. This is what the Word of God tells me and you how to live: *"Rid yourselves of all the offenses you have committed, and get a new heart and a new spirit. Why will you die, people of Israel? For I take no pleasure in the death of anyone, declares the Sovereign Lord. Repent and live!" (Ezekiel 18:31-32).*

"Then the nations around you that remain will know that I the Lord have rebuilt what was destroyed and have replanted what was desolate. I the Lord have spoken, and I will do it". (Ezekiel 36:26).

Here are some more heart-mending Scriptures to mend hurtful hearts:

"I will praise the Lord, who counsels me; even at night my heart instructs me. I keep my eyes always on the Lord. With Him at my right hand—I will not be shaken. Therefore, my heart is glad and my tongue rejoices; my body also will rest secure, because you will not abandon me to the realm of the dead, nor will you let your faithful one see decay. You make known to me the path of life; you will fill me with joy in your presence, with eternal pleasures at your right hand". (Psalm 16:7-11).

"The eyes of the Lord are on those who fear Him, on those whose hope is in His unfailing love, to deliver them from death and keep them alive in famine. We wait in hope for the Lord; He is our help and our hearts rejoice, for we trust in His holy name. May your unfailing love be with us, Lord, even as we put our hope in you". (Psalm 33:18-22).

"Lord, I wait for you; you will answer, Lord my God". (Psalm 38:15).

"As the deer pants for streams of water, so my soul pants for you, my God". (Psalm 42:1).

"Deep calls to deep in the roar of your waterfalls; all your waves and breakers have swept over me. By day the Lord directs His love, at night His song is with me—a prayer to the God of my life". (Psalm 42:7-8).

"Hope deferred makes the heart sick, but a longing fulfilled is a tree of life. Whoever scorns instruction will pay for it, but whoever respects a command is rewarded. The teaching of the wise is a fountain of life, turning a person from the snares of death. Good judgment wins favor, but the way of the unfaithful leads to their destruction". (Proverbs 13:12-15).

"Those who hope in the Lord will renew their strength. They will soar on wings like eagles; they will run and not grow weary, they will walk and not faint". (Isaiah 40:31).

"'For I know the plans I have for you', declares the Lord, 'plans to prosper you and not to harm you, plans to give you hope and a future. Then you will call on me and come and pray to me, and I will listen to

you'". (Jeremiah 29:11).

"For in this hope we were saved. However, hope that is seen is no hope at all. Who hopes for what they already have? But if we hope for what we do not yet have, we wait for it patiently". (Romans 8:24-25).

"Love must be sincere. Hate what is evil; cling to what is good. Be devoted to one another in love. Honor one another above yourselves. Never be lacking in zeal, but keep your spiritual fervor, serving the Lord. Be joyful in Hope, patient in affliction, faithful in prayer. Share with the

Lord's people who are in need. Practice hospitality". (Romans 12:9-13).

"How much more, then, will the blood of Christ, who through the Eternal Spirit offered Himself unblemished to God, cleanse our consciences from acts that lead to death, so that we may serve the living God!" (Hebrews 9:14).

After you absorb these mending Scriptures, absorb these Scriptures to guard and protect your heart: *"My brothers and sisters, pay attention to what I say; turn your ear to my words. Do not let them out of your sight; keep them within your heart, for they are Life to those who find them and health to one's whole body. Above all else, guard your heart for everything you do flows from it. Keep your mouth free of perversity; keep corrupt talk far from your lips. Let your eyes look straight ahead; fix your gaze directly before you. Give careful thought to the paths for your feet and be steadfast in all your ways. Do not turn to the right or the left; keep your foot from evil". (Proverb 4:20-27).*

"He gave them these orders: 'You must serve faithfully and wholeheartedly in the fear of the Lord'". (2 Chronicles 19:9).

"Listen, my son, and be wise, and set your heart on the right path: Do not join those who drink too much wine or gorge themselves on meat, for drunkards and gluttons become poor, and drowsiness clothes them in rags". (Proverb 23:19-21).

"This is the message we have heard from Him and declare to you: God is Light; in Him there is no darkness at all. If we claim to have fellowship with Him and yet walk in the darkness, we lie and do not live out the truth. But if we walk in the Light, as He is in the Light, we have fellowship with one another, and the blood of Jesus, His Son, purifies us from all sin". (1 John 1:5-7).

"For this reason I kneel before the Father, from whom every family in heaven

and on earth derives its name. I pray that out of His glorious riches He may strengthen you with power through His Spirit in your inner being, so that Christ may dwell in your hearts through faith. And

I pray that you, being rooted and established in love, may have power, together with all the Lord's holy people, to grasp how wide and long and high and deep is the love of Christ and to know this love that surpasses knowledge—that you may be filled to the measure of all the fullness of God. Now to Him is able to do immeasurably more than all we ask or imagine, according to His power that is at work within us, to Him be glory in the church and in Christ Jesus throughout all generations, forever and ever! Amen". (Ephesians 3:14-21).

To prevent anything dirty or evil that may want to enter my heart, I need to keep my eyes fixed on Jesus—who leads me down the path of riches and honor and peace. All for the glory of His Father. With Jesus walking with me, I can stay on the righteous path. As the Word of God tells me to: *"Pay attention and turn your ear to the sayings of the wise; apply your heart to what I teach, for it is pleasing when you keep them on your lips. So that your trust may be in the Lord. I will teach you today, even you". (Proverb 22:17-19).*

When burnout shows its ugly head:

Sometimes, learning from my failures brought me into burnout (spiritual burnout). I was always trying to figure out the reasons why uncomfortable things happened to me. I know that we all experience some kind of burnout, one way or another. I set out to explore the meaning behind burnouts (and its causes). Because no one likes to go through burnouts (I sure did not).

Burnout leads to diminished health, social withdrawal, depression, and spiritual emptiness. In our human stage, we tend to take on more than we can handle and try to solve every problem on our own. Doing this keeps us in the state of burnout and gives entrance to Satan, who just thrives on our downfalls. For he is the one who makes us feel empty and burned out. The struggles and difficulties of this world are overwhelming, making you feel like you are spinning like a top that never stops. This is the way I felt (most of the time) when the things of this world tried to defeat me. The things of this world are the weapons of Satan, which keeps us from obeying

God's commands and instructions, from attending a church faithfully, from spending time in prayer and reading the Bible (God's Word). Finally, Satan really loves it when his weapons make us too fatigued to please God for His approval.

Listen up, brothers and sisters, Jesus is with us, and He says: ***"I am the way, the truth and the life. No one comes to the Father except through Me"***. *(John 14:6).*

"Through Him we both have access to one Spirit to the Father". (Ephesians 2:18). "Consequently, He is able to save to the uttermost those who draw near to God through Him, since He always lives to make intercession for them". (Hebrews 7:25).

"I am the door. If anyone enters by Me, he will be saved and will go in and out and find pasture"*. (John 10:9).* Resting in the refuge of God's compassion is just enough to calm any stressful situation in this world.

True Spiritual maturity is this: when you give up your sin and weaknesses, and live by faith, and trust that He will carry you through life. I think of God's power as a river of love that I can ease into, and rest in the healing waters, and have the strength to endure all that I have to face in the course of my day. Our enemy (Satan) is prowling around, shooting his arrows of deceit and destruction. However, when Jesus (who is always right by my side) sees what Satan is doing to me, He then picks me up and places me on His shoulders and carries me, until I am confident enough that Satan's arrows will dissolve before they even come near me. I will always remember what Jesus tells me when I am overwhelmed with weariness and burdens:

"'Come to Me, all you who are weary and burdened, and I will give you rest. Take My yoke upon you and learn from Me, for I am gentle and humble in heart, and you will find rest for your souls. For My yoke is easy and My burden is light'"*. (Matthew 11:28-30).*

Satan's weapons are poisonous. Here are his most used weapons— bitterness, anger, and complaining. Bitterness is an expression of severe pain, grief, or regret. Satan sets out to stick this poisonous root of bitterness into our souls, and once he plants bitterness, it starts festering in our hearts, filling us up with anger and regret. When God showed me the bitterness that I had in me, He said it was hurting me and everyone around me. This was why I was feeling so ugly and empty inside. I had to rid myself of this poison, before I lose all who I care for.

Here is how I got rid of bitterness: I went straight to the Bible and looked up all the Scriptures that told me how to rid myself of bitterness. Here is what I found the Word of God (the Bible) says I should do: *"Get rid of all bitterness, rage and anger, brawling and slander, along with every form of malice. Be kind and with one compassionate to one another, forgiving each other, just as in Christ God forgave you". (Ephesians 4:31-32). "See to it that no one falls short of the Grace of God and that no bitter root grows up to cause trouble and defile many". (Hebrews 12:15). "For it is better if it is the Will of God, to suffer for doing good, than for doing evil". (1 Peter 3:17).*

Holding on to bitterness can also lead you to doubting your relationship with Jesus (which is what Satan wants), which leads you to turning away from living out God's Commands and Instructions, which leads you into sin, which leads you to hurting yourself and others (family and friends), which then leads away from being the salt of the earth for our Heavenly Father. Being the salt of the earth, we must stay close to our Lord Jesus so He can teach us how we can preach the gospel and be the salt for those in need. The Bible says: "He said to them, **'Go into the world and preach the gospel to all creation. Whoever believes and is baptized will be saved, but whoever does not believe will be condemned'".** *(Mark 16:15-16). "Then the disciples went out and preached everywhere, and the Lord worked with them and confirmed His Word by the signs that accompanied it". (Mark 16:20).*

To be the salt of the earth, we need to pay close attention to the Attributes and the Characteristics of our Lord Jesus. Bitterness is nowhere in our Heavenly Father and His Son Jesus. This world is what gives us bitterness. Too much bitterness goes undetected and we many times do not see how it pulls us away from our walk with Jesus. Bitterness—when left undetected—keeps us from telling the good news of the Gospel and all that God can do and give us.

When we receive our Lord Jesus, we receive the salt that we need to preserve our lives and live in peace with His Father. When we let bitterness creep into our lives, we give control to Satan (who is full of bitterness). Satan is always prowling around, just waiting for the opportunity to sip right into our lives. I never thought I had bitterness until I went to the Bible (God's Word) to find out that I was harvesting bitterness. I kept on reading all the Scriptures that pertained to bitterness and how to get free of it. Jesus told me not to stress about it too much. As long as I follow His example, all will go right with His Father in Heaven.

Before Jesus came into my life, my life seemed to be tasteless and empty, just like food is without seasoning (salt). Foods made with no salt are bland, bitter, and flavorless and not a joy to eat. Even when food has too much salt, you cannot eat the food, and you have to throw it away. However, when we have Jesus, we always have the right amount of seasoning (salt) to live a peaceful and loving life. There is no such thing as too much Jesus. We need all of Jesus to have all of His Father's Love. The moment our hearts take Jesus as Lord and Savior, we can never again walk in darkness. Our Lord Jesus is not only our light; He is our salt. Without Him, we become bland and bitter, like the food does with no salt, and we become huge targets for Satan. For Satan wants us to be bland and bitter, for he is bland, cold, and bitter. Satan is the cause of us losing our saltiness. However, the more we saturate ourselves with God's Word, the harder it is for Satan to steer us away from walking the righteous path with Jesus. God's Word gives us wisdom, hope, joy, and love to bring light to those who are still walking in the darkness of this world. In the Bible, Jesus tells us, *"**You are the salt of the earth. However, if the salt loses its saltiness, how can it be made salty again? It is no longer good for anything except to be thrown out and trampled underfoot. You are the light of the world. A town built on a hill, cannot be hidden. Neither do people light a lamp and put it under a bowl. Instead, they put it on its stand, and it gives light to everyone in the house. In the same way, let your light shine before others so that they may see your good deeds and glorify your Father in Heaven'**". (Matthew 5:13-16).

Here are some ways that Satan tries to get us to lose our saltiness. Read each Scripture verse and begin to rid yourselves of bitterness, anger or rage, selfishness, pride or arrogance, and unforgiveness.

<u>Bitterness is what Satan uses</u>. We must take notice of this weapon (bitterness) that Satan uses. For unresolved bitterness leads to hatred, anger, jealousy, and revenge. Bitterness keeps us from fellowship with our Heavenly Father and Creator, His Son Jesus, and other fellow believers. Bitterness blinds us to the blessings that God has for us. Study these Scripture verses to overcome bitterness.

"Repent of this wickedness and pray to the Lord in the hope that He may forgive you for having such a thought in your heart. For I can see that you are full of bitterness and captive by sin". (Acts 8:22-23).

"I have told you these things, so that in Me you may have peace. In this world, you will have trouble—but take heart! I have overcome the world". (John 16:33).

"Create in me a pure heart, O God, and renew a steadfast spirit within me. Do not cast me from your presence or take your Holy Spirit from me. Restore to me the joy of your salvation and grant me a willing spirit, to sustain me". (Psalm 51:10-12).

"Whoever conceals their sins does not prosper, but the one who confesses and renounces them, finds Mercy. Blessed is the one who always trembles before God, but whoever hardens their heart falls into trouble". (Proverb 28:13-14).

"Get rid of all bitterness, rage and anger, brawling and slander, along with every form of malice. Be kind and compassionate to one another, forgiving each other, just as in Christ God forgave you". (Ephesians 4:31-32).

"Therefore, as God's chosen people, holy and dearly loved, clothe yourselves with compassion, kindness, humility, gentleness and patience. Bear with each other and forgive one another if any of you has a grievance against someone. Forgive as the Lord forgave you. In addition, over all these virtues put on love, which binds them all together in perfect unity. Let the peace of Christ rule in your hearts, since as members of one body you were called to peace—and be thankful. Let the message of Christ dwell among you richly as you teach and admonish one another with all wisdom through psalms, hymns, and songs from the Spirit, singing to God with gratitude in your hearts. And whatever you do, whether in

word or deed, do it all in the name of the Lord Jesus, giving thanks to God the Father through Him". (Colossians 3:12-17).

"Each heart knows its own bitterness, and no one else can share its joy." The house of the wicked will be destroyed, but the tent of the upright will flourish". (Proverb 14:10-11).

Anger or Rage is the result of bitterness: We should deal with anger or rage quickly before it becomes—bitterness, hatred or revenge. We must also seek out the root of our anger or rage. One tool that I found to be the root of my anger turns out to be the same as bitterness: Satan. Once again, I tell you, Satan thrives on bringing us down to his low-down, filthy ways. I was kind and soft spoken, not wanting to hurt anyone, which made me the perfect target for Satan to mold me into one of his followers. Satan started having my classmates, friends, and yeah, even family say and do things that would make me angry and since I was shy and never wanted to hurt anyone's feelings I held my anger inside turning that anger into bitterness. My Star Team saw what was happening to me and came to help me change that bitterness into kindness and had me walk away before I lashed out at them. I now draw strength from my Star Team to keep on walking through the hurt instead of getting angry. Jesus gives me the strength to live as He does—with love, joy, peace, and kindness. Of course, I was somewhat not that popular (being quiet and all), but I was popular with my Star Team – who is always with me to keep me company to this day. As long as I keep hold of Jesus's hand, I will never be without company.

Here are some Scripture verses that I read all the time to overcome anger or rage and not fall into the pit of bitterness. The path that leads to my Heavenly Father—the One who gave me His Son Jesus to walk with – does not have bitterness.

"In your anger do not sin: Do not let the sun go down while you are still angry, and do not give the devil a foothold". (Ephesians 4:26-27).

"Do not let any unwholesome talk come out of your mouths, but only what is helpful for building others up according to their needs; that it may benefit those who listen. In addition, do not grieve the Holy Spirit of God, with whom you were sealed for the day of redemption. Get rid of all bitterness, rage and anger, brawling and slander, along with every form of malice. Be kind and *compassionate to one another, forgiving each other, just as in Christ God forgave you". (Ephesians 4:29-32).*

"Be still before the Lord and wait patiently for Him; do not fret when people succeed in their ways, when they carry out their wicked schemes. Refrain from anger, and turn from wrath; do not fret—it leads only to evil. For those who are evil will be destroyed, but those who hope in the Lord will inherit the land". (Psalm 37:7-9).

"My shield is God Most High, who saves the upright in heart. God is a righteous judge, a God who displays His wrath every day". (Psalm 7:10-11).

"Whoever fears the Lord walks uprightly, but those who despise Him are devious in their ways". (Proverb 14:2).

"A man of quick-temper does foolish things, and the one who devices evil schemes is hated". (Proverbs 14:17).

"Whoever is patient has great understanding, but one who is quick tempered displays folly. A heart at peace gives life to the body, but envy rots the bones". (Proverb 14:29-30).

"My dear brothers and sisters, take note of this: Everyone should be quick to listen, slow to speak and slow to become angry, because human anger does not produce the righteousness that God desires. Therefore, get rid of all moral filth and the evil that is so prevalent and humbly accept the word planted in you, which can save you". (James 1:19-21).

"Submit yourselves, then, to God. Resist the devil, and he will flee from you". (James 4:7).

"Brothers and sisters; do not slander one another. Anyone who speaks against a brother or sister or judges them speaks against the law and judges it. When you judge the law, you are not keeping it, but sitting in judgment on it". (James 4:11).

"You, my brothers and sisters, were called to be free. However, do not use your freedom to indulge the flesh; rather, serve one another humbly in love. For the entire law is fulfilled in keeping this on command: 'Love your neighbor as yourself.' If you bite and devour each other, watch out or you will be destroyed by each other. So I say, walk by the Spirit, and you will not gratify the desires of the flesh". (Galatians 5:13-16).

"I have been crucified with Christ and I no longer live, but Christ lives in

me. The life I now live in the body, I live by faith in the Son of God, who loved me and gave Himself for me". (Galatians 2:20).

"Fools give full vent to their rage, but the wise bring calm in the end". (Proverb 29:11).

"A hot-tempered person must pay the penalty; rescue them, and you will have to do it again". (Proverb 19:19).

"A gentle answer turns away wrath, but a harsh word stirs up anger". (Proverb 15:1).

"The eyes of the Lord are everywhere, keeping watch on the wicked and the good. The soothing tongue is a tree of life, but a perverse tongue crushes the spirit". (Proverb 15:3-4).

"A hot-tempered person stirs up conflict, but the one who is patient calms a quarrel". (Proverb 15:18).

"Better a patient person than a warrior, one with self-control than one who takes a city". (Proverb 16:32).

"Do not make friends with a hot-tempered person, do not associate with one easily angered, or you may learn their ways and get yourself ensnared". (Proverb 22:24-25).

"Do not be quickly provoked in your spirit, for anger resides in the lap of fools". (Ecclesiastes 7:9).

"But now you must also rid yourselves of all such things as these: anger, rage, malice, slander, and filthy language from your lips". (Colossians 3:8).

"You have heard that it was said to the people long ago, 'You shall not murder and anyone who murders will be subject to judgment'. But I tell you that anyone who is angry with a brother or sister will be subject to judgment". (Matthew 5:22a).

The emotions that link to anger or rage are un-forgiveness, selfishness, and pride or arrogance. These are toxins to your body, making you lose your strength and willingness to obey God, which in turn leads you to sin and death. To make sure you do not lose your willingness to obey God, you must read His word—the Bible (God's Word). Keeping your eyes fixed on His Son Jesus, and most of all keep your ears open to God's instructions, for He is always speaking. You must obey God's instructions if you want to live a peaceful and joyful life. Therefore, listen and do what your Heavenly Father asks you to do; He then will season you with His love (salt), joy, and peace. We then can spread them among all of His children. We serve an awesome God that will always be with us and protect us—no matter what kind of destructive arrows Satan throws our way. Walking in step with Jesus and living like He lives, we will never lose our saltiness. Just remember these verses and you cannot go wrong:

"Your word is a lamp for my feet, a light on my path". (Psalm 119:105).

"To shine on those living in darkness and in the shadow of death, to guide our feet into the path of peace". (Luke 1:79).

"My heart is set on keeping your decrees to the very end". (Psalm 119:112).

"My flesh and my heart may fail, but God is the strength of my heart and my portion forever". (Psalm 73:26).

A prayer of thanks to God:

Thank you, Father, for showing me Your Heart. And for changing my angry heart into Your Loving Heart. I will praise You all the days of my life. I pray this in Your Son's Glorious Name, Jesus. Amen.

Trials—Testing of Faith

----

*T*rials are inevitable in this world that we are journeying in. Trials test our Faith. How do I know this is true? Because whenever I begin to feel that "black cloud" hovering over my head, I know that I am not relying on God to carry me through my day. However, the moment I called out to my Star Team for help, the black cloud turned into a sunshine of strength, making me able to walk right on through that trial (situation) that so filled me with fear.

God uses these fearful trials to test my faith and teach me to trust Him and have patience and love Him above all else in this world. It is very important for me to stand firm in my Faith, for it keeps the enemy away. It also puts a smile on God's face, and it glorifies Him. To me, everything I do is to glorify my Heavenly Father; this is what I live for to shine His glory and let Him hear me say: "I will praise you in this storm, no matter what Satan tries to throw at me, to knock me off the path of righteousness".

My Lord Jesus is more powerful than any destructive arrows that Satan has. Jesus lives in me and defends me whenever He sees fit to intercede. Believing that God is working through me in the troubles that I face is satisfying enough for me. I will always find joy in the midst of my trials. This joy will always happen as I keep my eyes fixed on Him and not on my troubles. Jesus is my Lord over my life; there is nothing on this earth that can change that. I will always remember to let the One who calms the storms in my life and that hears my cry for help have total control. I owe Jesus that much for all He went through for me. I have Faith in my Lord Jesus! Faith is no matter what you are going through, you believe that Jesus is at your side walking you through the fire without getting burned. The Bible says, *"Now faith is confidence in what we hope for and assurance about what we do not see". (Hebrews 11:1).*

Trials make our Faith stronger. We need Faith because trials are full of suffering, distress, affliction, misery, and pain. Here is what God's Word tells us to do about trials:

"Consider it pure joy, my brothers and sisters, whenever you face trials of many kinds, because you know that the testing of your faith produces perseverance. Let perseverance finish its work so that you may be mature and complete, not lacking nothing". (James 1:2-4).

"Blessed is the one who perseveres under trial because, having stood the test, that person will receive the crown of life that the Lord has promised to those who love Him". (James 1:12).

"Love is patient, love is kind. It does not envy, it does not boast, it is not proud". (1 Corinthians 13:4).

"Every good and perfect gift is from above, coming down from the Father of the heavenly lights, who does not change like shifting shadows. He chose to give us birth through the Word of Truth that we might be a kind of first-fruits of all He created". (James 1:17-18).

In these times of the troubles of this world, having Jesus walking along with us, gives us the strength to endure. The Book of James made my mind much clearer and less foggy, ready to face the next test and trial of faith. I look at my trials as a constant "pop quiz." Just like when I was in school, I used to ask God these questions when my mind was foggy and confused; and He of course answered me through His Word. Here is what He answered:

1.) How do I count the "pain" that hurts so much, as joy? Because when I do, I am *"blessed to be the one who perseveres under trial because, having stood the test, that person will receive the crown of life that the Lord has promised to those who love Him". (James 1:12). "And the God of all grace, who called you to His Eternal Glory in Christ, after you have suffered a little while, will Himself restore you and make you strong, firm and steadfast". (1 Peter 5:10).*

2.) What do I need to learn from this test? To learn that—*"because you know that the testing of your faith produces perseverance. Let perseverance finish its work so that you may be mature and complete, not lacking anything". (James 1:3-4).*

3.) What is the purpose for me being patient? To get rid of pride. Impatience is caused by pride and patience burns pride out of your life. As the Bible says: *"The end of a matter is better than its beginning, and patience is better than pride". (Ecclesiastes 7:8).*

4.) How does patience make me perfect and complete and lacking nothing? By receiving our Lord Jesus Christ. *"If any lacks wisdom, you should ask God, who gives generously to all without finding fault, and it will be given to you". (James 1:5).* God gives us wisdom and patience to be able to teach others who He is. We sometimes do not realize we have pride until God reveals to us a situation that shows that we have pride in us. The Bible says: *"Pride goes before destruction and a haughty spirit before a fall. Better to be lowly in spirit along with the oppressed than to share plunder with the proud". (Proverbs 16:18-19).*

Whenever we go through the time of testing, we need to repent of any pride that may be involved; for pride can make us think we deserve better and make us angry at God for what is happening to us. Pride can have us develop an attitude that is not acceptable to God. Pride can make us show anger to others rather than love others. God tests us to see what is in our hearts. However, Satan uses pride to turn us away from following God's way of living. I for one do not want to be like Satan, for Satan is dark and depressing. I want to be like Jesus, God's Son; for Jesus is Light and Joyful. When I live like Jesus in the Light, I am living in His Father's Love.

The teaching of patience perfects you, and patience is the process of perfection. Praising God is the best thing to do when trials come your way. A joyful and thankful heart is all God wants us to have. Also, remember this: God is always watching over us, and He is always with us. We must always acknowledge God in everything you go through.

I have learned that I had to (and still do) find ways to encourage myself, to keep myself fixed on Jesus. The Holy Spirit gave me these sayings to get me out of my despair. I say these every time I need encouragement to get through the fiery trials that are before me.

"I am not my past."

"I am not my failures."

"I am a daughter of the One True God."

"I am smart."

"I am important."

"I am brave and courageous."

"I am fearfully and wonderfully made."

"I am beautiful."

"I am called by God to do great things."

"I am strong."

"I am a finisher."

"I am a winner."

"I am an overcomer."

"Greater is He than he who is in the world."

"I matter to God."

"I am strong in the face of adversity."

"I am patient and kind."

"I am honest."

"I am humble."

"I am hidden in Christ."

"I am wise to wear God's Grace."

"I am whom my Heavenly Father says I am, and I will do whatever He says to do."

"I am loved."

"I am blessed with God's Grace."

"I belong."

"I am rooted and grounded in my Lord."

"I am treasured."

"I will not give up. I am not a quitter."

"I will make it."

"I am a masterpiece."

Now, here are some encouraging Scriptures to lift you out of the pit of self-pity. These and many more from the Bible are my encouragement. Always and forevermore!

"My flesh and my heart may fail. But God is the strength of my heart and my portion forever". (Psalm 73:26).

*"And God says: **'Be still and know I am God. I will be exalted among the nations. I will be exalted in the earth'***". (Psalm 46:10).*

"The Name of the Lord is a Fortified Tower; the righteous run to it and are safe". (Proverb 18:10).

I Call These the Words God Speaks:

*"**'Do not fear, for I am with you; do not be dismayed, for I am you God. I will strengthen you and help you; I will uphold you with My Righteous right hand'**". (Isaiah 41:10).*

"Do not let any unwholesome talk come out of your mouths, but only what is helpful for building others up according to their needs, that it may benefit those who listen". (Ephesians 4:29).

*"**'Peace I leave with you; My Peace I give you. I do not give to you as the world gives. Do not let your hearts be troubled and do not be afraid'**". (John 14:27).*

*"**'I have told you these things, so that in Me you may have Peace. In this world, you will have trouble. However, take heart! I have overcome the world'**". (John 16:33).*

"God is our refuge and strength, an ever-present help in trouble. Therefore, we will not fear, though the earth gives way and the mountains fall into the heart of the sea, though its waters roar and foam and the mountains quake with their surging". (Psalm 46:1-3).

"For the Spirit God gave us does not make us timed, but gives us power, love and self-discipline". (2 Timothy 1:7).

"I keep my eyes always on the Lord. With Him at my right hand, I will not be shaken. Therefore, my heart is glad and my tongue rejoices; my body also will rest secure, because you will not abandon me to the realm of the dead, nor will you let your faithful one see decay. You make known to me the path of life; you will fill me with joy in your presence, with eternal pleasures at your right hand".

(Psalm 16:8-11).

"Cast your cares on the Lord and He will sustain you; He will never let the righteous be shaken". (Psalm 55:22).

"Humble yourselves, therefore, under God's mighty hand, that He may lift you up in due time. Cast all your anxiety on Him because He cares for you". (1 Peter 5:6-7).

"You will keep in perfect peace those whose minds are steadfast, because they trust in you. Trust in the Lord forever, for the Lord, the Lord Himself, is the Rock eternal". (Isaiah 26:3-4).

"I was pushed back and about to fall, but the Lord helped me. The Lord is my strength and my defense; He has become my salvation". (Psalm 118:13-14).

"You are my refuge and my shield; I have put my hope in your word." Away from me, you evildoers that I may keep the commands of my God!" (Psalm 119:114-115).

"I am laid low in the dust; preserve my life according to your word. I gave an account of my ways and you answered me; teach me your decrees. Cause me to understand the way of your precepts so that I may meditate on your wonderful deeds. My soul is weary with sorrow; strengthen me according to your word. Keep me from deceitful ways; be gracious to me and teach me your law. I have chosen the way of faithfulness; I have set my heart on your laws. I hold fast to your statutes, Lord; do not let me be put to shame. I run in the path of your commands, for you have broadened my understanding". (Psalm 119:25-32).

"Remember Your Word to Your servant, for You have given me hope. My comfort in my suffering is this: Your promise preserves my life". (Psalm 119:49-50).

"It was good for me to be afflicted, so that I might learn your decrees. The law from your mouth is more precious to me than thousands of pieces of silver and gold". (Psalm 119:71-72).

"I call on the Lord in my distress, and He answers me". (Psalm 120:1).

"It is You alone who is to be feared. Who can stand before You when You are angry?" (Psalm 76:7).

"Make vows to the Lord your God and fulfill them; let all the neighboring lands bring gifts to the One to be feared. He breaks the spirit of rulers; He is *feared by the kings of the earth". (Psalm 76:11-12).*

"My flesh and my heart may fail, but God is the strength of my heart and my portion forever. Those who are far from You will perish; You destroy all who are unfaithful to You. But as for me, it is good to be near god. I have made the Sovereign Lord my refuge; I will tell of all Your deeds". (Psalm 73:26-28).

*"He says, **'Be still and know I am God; I will be exalted among the nations; I will be exalted in the earth'".** (Psalm 46:10).*

DOUBT—We All Experience It

How am I to draw close to God? This question has always plagued my thoughts. However, one day, when I found out what this question meant, I had doubts about my relationship with God. So, I took it to my Star Team (my Counselor) and found out the truth of having a little doubt, which was not so little; it was much bigger than I thought. Doubt is a word that tells God that you do not trust Him. Having doubt you are sinning against God; and that is exactly what the enemy (Satan) wants you to do.

What is "doubt" anyway? Doubt is one explosive weapon of Satan, the maker of such destructive weapons. Doubt draws us away from getting closer to God (which Satan wants). Doubt is not only a one-word weapon; it is a five-word weapon. All of the five words Satan uses to turn us away from our walk with Jesus.

Here is my explanation of DOUBT in the five words that Satan uses to make us stumble:

D—Deceive—to make us believe something that is not true.

O—Obstacle—to block the path that leads to righteousness.

U—Unsure—to take away our confidence that God loves us.

B—Bewildered—to confuse us, causing us to lose our bearings (strength).

T—Taken-down—the action or act of taking down and turning us away from living in Peace.

These five words I was very aware of, for they were words that the enemy used all through my life. I have been <u>deceived</u> by not only strangers but by my own family. I had <u>obstacles</u> that I encountered to go around, to complete the work I was assigned. I was <u>unsure</u> of loved ones that they were not telling the truth, making me <u>bewildered</u> (confused); which <u>took me down</u> to a level that was hard to get out of to receive the Peace of God. However, ten years ago, I found my way out and dissolved them enough to walk right through them. I answered the knock that was at my heart, letting Jesus into my life. I then absorbed myself into God's Word when things become rough. This was the best thing I have ever done. The Bible (God's Word) was the place I found to go to when there was no one around to ask for advice. Today, I am stronger than I have ever been before.

Here are some Scripture verses that helped me dissolve all the doubt that Satan tried to use to knock me off my feet. They can and will surely help you too.

"I rise before dawn and cry for help; I have put my hope in Your Word". (Psalm 119:147).

"Sustain me, my God, according to Your Promise, and I will live; do not let my hopes be dashed". (Psalm 119:116). And the Lord says: ***"I am with you and will watch over you wherever you go, and I will bring you back to this land. I will not leave you until I have done what I have promised you"***. (Genesis 28:15).

"If any of you lacks wisdom, you should ask God, who gives generously to all without finding fault, and it will be given to you. However, when you ask, you must believe and not doubt, because the one who doubts is like a wave of the sea, blown and tossed by the wind. That person should not expect to receive anything from the Lord. Such a person is double-minded and unstable in all they do". (James 1:5-8).

"Whoever believes and is baptized will be saved, but whoever does not believe will be condemned". (Mark 16:16).

"You will say then, 'Branches were broken off so that I could be grafted in'. Granted. But they were broken off because of unbelief, and you stand by Faith. Do not be arrogant, but tremble. For if God did not spare the natural branches, He will not spare you either. Consider". (Romans 11:19-22).

"Jesus immediately reached out His hand and took hold of him, saying to

him, *'O you of little faith, why did you doubt?'"* *(Matthew 14:31).* Jesus will always be with us when we begin to get swallowed up in the evil waves of this angry and rushed world. So then, when you need confidence and encouragement, go to the Scriptures—the source of proof that God will always be there for you, no matter what or who comes against you. Take time out right now, and let God's Word speak to you to encourage and lift you up closer to your Heavenly Father who will always be there for you and loves you, unconditionally.

"I can do all things through Christ who strengthens me". (Philippians 4:13).

"Therefore, do not set your heart on what you will eat or drink; do not worry about it. For the pagan world runs after all such things, and your Father knows that you need them. However, seek His kingdom and these things will be given to you as well. Do not be afraid, little flock, for your Father has been pleased to give you the kingdom". (Luke 12:29-32).

"So we may boldly say: 'The Lord is my helper; I will not fear. What can man do to me?'". (Hebrews 13:6).

"Be confident of this very thing that He who has begun a good work in you will complete it until the day of Christ Jesus". (Philippians 1:6).

"The Lord God is my strength; He will make my feet like the feet of a deer, He enables me to tread on the heights". (Habakkuk 3:19).

"Yet, in all these things we are more than conquerors through Him who loved us". (Romans 8:37).

*"**When you pass through the waters, I will be with you; and the rivers, they shall not overflow you. When you walk through the fire, you shall not be burned, nor shall the flames scorch you'".** (Isaiah 43:2).*

"For the Lord will be your confidence, and will keep your foot from being caught". (Proverbs 3:26).

"In Him and through faith in Him we may approach God with freedom and confidence. I ask you, therefore, not to be discouraged because of my sufferings for you, which are your glory". (Ephesians 3:12-13)

We must choose to reject doubt if we want to live our lives the way God intended us to live. We must not have any doubt; for whenever doubt starts creeping into our lives, we must go straight to the Bible and discover the Power of God's Word and say, "I refuse to allow doubt to set up camp in my soul". Then read God's Word until you feel that doubt fall away from your thoughts. Scripture is the best medicine to keep your soul and mind free from doubt and any other negative thoughts. Faith is a Spiritual choice. Doubt is a choice of the flesh. We can choose to have Faith in God and His Word. When you have doubt at any time, get on your knees and confess it to God as sin. Ask Him, in Jesus' name, to remove that doubt and give you strength to reject doubt.

Check out this chart of how Scripture changed my reason for having doubt to God's Reason for having Faith in Him.\

My Reason for having Doubt	God's Reason for having Faith in Him
I'm feeling weak, and I'm doubting I can handle what I am doing.	*"I can do all things through Christ who strengthens me".* (Philippians 4:3).
What just happened to me is a disaster; and I doubt I can recover from it.	*"All things work together for good to those who love God, who are called according to His purpose".* (Romans 8:28).
I'm afraid of what could happen.	*"Perfect Love casts out fear".* (1 John 4:18).
Not knowing if God will answer my prayers.	*"If you ask anything in My name, I will do it".* (John 14:14).

Prayer:

Father, increase my faith every day that I read your Word. Give me strong faith, enough to help anyone I come across, to believe that You are everything You say You are. Help me to trust You with all my heart and not relying on my own understanding. I will acknowledge Your ways and depend on You to direct my path. Help me to trust You every day and to keep me from doubting You and Your Word. Thank you, Father, for helping me to reflect who You are, to show this world the proof of Your Love. Thank you for keeping me focused on living out Your Word and keeping Your Word in my heart. In the Name of Your Glorious Son Jesus, I pray. Amen.

I will always continue to build up my faith in God, so I can have the strength and discernment to fight off any sin that comes my way. I want to show and teach others that being faithful to God and His promises will break those chains of doubt. <u>We must all live out God's Word</u>. This will please Him, and it will bring Him Glory. God is everything to me. Because of Him, I will never be without His Love, Joy, Peace, Hope, Power, Courage and Protection. God lifts me above my situations so I could live in peace in the shadow of His wings. God has opened my eyes to His Truth and helped me to live out His Ways and His Word.

We are to always reflect on all the characters of God. The only place to seek out God's characters is to open your Bible. The place to start reading and seeking out the Characters of God is found in Book 1 Corinthians, describing just who God is and how He works.

"Love is patient, love is kind. It [Love] does not envy, it [Love] does not boast, it [Love] is not proud. It [Love] does not dishonor others; it [Love] is not self-seeking, it [Love] is not easily angered, and it [Love] keeps no record of wrongs. Love does not delight in evil but rejoices with the truth. It [Love] always protects, always trusts, always hopes, always perseveres—Love never fails. However, where there are prophets—they will cease; where there are tongues, they will be stilled; where there is knowledge—it will pass away. For we know in part and we prophesy in part, but when completeness comes, what is in part disappears. When I was a child, I talked like a child; I thought like a child, I reasoned like a child. When I became a man, I put the ways of childhood behind me. For now we see only a reflection as in a mirror; then we shall see face to face. Now I know in part; then I shall know fully, even as I am fully known. However, these three remain: faith, hope and love. But the greatest of these is LOVE". (1 Corinthians 13:4-13).

In addition:*"The Fruit of the Spirit is Love, Joy, Peace, Patience, Kindness, Goodness, Faithfulness, Gentleness and Self-control. Against such things, there is no law. Those who belong to Christ Jesus have crucified the flesh with its passions and desires. Since we live by the Spirit. Let us not become conceited, provoking and envying each other". (Galatians 5"22-26).*

These nine characters are to be remembered and used when they are needed in this life on this earth. The Bible is the best place to learn God's characters and to learn how to live them out, in this cold, dark world. They are worth repeating: love, joy, peace, patience, kindness, goodness, gentleness, faithfulness, and self-control. The most important character to work into your life is love. If you do not have God's love, you do not have Jesus living in you, and you will not be able to love others like His Father commands us to love others.Without these characters (fruits) of God in us, we will not be able to endure the hills and valleys of this dark and cold world that we are walking. God's love is what strengthens us when we become weary and want to give up. Having Jesus walk with us in every moment of our life is that love-strength that we need.

Life with Jesus is having peace in the difficulties that we are facing. Joy is the result of faithful and obedient living. Trust is accepting God's will, even in those difficult times. I have learned to trust God with all my difficulties, to teach me how to live and depend on Him, always. With God having total control over my life, I can stay calm and receive the joy of His presence. Being calm, no matter what comes my way, is how Jesus lives. I (we) owe it to Jesus, for our Lord Jesus died for us—a death that He (God's Son) did not deserve.

This life on this earth is full of difficulties (hills and valleys), but God was, is, and always will be faithful to us. God created a special way for us—that is His Son Jesus Christ. For the Bible says:

"I am the way, the truth and the life. No one comes to the Father except through Me". (*John 14:6*).

"I will not leave you as orphans; I will come to you. Before long, the world will not see Me anymore, but you will see Me. Because I live, you also will live. On that day, you will realize that I am in My Father, and you are in Me, and I am in you. Whoever has My commands and keeps them is the one who loves Me. The one who loves Me will be loved by My Father, and I too will love them and show Myself to them". (*John 14:18-21*).

"I am the Light of the world. Whoever follows Me will never walk in darkness, but will have the Light of life". (*John 8:12*).

We are confident (with these Scriptures) that we are not walking the path alone. Every step we take must be in step with Jesus, teaching us, instructing us, and directing us the course of life, which leads us to victory. So take hold of Jesus's hand and open your ears. For God is speaking to us always His instructions—all the time and in every step we take with Him.

In this world, we have our enemy—Satan and his "puppets"—rising against us. However, fear not and trust in the Lord. Who is our shield and protector and will pull us out of our slimy pit that we seem to always get ourselves to fall into. Have faith and keep on believing that God is manifesting Himself in your life. Speak aloud and very clearly (so Satan can hear you): "Jesus is Lord, and I will see the goodness that He is doing in my life. Satan, you cannot stop me from following my Lord and Savior Jesus Christ." Then watch Satan go fleeing away from you with his tail between his legs.

If we stay connected and focused on Jesus, reading our Bibles, and praying continually, we will receive strength and discernment, to do all that our Heavenly Father asks us to do. Bringing glory to God that He so much deserves. Our awesome God is watching all the time.

As you know, God knows every move that Satan makes, and Satan cannot win against God. Satan is out there prowling around just waiting for us to come unraveled, so he can get his foot in the door, to watch us fall to his schemes. Jesus is Lord, and He will never leave our side. Jesus defeated Satan, and Satan is afraid of Him. This is where the fruit of patience comes in—to wait and walk alongside Jesus and watch Him defeat Satan's arrows that he has been throwing at us. God (who loves you) is watching; and He will never let Satan hurt you by his lies and destructions. Jesus is with you all the time; you have no need to feel the strain of this life, for Jesus overcame this world.

Here are some Scriptures that help me feel the Joy of God:

"O God, you are my God, earnestly I seek you, my soul thirsts for you, my body longs for you, in a dry and weary land, where there is no water. I have seen you in the sanctuary and beheld your power and your glory". (Psalm 63:1-2).

"God is our refuge and strength, an ever-present help in trouble. Therefore,

do not fear, though the earth gives way and the mountains fall into the heart of the sea, though its waters roar and foam and the mountains quake with their surging". (Psalm 46:1-3).

"God says, **'Be still, and know I am God; I will be exalted in all the nations. I will be exalted among the earth'**". (Psalm 46:10).

"See, the Sovereign Lord comes with power and His arm rules for Him. See, His reward is with Him, and His recompense accompanies Him. He tends His flock like a shepherd: He gathers the lambs in His arms and carries them close to His heart; He gently leads those that have young". (Isaiah 40:10-11).

"Even youths grow tired and weary, and young men stumble and fall; but those who hope in the Lord will renew their strength. They will soar on wings like eagles; they will run not grow weary, they will walk and not be faint". (Isaiah 40:30-31).

"For you have been my hope, O Sovereign Lord, my confidence since my youth. From birth I have relied on you; you brought me forth from my mother's womb. I will ever praise you". (Psalm 71:5-6).

"My heart and flesh may fail, but God is the strength of my heart and my portion forever". (Psalm 73:26).

These five Scriptures are just some examples that show me how spending time in God's Word is so refreshing and uplifting. The Bible is the only place I can go to when I need to be comforted. This One Scripture really gave me comfort in a situation that was wrong in God's eyes. I turned to Him, got on my knees, and confessed of the sin and asked Him to—"Please forgive me, Father, I come to You to: *"Blot out my transgression. Wash me thoroughly from my iniquity and cleanse me from my sin". (Psalm 51:1-2).* In Jesus's Name, I pray. Amen".

This verse is part of a prayer that King David prayed when he sought after another man's wife, Bathsheba. Not only did he lay with her but also he had her husband killed to try to cover up his sin. God still used David. Read for yourself the details of David's actions. It is in 2 Samuel 11 and 12.

I have not done nothing like that, but sometimes when things go wrong, I feel a pain in my heart that feels like ten thousand pins, making me turn to God and say, "I'm sorry. Forgive me," even if it was not my fault. God knows my heart, and if the sin that I confessed to Him is of my doing, then He will tell me my punishment. If it is not of my doing, then He will tell me that I should not worry about it and let it fade away so that it can go back to where it came from.

Only God knows our hearts. When we confess something we did wrong, God will know if we really mean our confession. How can He tell? One thing is that God is omniscient, knowing everything that goes on in our lives. The second thing is He has His Son Jesus to tell Him if you are sincere in your confession. This is the power of forgiveness, as Jesus told the adulteress woman, *"Until only Jesus was left, with the woman still standing there. Jesus straightened up and asked her,* **'Woman, where are they? Has no one condemned you?'** *'No one, Sir,' she said.* **'Then neither do I condemn you',** *Jesus declared.* **'Go now and leave your life of sin'"**. *(John 8:8-11)*. Jesus knew she was deeply sorry. God is the only One that can see and cleanse the heart of sin. God is the only One that can restore the heart of sin. God is the only One that can bless the heart with mercy and grace. When you confess your sin, you are affirming to God that you sinned against Him. This is why it is very, very important to have a good relationship with Jesus.

Right now, I have this leading of the Holy Spirit, to pray this prayer for all who might not realize that sin (pride and doubt) is hanging around inside.

Prayer

Dear Heavenly Father, I come to you to thank you for watching over us. Thank you for protecting us, forgiving us, and most of all loving us. Please continue searching our hearts, minds, and souls, removing anything evil that creeps into our hearts. Show us what it is, so we can confess it, repent it, and turn away from it. Keep our hearts humble and strong to endure all that Satan is throwing at us in this dark and corrupt world. Make us able to rebuke any pride and doubt that is waiting to enter into our lives. I thank you always for your faithfulness and love. Enable us to live out Your

Command to love with our whole heart, loving others as You love us. Thank you. In Jesus's Name, I pray. Amen!

Mentors—who are they?

Who are mentors? They are loyal friends, wise advisers, teachers, parents, and guardians. We all need mentors. Why? Because they are the ones that we take examples from and look to them for advice. These mentors are walking among us, living out what they have <u>learned</u>.

They <u>learned</u> to face challenges and have overcome them.

They <u>learned</u> to grow through the struggles and persevere.

They <u>learned</u> to see God working in their lives.

They <u>learned</u> how to get through hard times and experienced God's Presence.

They <u>learned</u> how to pass on the active Word of God and show that He walks among us.

They <u>learned</u> how to walk the roads of life and pass on the Knowledge they have gained.

These are people I never met until I opened the door to my Lord. The deeper I read my Bible, the more I found that my Lord Jesus is, was, and always will be my Mentor. When Jesus speaks, you listen. By the Power of His Father in Heaven, Jesus walked this earth sinless. Jesus is the best example of a mentor, showing how to forgive, to love and to live a peaceful life.

The Scriptures confirm my seeking of how Jesus is the best example (mentor):

"We know that we have come to know Him if we keep His commands. Whoever says, 'I know Him,' but does not do what He commands is a liar, and the Truth is not in that person. However, if anyone obeys His Word, love for God is truly made complete in them. This is how we know we are in Him: Whoever claims to live in Him must live as Jesus did". (1 John 2:3-6).

"To this you were called, because Christ also suffered for you, leaving you an

example that you should follow in His steps. He committed no sin, and no deceit was found in His mouth". (1Peter 2:21-22).

I tell you brothers and sisters: *"Follow God's example, therefore, as dearly loved children and walk in the way of Love, just as Christ loved us and gave Himself up for us as a Fragrant Offering and Sacrifice to God". (Ephesians 5:1-2).*

"In your relationships with one another, have the same mindset as Christ Jesus: Who, being in very the nature of God, did not consider equality with God something to be used to His own advantage; rather, He made Himself nothing by taking the very nature of a servant, being made in human likeness. And being found in appearance as a man, He humbled Himself by becoming obedient to death—even death on a cross!" (Philippians 2:5-8).

"I have set you an example that you should do as I have done for you. Very truly, I tell you, no servant is greater than his master is, nor is a messenger greater than the One who sent Him. Now that you know these things, you will be blessed if you do them". (John 13:15-17).

Our Lord Commands: ***"A new command I give you: Love one another. As I have loved you, so you must love one another. By this everyone will know that you are My disciples, if you love one another"'.*** *(John 13:34-35).*

"This is how we know what love is: Jesus Christ laid down His life for us. In addition, we ought to lay down our lives for our brothers and sisters". (1 John 3:16).

"May the God who gives endurance and encouragement give you the same attitude of mind toward each other that Christ Jesus had, so that with one mind and one voice you may glorify the God and Father of our Lord Jesus Christ. Accept one another, then, just as Christ accepted you, in order to bring praise to God". (Romans 15:5-7).

"Therefore, as God's chosen people, holy and dearly loved, clothe yourselves with compassion, kindness, humility, gentleness, and patience. Bear with each other and forgive one another if any of you has a grievance against someone. Forgive as the Lord forgave you. In addition, over all these virtues put on love, which binds them all together in perfect unity. Let the peace of Christ rule in your hearts. Since as members of one body you were called to peace and be thankful.

Let the message of Christ dwell among you richly as you teach and admonish one another with all wisdom through psalms, hymns, and songs from the Spirit, singing to God with gratitude in your hearts. And whatever you do, whether in word or deed, do it all in the name of the Lord Jesus, giving thanks to God the Father through Him". (Colossians 3:12-17).

"Make every effort to live in peace with everyone and to be holy; without holiness no one will see the Lord. See to it that no one falls short of the grace of God and that no bitter root grows up, to cause trouble and defile many". (Hebrews 12:14-15).

These Scriptures were (and still are) what keeps me fixed on who Jesus was, is, and always will be. Still, today, I have no physical mentor to look up to, but I am okay with that, because I have my Star Team to show me how to stay faithful and strong to endure all the chaos this world offers. I will always look up to Jesus's example of how to live out God's Will and Purpose.

As I am keeping my eyes fixed on Jesus, I am always continually checking on how I speak. This was hard for me, seeing that I was quiet and shy, with no friends or family to talk to, making me feel very lonely. I would sit, many times, at the park talking to the geese that were there swimming in the pond. This comforted me a lot. I knew that the geese's presence was God teaching me His calming methods. God's Word (the Bible) is not the only way to ease the chaos of this world, just looking to all He created is the most calming and life giving. When we speak the Words of God, we speak Life and when we breathe in God's Creation, we live His Life.

We tend to speak the world's words—doubt, ugly, dumb, and loser. We bring ourselves into the darkness (a place where Satan loves to see us). Continually speaking these words of the world is what keeps us in the world of darkness; and we then grieve the Spirit of God (which by the way is sinning against God). To get us out of that darkness, we must speak the Words of God—Hope, Love, Comfort, and Encouragement. God intends for us to speak these words, making His Heart smile with Love, so the whole world sees His Love is in us; making Him alive in us. Feeling God's Love will always lift me up; and it will lift up any person who is in despair and discomfort.

My Lord Jesus reached down and pulled me out of the pit that I was in when I was younger. Jesus took me by the hand, telling me that He will not only be my mentor, but He will teach me how to mentor someone who needs mentoring. For forty-five years, I believed that I had no friend, no help, no mentor to follow the example. Nevertheless, I had the greatest mentor—my Lord and Savior Jesus Christ.

All this time, Jesus was with me, loving me and teaching me the ways of His Father. From the time I was five to my present age of fifty-five, it seemed that I was always looking for love, companionship, comfort, and compassion in the wrong places. I always found emptiness and hatred. Jesus was knocking at my heart's door, all this time, but I did not recognize the knock. I was distracted by Satan's ways. God then started calling my name to see if that would work. I heard Him calling, but I always thought it was my family or someone at my work, wanting me. Then in 2005, Jesus called out my name and shined the brightest light I ever did see—just to get my attention. It worked, and I never looked any more for that mentor. Through that light, I heard my name, by a soft and gentle voice, and as I turned to see who was calling, I saw a hand reaching out to me. It was Jesus's Hand wanting me to grab hold of it as He pulled me out of the pit of this world and into a Life-learning world of Love, Comfort, and Compassion.

As I grabbed on to Jesus's hand, He lifted me out and up and set me on the rock, where on that rock, I could stand firm on—the foundation of His Father's Grace, Truth, and Love. I now, to this day, stand on that Rock of confidence to endure the battle that is before me every morning, noon, and night. That day, when God poured His Light into me, wrapping me in His Loving Embrace, I knew that I will never walk in the darkness of this world again. There is nothing more beautiful than the Love, Compassion, and Companionship of my Lord and Savior Jesus Christ. Today, I hold on ever so tightly to Jesus' hand and walk with Him through the shadows of this world. I thrive to live out this promise: *"I can do all things with Christ who strengthens me". (Philippians 4:13).* Together, Jesus and I, can draw others to walk confidently in the Light of God. And meditating on these Scriptures of truth will always make me and you feel that love, compassion, and companionship of our Lord and Savior Jesus Christ:

*"The Lord appeared to us in the past saying; **'I loved with an everlasting love; I have drawn you with unfailing kindness'***". *(Jeremiah 31:3).*

"I delight greatly in the Lord; my soul rejoices in my God. For He clothe me with garments of salvation and array me in a robe of righteousness as a bridegroom adorns his head; like a priest and as a bride adorns herself with her jewels. For as the soil makes the sprout come up and a garden causes seeds to grow, so the Sovereign Lord will make righteousness and praise spring up before all nations". (Isaiah 61:10-11). "But you are a chosen people, a royal priesthood, a holy nation, God's special possession, that you may declare the praises of Him who called you out of darkness into His wonderful light". (2 Peter 2:9).

As I approached God in stillness and trust, God strengthened and protected me. With the protection that surrounds me now, it helps me stay focused on the things that are unseen and are in Heaven. Keeping my eyes on the prize—God's Glory, which reflects in the eyes of His children that sees, hears, and obeys His Commands. The best way to open your eyes and ears to God's Glory is to spend time in His presence. Nothing is more satisfying than to rest in His Presence.

As we live in this world of chaos, we need to focus more on the unseen. So that we can feel the joy of the Lord and to be able to stand firm on His rock of strength. God enables us with that strength, for us to carry out His assignment. As I walk along this journey with Jesus, I face all kinds of chaos that this world has become. Jesus is with me always and will never leave me. "I will not be moved!" It is God's Word (the Bible) which tells me and you to not be shaken by the evil ways of this evil world that you and I are currently journeying – *"Fixing our eyes not on what is seen but on what is unseen, since what is seen is temporary, but what is unseen is Eternal". (2 Corinthians 4:18).* Calling to one another: *'Holy, Holy, Holy is the Lord Almighty; the whole earth is full of His Glory'". (Isaiah 6:3).* Therefore: *"I wait for the Lord, my whole being waits, and in His Word I put my hope. I wait for the Lord more than watchmen wait for the morning". (Psalm 130:5-6).*

The 'our part' tools for a Christian to live in freedom of our Heavenly Father are these eight things that we must do to stay in step with Jesus and bring rest to our souls:

Love—*the object of attachment, devotion, or admiration –*

"Love the Lord your God with all your heart, and with all your soul, and with your entire mind, and with all your strength. The second is this: Love your neighbor as yourself. There is no commandment greater than these". (Mark 12:30-31).

Generosity—*the quality or fact of being abundantly generous –*

"Command those who are rich in this present world, not to be arrogant nor to put their hope in wealth, which is uncertain, but to put their hope in God—who richly provides us with everything for our enjoyment. Command them to do good, to be rich in good deeds, and to be generous and willing to share. In this way they will lay up treasure for themselves as a firm foundation for the coming age, so that they may take hold of the life that is truly life". (1 Timothy 6:17-19).

Worship—*reverence to a divine being: an act of expressing such reverence –*

"But I, through the abundance of your steadfast love, will enter your house. I will bow down toward your holy temple in the fear of you". (Psalm 5:7).

"But the hour is coming, and is now here, when the true worshipers will worship the Father in spirit and truth, for the Father is seeking such people to worship Him". (John 4:23).

Service—*the work performed by one that serves: in deed or worship –*

"No one can serve two masters; for either he will hate the one and love the other, or he will be devoted to one and despise the other. You cannot serve God and wealth". (Matthew 6:24).

Giving—*to make a present of, to grant or bestow by formal action –*

"Give to everyone who asks you, and if anyone takes what belongs to you, do not demand it back. Do to others as you would have them do to you". (Luke 6:30-31).

"Those who give to the poor will lack nothing—but those who close their eyes to them receive many curses." (Proverbs 28:27).

Contemplation—*concentration on spiritual things as a form of private devotion* –

"But his delight is in the Law of the Lord, and in His Law he meditates day and night". (Psalms 1:2).

"Tremble and do not sin; when you are on your beds, search your hearts and be silent". (Psalm 4:4).

"Be still and know I am God. I will be exalted among the nations. I will be exalted in the earth". (Psalm 46:10).

"Great are the works of the Lord; they are studied by all who delight in them". (Psalm 111:2).

Gratitude—*the state of being grateful, thankfulness.*

"Through Him then let us continually offer up a sacrifice of praise to God, that is, the fruit of lips that acknowledge His name". (Hebrews 13:15).

"The Lord has done it this very day—let us rejoice today and be glad". (Psalm 118:24).

"Rejoice always, pray continually; give thanks in all circumstances; for this is God's will for you in Christ Jesus. Do not quench the Spirit". (1Thessalonians 5:16-19).

"And whatever you do, whether in word or deed, do it all in the Name of the Lord Jesus; giving thanks to God the Father through Him". (Colossians 3:17).

"I have not stopped giving thanks for you, remembering you in my prayers". (Ephesians 1:16).

"Speaking to one another with psalms, hymns, and songs from the Spirit. Sing and make music from your heart to the Lord—always giving thanks to God the Father for everything—in the name of our Lord Jesus Christ". (Ephesians 5:20).

"Let us come before Him with thanksgiving and extol Him with music and song. For the Lord is the great God, the great King above all gods". (Psalm 95:2-3).

"I will give thanks to the Lord, because of His righteousness; I will sing the praises of the name of the Lord Most High". (Psalm 7:17).

"The Lord is my strength and my shield; my heart trusts in Him and He helps me". *(Psalm 28:7).*

Teaching—something taught, especially; doctrine –

"All Scripture is God-breathed and is useful for teaching, rebuking, correcting and training in righteousness, so that the servant of God may be thoroughly equipped for every good work". (2 Timothy 3:16-17).

Fellowship—a company of equals or friends: an organization of persons having a common interest –

"But if we walk in the light, as He is in the light, we have fellowship with one another, and the blood of Jesus His Son cleanses us from all sin". (1 John 1:7).

Prayer—an address, a petition, to God in word or thought; the act of praying –

"The Lord is near to all who call on Him, to all who call on Him in truth". (Psalm 145:18).

"The Lord is far from the wicked, but He hears the prayer of the righteous". (Proverbs 15:29).

"You will seek me and find me. When you seek me with all your heart". (Jeremiah 29:13).

"When my life was fainting away, I remembered the Lord, and my prayer came to you, into your holy temple". (Jonah 2:7).

"Whatever you ask in my name, this I will do that the Father may be glorified in the Son". (John 14:13).

As we weave these eight things (our part) into our daily life; our Heavenly Father does His Part for us to receive His Grace.

What does God do (His Part)?

The things God does for us are the same things that I just mentioned earlier. But there are much, much more that He does – all because we believe in His Son Jesus Christ:

God Delivers –

"The righteous cry out, and the Lord hears them; He delivers them from all

their troubles. The Lord is close to the brokenhearted and saves those who are crushed in spirit. The righteous person may have many troubles, but the Lord <u>delivers</u> him from them all; He protects all his bones, not one of them will be broken. Evil will slay the wicked; the foes of the righteous will be condemned. The Lord will rescue His servants; no one who takes refuge in Him will be condemned". (Psalm 34:17-22).

"Consider it pure joy, my brothers and sisters, whenever you face trials of many kinds, because you know that the testing of your faith produces perseverance. Let perseverance finish its work so that you may be mature and complete, not lacking anything". (James 1:2-4).

"You, Lord, prepare a table before me in the presence of my enemy. You, Lord, anoint my head with oil; my cup overflows. Surely Your Goodness and Love will follow me all the days of my life, and I will dwell in the House of the Lord forever ". (Psalm 23:5-6).

"The eyes of the Lord are on those who fear Him, on those whose hope is in His Unfailing Love, to <u>deliver</u> them from death and keep them alive in famine". (Psalm 33:18-19).

God Covers –

"Hatred stirs up conflict, but Love [God] <u>covers</u> over all wrongs". Proverbs 10:12).

"Whoever dwells in the shelter of the Most High will rest in the shadow of the Almighty. I will say of the Lord, 'He is my Refuge and my Fortress, my God, in whom I trust'. Surely, He will save you from the fowler's snare and from the deadly pestilence. He will <u>cover</u> you with His Feathers, and under His wings you will find refuge; His Faithfulness will be your shield and rampart. You will not fear the terror of night, nor the arrow that flies by day, nor the pestilence that stalks in the darkness, nor the plague that destroys at midday. A thousand may fall at your side, ten thousand at your right hand, but it will not come near you. You will only observe with your eyes and see the punishment of the wicked". (Psalm 91:1-8).

"The Lord is my Shepherd, I lack nothing. He makes me lie down in green pastures, He leads me beside quiet waters, He refreshes my soul. He guides me

along the right paths for His Name's sake. Even though I walk through the darkest valley, I will fear no evil, for you are with me; Your Rod and Your Staff, they comfort me". (Psalm 23:1-4).

And the Lord says: *"**Since you have kept My Command to endure patiently, I will also keep you from the hour of trial that is going to come on the whole world to test the inhabitants of the earth'".** (Revelation 3:10).*

God Shields –

"You, Lord, are a <u>shield</u> around me, my glory, the One who lifts my head high. I call out to the Lord, and He answers me from His Holy Mountain". (Psalm 3:3-4).

"Praise be to the Lord, for He has heard my cry for mercy. The Lord is my strength and my <u>shield</u>; my heart trusts in Him, and He helps me. My heart leaps for joy, and with my song I praise Him. The Lord is the strength of His people, a fortress of salvation for His anointed one. Save Your people and Bless Your inheritance; be their Shepherd and carry them forever". (Psalm 28:6-9).

"We wait in hope for the Lord; He is our help and our <u>shield</u>. In Him our hearts rejoice, for we trust in His Holy Name. May Your Unfailing Love be with us, Lord, even as we put our hope in You". (Psalm 33:20-22).

*"Hear my prayer, Lord God Almighty; listen to me, God of Jacob. Look on our <u>shield</u>, O God; look with favor on Your anointed one. Better is one day in Your Courts than a thousand elsewhere; i would rather be a doorkeeper in the House of my God than dwell in the tents of the wicked. For the Lord God is a sun and <u>shield</u>; the Lord bestows favor and honor; no good thing does He withhold from those whose walk is blameless. Lord Almighty, blessed is the one who trusts in You ". (Psalm 84:8-12). And He the Lord speaks and says:"**Do not be afraid, for I am your <u>shield</u>, your very Great Reward'".** (Genesis 15:1).*

God Loves –

"This is how we know that we live in Him and He in us He has given us of His Spirit. And we have seen and testify that the Father has sent His Son to be the Savior of the world. If anyone acknowledges that Jesus is the Son of God, God lives in them and they are in God. And so we know and rely on the Love

God has for us. <u>God is Love</u>. Whoever lives in Love lives in God, and God lives in them. This is how Love is made complete among us so that we will have confidence on the Day of Judgment: In this world we are like Jesus. There is no fear in Love. But Perfect Love drives out fear, because fear has to do with punishment. The one who fears is not made perfect in Love". (1John 4:13-18).

"Whoever has My Commands and keeps them is the one who loves Me. The one who loves Me will be loved by My Father, and I too will love them and show Myself to them"*. (John 14:21).*

"As the Father has loved Me, so have I loved you. Now remain in My Love"*. (John 15:9).*

"The Father Himself loves you because you have loved Me and have believed that I came from Him"*. (John 16:27).*

"Therefore, I am convinced that neither death nor life, neither angels nor demons, neither the present nor the future, nor any powers, neither height nor depth, nor anything else in all creation, will be able to separate us from the Love of God that is in Christ Jesus our Lord". (Romans 8:38-39).

"Very rarely will anyone die for a righteous person, though for a good person someone might possibly dare to die. But God demonstrates His own love for us in this: While we were still sinners, Christ died for us". (Romans 5:7-8).

"Because of His Great Love for us, God, who is rich in mercy, made us alive with Christ even when we were dead in transgressions – it is by Grace you have been saved". (Ephesians 2:4-5).

Now, all we have to do is believe and accept His Son Jesus into our lives. Teaming up with Jesus was the best move I have ever made. It took me ten years to realize that Jesus was with me, all long and all through it all. It is our Heavenly Father and Creator that is the owner and provider of everything. So since all belongs to Him, we should be ready to be used for His purpose, waiting and ready for that call that comes so suddenly and so quickly that if your ears are not open to His voice, you will miss out on serving Him and any blessings that comes with it.

We are always seeking the mind and will of God for every decision, financial worries, property, time, or influence. God expects us to use all that we have to His glory.

"Remember this: Whoever sows sparingly will also reap sparingly, and whoever sows generously will also reap generously. Each of you should give what you should give what you have decided in your heart to give, not reluctantly or under compulsion, for God loves a cheerful giver. And God is able to bless you abundantly, so that in all things at all times, having all that you need, you will abound in every good work". (2 Corinthians 9:6-8).

"Whatever you do, work at it with all your heart, as working for the Lord, not for human masters. Since you know that, you will receive an inheritance from the Lord as a reward. You are serving the Lord Christ. Anyone who does wrong will be repaid for their wrongs, and there is no favoritism". (Colossians 3:23-25).

"'Do not store up for yourselves treasures on earth, where moths and vermin destroy, and where thieves break in and steal. But store up for yourselves treasures in Heaven, where moths and vermin do not destroy, and where thieves do not break in and steal. For where your treasure is, there your heart will be also'". *(Matthew 6:19-21).*

"Give and it will be given to you. A good measure, pressed down, shaken together and running over, will be poured into your lap. For with the measure you use, it will be measured back to you". (Luke 6:38).

"Dear friend, I pray that you may enjoy good health and that all may go well with you, even as your soul is getting along well". (3 John 1:2). "Therefore, seek first His kingdom and His righteousness, and all these things will be given to you". (Matthew 6:33).

Time for a Prayer

Thank you, Star Team for being with me and providing for me the wisdom and strength to do all You want me to do. I am forever thankful for You in doing Your part of this team effort that keeps me walking in Your Footsteps of Grace; and keeping me shielded from Satan's weapons of destruction. When I live out Your Word I am thanking You for accepting me on Your Team (the place of refuge) that will never leave me, nor forsake me. In Your Son's Name I pray that all Your peoples turn to You when they need Love, Compassion, Grace and Guidance. Thank you, always and forever. Amen.

The 'Me Disease'—What Is It?

*T*he 'me disease' is a virus of self-centeredness that spreads like a wildfire, through our soul, infecting all in its path. Its symptoms are as follows: a rude behavior, selfish conversations and sheer indifference to anyone else's needs. I know, you are probably saying, "I don't have it. I help out people who need help." This is just what the 'me disease' is—a total denial of the disease that so shines through the person that it effects. People think that they would never act the way of selfishness, but news flash: selfishness is what this world possesses. Satan looks for these selfish people to make them the prime candidates for him to use in his quest to "try" to defeat God.

Many of us fall prey to Satan's ways, taking on an attitude of their own selfish ways, thinking "their" way is the correct way, wanting all the attention and boasting how "righteous" they are. They also begin to get mad at God and have doubts about Him and His power. Most of all they start listening to the world and therefore driving a wedge between them and God.

People forget that when Jesus was preaching His Father's Words, He never once showed any kind of arrogance (a know-it-all to these worldly people). Never the victim of circumstance (on His way to the cross). Never wanted the center of attention (that glory was for His Father's). If Jesus would have done all these things, He would have sinned and thus not be the sacrifice for our sins that rekindled ourselves to His Father. Jesus was just following His Father's instructions—Jesus became a man of no sin who took our sins, then endured the cross so that we can walk in the confidence and love that His Father gives Him. Jesus was that friend that died for you and me. I thank Him every moment I can.

The only antidote for this 'me disease' is not that hard to accomplish.

It is to no longer "live for yourself," but live for Jesus who died for you and gives life everlasting. To live for Jesus is a simple, easy task that we can accomplish, which is nothing compared to what Jesus went through, and He was God's only Son. To have someone die for me is the greatest proof of love and endurance and friendship only the Son of God can accomplish. Jesus saved me (us) from a punishment no one should ever go through. Life is worth living for Jesus. As the Bible says:

"Jesus said; **'Truly I tell you, whatever you did for one of the least of these brothers and sisters of Mine, you did for Me'"**. *(Matthew 25:40).*

My goal, before I leave this earth, is to live for Jesus, doing the things He did.

Living as Jesus did is to:

1. Help a friend or person so they can just get some rest.
2. Give respect and dignity to anyone who feels worthless and ashamed, speaking those encouraging words.
3. Listen to that someone who needs that comforting friend to listen and not talk harshly back.
4. To cease living for "self" ("me") and live for Jesus. Always!

Just doing one of these things can ward off the "me disease."

We have the best example of how to act (in this crazy, mixed-up world), and that is our Lord Jesus Christ. This will open that door so that 'me disease' can float away, returning to where it came from—Satan the origin of the 'me disease'.

Here is what the Bible says about this 'me disease' (selfishness). Meditate on these Scriptures and live them out by sharing them with all who are heading down that road of selfish and arrogant behavior. I myself read these Scriptures repeatedly so that I could pass on by this path of selfishness and walk down the Humble Path with my Star Team.

"Command those who are rich in this present world—not to be arrogant nor to put their hope in wealth; which is so uncertain, but to put their hope in God, who richly provides us with everything for our enjoyment. Command them to do good, to be rich in good deeds and to be generous and willing to share. In this

way they will lay up treasure for themselves as a firm foundation for the coming age, so that they may take hold of the Life that is truly Life. Guard what has been entrusted to your care. Turn away from godless chatter and the opposing ideas of what is falsely called knowledge, which some have professed and in so doing have wandered from the faith. Grace be with you all". (1 Timothy 6:17-21).

"Since an overseer is entrusted with God's work, he must be blameless— not overbearing, not quick-tempered, not given to drunkenness, not violent, not pursuing dishonest gain. Rather, he must be hospitable, one who loves what is good, who is self-controlled, upright, holy and disciplined. He must hold firmly to the trustworthy message as it has been taught, so that he can encourage others by sound doctrine and refute those who oppose it". (Titus 1:7-9).

"Remind the people to be subject to rulers and authorities, to be obedient, to be ready, to do whatever is good, to slander no one, to be peaceable and considerate and to show true humility toward all men". (Titus 3:1-2).

"Who may ascend the hill of the Lord? Who may stand in His holy place? He who has clean hands and a pure heart; who does not lift up his soul to an idol or swear by what is false. He will receive a blessing from the Lord and vindication from God his Savior". (Psalm 24:3-5).

"He gives strength to the weary and increases the power of the weak....but those who hope in the Lord will renew their strength. They will soar on wings like eagles; they will run and not grow weary, they will walk and not faint". (Isaiah 40:29, 31).

"Do nothing out of selfish ambition or vain conceit. Rather, in humility value others above yourselves, not looking to your own interests but each of you to the interests of the others". (Philippians 2:3-4). "For where you have envy and selfish ambition, there you find disorder and every evil practice". (James 3:16).

"Those who live according to the flesh have their minds set on what the flesh desires; but those who live in accordance with the Spirit their minds set on what the Spirit desires. The mind governed by the flesh is death, but the mind governed by the Spirit is Life and Peace. The mind governed by the flesh is hostile to God; it does not submit to God's Law, nor can it do so. Those who are in the realm of the flesh cannot please God". (Romans 8:5-8).

"An unfriendly person pursues selfish ends and against all sound judgment starts quarrels. Fools find no pleasure in understanding, but delight in airing their own opinions". (Proverb 18:1-2).

"Woe to you, teachers of the law and Pharisees, you hypocrites! You clean the outside of the cup and dish, but inside they are full of greed and self-indulgence. Blind Pharisees! First clean the inside of the cup and dish, and then the outside also will be clean". (Matthew 23:25-26).

"Who is wise and understanding among you? Let them show it by their good life, by deeds done in the humility that comes from wisdom. However, if you harbor bitter envy and selfish ambition in your hearts, do not boast about it or deny the truth. Such 'wisdom' does not come down from heaven but is earthly, unspiritual, and demonic. For, where you have envy and selfish ambition, there you find disorder and every evil practice. However, the wisdom that comes from heaven is first pure; then peace-loving, considerate, submissive, full of mercy and good fruit, impartial and sincere. Peacemakers who sow in peace reap a harvest of righteousness". (James 3:13-18).

When I meditated on these Scriptures, I thirsted for knowing more of God. I am looking forward to the day that all I do is sit at Jesus's feet and listen to all He has to tell me. That will be a glorious day! Here are eight more things to know about our God—these might be eight things, but if I would put down all the things about our God, this book will never end.

1.) God is Good and is full of Goodness:

"Good and upright is the Lord". (Psalm 25:8).

"Surely God is good to Israel—To those who are pure in heart!" (Psalm 73:1).

"You are good, and what You do is good; teach me Your decrees". (Psalm 119:68).

2.) God is always on your side:

"The Lord is with me; I will not be afraid. What can man do to me? The Lord is with me; He is my helper. I will look in triumph on my enemies. It is better to take refuge in the Lord than to trust in man. It is better to take refuge in the Lord than to trust in princes". (Psalm 118:6-9).

97

"Then my enemies will turn back when I call for help. By this I will know that God is for me". (Psalm 56:9).

3.) God's Laws and Ways are for our benefits:

"The fear of the Lord is pure, enduring forever. The ordinances of the Lord are sure and altogether righteous". (Psalm 19:9).

"By them is your servant warned; in keeping them there is great reward". (Psalm 19:11).

4.) God is <u>always</u> with you:

"Keep your lives free from the love of money and be content with what you have, because God has said, 'Never will I leave you; never will I forsake you". (Hebrews 13:5).

5.) God will restore you to new things:

"For you, O Lord, have delivered my soul from death, my eyes from tears, my feet from stumbling, that I may walk before the Lord in the land of the living". (Psalm 116:8-9).

6.) God's promises will never fail:

"The earth is filled with your love, O Lord; teach me your decrees". (Psalm 119:64).

"You are good, and what you do is good; teach me your decrees". (Psalm 119:68).

"Your word, O Lord, is eternal; it stands firm in the Heavens. Your faithfulness continues through all generations; you established the earth, and it endures. Your laws endure to this day, for all things serve you". (Psalm 119:89-91).

7.) God always wins every battle:

"The Lord will march out like a mighty man, like a warrior He will stir up His zeal; with a shout He will raise the battle cry and will triumph over His enemies". (Isaiah 42:13).

8.) God is Love:

"Dear friends, let us love one another, for love comes from God. Everyone who loves, has been born of God and knows God. Whoever does not love does not know love does not know God, because God is love. This is how God showed His love among us; He sent His one and only Son into the world that we might live through Him". (1 John 4:7-9).

"This is love: not that we loved God, but that He loved us and sent His Son as an atoning sacrifice for our sins". (1 John 4:10).

The Desired Will of God

O ur Creator and Heavenly Father designs a specific plan for our lives that is unique in every believer and shown in the gifts, the talents, and even the situations that He puts us in. All for the good of His Kingdom. In His Presence, God shares His desired will so we can live successfully, for His Glory. As Jeremiah 29:11-14 says, ***"For I know the plans I have for you,'*** *declares the Lord,* ***'plans to prosper you and not to harm you, plans to give you hope and a future. Then you will call upon Me and come and pray to Me, and I will listen to you. You will seek Me and find Me when you seek Me with all your heart. I will be found by you, declares the Lord'"***. *(Jeremiah 29:11-14).*

There are three <u>must</u> desires that God wants us to do (and they are necessary):

<u>First, we must</u> follow the moral laws, like the Ten Commandments. These are for everyone to apply in their life so we can have joy, peace, and meaning to our lives.

<u>Second, we must</u> discover God's intentions for your personal life. One good example is vocation (your specific skills, talents, and spiritual gifts); that God has put in you. Your vocation may change, but with the Holy Spirit's guidance, your vocation will fit you perfectly for the glory of your Heavenly Father.

<u>Third, we must</u> put God's desired will in action in our daily lives. What interests God <u>must</u> interest you. In your prayers, you find contentment in the arms of your caring, loving Heavenly Father, who gives you rest and leads you right to the place He wants you to be—right in His presence and into His loving and comforting arms of love.

Here is now what the Word of God tells of what God Desires. Put these into action and live:

"Be joyful always; pray continually; give thanks in all circumstances, for this is God's will for you in Christ Jesus. Do not put out the Spirit's fire. Avoid every kind of evil". (1 Thessalonians 5:16-19, 22).

"Get rid of all bitterness, rage, and anger, brawling and slander, along with every form of malice. Be kind and compassionate to one another, forgiving each other, just as in Christ God forgave you. Be imitators of God, therefore, as dearly loved children and live a life of love, just as Christ loved us and gave Himself up for us as a fragrant offering and sacrifice to God". (Ephesians 4:31-32 and 5:1-2).

"Open the gates that the righteous nation may enter, the nation that keeps faith. You will keep in perfect peace those whose minds are steadfast, because they trust in you. Trust in the Lord forever, for the Lord, the Lord Himself, is the Rock eternal. He humbles those who dwell on high; He lays the lofty city low; He levels it to the ground and casts it down to the dust". (Isaiah 26:2-5).

"For anyone who enters God's rest also rests from their works, just as God did from His. Let us, therefore, make every effort to enter that rest, so that no one will perish by following their example of disobedience". (Hebrews 4:10-11).

"For Christ did not enter a sanctuary made with human hands that was only a copy of the true one; He entered Heaven itself, now to appear for us in God's presence". (Hebrews 9:24).

"In peace I will lie down and sleep, for you, Lord, make me dwell in safety". (Psalm 4:8).

"The Lord is my shepherd, I lack nothing. He makes me lie down in green pastures; He leads me beside quiet waters; He refreshes my soul. He guides me along the right paths for His Name's sake. Even though I walk through the darkest valley, I will fear no evil, for You are with me; Your Rod and Your Staff they comfort me". (Psalm 23:1-4).

"Yes, my soul, find rest in God; my hope comes from Him. Truly, He is my Rock and my Salvation; He is my fortress, I will not be shaken". (Psalm 62:5-6).

"Let your gentleness be evident to all. The Lord is near. Do not be anxious about anything, but in every situation, by prayer and petition, with thanksgiving, present your requests to God. And the peace of God—which transcends all

understanding—will guard your hearts and your minds in Christ Jesus". *(Philippians 4:5-7).*

"The fear of the Lord leads to life; then one rests content, untouched by trouble". (Proverbs 19:23).

"My flesh and my heart may fail, but God is the strength of my heart and my portion forever". (Psalm 73:26).

"God says: **'Be still and know I am God. I will be exalted among the nations. I will be exalted in the earth'".** *(Psalm 46:10).*

The Lord wants to work His Desires into our lives and have a loving relationship with every one of us. God will send blessings to those who follow in His Way. It is impossible to get less than the best when we do things God's Way. The best way to know God's Best is to believe in and follow His Son—Jesus. Also, reading His Word (the Bible). You will never feel lonely again.

Our Desires Turn into Arrogant and Selfish Ways

----

*O*ur desires lead to selfishness, which turns into arrogance. Arrogance is an attitude of an overbearing manner, relying on your own power. God does not like us to have an arrogant and selfish attitude. For this leads to not trusting in Him. When we do not trust the Lord, we are being arrogant and prideful, thinking that we know more than the Lord does. This never works out; it just prolongs the blessing that God has for us and it keeps us seemingly, standing in one place, preventing us from moving forward. As the Bible tells us:

"*Trust in the Lord with all your heart and lean not on your own understanding; in all your ways submit to Him*". *(Proverbs 3:5-6).*

"*Do not be wise in your own eyes; fear the Lord and shun evil. This will bring health to your body and nourishment to your bones*". *(Proverbs 3:7-8).*

To be wise is to put ourselves totally devoted to seeking to know God will always guard us from any kind of unwelcomed attitude that we may (unnoticing) possess. We must continually check ourselves if we are speaking kind words (God's Words). For a kind word (even just a smile) can lift up the most depressed person. It shows them (through you) that God really does love them.

God allows us to experience failures to show us how dependent we really are on Him. I found this very true in my life. When I would fail at a task that I was working on and the task was making me frustrated, making me feel weak, sad, and empty. I would ask God, "What went wrong and what is the lesson I am to learn from this"? Then He would gently lift my head up, look into my eyes, and say to me; *'I love you; you need not be discouraged, I am with you. I have this all under My control. Stay strong in Me and*

all will work out for good'. No person on this earth ever showed me this kind of compassion. I just stayed quiet and took in all that He was telling me. This one moment that I spent listening to Jesus was priceless. It really changed my life forever. Seeing my troubles in God's Light made me see more clearly the lessons I needed to learn and not the hurt that made me feel weak. I needed to hear all that Jesus was telling me and put them into action. Listening to God's Instructions opened my ears, making them more aware of His voice, giving all those "other voices" no voice, just a bunch of empty words of destruction.

Nowadays, I only hear God's Voice—'the Voice of Truth' The other voices are but a distant memory, tossed away never to be heard of again. Well, sometimes I would hear those other voices, but only hear empty air, flowing from their evil mouths. All thanks and glory go to my Father God, my Lord, my Savior, my Friend, my Teacher, my Light, my Deliver, my Redeemer – my Star Team – in whom I thank every day. The Bible (God's Word) says:

"For we are God's workmanship, created in Christ Jesus to do good works, which God prepared in advance for us to do". (Ephesians 2:10).

"He has shown you, O mortal, what is good. In addition, what does the Lord require of you? To act justly and to love mercy and walk humbly with your God". (Micah 6:8).

When you follow the Voice of God and obey His Instructions, you are building upon the Rock of His daily teaching and perfect will. As God's Word (the Bible) says:

"Therefore, everyone who hears these Words of Mine and puts them into practice is like a wise man who built his house on the Rock'". *(Matthew 7:24).*

When we open our ears to God's Voice, we can hear the answers to our troubled situations. There is nothing more comforting than to take refuge in the Presence of our Heavenly Father. This is why I will continue to absorb the Scriptures into my heart and my brain so I can encourage others and myself to rest in God's presence. This is also an act of obeying God and making us available for His work in us.

Obeying God's written Word, you will find the Instructions of how to live your life on this earth:

To obey how God says you are to treat people is to –

"Be devoted to one another in love. Honor one another above yourselves. Never be lacking in zeal, but keep your spiritual fervor, serving the Lord. Be joyful in hope, patient in affliction, and faithful in prayer. Share with the Lord's people who are in need. Practice hospitality". (Romans 12:10-13).

"Finally, all of you, be like-minded, be sympathetic, love one another, and be compassionate and humble. Do not repay evil with evil or insult with insult. On the contrary, repay evil with blessing, because to this you were called so that you may inherit a blessing. For whoever would love life and see good days, must keep their tongue from evil and their lips from deceitful speech. They must turn from evil and do good and they must seek peace and pursue it. For the eyes of the Lord are on the righteous and His ears are attentive to their prayer, but the face of the Lord is against those who do evil". (1 Peter 3:8-12).

To obey how God says you are to run from sexual sin is to do the following –

"Flee from sexual immorality. All other sins a person commits are outside the body, but whoever sins sexually, sins against their own body. Do you not know that your bodies are temples of the Holy Spirit, who is in you, whom you have received from God? You are not your own; you were bought at a price. Therefore, honor God with your bodies". (1 Corinthians 6:18-20).

"A man who commits adultery has no sense; whoever does so destroys himself". (Proverb 6:32).

To obey how God says you are to be a light in a dark world is to –

*"For this is what the Lord has commanded us: **'I have made you a light for the Gentiles that you may bring salvation to the ends of the earth'".** (Acts 13:47).*

"For you were once darkness, but now you are light in the Lord. Live as children of light (for the fruit of the light consists in all goodness, righteousness

and truth) and find out what pleases the Lord. Have nothing to do with the fruitless deeds of but rather expose them". (Ephesians 5:8-11).

"You are the salt of the earth. However, if the salt loses its saltiness—how can it be made salty again? It is no longer good for anything, except to be thrown out and trampled underfoot. You are the light of the world. A town built on a hill cannot be hidden. Neither do people light a lamp and put it under a bowl. Instead, they put it on its stand, and it gives light to everyone in the house. In the same way, let your light shine before others so that they may see your good deeds and glorify your Father in Heaven". (Matthew 5:13-16).

To obey how God says you are to forgive those who hurt you is to –

"Therefore, as God's chosen people, holy and dearly loved, clothe yourselves with compassion, kindness, humility, gentleness and patience. Bear with each other and forgive one another if any of you has a grievance against someone. Forgive as the Lord forgave you. In addition, over all these virtues put on love, which binds them all together in perfect unity. Let the peace of Christ rule in your hearts, since as members of one body you were called to peace and be thankful". (Colossians 3:13-15).

"Do not judge and you will not be judged. Do not condemn, and you will not be condemned. Forgive, and you will be forgiven". (Luke 6:37).

"Get rid of all bitterness, rage and anger, brawling and slander, along with every form of malice. Be kind and compassionate to one another, forgiving each other, just as in Christ God forgave you". (Ephesians 4:31-32).

To obey how God says you are to share Him with others is to—

*"He said to them, '**Go into the entire world and preach the gospel to all creation. Whoever believes and is baptized will be saved, but whoever does not believe will be condemned**'". (Mark 16:15-16).*

"Sing to the Lord a new song; sing to the Lord, all the earth. Sing to the Lord, praise His name; proclaim His salvation day after day. Declare His glory among the nations, His marvelous deeds among all peoples. For great is the Lord and most worthy of praise; He is to be feared above all gods". (Psalm 96:1-4).

"Through Jesus, therefore, let us continually offer to God a sacrifice of praise—the fruit of lips that openly profess His name. However, do not forget

to do well and to share with others, for with such sacrifices God is pleased". *(Hebrews 13:15).*

In our obedience to live out God's Word, it will give us great results in His kingdom. In addition, our Heavenly Father will shine His smile of grace to strengthen us to walk through the troubles of this earth. To obey God, you must listen to (and for) His soft voice that is continually speaking to you throughout your daily life. Open your ears and hearts to let in God's power (He so freely pours) to strengthen you and give you the wisdom and discernment to endure all that you go through on the journey that He sets before you. Saying yes to God's instructions and advice brings blessings into your life that you cannot get from anyone else but Him. Live by

God's Word (the Bible), and you will live long. Ignoring God's Word, you will not live long. In other words, listen to God and live; turn your back (and ears), you die. As the Bible says:

"Blessed are those whose ways are blameless, who walk according to the Law of the Lord. Blessed are those who keep His Statutes and seek Him with all their heart—they do no wrong but follow His ways. You have laid down precepts that are to be fully obeyed". *(Psalm 119:1-4).*

Here is what the Bible (God's Word) says about the troubles we face:

"The Lord is a refuge for the oppressed, a stronghold in times of trouble. Those who know your name will trust in you—for you, Lord, have never forsaken those who seek you". *(Psalm 9:9-10).*

"The salvation of the righteous comes from the Lord; He is their stronghold in time of trouble. The Lord helps them and delivers them; He delivers them from the wicked and saves them, because they take refuge in Him". *(Psalm 37:39-40).*

"God is our refuge and strength; an ever-present help in trouble. Therefore, we will not fear, though the earth gives way and the mountains fall into the heart of the sea, though its waters roar and foam and the mountains quake with their surging". *(Psalm 46:1-2).*

"Be still and know I am God; I will be exalted among the nations. I will be exalted in the earth". *(Psalm 46:10).*

"Give ear and come to me; hear me that your soul may live. I will make

an everlasting covenant with you, my faithful love promised to David". (Isaiah 55:3).

"Seek the Lord while He may be found; call on Him while He is near". (Isaiah 55:6).

"*I have told you these things, so that in Me you may have Peace. In this world, you will have trouble. However, take heart! I have overcome the world*"*. *(John 16:33).*

"Let your gentleness be evident to all. The Lord is near. Do not be anxious about anything, but in every situation, by prayer and petition, with thanksgiving, present your requests to God". (Philippians 4:5-6).

"For God so loved the world that He gave His one and only Son, that whoever believes in Him shall not perish but have eternal life". (John 3:16).

"Humble yourselves, therefore, under God's mighty hand, that He may lift you up in due time. Cast all your anxiety on Him because He cares for you. Be alert and of a sober mind. Your enemy, the devil prowls around like a roaring lion looking for someone to devour. Resist him, standing firm in the faith, because you know that the family of believers throughout the world is undergoing the same kind of sufferings. In addition, the God of all grace, who called you to His Eternal Glory in Christ, after you have suffered a little while, will Himself restore you and make you strong, firm and steadfast. To Him be the power forever and ever. Amen". (1 Peter 5:6-11).

"Do not conform to the pattern of this world, but be transformed by the renewing of your mind. Then you will be able to test and approve what God's will is—His good, pleasing and perfect will". (Romans 12:2).

When you do not understand why the things are happening in your life, you can go to the Father for understanding through His Son Jesus. We need not be afraid to enter into God's Presence, for our Lord Jesus is right at our side, helping us to be strong. Because Jesus loves us. We need not understand why things happen (good or bad) if we trust in God's work. I know that God is working all things out for my good. He has been working things out for me for fifty years (and counting). Sometimes those questions of 'whys' slip into my mind (by ways of Satan), and as quickly as they enter, I would be reminded to read these Scripture verses from my Bible to put off all negative thoughts.

*"**For My Thoughts are not your thoughts, neither are your ways My Ways'**, declares the Lord. '**As the Heavens are higher than the earth, so are My Ways higher than your ways and My Thoughts than your thoughts'**". (Isaiah 55:8-9).*

"Because of the Lord's great love, we are not consumed, for His compassions never fail. They are new every morning, great is your faithfulness". (Lamentations 3:22-24).

"Humble yourselves, therefore, under God's mighty hand that He may lift you up in due time. Cast all your anxiety on Him because He cares for you. Be self-controlled and alert. Your enemy, the devil, prowls around like a roaring lion looking for someone to devour. Resist him, standing firm in the faith, because you know that your brothers throughout the world are undergoing the same kind of sufferings. And the God of all grace, who called you to His eternal glory in Christ, after you have suffered a little while, will Himself restore you and make you strong, firm and steadfast". (1 Peter 5:6-10).

"Be joyful always; pray continually; give thanks in all circumstances, for this is God's will for you in Christ Jesus. Do not put out the Spirit's fire". (1 Thessalonians 5:16-19).

"And we know that in all things God works for the good of those who love Him, who have been called according to His purpose". (Romans 8:28).

"Finally, be strong in the Lord and in His mighty power. Put on the Full Armor of God, so that you can take your stand against the devil's schemes". (Ephesians 6:10-11).

Going through trials draws us closer to God, which is the first step in making us stronger to handle the trials and all the things that Satan throws our way. Satan will try anything to throw us off the path of peaceful living, which brings us to the door of our Heavenly Father. I am so grateful for having the opportunity to read the Word of God—the Bible. In many places in this world, people do not even own a Bible (not to mention read it). If I did not have my Bible to read, I would still be that weak, confused girl, not able to fight off the destructive arrows that Satan flings my way.

In my Bible, I find out more and more about who God is and how

He wants me to live a strong and peaceful life and how much He loves me. Having my Bible—along with my Star Team—gives me strength and understanding to live the Life that my Heavenly Father wants me to live. I am able to face the evil giants and climb the evil mountains that this earth offers. I am never alone in this climb and battle with these giants. For I have Jesus right here by my side, giving His encouraging words of love, trust, comfort, and strength.

As Jesus dwells in my heart all the way up the mountain, so do I dwell also in His victorious power to overcome all that may be holding me back from following Him. I can go ahead and face those struggles with all assurance of the guidance of my Lord Jesus Christ who leads me with the Light of Life that He so possesses. Jesus carries me on His shoulders when I am too weak and feeling faint. I never have to look back on past failures, never worry about tomorrow, for the guidance of Jesus is for today's struggles. Tomorrow's struggles will have different guidelines of its own. Just as the Bible says: *"Therefore, do not worry about tomorrow, for tomorrow will worry about itself. Each day has enough trouble of its own". (Matthew 6:34).*

"For this reason I say to you, do not be worried about your life, as to what you will eat or what you will drink; nor for your body, as to what you will put on. Is not life more than food and the body more than clothing? Look at the birds of the air that they do not sow, nor reap nor gather into barns, and yet, your Heavenly Father feeds them. Are you not worth much more than they are?" (Matthew 6:25-26).

I learned to laugh freely by not taking the situation or myself so seriously, because I am relaxed and trust that my Lord Jesus is with me through it all. This statement is a statement of how I desire God's Will above anything this world can offer. Letting God be in control of my life becomes much less threatening when I stop trying to monitor God's responsibilities (the things beyond my control). God's responsibility is to teach, warn, and instruct us on the way that we should go, who to follow, and how we should live. Too many times, we forget that God is the only one that knows everything; and the only One that can change things into good.

We intend to push aside His teachings and instructions. This is our problem: we "think" we know it all, so we "try" to tell God what to do. It does not work that way. I have learned that without God's help and teaching, I am just walking in a continuous circle of a heavy, dark fog. I learned that laughter lightens my heart and lifts me up into places that I could never get to without Jesus's help and encouragement. God delights in shining His Light into my life, making a way for you and me, to step out of that continuous dark fog and stop trying to do things on our own terms and start doing things His way (the best way). God smiles with joy, when we enjoy life, lightheartedly. I know I am never going to miss being in the joy of God's Presence, because I am never going to let go of Jesus's hand—as He is the One who is carrying me into His Father's world. God knows we are not that strong, so He wants us to give those heavy burdens to Him, and He will give us a Life of joy and comfort. As the Bible says: *"A cheerful heart is good medicine, but a crushed spirit dries up the bones" (Proverbs 17:20, 22).*

"She is clothed with strength and dignity; she can laugh at the days to come". (Proverbs 31:25).

"Come to Me, all you who are weary and burdened, and I will give you rest. Take My yoke upon you and learn from Me, for I am gentle and humble in heart, and you will find rest for your souls. For my yoke is easy and my burden is light". *(Matthew 11:28-30).*

The only way to receive God's calm into your life is to be still and know He is God. Your mind and body become stronger to conquer all that God tells you to conquer. So breathe in that stillness of God's presence every chance you get and feel the weight and fogginess of your burden being lifted off your shoulders and on to His shoulders.

Seek God always and walk in His ways, trusting Him in everything you do. God's rest is true and pure and can cease all struggle, making you calm, strong, and confident. Knowing that He will always have your back, then you can rest in His presence and His tender loving embrace that He has you in all the time. Let God's Presence purify your life.

All God wants us to do is contemplate Him in every chance we get. Contemplate means to think deeply or carefully about someone or something. Bingo! That is it! God wants us to think deeply about Him, all the time and in everything we do and say! Nothing is more important than acknowledging God in ultimate awe and reverence. Nothing!

Here are some Scripture verses that you can use to contemplate our Heavenly Father:

"In peace I will lie down and sleep, for you alone, Lord, make me dwell in safety". (Psalm 4:8).

"I will consider all your works and meditate on all your mighty deeds. Your ways, God, are holy. What god is our God? You are the God who performs miracles; you display your power among the peoples". (Psalm 77:12-14).

"Brothers and sisters, I do not consider myself yet to have taken hold of it. But one thing I do: Forgetting what is behind and straining toward what is ahead. I press on toward the goal to win the prize for which God has called me heavenward in Christ Jesus". (Philippians 3:13-14).

"Keep this Book of the Law always on your lips; meditate on it day and night, so that you may be careful to do everything written in it. Then you will be prosperous and successful". (Joshua 1:8).

"Finally, brothers and sisters, whatever is true, whatever is noble, whatever is right, whatever is pure, whatever is lovely, whatever is admirable—if anything is excellent or praiseworthy—think about such things". (Philippians 4:8).

After you meditate on these Scriptures and absorb every word into your heart, contemplate on how powerful the Star Team is. When I feel weak and don't know where to go or what to say to make me stronger again, I start calling out, 'Star Team, help me' – and no sooner do I speak out His Name, I feel a surge of energy enter into my body; making me able to get things done. The Star Team's Almighty Power only comes from Him who helps me in my time of need. Here are seven things that remind me of what happens with the Almighty Power of the Star Team (Jesus):

1. Miracles happen, when all seems bleak.
2. Drives away evil and leads me away from temptations.
3. Comforts me in the loneliness and gloom of this world.
4. Helps me conquer all my faults and mistakes.

5. He gives me Word Power to pray for others.

6. Brings me tenderness and mercy, drawing me closer to Him.

7. And, finally, is always with me all this time, through everything that happens to me.

These are just some of the things that help me remember that my Star Team is working in my life. All this started with me saying four simple words: 'Star Team, help me'. The moment I said those four words, the cloud of confusion lifted, and my mind was clear to listen and follow Him through the hard times and the good times. This is the true help of my Star Team.

A Prayer of Thankfulness:

My dear Star Team, I want to thank you for letting me rest a while in Your awe-some embrace.

As I rest, in your protection that you provide for me, I am Blessed. Father, as you are watching over me, please refresh me with Your Love and Strength. For Satan is throwing those arrows of doubt and unworthiness my way. I know that You see me worthy and strong. I thank You also for not letting go of me, for You are my Anchor to stay on the Your Righteous Path. I love you, and I am committed to You to complete the work that You put before me. I will always thank you, Father, for all that you have been doing and continue to do in and through me. I have no other source, for the strength and wisdom that You give me to walk this journey. *"Let the morning bring me word of Your Unfailing Love, for I have put my trust in you. Show me the way I should go, for to You I entrust my life. Rescue me from my enemies, Lord, for I hide myself in You". (Psalm 149:8-9).* In Your Name, I always pray. Amen.

A Prayer to Speak Life-Giving Words:

My dear Star Team, You are there in Heaven, and I am down here on earth. Let my words speak of Your Precious Life. Help condemn every negative and destructive word that the enemy (Satan) has been releasing against me. Help me to count those thoughts and words as dust. I rebuke them in the Your Precious Name of your precious Jesus Christ. Help me to rebuke the spirit of fear and confusion. They have no place in my heart and mind. Father, you have not given me that spirit of fear, but you have given me courage, love, hope, and a sound mind. Your Words are of victory and strength in my life. I am not going to let Satan pull me under when I have my Star Team to pull me over any obstacles. I will live and see Your Glory be manifested in my life. I thank you for Your Life-giving Power within me and for walking beside me to help me walk away from any temptations. When I am tempted to speak or even think negative things, help me to shake them off with your Positive and Life-giving Words, not negative, evil words.

Your words, Father, Satan cannot not stand. For Your Words are Life-giving to all who believe. In Name, I always pray. Amen.

Upon speaking these two prayers, I repented of any wrongdoings or thoughts that I may have done. I now proclaim in the Presence of God to walk the Godly life that He has designed for me to live. These are the words God speaks to me when I am feeling abandoned by family and friends: *"I am with you and will watch over you wherever you go, and I will bring you back to this land. I will not leave you until I have done what I have promised"*. *(Genesis 25:15)*.

God is always speaking to me. Be it through things of: Christian songs, on the radio, the clouds in the sky, the leaves, on the trees, and of course His Word (the Bible). I find Jesus always right beside me in everything I do and everything I see.

The moments that I seek God are the moments I find God. The moments I find God are the moments I love God. In these moments of God, I find the rest that I need for my soul. And when my soul is at rest, I find the Peace of God that surpasses all the evil that is in this world.

"Lord, our Lord, how Majestic is Your Name in all the earth! You have set Your Glory in the Heavens". *(Psalm 8:1)*.

"The Heavens declare the glory of God; and the firmament [the sky] *shows His handiwork. Day unto day utters speech, and night unto night shows knowledge"*. *(Psalms 19:1-2)*.

"When I consider Your Heavens, the work of Your fingers, the moon and

the stars, which you have set in place. What is mankind that You are mindful of—human beings that you care for?" (Psalm 8:3-4).

"Do you not know that your bodies are temples of the Holy Spirit, who is in you, whom you have received from God? You are not your own; you were bought at a price. Therefore, honor God with your bodies". (1Corinthians 6:19-20). Therefore: "Seek the Lord while you can find Him. Call on Him now while He is near". (Isaiah 55:6).

"'You will seek Me and find Me, when you seek Me with all your heart. I will be found by you' *declares the Lord,* **'and I will bring you back from captivity. I will gather you from all the nations and places where I have banished you'**, *declares the Lord,* **'and I will bring you back to the place from which I carried you into exile'"**. (Jeremiah 29:13-14).

"Listen to my voice in the morning, Lord. Each morning I bring my requests to you and wait expectantly". (Psalm 5:3).

As we are drawing closer to God, we are building the foundation that can withstand anything. You see, God calls to us every day to draw close to Him, to rest on His firm foundation. Jesus is that firm foundation. When I accepted Jesus into my life, I was able to relax and rejoice in His presence. In His presence, God points me in the right direction—where fear cannot intimidate me. On this earth, there is no one that can lead me to the glory of God. It is only His Son Jesus, who is the Way to the Truth, to life, and to the Glory of His Father in Heaven.

Here are some Bible verses to read and meditate on to get you even closer to the Father in Heaven; and enjoy His Peace:

"Let all who take refuge in you be glad; let them ever sing for joy. Spread your protection over them so that those who love your name may rejoice in you". (Psalm 5:11).

"He reached down from on high and took hold of me; He drew me out of deep waters. He rescued me from my powerful enemy, from my foes, who were too strong for me. They confronted me on the day of my disaster, but the Lord was my support. He brought me out into a spacious place; He rescued me because He delighted in me". (2 Samuel 22:17-20).

"Now to Him who is able to do immeasurably more than all we ask or imagine, according to His work within us, to Him be the Glory in the church and in Christ Jesus; throughout all generations, forever and ever. Amen". (Ephesians 3:20-21).

"To Him who is able to keep you from stumbling and to present you before His glorious presence without fault and great joy—to the only God our Savior be the glory, majesty, power and authority, through Jesus Christ our Lord, before ages now and forevermore. Amen". (Jude 24-25).

The biggest part of our faith-walk is to taste and see the Goodness of God in everything that He does for us. I experienced that taste of living in God's presence. Now, I feel confident in His Love and Goodness; which is with me always and forevermore. I do believe that we all tend to doubt God's work in our lives. Because most of us want to see the results quickly. This is what our enemy (Satan) wants – to get us to doubt God. Satan then sneaks into our lives and makes our lives a living hell (a place where only Satan is happy), turning us away from following our Lord Jesus. Instead of doubting, you should spend as much of your time as you can in God's Word, enjoying all that He is. Stop trying to fathom God's ways. Just absorb all of God's Promises, and he will do the rest. As the Word of God says:

"Taste and see that the Lord is good; blessed is the one who takes refuge in Him. Fear the Lord, you His holy people, for those who fear Him lack nothing". (Psalm 34:8-9).

"'For my thoughts are not your thoughts, neither are your ways my ways,' declares the Lord. 'As the heavens are higher than the earth, so are my ways higher than your ways and my thoughts than your thoughts'". (Isaiah 55:8-9).

"In you, Lord, I have taken refuge; let me never be put to shame; deliver me in your righteousness. Turn your ear to me; come quickly to my rescue; be my rock of refuge, a strong fortress to save me". (Psalm 31:1-2).

"How abundant are the good things that you have stored up for those who fear you that you bestow in the sight of all, on those who take refuge in you. In the shelter of your presence you hide them from all human intrigues; you keep

them safe in your dwelling from accusing tongues". (Psalm 31:19-20).

"Love the Lord, all His faithful people! The Lord preserves those who are true to Him, but the proud He pays back in full. Be strong and take heart, all you who hope in the Lord". (Psalm 31:23-24).

"I am like an olive tree flourishing in the house of God; I trust in God's unfailing love forever and ever. For what you have done, I will always praise you in the presence of your faithful people. And I will hope in your name, for your name is good". (Psalm 52:8-9).

"And do not grieve the Holy Spirit of God, with whom you sealed for the day of redemption. Get rid of all bitterness, rage and anger, brawling and slander, along with every form of malice. Be kind and compassionate to one another, forgiving each other, just as Christ God forgave you". (Ephesians 4:30-32).

"Be completely humble and gentle; be patient, bearing with one another in love. Make every effort to keep the unity of the Spirit through the bond of peace". (Ephesians 4:2-3).

Draw near to God through His Word, and let His Love stream through you. He then will remove all fear and doubt. God's Presence is always going to be with you, as long as you acknowledge Him in everything you see. Depending on God, throughout your day, brings a smile to His face and blessings to your heart. Walk hand in hand with Jesus and all darkness will turn to Light.

Holding Jesus's hand with trust and compassion as I walk through the valley of the shadows of this world will give me (and you too) the strength I need to not stumble. For it is Jesus's Light that fills my heart with joy and assurance that I am not alone. I can depend on my only friend Lord Jesus to help me when I need that help. There is nothing (or no one) on this earth that will satisfy me as much as my Lord Jesus. And my Lord tells me: ***"So do not fear, for I am with you; do not be dismayed, for I am your God. I will strengthen you and help you; I will uphold you with My righteous right hand. All who rage against you will surely be ashamed and disgraced; those who oppose you will be as nothing and perish"***. *(Isaiah 41:10-11).*

"Yes, my soul, find rest in God; my hope comes from Him. Truly, He is my Salvation; He is my Fortress. I will not be shaken. My salvation and my honor depend on God; He is my Mighty Rock, my Refuge. Trust in Him at all times, you people; pour out your hearts to Him, for God is our Refuge". (Psalm 62:5-8).

When you reach out your hand and open your heart to receive the precious gift from God that He gives you each day (when you arise), you can feel the pressure of this world, just melt away.

Many times in my life, I had to just stand still and breathe in the refreshing love that God displays. Using God's Word and His creation are the keys to the Peace (God's Peace) that surpasses all. I know there are people out there that do not believe me, but it is true. Jesus encountered the same thing—He would go away from the disciples and the crowd where He can be alone with His Father and refresh His strength. As it says in these Scriptures: *"Very early in the morning, while it was still dark, Jesus got up, left the house and went off to a solitary place, where He prayed". (Mark 1:35).*

"After He dismissed them, He went up on a mountainside by Himself to pray. When evening came, He was alone". (Matthew 14:23).

"One of those days Jesus went out to a mountainside to pray, and spent the night praying to God". (Luke 6:12).

"Now my soul is troubled, and what shall I say? 'Father, save me from this hour'? No, it was for this very reason I came to this hour. Father, glorify your name'! Then a voice came from Heaven, 'I have glorified it, and will glorify it again'" (John 12:27-28).

Here are some more Scripture verses to meditate on and learn:

"The Lord has done it this very day; let us rejoice today and be glad. Lord, save us, Lord, grant us success". (Psalm 118:24-25).

"Let us come before Him with thanksgiving and extol Him with music and song. For the Lord is the great God, the great King above all gods". (Psalms 95:2-3)

"The Lord your God is with you, the Mighty Warrior who saves. He will take great delight in you; in this love, He will no longer rebuke you, but will

rejoice over you with singing". (Zephaniah 3:17)

"Do not conform to the pattern of this world, but be transformed by the renewing of your mind. Then you will be able to test and approve what God's will is—His good, pleasing and perfect will". (Romans 12:2). ***"For I know the plans I have for you,' declares the Lord, 'plans to prosper you and not to harm you, plans to give you hope and a future. Then you will call on Me and come and pray to Me, and I will listen to you'".*** *(Jeremiah 29:11-12).*

"Love must be sincere. Hate what is evil; cling to what is good. Be devoted to one another in love. Honor one another above yourselves. Never be lacking in zeal, but keep your spiritual fervor, serving the Lord. Be joyful in Hope, patient in affliction, faithful in prayer. Share with the Lord's people who are in need. Practice hospitality. Bless those who persecute you; bless and do not curse. Rejoice with those who rejoice; mourn with those who mourn. Live in harmony with one another. Do not be proud, but be willing to associate with people of low position. Do not be conceited. Do not repay anyone evil for evil. Be careful to do what is right in the eyes of everyone. If it is possible, as far as it depends on you, live at peace with everyone. Do not take revenge, my dear friends, but leave room for God's Wrath, for it is written: **'It is Mine to avenge; I will repay'***". (Romans 12:9-19).*

Staying calm and focused on Jesus (no matter what comes your way) is a simple task that our Heavenly Father wants us to do. However, we tend to make it more difficult. All God asks you and me to do is (1) read the Bible to absorb it into our hearts and minds, (2) believe in His Son Jesus and let Him help you cope with your daily problems to receive His blessings that outweighs any kind of trouble, and (3) always be aware of God's Presence that brings joy and strength to endure all the burning arrows that Satan throws our way. As the Bible says:

"The Lord is my shepherd, I lack nothing. He makes me lie down in green pastures. He leads me beside quiet waters. He refreshes my soul. He guides me along the right paths for His namesake. Even through the darkest valley, I will fear no evil; for you are with me; your rod and staff, they comfort me". (Psalm 23:1-4).

"Therefore, we do not lose heart. Though outwardly we are wasting away, yet inwardly, we are being renewed, day by day. For light and momentary troubles are achieving for us an eternal glory that far outweighs them all. So, we fix our eyes not on what is seen, but on what is unseen; since what is seen is temporary, but what is unseen is eternal". (2 Corinthians 4:16-17).

What Is the Grace of God?

---

*T*he Grace of God is His Love-Light that never turns off.

It is His Grace that shines the way through the darkness of this present world.

It is His Grace that keeps you wanting to obey Him.

It is His Grace that lets you into a relationship with Him.

It is His Grace that teaches you to stay close to Him.

It is His Grace that never departs from you.

It is His Grace that shows He loves and protects you in everything you do.

It is His Grace that gives you rest from the hurts of this world.

It is His Grace that is a gift, wrapped up in His Love.

It is by His Grace that we are saved from the chains that bind us to this evil material world.

It is by His Grace that I can say: *"I waited patiently for the Lord to help me, and He turned to me and heard my cry". (Psalm 40:1).*

Obeying God's Commands, and trusting Him in all He says and does, He will shower you with His Grace,Peace, and Love. Be aware a;ways of God's Presence and Grace that He bestows upon you; from the moment you wake up in the morning to the moment you lay your head down at night. Don't forget to thank Him for each moment that you breathe in His Glorious Grace and Love. Take the time to acknowledge Him in everything you see, do, and say. God will reward you for doing so. In the Presence of God you will live humbly with His Son Jesus; the way God intended you to live.

When I trust my thoughts to God, my journey turns to a beautiful and peaceful scenery of bright lights, shining with bright colors. Any fears I have just melts away, leaving me stronger to keep pressing on forward to the finish line—where Jesus is standing there, waiting with that key to my house that He made ready for me.

As I take a deep breath of God's Grace, I can see all the colors of the rainbow across the sky (even on cloudy days), giving me assurance of His Presence and Love for me (an Everlasting Love). This assurance was (and still is) the wind beneath my wings, letting me soar like an eagle, through this journey on this earth.

Here are some of my favorite Promises of God that I hold deep in my heart when I am feeling the moments of weakness creeping in:

"God is our refuge and strength, an ever-present help in troubles". (Psalms 46:1).

"And God says: **Be still and know I am God. I will be exalted among the nations. I will be exalted in the earth'**". *(Psalm 46:10).*

"My flesh and my heart may fail, but God is the strength of my heart and my portion forever". (Psalm 73:26).

"He is your shield and helper and your glorious sword. Your enemies will cower before you, and you will tread on their heights".(Deuteronomy 33:29b).

"Hear my cry for help, my King and my God, for You I pray. In the morning, Lord, you hear my voice; in the morning, I lay my requests before you and wait expectantly. For you are not a God who is pleased with wickedness, with you, evil people are not welcome. The arrogant cannot stand in Your Presence. You hate all who do wrong; You destroy those who tell lies. The bloodthirsty and deceitful; you Lord, detest". (Psalm 5:2-6).

"O, God, you are my God, earnestly I seek you; my soul thirsts for you, my body longs for you, in a dry and weary land where there is no water". (Psalm 63:1).

"Enter His gates with thanksgiving and His courts with praise; give thanks to Him and praise His name. For the Lord is Good and His Love endures forever; His Faithfulness continues through all generations". (Psalm 100:4-5).

"Yet a time is coming and has now come when the true worshipers will worship the Father, in Spirit and in truth; for they are the kind of worshipers the Father seeks. God is spirit and His worshipers must worship in the Spirit and in Truth" (John 4:23-24).

"I can do everything through Him who gives me strength". (Philippians 4:13).

"And my God will meet all your needs according to His glorious riches in Christ Jesus. To our God and Father be glory forever and ever. Amen". (Philippians 4:19-20).

And again God says: ***"Have I not I commanded you? Be strong and courageous. Do not be afraid; do not be discouraged, for the Lord your God will be with you wherever you go"***. *(Joshua 1:9).*

"The Grace of the Lord Jesus Christ be with your spirit. Amen". (Philippians 4:23).

Building God's Truth into your life is very important. It creates in you all that God is. In addition, truthfulness is an essential character quality for believers to have. Truthfulness is one of God's characters that make up who God is. To establish God's character of ?Truthfulness, you must know how to speak His Truth. The Word of God says: *"For the law given through Moses; Grace and Truth came through Jesus Christ". (John 1:17).*

"Sanctify them in the truth; your word is truth". (John 17:17).

"Jesus said to him, 'I am the way, and the truth, and the life. No one comes to the Father except through Me". (John 14:6).

To know and to understand the Truth, you must be willing to accept the Truth and to speak the Truth as Jesus speaks the Truth. Even when the Truth causes discomfort. God's Truth never causes discomfort – it is the lies of Satan's that causes discomfort.

God is truth. It is based on His desires and His ways—the True reality. In addition, the reality of speaking honestly is a quality that overrides any uncomfortable or costly situation.

After I had an honest conversation with my Star Team about this, they told me the benefits of knowing and having God's Truth in my life. I wrote them down and memorized them. Here are the ones that I feel are essential for every believer to possess. These are very important:

The first benefit is that I have a firm foundation to build on, to keep me in God's Word, and to receive His Grace and Mercy, for strengthening me in the midst of trouble and despair. The Bible is the only source to find how to build a Foundation of Truth.

The second benefit is to know God's Truth reassuring me that His Protection is continually with me, whenever I am facing any kind of dangers that arise on this earth.

The third benefit is when I am ill and weak, when I cry to Him, He comes to heal and strengthen me. Jesus puts me on His shoulders and carries me until I am strong enough to walk again.

Jesus is the Anchor to His Father's Truth, for He is the One who is walking with me through these crucial times on this earth. Knowing that Jesus overcame these crucial times, I can walk in confidence. Life on this earth is distorted, but Jesus makes all things clear so that I can follow Him and not go astray and miss the blessings that His Father has for me (and you too).

God's Truth provides:

The Scriptures tell the benefits of knowing and living out God's Truth. There were many times when I just did not know where to go to find the answers to the questions that I was harvesting in my mind. Until I started reading the Bible. I cannot stress it enough that the Bible (which is God speaking to us) has all the answers to all the questions that we are harvesting in our minds. When I opened up my Bible, I turned on God's Light. That Light illuminated all the answers I needed.

Here are some of the Scriptures that encouraged me for the help I needed in my time of despair. When you start with these Scriptures, God will reveal to you more that He sees that you need to read—just like He did for me.

For Guidance to know the best way to go and what to do:

"Seek the Lord and His strength; seek His presence continually". (1Chronicles 16:11).

"He leads the humble in what is right, and teaches the humble His way". *(Psalm 25:9)*.

*"**I will instruct you and teach you in the way you should go; I will counsel you with my eye upon**"*. *(Psalm 32:8)*.

<u>For Wisdom</u> to know the difference between good and evil:.

"If any of you lacks wisdom, let him ask God, who gives generously to all without reproach, and it will be given to him". *(James 1:5)*.

"For our boast is this: the testimony of our conscience that we behaved in the world with simplicity and godly sincerity, not by earthly wisdom but by the Grace of God, and supremely so toward you". *(2 Corinthians 1:12)*.

"Listen to advice and accept instruction, so that you may gain wisdom in the future". *(Proverbs 19:20)*.

"If one gives an answer before he hears, it is his folly and shame". *(Proverbs 18:13)*.

"To know wisdom and instruction, to understand words of insight". *(Proverbs 1:2)*.

"The mouth of the righteous utters wisdom, and his tongue speaks justice". *(Psalms 37:30)*.

<u>For Strength</u> to enable you to endure all that the enemy (Satan) is throwing at you:

"God is our refuge and strength, a very present help in trouble". *(Psalm 46:1)*.

"For the Lord your God is He who goes with you to fight for you against your enemies, to give you victory". *(Deuteronomy 20:4)*.

"On the day I called, you answered me; my strength of soul you increased". *(Psalm 138:3)*.

*"**Fear not, for I am you; be not dismayed, for I am your God; I will strengthen you, I will help you, I will uphold you with my righteous right hand**"*. *(Isaiah 41:10)*.

"God, the Lord, is my strength; He makes my feet like the deer's; He makes me tread on my high places. To the choirmaster: with stringed instruments". *(Habakkuk 3:9)*.

"Come to me, all who labor and are heavy laden, and I will give you rest".

(Matthew 11:28).

"Keep your life free from love of money, and be content with what you have, for He has said, ***'I will never leave you nor forsake you'****". (Hebrews 13:5).*

"I can do all things through Him who strengthens me". (Philippians 4:13).

"Count it all joy, my brothers, when you meet trials of various kinds, for you know that the testing of your faith produces steadfastness. And let steadfastness have its full effect, that you may be perfect and complete, lacking in nothing". (James 1:2-4).

<u>For Courage</u> to motivate you to keep moving forward:

*"****Be strong and courageous. Do not fear or be in dread of them, for it is the Lord your God who goes with you. He will not leave or forsake you'****". (Deuteronomy 31:6).*

*"****Only be strong and very courageous, being careful to do according to all the Law that Moses My servant commanded you. Do not turn from it to the right or to the left, that you may have good success wherever you go'****". (Joshua 1:7).*

*"****Have I not commanded you? Be strong and courageous. Do not be frightened, and do not be dismayed for the Lord your God is with you wherever you go'****". (Joshua 1:9),*

"Be strong, and let your heart take courage, all you who wait for the Lord!" (Psalm 31:24).

"Therefore we will not fear though the earth gives way, though the mountains be moved into the heart of the sea". (Psalm 46:2).

"In God, whose word I praise, in God I trust; I shall not be afraid. What can flesh do to me?" (Psalm 56:4).

"The Lord is on my side; I will not fear. What can man do to me?". (Psalm 118:6).

"Trust in the Lord with all your heart, and do not lean on your own understanding". (Proverbs 3:5).

"For God gave us a spirit not of fear but of power and love and self-control". (2 Timothy 1:7).

"Therefore lift your drooping hands and strengthen your weak knees".

(Hebrews 12:12).

"Wait for the Lord; be strong, and let your heart take courage; wait for the Lord!". (Psalms 27:14).

For Comfort and Trust to know that God is working on your situation:

"Lord, you know the hopes of the helpless. Surely you will listen to their cries and comfort them". (Psalm 10:17).

"He who dwells in the shadow of the Most High will rest in the shadow of the Almighty. I will say to the Lord, 'My refuge and my fortress, my God, in whom I trust'". (Psalm 91:1-2).

"When doubts filled my mind, Your Comfort gave me renewed hope and cheer". (Psalm 94:19).

"Behold, God is my salvation; I will trust, and will not be afraid; for the Lord God is my strength and my song, and He has become my salvation". (Isaiah 12:2).

"My comfort in my suffering is this: Your Promise preserves my life". (Psalm 119:50).

"Trust in the Lord forever, for the Lord God is an everlasting rock". (Isaiah 26:4).

"Now let your unfailing love comfort me, just as you promised me, your servant". (Psalm 119:76).

"Ah, Lord God! It is you, who has made the Heavens and the earth by Your Great Power and by Your outstretched arm! Nothing is too hard for You". (Jeremiah 32:17).

"The Lord is good, a stronghold in the day of trouble; He knows those who take refuge in Him". (Nahum 1:7).

For Faith to help you act on God's Truth:

"Behold, his soul is puffed up; it is not upright within him, but the righteous shall live by Faith". (Habakkuk 2:4).

*"Jesus turned, and seeing her He said, **'Take heart, daughter, your faith has made you well'**. And instantly the woman was made well". (Matthew 9:22).*

*"Then He touched their eyes, saying, **'According to your faith be it done***

to you'". *(Matthew 9:29).*

"He said to them, 'Why are you so afraid? Have you still no faith?'" (Mark 4:10).

*"And Jesus answered them, **'Have faith in God'**" (Mark 11:22).*

"For we walk by faith, not by sight". (2 Corinthians 5:7).

"For in Christ Jesus you are all sons of God, through faith". (Galatians 3:26).

"And the fruits of the Spirit are Love, Joy, Peace, Patience, Kindness, Goodness, Gentleness, Faithfulness, and Self-control". (Galatians 5:22).

"For by Grace you have been saved through Faith. And this is not your own doing; it is the gift of God". (Ephesians 2:8).

"Now faith is the assurance of things hoped for, the conviction of things not seen". (Hebrews 11:1).

The list goes on and on of all truths that God provides. I pray that you will take these Scripture verses and feel God's Spirit move through you, giving you the encouragement to live out God's Word and Ways, for this world has ways that only last but a moment, then turns into dust. There is one more huge encouragement that our Heavenly Father provides for us—that is His Son Jesus Christ.

This is a little something I put together to remind me of all what our Lord Jesus stands for:

Jesus stands for Love: To love me like no other.

Jesus stands for Guidance: To guide me with the Light of Life.

Jesus stands for Companionship: To walk with me when I feel lonely.

Jesus stands for Obedience: To teach me His Father's Commands and ways.

Jesus stands for Shield: To protect me from the fiery arrows of Satan.

Jesus stands for Courage: To fight for me when the battle is too rough.

Jesus stands for Prayer: To listen to me when no one else would.

Jesus stands for Strength: To carry me when I am feeling weak with despair.

Jesus stands for Safety: To catch me when I stumble and fall.

With all the things that our Heavenly Father provides and gives us, we have no reason to disobey Him. When He gave us His Son Jesus, He gave us Comfort for all of the times when we need to be comforted and to renew our relationship that our sin had severed us from Him.

Do you know what happens when you fail to open the door for Jesus? Well, let me tell you what happened to me when I kept denying hearing that knock. I started:

Believing in worldly advice; rather than the Word of God (the Bible) for the true, righteous advice for living, which landed me right in the pit of despair.

>>>Which then led me in developing evil habits – where I gave into Satan's actions and deceitful ways.

>>>Which then led me to living in emotional bondage—where absorbing all of the lies that Satan dangled in front of me that turned my self-esteem into a deadly toxin that blackened my soul. In addition, Satan used friends, coworkers, and family to keep those lies coming at me until I got so wrapped up in them, I became them, instead of becoming what God designed me to be. I see now that there is no such thing as a harmless lie or even a little lie, for all the lies turned me into an emotional mess, keeping me from living in the Light of God's Peace and turning me away from following Jesus.

>>>Which then led me to lacking Spiritual growth—being wrapped up in emotional lies blinded me to God's Truth and kept me from maturing in the Lord.

>>>Which then led me to being off balance, emotionally and physically. Dishonesty always leads to conflict, giving you a sense of unworthiness and living in that state of lying always. Which then led to destroying any kind of good reputation.

>>>When living a life of lies, the lies make others not believe you, when you tell them something that would hurt them. People tend to remember you more in telling lies]. This life of lies will always lead to grieving God's heart. In God's eyes telling lies are not acceptable. God wants us to always speak His truth and in turn bring others to Him. If you are telling lies, it hinders

you from doing God's work, which grieves Him terribly. You then suffer continuously in disappointment. You cannot lie and expect to have peace in your heart—it just can never happen.

You will always feel dissatisfied.

>>>Which then leads to poor relationships with others and with God. Telling lies will always give you trouble in making friends. People will stay as far away from you as possible. Even if Jesus would turn His back on you, He will never leave you, but He will be disappointed in you. >>>This then leads to hurting your self-image. Speaking and listening to lies will make you start to give into them and look like them.

>>>Which then leads to dwelling on past failures. When you keep remembering your past failures, it throws you off the path of moving forward and not living out God's truth, way, and Life.

>>>Which then leads to failure in reaching your full potential. Keeping you from achieving all the plans God has for you. Making you feel that you are standing still in a deep mud puddle—unable to move in any direction.

Satan's temptations and lies always lead to speaking and doing evil things. However, the Holy Spirit will lead you to speaking and doing good things. This is why it is very important for you to keep your ears open at all times and listen very carefully for that Voice of Truth— which is God whispering instructions of how to follow the Holy Spirit's leading and living in the Peace that surpasses all. All for God's Glory and Victory. God's Words of Truth speak Life, and His leading leads you out of the dark, cold places of which this world provides.

Here now is what God's Word (the Bible) says about speaking lies:

"You shall not bear false witness against your neighbor". (Exodus 20:16).

"Who is the man who desires life and loves the length of days that he may see well? Keep your tongue from evil and your lips from speaking deceit". (Psalm 34:12-13).

"Therefore, laying aside falsehood, speak TRUTH, each one of you, with your neighbor, for we are members of one another". (Ephesians 4:25).

"Lying lips are an abomination to the Lord, but those who deal faithfully are

His delight". (Proverb 12:22).

"Do not steal. Do not lie. Do not deceive one another". (Leviticus 19:11).

"A false witness will not go unpunished, and he who tells lies will perish". (Psalm 19:9).

"But You, O God, will bring them down to the pit of destruction; men of bloodshed and deceit will not live out half their days. But I will trust in You". (Psalm 55:23).

"Enemies disguise themselves with their lips, but in their hearts they harbor deceit. Though their speech is charming, do not believe them, for seven abominations fill their hearts. Their malice may be concealed by deception, but their wickedness will be exposed in the assembly. Whoever digs a pit will fall into it; if someone rolls a stone, it will roll back on him or her. A lying tongue hates those it hurts, and a flattering mouth works ruins". (Proverbs 26:24-28).

"The Spirit clearly says that in later times some will abandon the faith and follow deceiving spirits and things taught by demons. Such teachings come through hypocritical liars, whose consciences have been seared with a hot iron". (1 Timothy 4:1-2).

"We know that we have come to know Him if we keep His Commands. Whoever says, 'I know Him,' but does not do what He commands, is a liar and the Truth is not in that person". (1 John 2:3-4).

"Who is a liar? It is whoever denies that Jesus is the Christ. Such a person is the antichrist—denying the Father and the Son. No one who denies the Son has the Father; whoever acknowledges the Son has the Father also". (1 John 2:22-23).

"We love each other because He first loved us. Whoever claims to love God yet hates a brother or sister is a liar. For whoever does not love their brother and sister, whom they have seen, cannot love God, whom they have not seen. And He has given us this Command: **'Anyone who loves God must also love their brother and sister'***". (1 John 4:19-21).*

"An honest witness does not deceive, but a false witness pours out lies. The mocker seeks wisdom and finds none, but knowledge comes easily to the discerning. Stay away from a fool, for you will not find knowledge on their lips". (Proverb 14:5-7).

"There are six things the Lord hates, seven that are detestable to Him: haughty

eyes, a lying tongue, hands that shed innocent blood, a heart that devises wicked schemes, feet that are quick to rush into evil, a false witness who pours out lies and a person who stirs up conflict in the community". (Proverbs 6:16-20).

"May these words of my mouth and this meditation of my heart, be pleasing in your sight, Lord, my Rock and my Redeemer". (Psalm 19:14).

"If I speak in the tongues of men or of angels, but do not have love, I am only a resounding gong or a clanging cymbal. If I have the gift of prophecy and can fathom all mysteries and all knowledge, and if I have a faith that can move mountains, but do not have love, I am nothing. If

I give all I possess to the poor and give over my body to hardship that I may boast, but do not have love, I gain nothing". (1 Corinthians 13:1-3).

"Be very careful, then, how you live—not as unwise, but as wise, making the most of every opportunity, because the days are evil. Therefore, do not be foolish, but understand what the Lord's will is. Do not get drunk on wine, which leads to debauchery. Instead, be filled with the

Spirit, speaking to one another with psalms, hymns, and songs from the Spirit. Song and make music from your heart to the Lord, always giving thanks to God the Father for everything, in the name of our Lord Jesus Christ". (Ephesians 5:15-21).

"Do not let any unwholesome talk come out of your mouths, but only what is helpful for building others up according to their needs, that it may benefit those who listen". (Ephesians 4:29).

"Blessed are those who wash their robes, that they may have the right to the tree of life and may go through the gates into the city. Outside are the dogs, those who practice magic arts, the sexually immoral, the murderers, the idolaters and everyone who love and practices falsehood".

(Revelation 22:14-15).

These Scriptures from the Bible are the Words of God's Truth that heal and destroy Satan's burning arrows that are continually flying through the air of this world; right at all who are following Jesus. Recognizing and speaking God's Truth will help build on the foundation to live and breathe the Life God created for us to live. Therefore, I tell you, a truth I learned to do, to keep me moving forward and achieving all the plans that God has for me; and dodging those arrows of lies of Satan: Through the early years of my life, I always walked around feeling alone and envying other people that seem to be living a 'glamorous life', which I thought was the way I needed to live. Since then, I let Jesus into my life, and He showed me that living that 'glamorous life' (worldly life) was living a life of lies (as you read in the Scriptures above). Jesus also showed me when living with Him, all worldly desires would disappear, and I would find a better life in His Father's Love and Peace that He created me to live, leaving behind the ways of this 'glamorous world in the dust.

The life other people were living was what this world wanted me to live (which is temporary, not eternal). However, living in God's Truth is Life Eternal. God's Word started to absorb into my mind and heart, giving me a strength that was beyond anything I could have ever imagined.

I found the truthfulness of God for my life in the Bible, and I accepted it and believe in it for being my guide in living out God's Ways. Therefore, I chose to speak the words that build up instead of the words that tear down. I started examining my past failures, asking God to identify any areas of weakness. God revealed Scriptures that lifted me up from the pit and stopped the slipping down action that I started progressing. I have been reading all that He revealed to me (and then some), absorbing them all in my mind and heart. God put in my heart to be a trustworthy, reliable person, whose words speak truth, always remembering that Jesus is the Way, the Truth, and Life. He has set me free indeed. Free from any desires of this world.

God does His best work in us when we sit in the stillness of His Presence; where we can focus our eyes on Him and on Him alone. In the time you spend with God, you gain His Prospective for your life, heavy burdens are carried away, unscrambled thoughts are smoothed out, and you feel His Love and Comfort that He so freely gives to those who love Him.

Meditate on these Scriptures of the Truthfulness of God:

"Be sure to fear the Lord and serve Him faithfully, with all your heart; consider what great things He has done for you". (1 Samuel 12:25).

"Let all creation rejoice before the Lord, for He comes, He comes to judge the

earth. He will judge the world in righteousness and the peoples in his faithfulness". (Psalm 96:13).

"The Lord detests lying lips, but He delights in people who are trustworthy". (Proverbs 12:22).

"The Word became flesh and made His dwelling among us. We have seen His glory of the one and only Son, who came from the Father, full of grace and truth...For the law was given through Moses; grace and truth came through Jesus Christ. No one has ever seen God, but the one and only Son, who is Himself God—and is in closest relationship with the Father—has made Him known". (John 1:14, 17).

"God is spirit and His worshipers must worship in the Spirit and in Truth". (John 4:24).

"Stand firm then, with the Belt of Truth, buckled around your waist; with the Breastplate of Righteousness in place". (Ephesians 6:14).

"All Your words are true; all Your righteous laws are Eternal". (Psalm 119:160).

"He chose to give us birth through the word of truth that we might be a kind of first-fruits of all He created. My dear brothers and sisters, take note of this: Everyone should be quick to listen, slow to speak and slow to become angry, because human anger does not produce the Righteousness that God desires. Therefore, get rid of all moral filth and the evil that is so prevalent and humbly accept the word planted in you, which can save you. Do not merely listen to the word, and so deceive yourselves. Do what it says". (James 1:18-22).

"Show me Your Ways, Lord, teach me Your Paths. Guide me in Your Truth and teach me, for You are God my Savior, and my hope is in You all day long". (Psalm 25:4-5).

"Therefore, each of you must put off falsehood and speak truthfully to your neighbor, for we are all members of one body". (Ephesians 4:25).

"Do not let any unwholesome talk come out of your mouths, but only what is helpful for building others up according to their needs; that it may benefit those who listen. In addition, do not grieve the Holy Spirit of God, with whom you were sealed for the day of redemption. Get rid of all bitterness, rage and anger, brawling and slander, along with every form of malice. Be kind and

compassionate to one another, forgiving each other, just as in Christ God forgave you". (Ephesians 4:29-32).

The Bible is a great place to go when you are in the state of confusion and lacking knowledge of how to handle the ways of this dark, cold and confusing world. Situations will come and go, but the Word of God will live on forever. It is how you endure them that matters. The best way to endure your situation, that seems to be weighing you down, is to call out to Jesus, and He will reach out and give you that helping hand. Because <u>Jesus knows all</u> you are going through; and He overcame all that you are going through. Jesus is the Way to Righteous living with His Father in Heaven. <u>Jesus will teach</u> you all He knows and protect and defend you at the same time. You need not fear; for fear is a lie. Just trust the Lord that He is with us and He will never leave us.

This is the Will of God: Confess any sin that you might be hiding and repent of it. For repentance gets you on the path to joy—all on the wings of Love and Grace.

Repentance is the change of the mind to walk away from your sin and out of the darkness (your desires) of this world. The choice to confess and repent is the choice well taken to walk in the Light of Love, Joy and Grace – the Star Team.

I completely turned from my wrongdoings (sin) and handed them over to the One in Heaven, who overcame this world and He fights my battles for me. The Bible says:

"Blessed is he whose transgressions are forgiven, whose sins are covered.

Blessed is the man whose sin the Lord does not count against him and in whose spirit is no deceit. When I kept silent, my bones wasted away through my groaning all day long.

For day and night, your hand was heavy upon me; my strength was sapped as in the heat of summer. Then, I acknowledged my sin to You and did not cover up my iniquity. I said, 'I will confess my transgressions to the Lord'—and you forgave the guilt of my sin. Therefore, let all the faithful pray to You, while you may be found; surely the rising of the mighty waters will not reach them. You are my hiding place; You will protect me from trouble and surround me with songs of deliverance. 'I will instruct you and teach you in the way you should go; I will counsel you with My loving eye on you'. Do not be like the horse or the mule, which have no understanding, but must be controlled by bit and bridle or they will not come to you. Many are the woes of the wicked, but the Lord's Unfailing Love surrounds the one who trusts in Him. Rejoice in the Lord and be glad, you righteous; sing, all you who are upright in heart!" (Psalm 32:1-11).

There are many battles that we need to fight on this earth that are trying to turn us away from following Jesus. Here are three of the battles that I am continually battling:

<u>Battle one</u> is of your own desire to slack off and not do what God is telling us to do.

<u>Battle two</u> is about dealing with Satan's daily burning arrows (repeatedly occurring) to distract us from walking with Jesus.

<u>Battle three</u> is the pressure from your family members, your friends, and yeah even your own inner self.

Fighting these battles (and many others) weakened me a lot because I was trying to go it alone, thinking I could face these 'giants'. Then, I remembered what the Lord said in His Word:

"Be strong and courageous. Do not be afraid or terrified because of them, for the Lord your God goes with you; He will never leave you nor forsake you". *(Deuteronomy 31:6).*

"Have I not commanded you? Be strong and courageous. Do not be afraid; do not be discouraged, for the Lord your God will be with you wherever you go". *(Joshua 1:9).*

I instantly felt myself getting stronger and making those 'giants' weaker. Being totally devoted to God gave me confidence to face the battles of this world; this pleased Him and made Satan flee away from me. Ever since I grabbed hold of Jesus's hand, I gained the strength to endure the fight and to trust in Him to help me through these battles. This all happened when I answered His knocking on my heart's door and welcomed Jesus into my life (giving Him total control). My relationship with Him has gotten stronger—

making it very impossible for anything to draw me away from Him. As the Bible says: *"For nothing will be impossible with God". (Luke 1:37).*

"I can do all things through Him who strengthens me". (Philippians 4:13).

There is no one on earth that could even come close to being more trustworthy than God is. I have learned to be relaxed and enjoy all the blessings that God is laying out before me. I do not have to worry about Satan's burning arrows, for God placed a protective shield around me, so those arrows cannot get through. I tell you that trust and obedience is the key to everlasting protection from our Father God, Creator and Savior. I can walk with a smile on my face and love in my heart that my Lord will be with me always and forevermore. I will always have these Scriptures (and many others) from the Bible in my heart so I can speak and remember them when I need encouragement:

"For I am convinced that neither death nor life, neither angels nor demons, neither the present nor the future, nor any powers, neither height nor depth, nor anything else in all creation, will be able to separate us from the love of God that is in Christ Jesus our Lord". (Romans 8:38-39).

"When I am afraid, I put my trust in you—in God whose word I praise—in God I trust and am not afraid. What can mere mortals do to me?" (Psalm 56:3-4).

"See, I am doing a new thing! Now it springs up; do you not perceive it? I am making a way in the wilderness and streams in the wasteland". (Isaiah 46:19).

I now trust God with <u>all</u> my battles. The world tries to get me to go with them in their ways of living, but I know that Jesus is the way for me. In addition, I know that Jesus will never leave me or let me get hurt. For He is always with me in <u>all</u> the moments of my life.

It all started fifty years ago when I did not know all that I know now about God. When I thought I was alone, afraid, and confused. When I thought I had no one to go to and teach me how to live the right way (God's way). Without God's guidelines and instructions of how to live my life, I was lost. This was all when my relationship with my Heavenly Father (or even any relationship with anyone) was pretty slim pickings. However, when I read my Bible more and accepted Jesus into my life as my Lord and Savior, I found the real me that God created me to be. I now am seeking (every chance I have) to know <u>all</u> about God the Father and Creator and His Son Jesus. In this seeking, I needed to put aside <u>all</u> thoughts of this world and place God above <u>everything</u> (even if it hurt me to do so). Doing this, I found the blessings that God had for me. Now, some people would take this statement and think that God will bless them with material things. I was one of those people. God does not bless that way. He blesses with His Grace, Love, and Peace (the unseen). Well, if that leads to wealth, then that is an extra bonus.

It is God who directs my life. This is the only way to walk this journey on this earth. God sees how your heart is. If your heart has anything that God does not approve of, then He will tell you about it. This is why it is important to have that relationship with Him (through His Son Jesus).

You must open your heart and mind so that God can search them and remove anything that is not of Him. Opening the door for Jesus was the best thing I ever did. I now have someone to walk and talk with when I need a friend that can strengthen me instead of breaking me down.

Teaming up with Jesus creates here on earth the blessings that lead to the Glory that awaits me in Heaven. In addition, when I look in the mirror, I do not see that poor image of myself; the mirror now reflects the new me that I am in Christ. Read these Scriptures from the Bible that I read to remember who trusts me, loves me, and gives me refuge in Him:

"If you remain in Me and My Words remain in you, ask whatever you wish and it will be done for you. This is to My Father's Glory that you bear much fruit, showing yourselves to be My disciples". *(John 15:7-8).*

"The Lord is a refuge for the oppressed, a stronghold in times of trouble. Those who know your name trust in you, for you, Lord, have never forsaken those who seek you". (Psalm 9:9-10).

"Taste and see that the Lord is good; blessed is the one who takes refuge in Him. Fear the Lord, you His holy people, for those who fear Him lack nothing". (Psalm 34:8-9).

"How priceless is your Unfailing Love, O God! People take refuge in the

Shadow of Your Wings. They feast on the abundance of Your House; You give them drink from Your river of Delights. For with You is the Fountain of Life; in Your Light we see Light". (Psalm 36:7-9).

"I am like an olive tree flourishing in the house of God; I trust in God's unfailing love for ever and ever. For what you have done I will always praise you in the presence of your faithful people, and I will hope in your name, for your name is good". (Psalm 52:8-9).

"Whoever dwells in the shelter of the Most High will rest in the shadow of the Almighty. I will say of the Lord, 'He is my refuge and my fortress, my God, in whom I trust. Surely, He will save you from the fowler's snare and from the deadly pestilence. He will cover you with His Feathers, and under His Wings, you will find refuge; His Faithfulness will be your shield and rampart. You will not fear the terror of night, nor the arrow that flies by day, nor the pestilence that stalks in the darkness, nor the plague that destroys at midday. A thousand may fall at your side, ten thousand at your right hand, but it will not come near you". (Psalm 91:1-7).

"Those who trust in the Lord are like Mount Zion, which cannot be shaken but endures forever. As the mountains surround Jerusalem, so the Lord surrounds His people both now and forevermore". (Psalm 125:1-2).

"Let love and faithfulness never leave you; bind them around your neck, write them on the tablet of your heart. Then you will win favor and a good name in the sight of God and man. Trust in the Lord with all your heart and lean not on your own understanding; in all your ways submit to him, and he will make your paths straight. Do not be wise in your own eyes; fear the Lord and shun evil. This will bring health to your body and nourishment to your bones. Honor the Lord with your wealth, with the first-fruits of all your crops; then your barns will be filled to overflowing, and your vats will brim over with new wine". (Proverbs 3:3-10).

"Whoever gives heed to instruction prospers, and is blessed is the one who trusts in the Lord. The wise in heart are called discerning, and gracious words promote instruction. Prudence is a fountain of life to the prudent, but folly brings punishment to fools. The hearts of the wise make their mouths are prudent, and their lips promote instruction". (Proverbs 16:20-23).

"Whoever fears the Lord has a secure fortress, and for their children it will

be a refuge. The fear of the Lord is a fountain of life, turning a person from the snares of death". (Proverbs 14:26-27).

"Trust in the Lord forever, for the Lord, the Lord Himself, is the Rock eternal". (Isaiah 26:4).

"The Lord is good, a refuge in times of trouble. He cares for those who trust in Him". (Nahum 1:7).

"And God says: **'Be still and know I am God. I will be exalted among the nations. I will be exalted in the earth'**". (Psalm 46:10).

This is how I spend my free time, absorbing God's Word, so that I can remember I am never alone in facing what this world comes at me; all to bring me down. I may be no expert on fixing problems, but I tell you this: I learned from my Star Team that I had to stop worrying and complaining and start relaxing in God's Strength, Compassion, and Refuge; which is being in His Glorious Presence.

Not all that worrying and complaining solves anything; they just delay any blessings that God has for you. So then, when you enter God's Presence, leave the worries and complain outside in the cold. Bring only yourself, ready to listen and receive all that God has to say to you. When you are in God's Presence, do not speak too many words. It just makes you out to be a fool, and you will not be able to hear Him speaking to you. God is always speaking in a soft and gentle voice, and it is very difficult to hear Him when you are continually talking many words. This was my biggest sin. I always 'thought' that when I prayed, I had to keep on talking to have God hear me.

Then, one time as I was praying, I had no words to speak to Him. I was speechless. I was without words. All I could say to Him was, 'Thank you for Your protection and I love you. Amen'. Then, I heard Him say to me: *'Be not afraid or worried, for I am with you. I am clearing the way for you. Take hold of My hand and walk with Me, and I will be your guide and shield'*. After these words were spoken, my ears were tuned in to His Voice every time I prayed. I never, again, spoke too many words. The Word of God tells me: "Guard your steps when you go to the House of God. Go near to listen rather than to offer the sacrifice of fools, who do not know that they do wrong. Do *not be quick with your mouth, do not be hasty in your heart to utter anything before God. God is in Heaven and you are on earth, so let your words be few. A dream comes when there are many cares, and many words mark the speech of a fool". (Ecclesiastes 5:1-3).* So, I did just as He said and changed my ways from a 'talkie prayer person' to a 'listening prayer person' whenever I was in His Presence giving Him the Respect, Love, and Glory that He so deserves.

Your words and thoughts are no match to God's Words and Thoughts. God wins every time: It is He who clears the air of our many words; so we can hear His Words of Truth that bring Wisdom, Knowledge,and Victory into our lives. God's Words are what you need to overcome the ways of this world that is full of 'talkie people'. When your mind is quiet, all the thoughts of this world transform into God's Thoughts. This is the first step of the transformation and renewal that God (our Creator) does to have you live His Way of living and thinking like Him. Since God changed my words and thoughts to His, I am more confident to accomplish the work that He has given me. Today, I now thank Him every day for His Teaching, Comfort, and most of all His Love/Grace. I found out when I pray, I should not mention any of my performance pressures—for He looks at my heart, not my deeds.

Your heart tells everything about you—that is why you must have good and pure thoughts in your heart. This will benefit you in your journey through this world. One benefit is the Joy of a True Friendship with that Someone you can trust completely; to feel free to be the real you that God created you to be. Jesus, His Son, is that Someone to trust—He knows the worst about you and the best about you. And He still desires to be your True Friend. Jesus brings out the best in me (and you too) so I can live and love the best in Him. Just take a look at these Scriptures that backs up what I just said:

"Do not conform any longer to the pattern of this world, but be transformed by the renewing of your mind. Then you will be able to test and approve what God's will is—His good, pleasing and perfect will". (Romans 12:2).

"My Command is this: Love each other as I loved you. Greater love has no one than this; that He laid down His life for His friends. You are my friends if you do what I command. I no longer call you servants,

because a servant does not know his master's business. Instead, I have called you friend, for everything that I learned from my Father, I have made known to you. You did not choose me, but I chose you and appointed you to go and bear fruit—fruit that will last. Then the Father will give you whatever you ask in My Name. This is My Command: Love each other'". (John 15:12-17).

"*Love is patient, Love is kind. Love does not envy, Love does not boast, Love is not proud. Love does not dishonor others, Love is not self-seeking; Love is not easily angered. It keeps no record of wrongs. Love does not delight in evil but rejoices with the Truth. Love always protects, always trusts, always hopes, and always perseveres. Love never fails….And now these three remain: Faith, Hope, and Love. But the Greatest of these three is Love". (1 Corinthians 13:4-7, 8a, 13).*

These verses describe the very nature and character of God. I want to live (and love) out these verses and become like Jesus. There is no other example than Jesus to walk as He walks and talk as He talks. Jesus came down from on high to show us how to live and breathe His Father's ways. Living this world's ways, you are left confused and walking in circles. However, living God's Way, you can walk with confidence, down the straight Path of Love that God prepared before you. "***Then Jesus again spoke to them saying: 'I am the light of the world; he who follows me will not walk in the darkness, but will have the light of life'"***. (John 8:12).

And then I prayed this Psalm: *"Let the words of my mouth and the meditation of my heart be acceptable in your sight, O Lord, my Rock and my Redeemer". (Psalm 19:14).* Amen!

I just keep holding on to these two promises. God will tell us 'when' and 'how' that He sees best for us to live out His ways. So I will always listen to God speak and follow His Commands in <u>all</u> things. I will then have God's Peace that surpasses all. The way of sin will definitely end in sorrow. Most people that live in this world have somehow lost the awareness of how sin and guilt can bring the consequences of losing the life in living in the purity that the Bible speaks of: *"Blessed are the pure in heart, for they shall see God". (Matthew 5:8).*

"Behold, You desire truth in the innermost being, and in the hidden part You will make me know wisdom". (Psalm 51:6).

"Surely God is good to Israel, to those who are pure in heart!" (Psalm 73:1).

"My flesh and my heart may fail, but God is the strength of heart and my portion forever". (Psalm 73:26). "Therefore, consider the members of your earthly body as dead to immorality, impurity, passion, evil desire, and greed, which amounts to idolatry". (Colossians 3:5).

"Create in me a clean heart, O God, and renew a steadfast spirit within me". (Psalm 51:10).

"This is the message we have heard from Him and announce to you, that God is Light, and in Him there is no darkness at all". (1 John 1:5). "And everyone who has this hope fixed on Him purifies himself, just as He is Pure". (1 John 3:3).

One of the ways that brings death to your soul is when you start complaining about how others are doing things or saying things and not even realizing that you are hurting the people around you. I found this to be true when I heard some people complaining about me; it made me feel ill inside, an illness that made me feel shameful. I had no one to go to (so I thought) to ask what to do. I went to the one place that I knew would make me feel better and tell me everything that I was doing wrong—my Bible (God's Words of healing). As I opened up my Bible, I asked my Heavenly Father, "What should I do instead of complaining about others who are hurting me?" Then, He led me to these Scriptures, in which answered my question, and now when I get the need to complain, I would read them until the ill feeling of complaining would go away.

"Continue to work out your salvation with fear and trembling, for it is God who works in you to will and to act in order to fulfill His good purpose. Do everything without grumbling or arguing, so that you may become blameless and pure, 'children of God without fault in a warped and crooked generation'. Then you will shine among them like stars in the sky as you hold firmly to the Word of Life. And then I will be able to boast on the Day of Christ that I did not run or labor in vain". (Philippians 2:12b-16).

"Why should the living complain when punished for their sins? Let us examine our ways and test them, and let us return to the Lord". (Lamentations 3:39-40).

"Do not judge and you will not be judged. Do not condemn, and you will not be condemned. Forgive, and you will be forgiven. Give, and it will be given to you—A good measure, pressed down, shaken together and running over—will be poured into your lap. For with the measure you use, it will be measured to you. He also told them this parable: Can the blind lead the blind? Will they not both fall into a pit? The student is not above the Teacher, but everyone who is fully trained will be like their Teacher. Why do you look at the speck of sawdust in your brother's eye and pay no attention to the plank in your own eye?" (Luke 6:37-41).

"Do not let any unwholesome talk come out of your mouths, but only what is helpful for building others up according to their needs, that it may benefit those who listen. In addition, do not grieve the Holy Spirit of God, with whom you were sealed for the day of redemption. Get rid of all bitterness, rage and anger, brawling and slander, along with every form of malice. Be kind and compassionate to one another, forgiving each other, just as in Christ God forgave you". (Ephesians 4:29-32).

In the end, complaining hurts others, and no one (but no one) likes to be around complainers. Especially, our Heavenly Father—it just breaks His heart. Complaining leads to slandering, gossiping, bitterness, doubting, and rage, which leads us away from our Lord Jesus and a Life of Love and Peace. This is what the Bible says: *"God gives us more Grace. That is why Scripture says: 'God opposes the proud but shows favor to the humble'. Submit yourselves, then, to God. Resist the devil, and he will flee from you. Come near to God and He will come near to you. Wash your hands, you sinners, and purify your hearts, you double-minded. Grieve, mourn and wail. Change your laughter to mourning and your joy to gloom. Humble yourselves before the Lord, and He will lift you up. Brothers and sisters do not slander one another. Anyone who speaks against a brother or sister or judges them speaks against the law and judges it. When you judge the law, you are not keeping it, but sitting in judgment on it. There is only one Lawgiver and Judge, the One who is able to save and destroy. But you—who are you to judge your neighbor?" (James 4:6-12).*

"Be patient and stand firm, because the Lord's coming is near. Do not grumble against one another, brothers and sisters, or you will be judged. The Judge is standing at the door!" (James 5:8-9).

"As you know, we count as blessed those who have persevered. You have heard of Job's perseverance and have seen what the Lord finally brought about. The Lord is full of compassion and mercy. Above all, my brothers and sisters do not swear—not by heaven or by earth or by anything else. All you need to say is a simple 'Yes' or 'No.' Otherwise, you will be condemned". (James 5:11-12).

God's comforting touch is near all of time for all who are hurting and feel alone. God knows and sees all, for He is hovering over our lives and renewing us all the time. God knows that we are weak and cannot handle this world's corrupt ways. Because the enemy (Satan) is continually prowling around shooting those arrows of temptations and deceptions at us, trying to knock us off the path that leads to the Eternal Life that God has for us. However, if we continue to fix our eyes on Jesus and hold on to His hand, we can dodge those arrows and walk through the fire without feeling the heat. The Bible says:

"See, the Sovereign Lord comes with power, and He rules with a mighty arm. See, His reward is with Him, and His recompense accompanies Him. He tends His flock like a shepherd: He gathers the lambs in His arms and carries them close to His heart; He gently leads those that have young". (Isaiah 40:10-11).

"Lift up your eyes and look to the heavens: Who created all these? He who brings out the starry host one by one and calls forth each of them by name. Because of His great power and mighty strength, not one of them is missing. Why do you complain, Jacob? Why do you say, Israel,

'My way is hidden from the Lord; my cause is disregarded by my God'? Do you not know? Have you not heard? The Lord is the everlasting God, the Creator of the ends of the earth. He will not grow tired or weary, and His understanding no one can fathom. He gives strength to the weary and increases the power of the weak. Even youths grow tired and weary, and young men stumble and fall; but those who hope in the Lord will renew their strength. They will soar on wings like eagles; they will run and not grow weary, they will walk and not be faint". (Isaiah 40:26-31).

Forgiveness

We must persevere in all God tells us to do, and God is telling us to love and forgive others. Forgiveness was (and still is) the one thing that I seemed to do well. Here are two moments where I needed to set me free of the emotional turmoil; saying as Jesus said when He was being slander. I have been saying this all through my life:*"Jesus said,* **'Father, forgive them, for they do not know what they are doing'***". (Luke 23:34a).*

The first moment: All through my school days, my classmates were not very kind to me and hurt me very badly (emotionally). They would make fun of my appearance – my clothes, my look, the way I talked and not talked. However, I still forgave them, because I knew that holding any kind of grudge toward someone would hurt me worse than how they hurt me, so I forgave them.

The second one: It was at the bedside of my dying dad; he asked me to forgive him of how he was not the dad to me, the way he should have been. I thought for a moment, and in that moment, I recalled all the moments that my dad was there for me and all the times he was not there for me. The one time that really stuck was the time my dad disappointed me when he lied to me right in front of my face. I asked him about that time, and he then explained, in full detail. I gave him a hug and told him that I forgave him. Later that night, I went home and told my son that Grandpa died, and as I pointed at the one star that was out, before I could finish my sentence, he turned to me and said these words (that I will never forget): 'Grandpa is tied up somewhere'. I did not understand what my son was saying (he was only three), until ten years later when I answered the knock of my Lord Jesus and let Him into my life. My Lord sat with me and explained what my son said to me. He told me that it was not my son telling me that my dad is tied up somewhere; it was Him telling me that I haven't forgiven my dad wholeheartedly and I was the one bound in chains. As I sat there with Him, I was so in awe of His presence that my voice made no sound, and I just kept on listening to all He was speaking to me. I soon found myself on my knees, forgiving everyone that He showed me that I have not forgiven wholeheartedly, which included: my dad, my mom, my grandma, my classmates, my coworkers, my husband and his family, my brothers and sisters, and my children.

Once I finished, I felt a sense of Grace and Peace flow through my whole body and that huge gray cloud disappeared. As tears rolled down my face, I felt the healing touch and comfort of God that had comforted me before, and now He was doing it again. I tell you, I will always be thankful to my Lord for staying with me all this time. I now acknowledge my Heavenly Father and my Lord Jesus and the Holy Spirit (Star Team) in everything I see and in every situation that happens. It is very important in God's Sight to see His children loving and forgiving each other—even if it hurts too much to do so.

Read these Scriptures, and you will know why it is important to forgive.

"Forgive us our debts, as we also have forgiven our debtors". (Matthew 6:12).

"For if you forgive other people when they sin against you, your Heavenly Father will also forgive you. But, if you do not forgive others their sins, your Father will not forgive your sins". (Matthew 6:14-15).

"Blessed are the merciful, for they will be shown mercy". (Matthew 5:7).

*"Peter came to Jesus and asked, 'Lord, how many times shall I forgive my brother or sister who sins against me? Up to seven times?' Jesus answered, **'I tell you, not seven times, but seventy-seven times seven'**". (Matthew 18:21-22).*

"This is how my heavenly Father will treat each of you, unless you forgive your brother or sister from your heart". (Matthew 18:35). "Do not judge and you will not be judged. Do not condemn, and you will not be condemned. Forgive, and you will be forgiven". (Luke 6:37). "So watch yourselves". (Luke 17:3). "I urge you, therefore, to reaffirm your love for Him. Another reason I wrote to you was to see if you would stand the test and be obedient in everything. Anyone you forgive, I also forgive. And what I have forgiven—if there was anything to

forgive—I have forgiven in the sight of Christ for your sake, in order that Satan might not outwit us. For we are not unaware of his schemes".(2 Corinthians 2:8-11).

I tell you brothers and sisters, you must:*"Get rid of all bitterness, rage and anger, brawling and slander, along with every form of malice. Be kind and compassionate to one another, forgiving each other, just as in Christ God forgave you". (Ephesians 4:31-32).*

<u>Prayer Time:</u>

To my Awesome Heavenly Father:

I want to thank You for forgiving me. With Your forgiveness I can forgive, wholeheartedly, all who have hurt me in the past and present. So I can continue my walk with You. I thank You also for walking with me through this journey that You have made for me. I love walking in the Light of Your Footsteps of Grace. I pray this in Your Son's Gracious Name Jesus. Amen.

Relationships—Friendships

O nce our Heavenly Father forgives our sins and welcomes us into His Presence, we begin our relationship with Him. This is where I finally felt loved and accepted—where I found friendship. You see, when I was growing up, I was never accepted and really never had much as this world calls friends. I didn't even know how to make friends. In fact, I never had that 'best friend' that most people have when they are growing up. With me, my social skills were not very sharp (not knowing how to be social), making it very hard for me to talk to people. I always had to have the other person start the conversation (if I had found someone to talk to). I would always jumble my words, and it would always make me stutter, giving them a chance to laugh and make fun of me. Therefore, I just kept quiet and only spoke when I was spoken to—this is why I considered myself an observer; watching how people conducted themselves.

I then became a waitress at the age of sixteen, so I can learn how to talk with people (thinking that would teach me). I became a good waitress; for all I had to do was to take their order and then serve it to them. I love serving people. But being a waitress did not teach me how to talk to people. Even with my family, my talking skills were lacking. I thought your family should be the easiest to talk with. I guess I was wrong in thinking that waitressing would teach me how to talk to people and make friends.

When I wasn't working, I stayed in my own space being quiet; not letting anyone in so I didn't get hurt. To everyone, my opinion did not seem to matter for any kind of subject of concern. They all still thought of me as an idiot (a name that makes me shatter every time I say it or hear it). I then would put myself in the corner of the room never getting in on the topic that was being discussed. Oh, don't get me wrong, I had people talking to me but with their problems – only as a soundboard, a vent-board, a good listener type of a deal; that never talked back so that the other person can get off their chest what they needed to, to make them feel better. In other words, an unpaid counselor. As you can say they were using me for their own benefits. As long as I did not speak of my problems. People thought since I was quiet and a good listener, I didn't have any problems. However, when I reached out and opened that door for Jesus to come into my life, I found the one and only friend that was always there for me, ready to listen and help me. My friend, Lord and Savior Jesus Christ—He has been teaching me ever since that Glorious Day. Now, I read my Bible all the time; to get me through all the times when I was feeling alone and empty inside and abandoned.

When I was growing up, I did not read much of the Bible. But yet, I was somehow drawn to reading the four Gospel Books (the Books of God's Message). These Books of Gospel are Matthew, Mark, Luke, and John. I mostly read the Gospel of John, because in some way I felt the connection that John had between himself and Jesus.

When I was reading the Gospel of John, in chapter 15, where Jesus was teaching about the vine and the branches, I came to understand the connection that John and the other disciples had with Jesus.

Here is the explanation of how me and you can have that same connection that the disciples had:

"I am the True Vine, and My Father is the Gardener. He cuts off every branch in Me that bears no fruit, while every branch that does bear fruit He prunes so that it will be even more fruitful. You are already clean because of the Words I have spoken to you. Remain in Me, and I will remain in you. No branch can bear fruit by itself; it must remain in the Vine. Neither can you bear fruit unless you remain in Me. I am the Vine—you are the branches. If a man remains in Me and I in him, he will bear much fruit; apart from Me you can do nothing. If you remain in Me and My Words remain in you, ask whatever you wish and it will be given you. This is to My Father's Glory, that you bear much fruit, showing yourselves to be My disciples. If you obey My Commands, you will remain in My love, just as I have obeyed my Father's Commands

and remain in His Love. My Commands is this: Love each other as I have loved you. Greater Love has no one than this; that He lay down His Life for His friends. You are My friends if you do what I Command. I no longer call you servants, because a servant does not know his master's business. Instead, I have called you friends, for everything that I learned from My Father, I have made known to you. You did not choose me, but I chose you and appointed you to go and bear fruit—fruit that will last. Then the Father will give you whatever you ask in My Name. This is My Command: LOVE EACH OTHER! If the world hates you, keep in mind that it hated Me first". *(John 15:1-17).*

After I read these verses, I felt the connection that Jesus who was, is and always will be my Friend who will be there for me when I need a friend to talk over problems with. As I hold on to Jesus's hand, I know that I could walk this journey (never alone), with strength and wisdom (and discernment) that only my Star Team can supply. As I walk the walk I am supposed to walk, I will achieve all that I need to achieve to receive that reward that is waiting for me at the finish line in Heaven. For the Bible says: *"Finally, be strong in the Lord and in His Mighty Power. Put on the full Armor of God, so that you can take your stand against the devil's schemes. For our struggle is not against flesh and blood, but against the rulers, against the authorities, against the powers of this dark world, and against the spiritual forces of evil in the heavenly realms. Therefore, put on the full Armor of God, so that when the day of evil comes, you may be able to stand your ground, and after you have done everything, to stand. Stand firm then, with the Belt of Truth buckled around your waist with the Breastplate of Righteousness in place, and with your feet fitted with the Readiness that comes from the Gospel of Peace. In addition to all this, take up the Shield of Faith, with which you can extinguish all the flaming arrows of the evil one. Take the Helmet of Salvation and the Sword of the Spirit, which is the Word of God. In addition, pray in the Spirit on <u>all</u> occasions with all kinds of prayers and requests. With this in mind, be alert and always keep on praying for <u>all</u> the Lord's people"*. *(Ephesians 6:10-18).*

This is my best defense (putting on that whole Armor of God); which will never come off, as long as I keep reading my Bible and spending time in His Presence (praying), gathering up the strength that I need for the days of destruction and despair that lay before me. As I walk along these paths of hurt, guilt, loneliness and anger; aren't so bad when I have the One beside me, who overcame the world, and is giving me His Grace that is enough to achieve His Victory.

After I adorned the whole Armor of God, I started walking the best route (following Jesus) to avoid any stumbling stones that would cause me to fall. Every morning I go straight to my Bible for all the guidelines and routes that will fill up my emptiness and strengthen me for the road ahead. I get inspired and encouraged from reading my Bible. It helps me discern all the confusion that is around me. It clears the air and straightens the path that leads me to live the life my Heavenly Father designed for me. The Bible is the best place where you can find the most 'maps' and 'guidelines' for a clear path for your journey on this earth. I do believe that this is true. Because I have looked most of my life for a way to a joyful, peaceful, slow-paced, and loving place of rest from the hurriedness of this world. And the only way through the hurts, guilt, hurriedness, and joys is through the Bible, where Jesus is directing and teaching the route to

His Father's Presence—where the Love, Joy, and Peace flow like honey flowing down the side of the tree. As the Bible says: *"**I said you; 'You will possess their land; I will give it to you as an inheritance, a land flowing with milk and honey. I am the Lord your God, who has set you apart from the nations'**". (Leviticus 20:24).*

In this world is the land of unwavering trust, confusion, and misunderstanding. Also this world is a raging storm that is full of angriness, bitterness, selfishness, and hurriedness that seem to whirl around in one place (like a tornado), leaving destruction as it rushes through. This is what happens when we worry and hurry through our daily walk through this cold and dark world. Nothing comes out of rushing through life. It just blinds us to the Truth of who God is.

At some point on this journey-walk, I took my eyes off Jesus for just only but a moment and found myself drifting out to sea—far, far away from the shoreline Jesus was waiting for my return. This drifting was the result of my enemy (Satan), who weakened and distracted me enough to allure me away from my focus on Jesus. I eventually made my way back (with a lot of hurdle jumping and mountain climbing), but later than I would have with Jesus guiding the way. This lost time is lost energy, making me weak to face the giants that came at me. As soon as I realized what was happening (my drifting off into the open wild sea), I did cry out, "I need you Jesus!" (saying it with a wholehearted trust), and Jesus appeared with His hand stretched out saying, *'Do not fear, for I am with you. Grab on to My hand and walk with Me'.*

My Lord Jesus has been leading me ever since. Oh yeah, my feet still slip at times, but Jesus is always right there to keep me from falling and drifting away (He is my Anchor). I have the best Guide and Best Friend a person can have. I will always be so grateful for His Love, Protection, and Comfort that will never leave me or forsake me. Thank you, Jesus, my Star Team, for being with me all this time.

My Star Team is always available for me wherever and whenever I call on Him. The Bible is full of His promises to be with me (us), watching over me (us). No matter what I (we) lose in this lifetime, I will gain Grace and Love in my relationship with my Heavenly Father as long as I hold tightly to His Son's hand and trust Him that He is in control of everything. Opening the door to Jesus and letting Him into my life is the best move that I ever made. Do not get me wrong, my family is very important to me, but my relationship with God is much much more important. Each day, when I wake to God's Light shining in my life, I know that His Grace and Love is with me—to comfort me in the moments I need Him. This is Grace winning every time!

I now realize and proclaim that Jesus has been with me all through the good and the bad, giving me that special comfort He alone possesses. I will always rejoice for everything that God has done for me. Even in those hard times (when I thought I was alone) when I needed Him the most. This world throws at me the arrows of distraction, to get me to turn away from following Jesus and taking refuge in His Compassionate Embrace. My God is real, and He is with me (us) always and forever. I cannot stop smiling when I see the works of God in my life, shining the sun on all of His creation. God's Love always gets me through the good days and the bad days that I face on this earth. I am ever so grateful for the precious gift of His Son, Lord and Savior Jesus Christ. For Jesus is the peace that surpasses all.

In the quietness of God's Presence, I receive His Peace to demolish any strongholds that Satan is throwing at me—to stop me from getting closer to God. My best defense against Satan is the power of Jesus living in my heart. Jesus is my Stonewall that Satan cannot break through.

Here are some Scriptures to meditate on, to hold on to, and to encourage you to fix your eyes on the One who can lead you with Love, Joy, and Peace that surpasses all. God wants us to trust Him, even when we are low in the Faith of God's Presence. Faith is never taking your eyes off Jesus and trusting that He will always be by our sides. God warns us not to choose the wrong way (Satan's way) because it leads to destruction. God's Words are of healing and strength and most of all Love that refreshes our hearts, minds, and souls. God's Words are the sword and shield that we need to fight the enemy that prowls around in this world.

"My son, do not forget my teaching, but keep my commands in your heart, for they will prolong your life many years and bring you peace and prosperity. Let love and faithfulness never leave you; bind them around your neck, write them on the tablet of your heart. Then you will win favor and a good name in the sight of God and man. Trust in the Lord with all your heart and lean not on your own understanding; in all your ways submit to Him, and He will make your paths straight. Do not be wise in your own eyes; fear the Lord and shun evil. This will bring health to your body and nourishment to your bones". (Proverbs 3:1-8).

"Like snow in summer or rain in harvest, honor is not fitting for a fool". (Proverb 26:1).

"As a dog returns to its vomit, so do fools repeat their folly". (Proverb 26:11).

"Do you see a person wise in their own eyes? There is more hope for a fool than for them". (Proverbs 26:12).

"Though the mountains be shaken and the hills be removed, yet my unfailing love for you will not be shaken nor my covenant of peace be removed," says the Lord, who has compassion on you". (Isaiah 54:10).

*"**I am with you and will watch over you wherever you go, and I will bring you back to this land. I will not leave you until I have done what I have promised you**". (Genesis 28:15).*

"Therefore, go and make disciples of all nations, baptizing them in the name of the Father and of the Son and of the Holy Spirit, and teaching them to obey everything I have commanded you. And surely I am with you always, to the very end of the age". (Matthew 28:19-20).

"Rejoice in the Lord always. I will say it again: Rejoice! Let your gentleness be evident to all. The Lord is near. Do not be anxious about anything, but in every situation, by prayer and petition, with thanksgiving, present your requests to God. In addition, the peace of God, which transcends all understanding, will guard your hearts and your minds in Christ Jesus. Finally, brothers and sisters, whatever is true, whatever is noble, whatever is right, whatever is pure, whatever is lovely, whatever is admirable—if anything is excellent or praiseworthy—think about such things. Whatever you have learned or received or heard from me, or seen in me—put it into practice. And the God of peace will be with you". (Philippians 4:4-9).

"I am not saying this because I am in need, for I have learned to be content whatever the circumstances. I know what it is to be in need, and I know what it is to have plenty. I have learned the secret of being content in any and every situation, whether well fed or hungry, whether living in plenty or in want. I can do everything through Him who gives me strength". (Philippians 4:11-13).

"You remain the same, and your years will never end". (Psalm 102:27).

*"Jesus answered: '**I am the Way, the Truth and the Life. No one comes to the Father except through me**'". (John 14:6). Therefore: "'**Do not let your hearts be troubled. You believe in God; believe also in Me. My Father's house has many rooms; if that were not so, would I have told you that I am going there to prepare a place for you? In addition, if I go and prepare a place for you, I will come back and take you to be with Me so that you also may be where I am. You know the way to the place where I am going'**". (John 14:1-4).*

*"**All this I have spoken while still with you. However, the Advocate, the Holy Spirit, whom the Father will send in My Name, will teach you all things and will remind you of everything I have said to you. Peace***

I leave with you; My Peace I give you. I do not give to you as the world gives. Do not let your hearts be troubled and do not be afraid. You heard Me say; 'I am going away and I am coming back to you'. If you loved Me, you would be glad that I am going to the Father, for the Father is greater than I'". (John 14:25-28).

"This is what the Sovereign Lord, the Holy One of Israel says: 'In repentance and rest is your salvation, in quietness and trust is your strength'". (Isaiah 30:15).

"The weapons we fight with are not the weapons of the world. On the contrary, they have divine power to demolish strongholds. We demolish arguments and every pretension that sets itself up against the knowledge of God, and we take captive every thought to make it obedient to Christ. And we will be ready to punish every act of disobedience, once your obedience is complete". (2 Corinthians 10:4-6).

Let these verses absorb into your heart and mind so you can inspire others that just do not have a clue of how to get through their troubled day. There is no one else that has the expertise that our Heavenly Father has. God is the One (and only) who created all knowledge. God has Unending Wisdom and Unending Love; and He is willing to share it with you and me.

Do not run to God as an afterthought. Start with Him. He is all you will ever want and need. God controls the outcome of every situation and every individual's outcome. Therefore, you might as well go to Him for <u>all</u> the advice that you need. I did, and I am a better person for doing so. As long as I live, I will live out His Word and not fear what this world has to offer. For what God offers will last and what this world offers will fade and melt away.

<u>Here are some more Scriptures of Truth to absorb into your hearts and minds</u>:

"Blessed are those whose help is the God of Jacob, whose hope is in the Lord their God. He is the Maker of heaven and earth, the sea, and everything in them—He remains faithful forever. He upholds the oppressed and gives food to the hungry. The Lord sets prisoners free, the Lord gives sight to the blind, the Lord lifts up those who are bowed down, and the Lord loves the righteous. The Lord watches over the foreigner and sustains the fatherless and the widow, but

He frustrates the ways of the wicked. The Lord reigns forever your God, O Zion, for all generations. Praise the Lord". (Psalm 146:5-10).

*"God is our refuge and strength, an ever-present help in trouble. Therefore, we will not fear, though the earth gives way and the mountains fall into the heart of the sea, though its waters roar and foam and the mountains quake with their surging. There is a river whose streams make the City of God, the Holy Place where the Most High dwells. God is within her, she will not fall; God will help her at break of day. Nations are in uproar, kingdoms fall; He lifts His voice, the earth melts. The Lord Almighty is with us; the God of Jacob is our fortress. Come and see what the Lord has done, the desolations He has brought on the earth. He makes wars cease to the ends of the earth. He breaks the bow and shatters the spear; He burns the shields with fire. He says, **'Be still and know I am God; I will be exalted among the nations, I will be exalted in the earth'.** The Lord Almighty is with us; the God of Jacob is our fortress". (Psalm 46:1-11).*

"How precious to me are Your Thoughts, God! How vast is the sum of them! Were I to count them, they would outnumber the grains of sand. When I awake, I am still with you". (Psalm 139:17-18).

"But He gives us more grace. That is why Scripture says: 'God opposes the proud but shows favor to the humble'". (James 4:6).

Pray now with perseverance to strengthen you; it will crush Satan's power and send him running with his tail between his legs. To see this happen, you must: *"Submit yourselves, then, to God. Resist the devil, and he will flee from you. Come near to God and He will come near you. Wash your hands, you sinners, and purify your hearts, you double-minded". (James 4:7-8).*

A simple way to Honor Our Heavenly Father.

The simplest way to Honor the Father is to bring Life, Love, and Joy and send away any evil that is hanging around. Just remember God's son Jesus. As the Bible says:*"For God so loved the world that He gave His one and only Son that whoever believes in Him shall not perish but have eternal life". (John 3:16).* Remembering this one Scripture and obeying all of God's Commands (and living them out) gives Honor and Glory to Him. However, we tend to forget these four simple ways that also honor God. They are:

_Number 1:_Loving God unconditionally (as well as all others):

"Love the Lord your God with all your heart and with all your soul and with all your strength". (Deuteronomy 6:5).

"God demonstrates His own love for us in this: While we were still sinners, Christ died for us" (Romans 5:8).

"The Lord appeared to us in the past, saying: **'I have loved you with an everlasting love; I have drawn you with unfailing kindness'**". _(Jeremiah 31:3)._

"'Love the Lord your God with all your heart, and with all your soul, and with all, your mind, and with all your strength'. The second is this: 'Love your neighbor as yourself. There is no commandment greater than these'" (Mark 12:30-31).

Number 2: Forgiving compassionately (as your Heavenly Father forgives you):

"Get rid of all bitterness, rage and anger, brawling and slander, along with every form of malice. Be kind and compassionate to one another, forgiving each other, just as in Christ God forgave you". (Ephesians 4:31-32).

"Consequently, just as one trespass resulted in condemnation for all people, so also one righteous act resulted in justification and life for all people". (Romans 5:18).

"So watch yourselves. If your brother or sister sins against you, rebuke them; and if they repent, forgive them. Even if they sin against you seven times in a day and seven times come back to you saying, "I repent" you must forgive them". (Luke 17:3-4).

"For if you forgive other people when they sin against you, your Heavenly Father will also forgive you. But if you do not forgive others their sins, your Father will not forgive your sins". (Matthew 6:14-15).

Number 3: Remembering to be forever thankful to God (with a wholehearted heart):

"I will praise God's name in song and glorify Him with thanksgiving. This will please the Lord more than an ox, more than a bull with its horns and *hooves". (Psalm 69:30-31).*

"Come, let us sing for joy to the Lord; let us shout aloud to the Rock of our salvation. Let us come before Him with thanksgiving and extol Him with music and song". (Psalm 95:1-2).

"Enter His Gates with thanksgiving and His Courts with praise; give thanks to Him and praise His Name. For the Lord is Good and His Love endures forever; His Faithfulness continues through all generations". (Psalm 100:4-5).

"Give thanks to the Lord, for He is good. His love endures forever". (Psalm 136:1).

"The sting of death is sin, and the power of sin is the law. However, thanks be to God! He gives us victory through our Lord Jesus Christ. Therefore, my dear brothers and sisters, stand firm. Let nothing move you. Always give yourselves fully to the work of the Lord, because you know that your labor in the Lord is not in vain". (1 Corinthians 15:56-58).

"Do not be anxious about anything, but in every situation, by prayer and petition, with thanksgiving, present your requests to God. And the peace of God, which transcends all understanding, will guard your hearts and your minds in Christ Jesus". (Philippians 4:6-7).

"Rejoice always, pray continually, and give thanks in all circumstances; for this is God's will for you in Christ Jesus. Do not quench the Spirit". (1 Thessalonians 5:16-19).

Number 4: Treating God kindly and lovingly (which enable you to treat others with kindness):

"Do not let any unwholesome talk come out of your mouths, but only what is helpful for building others up according to their needs, that it may benefit those who listen". (Ephesians 4:29).

"Be kind and compassionate to one another, forgiving each other, just as in Christ God forgave you". (Ephesians 4:32).

"Do not gloat when your enemy falls; when they stumble, do not let your heart rejoice, for the Lord will see and disapprove and turn His Wrath away from them". (Proverbs 24:17-18).

"Love must be sincere. Hate what is evil; cling to what is good. Be devoted

to one another in love. Honor one another above yourselves. Never be lacking in zeal, but keep your spiritual fervor, serving the Lord. Be joyful in hope, patient in affliction, and faithful in prayer. Share with the Lord's people who are in need. Practice hospitality". (Romans 12:9-13).

"Therefore, as God's chosen people, holy and dearly loved, clothe yourselves with compassion, kindness, humility, gentleness and patience. Bear with each other and forgive one another if any of you has a grievance against someone. Forgive as the Lord forgave you. And over all these virtues put on love, which binds them all together in perfect unity". (Colossians 3:1-14).

"Show proper respect to everyone, love the family of believers, fear God, and honor the emperor". (1 Peter 2:17).

"My brothers and sisters, believers in our glorious Lord Jesus Christ must not show favoritism". (James 2:1).

"If you really keep the royal law found in Scripture, 'Love your neighbor as yourself,' you are doing right. But if you show favoritism, you sin and are convicted by the law as lawbreakers". (James 2:8-9).

"Do not rebuke an older man harshly, but exhort him as if he were your father. Treat younger men as brothers, older women as mothers, and younger women as sisters, with absolute purity". (1 Timothy 5:1-2).

When we honor God in all we do, it keeps us strong to endure any struggles that we face along this journey that we are to walk on this earth— all for His glory.

Adversity Is Something that We All Have to Go Through.

God chooses adversity to build up spiritual character (our faith) into our lives. Until we experience heartaches, disappointment, and pain, we will not be equipped for service.

So I had to ask myself these three questions (you can too):

Question (1) Have I experienced a heartache?

Question (2) Have I experienced disappointment?

Question (3) Have I experienced pain?

Before I give you my answers to these questions, I have to explain the meanings behind each one of these words: heartache, disappointment, and pain. Because I had to find out for myself the meanings, before I knew if I experienced them.

Heartache is a strong feeling of sadness, anguish of the mind (sorrow).

Disappointment is a feeling of being displeased with someone or something.

Pain is a feeling caused by disease, injury, and something (or someone) that hurts the body or mind. Pain is also the result of emotional distress or suffering.

After reading the meanings of heartache, disappointment, and pain, my answer to the three questions above is a yes – I have gone through heartache, disappointment and pain. As I think back to the situations, they were very confusing. They were situations that no one can handle on their own. As much as I tried I was not able to heal myself of these situations of heartache, disappointment and pain; I had a hard time. Before I was saved by Jesus, I always thought I had no one to help me. But then my Lord found the method that helped me endure the trials (adversity) of this world that caused me to stumble—the Bible. The method the Bible says is this: *"Consider it pure joy, my brothers and sisters, whenever you face trials of many kinds, because you know that the testing of your faith produces perseverance. Let perseverance, finish your work so that you may be mature and complete, not lacking anything. If any of you lacks wisdom, he should ask God, who gives generously to all without finding fault, and it will be given to you, but when ask; you must believe and not doubt, because the one who doubts is like a wave of the sea, blown and tossed by the wind. That person should not expect to receive anything from the Lord. Such a person is double-minded and unstable in all they do".* *(James 1:2-8).*

When I read this for the first time and where it said, "Consider it all joy," I could not fathom the fact to consider anything hurtful joyful. This Scripture many times is not that easy to discern any kind of benefits of suffering, not to say considering joy in the suffering. Because many times the trials we go through are so hurtful to deal with, we just want relief from them. We must understand that when we consider our trials as joy, we are not being happy in the hurt, we are seeing God's purpose in the hurt. To consider means to evaluate, a look at something or someone through a different perspective other than your own. The best perspective to consider is God's Perspective, placing the proper value on the difficulties, to bring a better outcome than what human perspective sees even if that difficulty is painful.

Our Heavenly Father knows that we are weak, and He wants us to come to Him for the strength that we need to get through that trial. Meditate on this statement: Trials do hurt, but the Lord will ease the pain with one single touch of comfort, compassion, and most of all love.

God is just waiting for us to ask Him for help. For the testing of our Faith accomplishes His purpose through the adversities of this world, which produces endurance and spiritual maturity. I found out, in my fifty years, that God hides precious character gems, among my struggles, that I will receive upon the response that I fulfill in the midst of that struggle. This is what Jesus says: *"**Keep on asking, and you will receive what you ask for. Keep on seeking, and you will find.***

***Keep on knocking, and the door will be opened to you'"*. *(Matthew 7:7)*.

The biggest benefit in enduring trials is that we are drawing closer to our Heavenly Father, while being transformed into the likeness of His Son Jesus. So let us start digging deeper to find that precious character gem that our Heavenly Father has hidden in the struggles that we are going through. Take one precious moment out of your busy day and discover the joy of God.

Trials will come and go; they are unavoidable in this corrupt and fallen world. However, as long as you have Jesus by your side, you can endure anything and everything. As the Bible says:

"Truly, He is my rock and my salvation; He is my fortress, I will never be shaken". *(Psalm 62:2)*.

"The bolts of your gates will be iron and bronze, and your strength will equal your days". *(Deuteronomy 33:25)*.

To profit from our struggles (trials) with Joy and Victory (Star Team), we must understand the Truth that is in them. Therefore:

<u>We must understand</u> – that God is in full *Control* of the timing and intensity of our trials.

<u>We must understand</u> – that God has a *Purpose* for our suffering that is for our benefit in our relationship with Him.

<u>We must understand</u> – in how submitting to God is to *Trust* that He *will* get us through our struggles (trials).

<u>We must understand</u> – that many struggles (trials) are moments for our *Faith* to grow stronger and genuine.

<u>We must understand</u> – that God is *always* demonstrating *His Power* to the watching world.

<u>We must understand</u> – that God uses our difficulties (trials) to produce a *Christlike Character.*

<u>We must understand</u> – that God will walk with us through the struggles (trials). Making every step we make, assures us that we are never alone.

<u>We must understand</u> – that the Holy Spirit is always going to *Help* us survive this cruel, corrupted world we live in; to conqueror to the end.

Check out the scriptures that might help you understand why we need to go through the struggles of this world:

"Do not conform to the pattern of this world, but be transformed by the renewing of your mind. Then you will be able to test and approve what God's will is—His good, pleasing and perfect will. For by the grace given me I say to every one of you: Do not think of yourself more highly than you ought, but rather think of yourself with sober judgment, in accordance with the faith God has distributed to each of you". (Romans 12:2-3).

"A faith and knowledge resting on the hope of eternal life, which God, who does not lie, promised before the beginning of time, and His appointed season He brought His word to light through the preaching entrusted to me by the command of God our Savior". (Titus 1:2-3).

As I lay myself at the foot of the Cross, surrendering it all to the point of death, of my self's will into the will of God, I will proclaim this Truth from the Bible: *"I eagerly expect and hope that I will in no way be ashamed, but will have sufficient courage, so that now as always, Christ will be exalted in my body, whether by life or by death".(Philippians 1:20).*

I will yield to Jesus the areas of my life that are hindering me from my walk with Him. This "yielding" is an act of willing to do what other people want. In other words, a matter of surrendering my will for God's will. You know what kept me from the decision to surrender to God. I was getting too comfortable in the life here on this earth (that I had thought was a wonderful life). What changed my mind? It is not "what" that changed my mind, but it was "who" changed my mind. God opened my heart and eyes to the destruction that was ahead of me. The more I was living the life of this world, the more I was hurting God. I was being disobedient to the One that gave me life and the One who saved my life. I had to shut out every thought that Satan was throwing my way and place myself before God, determined to be absolutely and entirely His alone, making the distractions of Satan turn to dust. The moment I made that decision to do exactly what God wants me to do, I felt a great weight off my shoulders; my heart became pure, and my mind became unscrambled. So I tell you to make a point to be determined to do all you can to let nothing stop you from doing exactly what God wants you to do to further His kingdom. When a crisis happens in your life that brings you to the crossroad, surrender it to God, totally and absolutely. You will be cleaner than the whiteness of the first fallen snow. As the Bible says:

"For I know the plans I have for you,' declares the Lord, 'plans to prosper you and not to harm you, plans to give you hope and a future. Then you will call on me and come and pray to me, and I will listen to you'". *(Jeremiah 29:11-12).*

"We wait in hope for the Lord; He is our Help and our Shield. In Him, our hearts rejoice, for we trust in His Holy Name. May Your Unfailing Love be with us, Lord, even as we put our hope in you". (Psalm 33:20-22).

The only thing we need to know is that God is in charge, and He knows what He is doing. We are to continually examine our attitude toward God, making sure there is nothing in the way of 'going out' for His purpose. Make sure that you examine every area of your life. If you are not sure of what to look for, then ask God to show you so you can surrender it properly. Keep trusting and depending on God entirely. Doing this keeps me (and you) from wandering away from living in God's love. Do not worry about the things that concern the ways of the world. Just put your trust in God who is always in control of every situation and will work it out for our good. Believe God always! Believe Jesus is always beside you helping fight off Satan's burning arrows. Keep on believing that to go through the valley of darkness is to get to the mountaintop of glory. Stop worrying and let God fight the battles that are too hard for you. Let the attitude of your heart continually want to do the Will of God. Remember, that being depended on God does not mean you are weak. For the Bible says: *"That is why, for Christ's sake, I delight in weaknesses, in insults, in hardships, in persecutions, in difficulties. For when I am weak, then I am strong"*. *(2 Corinthians 12:10)*.

Come to the point in your faith where there is nothing between you and God. Relax in God's presence, knowing that nothing can separate you from His love. For God's love is a pure gift that flows like a river from His heart to yours. When you believe it, you will achieve it. That is what overcomes all struggles. When facing the giants in your life, remember to always praise God in the storm. Praise can go a long way. Also, remember Jesus overcame this world, and His strength and compassion is available at any time you need it. Every time I read my Bible, God points out

Scriptures that pertain to the situation that I am presently dealing with. Here are some of the Scriptures that speak to me and keep me grounded in the presence of God:

"Look to the Lord and His strength; seek His face always". *(Psalm 105:4)*.

"Sing to Him, sing praise to Him; tell of all His wonderful acts". *(Psalm 105:2)*.

"For I am convinced that neither death nor life, neither angels nor demons, neither the present nor the future, nor any powers, neither height nor depth, nor anything else in all creation, will be able to separate us from the love of God that

is in Christ Jesus our Lord". *(Romans 8:38-39).*

"'The thief comes only to steal and kill and destroy; I have come that they may have Life, and have it to the full'". *(John 10:10).*

"I have told you these things, so that in Me, you may have peace. In this world, you will have trouble. However, take heart! I have overcome the world'". *(John 16:33).*

"Then Jesus said to His disciples: **'Therefore, I tell you, do not worry about your life, what you will eat; or about your body, what you will wear. For life is more than food and the body more than clothes'".** *(Luke 12:22-23).*

Called by God

There are battles that are out there in this world that need God's attention. Yeah, you are probably saying, "God sees all that is happening. He can fix it." Yeah, you're right, but God calls us to be His hands and feet. To do the legwork, as they may call it. The call by God is not just for the selected few but also for everyone that hears Him calling out their name. For the longest time, God was calling my name, and it was always when He saw me about to do something that He did not approve of. I never completed that. To hear God's Voice depends on the condition of your ears (no blockage of the other voices of this world) and the condition of your spiritual attitude of the heart for God. For God does see all, and He mostly sees the condition of our hearts. We can look like we are being obedient to Him, but if our hearts have anything evil in them, God will know. Nothing gets past God; you cannot hide anything from Him. God knows all and sees all. As the Bible says: *"Many are called, but few are chosen". (Matthew 22:14).*

The chosen are those who have an intimate relationship with God through His Son Jesus Christ. Our ears are opened the moment we accept Jesus into our lives, igniting the flame to the Spiritual conditioning that is needed to build us up to do God's work. We must allow the Holy Spirit to bring us face-to-face with God, to hear Him speak to our hearts. Therefore, we can say as Isaiah said, *"Here I am. Send me!". (Isaiah 6:8b).* The first time I heard God's Voice calling out my name, I thought it was a family member saying my name; wanting me to do something for them. It took three times for God to say my name until finally I was brought to my knees and recognized that it was God calling me to His Presence. Once I was there in His Presence, I was able to hear Him clearly. I received His message and thanked Him for choosing me for the task.

When you hear God calling your name, you must deal with it, not going to other people and asking them what to do. When God calls your name, He is calling you for a purpose—to have an intimate relationship with you and to have you go out and tell the unbelieved world about Him.

The assignments that God wants you to do for Him will bring His children that are lost back to Him or to Him. This is why it is necessary to read the Bible (God's Word) and pray to distinguish between God's Voice and the enemy's voice. Satan will try anything to distract our minds. To fight this battle is to hold firm to all of God's *Promises* and keep your eyes fixed on Jesus.

I personally like to sit quietly and talk out all that concerns me with my Star Team (the Father, Jesus, and the Holy Spirit). This is the best way for me to draw strength for the battles of this cold, angry, selfish and rushed world. Communication with Father (through His Son Jesus) is the most important weapon that helps me walk through this journey on this earth. Because taking my eyes off Jesus and not talking with Him weakens me and leaves the door open for Satan to slither in with all his distractions. Only Jesus can help me stay fixed on the *Prize* awaiting me in Heaven. Every step away from Jesus is a step toward destruction.

We must refuse to worry about the ways of this world; and stay alert to the fact that Satan is out there just waiting for that weak (worrying) moment to draw us away from the *Life of Peace* that God so freely gives to those who follow in the *Footsteps* of His Son Jesus Christ.

Read now, these Scripture verses that I read to stay fixed on my Star Team:

"God raised us up with Christ and seated us with Him in the Heavenly Realms in Christ Jesus". (Ephesians 2:6).

"My heart says to you 'Seek His face!' Your face, Lord, I will seek". (Psalm 27:8).

"The mind of sinful man is death, but the mind controlled by the Spirit is Life and Peace".

(Romans 8:6).

"For the law was given through Moses; Grace and Truth came through Jesus Christ".

(John 1:17).

The Truths that Jesus taught His disciples are to teach the disciples (and us) where they can find joy. In addition, any overflow of joy they found would fall onto us. This teaches us that wherever Jesus is, joy is there. Jesus waits for us always to share His Wisdom, Compassion, and Joy (for these are who He is). All we have to do is reach out and grab hold of His hand, and He will lead us all the way to His Father's House. This is a guarantee that will never get lost in the shuffle of this crazy mixed up world. So, take it from me, who walked in the bitterness of this dark world for so long; it is better to live in the Life of Love, Joy and Peace – the Star Team.

These Scriptures will remind you that Jesus is the only True Vine. It is the Words of the Star Team (Jesus) who is speaking to us all of the time:

"I am the True Vine and My Father is the Gardener. He cuts off every branch in Me that bears no fruit, while every branch that does bear fruit He prunes so that it will be even more fruitful. You are already clean because of the Word I have spoken to you. Remain in Me, as I also remain in you. No branch can bear fruit by itself; it must remain in the Vine. Neither can you bear fruit unless you remain in Me. I am the Vine; you are the branches. If you remain in Me and I in you, you will bear much fruit; apart from Me you can do nothing. If you do not remain in Me, you are like a branch that is thrown away and withers; such branches are picked up, thrown into the fire and burned. If you remain in Me and My Words remain in you, ask whatever you wish, and it will be done for you. This is to My Father's Glory, that you bear much fruit, showing yourselves to be My disciples'". (John 15:1-8).

What serving My Star Team does for Me?

– overflows my life, with Love, Compassion, and devotion to Him.

– brings me into a closer proper relationship with the Father; through His Son Jesus Chrisst.

– becomes part of my life; all for His Will and Purpose.

– accomplishes that the Son of God lives in me.

Therefore, when you receive the Call from the Father to serve, you join up with His Son Jesus and become one with Him. This is called a total Devotion and Love to the Father. Since I accepted Jesus into my life I have been able to make serving my Star Team a daily habit and a way of life, all for His Glory. Which brought me the Peace that demolishes all the flaming arrows of the enemy. Being at Peace (through serving) is how God made me to be. I am a servant of God that will serve others, with His Love and Compassion.

This world wants me to be coldhearted, which is the total opposite of how my Creator made me to be. The Bible says, *"For we are God's handiwork, created in Christ Jesus to do good works, which God prepared in advance for us to do". (Ephesians 2:10). "For He Himself is Peace, who has made the two groups and has destroyed the barrier, the dividing wall of hostility, by setting aside in His flesh the law with its commands and regulations. His purpose was to create in Himself one new humanity out of the two, thus making peace, and in one body to reconcile both of them to God through the cross, by which He put to death their hostility. He came and preached peace to you who were far away and peace to those who were near. For through Him we both have access to the Father by one Spirit". (Ephesians 2:14-18).*

In my younger years, when I had a situation that was causing me pain, I would try to find someone who had gone through the same situation (and survived). However, all I found were people telling me either hash words or they were too busy and told me to come back another time when they were less busy (that day never came), which made me hurt more that I would sink deeper into my shell of darkness, never going to anyone for advice again.

Peers (and even family) can be cruel when they lash out words that they think helps a person but really belittles them. However, one night when I was just sitting there thinking of ways to solve my problem, all of sudden I got the sense to open my Bible and start reading. Right where I opened it up, the Holy Spirit led me to Scriptures on flaws and failures, where they told me how to correct my flaws and failures and did not belittle me. Here are some of the Scripture verses that that I read; and helped me walk right lon through the flames of my flaws and failures (not getting burned): *"As for you, you were dead in your transgressions and sins, in which you used to live when you followed the ways of this world and of the ruler of the kingdom of the air, the spirit who is now at work in those who are disobedient. All of us also lived among them at one time, gratifying the cravings of our flesh and following its desires and thoughts. Like the rest, we were by nature deserving of wrath. But because of His Great Love for us, God, who is rich in Mercy, made us alive with Christ even when we were dead in transgressions—it is by grace you have been saved. And God raised us up with Christ and seated us with Him in the heavenly realms in Christ Jesus".* (Ephesians 2:2-7).

"These people are springs without water and mists driven by a storm. The blackest, darkness is reserved for them, for they mouth empty, boastful words and, by appealing to the lustful desires of the flesh, they entice people who are just escaping from those who live in error. They promise them freedom, while they themselves are slaves of depravity—for 'people are slaves to whatever has mastered them'". (2 Peter 2:17-19).

"But who can discern their own errors? Forgive my hidden faults. Keep Your servant also from willful sins; may they not rule over me. Then I will be blameless, innocent of great transgression. May these words of my mouth and this meditation of my heart be pleasing in Your sight,

Lord, my Rock and my Redeemer". (Psalm 19:12-14).

"Do not be deceived: God cannot be mocked. A man reaps what he sows. Whoever sows to please their flesh, from the flesh will reap destruction; whoever sows to please the Spirit, from the Spirit will reap Eternal Life. Let us not become weary in doing good, for at the proper time we will reap a harvest if we do not give up. Therefore, as we have opportunity, let us do good to all people, especially

to those who belong to the family of believers". (Galatians 6:7-10).

"Therefore, confess your sins to each other and pray for each other so that you may be healed. The prayer of a righteous person is powerful and effective". (James 5:16).

"My brothers and sisters, if one of you should wander from the truth and someone should bring that person back, remember this: Whoever turns a sinner from the error of their way will save them from death and cover over a multitude of sins". (James 5:19-20).

"And, He who searches our hearts knows the mind of the Spirit, because the Spirit intercedes for God's people in accordance with the will of God. In addition, we know that in all things God works for the good of those who love Him, who have been called according to His purpose. For those God foreknew he also predestined to be conformed to the image of His Son, that he might be the firstborn among many brothers and sisters. And those He predestined, He also called; those He called, He also justified; those He justified, He also glorified" (Romans 8:27-30).

"Submit yourselves, then, to God. Resist the devil, and he will flee from you" (James 4:7).

"Humble yourselves before the Lord, and He will lift you up. Brothers and sisters do not slander one another. Anyone who speaks against a brother or sister or judges them speaks against the law and judges it. When you judge the law, you are not keeping it, but sitting in judgment on it. There is only one Lawgiver and Judge, the one who is able to save and destroy. But you—who are you to judge your neighbor?" (James 4:10-12).

"Therefore, since we have been justified through faith, we have peace with God through our Lord Jesus Christ, through whom we have gained access by faith into this grace in which we now stand. In addition, we boast in the hope of the glory of God. Not only so, but we also glory in our sufferings, because we know that suffering produces perseverance; perseverance, character; and character, hope. In addition, hope does not put us to shame, because God's love has been poured out into our hearts through the Holy Spirit, who has been given to us. You see, at just the right time, when we were still powerless, Christ died for the ungodly. Very rarely will anyone die for a righteous person, though for a good person someone might possibly dare to die. However, God demonstrates His own love for us in *this: While we were still sinners, Christ died for us. Since we have now been justified by His blood, how much more shall we be saved from God's wrath through Him! For if, while we were God's enemies, we were reconciled to Him through the death of His Son, how much more, having been reconciled, shall we be saved through His life! Not only is this so, but we also boast in God through our Lord Jesus Christ, through whom we have now received reconciliation". (Romans 5:1-11).*

After I read all the Scriptures that my Father spoke to my heart, I took my hurting and feeling lonely (even with loved ones around) and started to correct my flaws. I then heard that knocking sound at my heart's door, along with Jesus's Voice calling out my name. I Turned around and opened that door, and lo and behold, there stood Jesus, and He was holding out His hand to me. As I reached out to Him, I fell to my knees in awe. Jesus lifted my head and said, 'Don't be afraid. I am always with you. Be strong. Come, I will show a Life of Peace. Not the peace the world offers, but my Father's Peace that will be with you always. The Peace that will never hurt you but make you stronger and more confident, to keep moving forward'. As a tear was running down my face, Jesus took His finger and took that one tear of pain and turned into a tear of joy. At that moment, I got my answer to my prayer. I just had to let Jesus into my life and help me better myself.

I had the radio on; the radio went silent (while Jesus was speaking), but as soon as I let Jesus into my life, the radio started playing the song "I Will Rise" by Chris Tomlin. Tears started falling and again I fell down to my knees in awe and thankfulness. Just then, that dark cloud that was over me turned into sunshine – the whole lit up. From that moment on, God's Peace and my Star Team was with me, wherever I went. To this day, when troubles come my way, I remember that time that Jesus rescued me from under that dark cloud of despair and hurt. Jesus has been with me ever since. I now read my Bible and pray continually for strength to face the giants of this cold evil world. I am a better person for always taking the time to spend quality time with my Star Team—the Father, His Son Jesus, and the Holy Spirit. In this time that I spend with my Star Team, I get to know myself—in the eyes of my Heavenly Father. Only God can reveal the true me, because He is the

One who designed me. God is the only one that will love me, even with all my flaws. And God is the only one who can turn my hurt into Joy (Jesus).

This was the moment I died to self and gained an Everlasting Friend— my Lord and Savior Jesus – the Friend that made me flawless, turning them into strength, comfort, and most of all love. I am forever grateful to my Lord.

Dying to Self.

I just talked about this a little earlier when I was talking about the 'me disease'. Every person has a 'me' that we think we should be and that 'me' is always wrestling with God. Because that 'me' is the opposite of 'who' God made us to be, it can be hard to let go of the self that you got so accustomed to that this world so possesses. Most of the time, letting go feels like death. Exactly! Because you have to die to live in the Life that our Creator designed for us. Dying to self is dying to pride, anger, lust, and the desires of this world. When you let go of these things and lay them at the foot of God, He takes them and starts the process of replacing them with equipment to live in His freedom.

Along the journey that I am on, I needed to bury that 'old self' and focus on listening to His Voice of Truth that is whispering in my ear: *"This is the way; walk in it'"*. *(Isaiah 30:21b)*. However, I cannot hear His voice if I am still living in the 'self' of this world. This is why it is very important to read the Bible (God's Word), so the voices of this world are drowned out and fade away. In keeping God's Word in my heart, it helps me to be prepared to defend myself against the words of Satan, which are words that turn me into the person no one wants to be around.

God is Working the Inside and Outside.

Our outer body is being shaped by the way we eat, drink, sleep, exercise, and live. The inner you is being shaped by what you see, read, hear, think, and do. The outer self (flesh) is continually rebelling against the inner self (spiritual) for control. This is what the Bible calls 'wrestling with God' (see

Genesis 32:22-32). The more we rebel against God, the longer it takes to receive blessings from Him. You can only flourish when you are rooted in the Word of God and shaped by God. For God wants to be the only one that shapes and designs us, that fits to fulfill His purpose. God makes it clear to us to do His will. The dependence on God leads to a quiet confident spirit. We read in the Bible:

"Better to live on a corner of the roof than share a quarrelsome wife". *(Proverbs 25:24).*

"In quietness and confidence shall be your strength", *(Isaiah 30:15).*

"Your ears shall hear a word behind you, saying: 'This is the way; walk in it' *(Isaiah 30:21b).*

"A man's steps are directed by the Lord. How can anyone understand His Way?" (Proverbs 20:24).

"Wait for the Lord, and He will deliver you" (Proverbs 20:22b).

"Give ear to my words, O Lord, consider my sighing. Listen to my cry for help, my King and my God, for to you I pray. In the morning, O Lord, you hear my voice; in the morning I lay my requests before you, and wait in expectation". *(Psalm 5:1-3).*

What is my 'Egypt' or 'Source' that I am turning to?

In the Bible 'Egypt' is a place of refuge and a threat to the Lord's people. Also, 'Egypt' was a place of important cultural (refinement) for the Israelites, a place of depending on wealth to make them happy. The Israelites got so used to it that when they left it, they missed it. For they did not know how to survive in the wilderness without it (the means of money or material things).

Today, we all do something as the Israelites did—accepting the ways of this world. Why? Because it is all that we seem to know – not knowing God – not realizing that the ways of this world will not last; which would fade away like the sun does, when it sets. The world's ways are the ways that can darken our hearts and kill our souls, opening the door for Satan to refine us into the likeness of him. However, when we seek after God and let Him provide for our needs, He then showers us with His grace to refine us back into the Glory that will take us into Eternity—where Satan cannot enter and steal us away from Him.

Sometimes, when I am walking down the path that God had provided for me to walk, it takes me to a crossroad or steep, a steep hill that looks pretty scary and slippery—a place where my burden was heavy and loaded up with guilt (weighing me down); which was making it difficult to climb up those steep hills, causing my feet to slip and not face my giants. However, I remembered suddenly that I had my Star Team by my side. As I cried out His Name, I felt His hand grab my hand, enabling me to walk with solid steps. I held on to Jesus's hand as tight as I could, and Jesus took that guilt I was carrying and buried it so deep that it turned into dust.

My act of reaching out to Jesus really straightened me upright from that hunchback I was beginning to walk. I looked to my Lord and gave Him my trust to bear my burden, turning my shame and darkness into Love and Light. Now, I am able to move forward with Love and Kindness. The Bible (God's Word) says:

"Praise be to the Lord, to God our Savior, who daily bears our burdens". (Psalm 68:19).

"This is the message we have heard from Him and declare to you: God is Light; in Him there is no darkness at all. If we claim to have fellowship with Him and yet walk in the darkness, we lie and do not live out the Truth. However, if we walk in the Light, as He is in the Light, we have fellowship with one another, and the blood of Jesus, His Son, purifies us from all sin. If we claim to be without sin, we deceive ourselves and the Truth is not in us. If we confess our sins, He is Faithful and just and will forgive us our sins and purify us from all unrighteousness. If we claim we have not sinned, we make Him out to be a liar and His Word is not in us". (1 John 1:1-10).

"There is no fear in love. However, perfect love drives out fear, because fear has to do with punishment. The one who fears is not made perfect in Love. We love because He first loved us". (1 John 4:18-19).

To rediscover the Good (Pure) Life God has offered us, we have to fulfill what Jesus says in the Gospel of John: *"On the last and greatest day of the Feast, Jesus stood and said in a loud voice;* **'If anyone is thirsty, let him come to Me and drink. Whoever believes in Me, as the Scripture has said, streams of living water will flow from within him'**". *(John 7:37-38).*

When we feed on God's Word, we will fill our bellies with His living water and never have to feel empty again—with disappointment and discouragement (for these are what this world brings). We thrive when we listen and live the ways of God. Therefore, as for me, I will seek more of God and be filled with the living water that He supplies for me (us) to live in His peace. I am ever so thankful for the living water that my Heavenly Father gives me. The more I read my Bible (God's Word and living water), I discover this: The more I seek Him, the more I know Him; the more I know Him, the more I love Him, and the more I love Him, the more I understand His ways. Reading the Word of God (the Bible) and praying continually keeps my Faith strong and ready to face the struggles of this world.

Back when I did not read the Bible that much, I struggled a lot with the ways of this world; making my life empty and lost. But now, since I opened my Bible more, I also opened up my heart and mind to the Greatest Love of all:

The <u>Love</u> that was always with me.

The <u>Love</u> that died for me and made me flawless.

The <u>Love</u> that will never leave me.

The <u>Love</u> of my Star Team.

There is no other love that comes even closer than the <u>Love</u> of God.

"So we know and rely on the <u>Love</u> God has for us. <u>God is Love</u>. Whoever lives in Love lives in God, and God in them". (1 John 4:16).

The Landmines of Discouragement, Despair, Dismayed, Belittling, Complaining, Guilt and Shame

andmines were in the Korean War and in World War I and II. Landmines are explosives hidden underground, scattered about in the fields of war – many lives were lost with these landmines. In this world there are also many landmines hidden; and they are not hidden in the ground. Discouragement and despair are two of many landmines that are scattered about in this world. I picked these two because they are the ones that I have experienced mostly in my life. I know that they will always be out there, for Satan knows that he can use them against me to make me feel belittled and dismayed and to make me complain and feel guilty of all my wrongdoings. Satan uses these landmines on all of us, because nothing else works for him.

These seven landmines are the landmines that can pierce a hole into your heart and torment you for a very long time—that is, if you do not have Jesus (the Star Team) walking by your side to comfort and help you:

Discouragement—a feeling of having lost hope or confidence (unconfident).

Despair—to have no hope or belief of a situation that will change or improve (hopeless).

Dismayed—to cause (someone) to feel very worried or upset (unsure).

Belittled—to describe (someone or something) as little or unimportant (shameful).

Complaining—to express grief, pain, or discontent (grumpy).

Guilt—the state of one who has committed an offense, especially consciously (blameful).

Shame—a condition of humiliating disgrace or disrepute (pity).

If you notice, these meanings are all the same but worded differently. We must learn to recognize and deal with each of these negative thoughts and reactions. Because when they fester inside your heart, they turn us into bitter souls. For when we are bitter, we are prime targets for the enemy's attacks, which is exactly Satan's plan (wanting us to feel bitter just like he is). Satan has many attacks, scattered about this world – always shooting these arrows of negative thoughts our way.

All through my life, I had to deal with people making me feel what I call the 'un' words: <u>un</u>important, <u>un</u>confident, and <u>un</u>sure. These words were making me very <u>un</u>worthy and <u>un</u>loved (two more 'un' words). However, when I took the Hand of my Lord Jesus and started walking with Him, all these negative words got easier to deal with. Every moment I sit with my Star Team, I am sitting in Comfort and Love. In these Sessions of Comfort and Love, Jesus is always telling me that I do not have to fear these 'un' words or even have to deal with them alone. That is why He took the cross for me (and you too). I am never alone to deal in my shame. Jesus overcame the shame and replaced it with Compassion, Joy, Hope, Peace, and of course Love. Without the Love of God, we are too weak to endure <u>all</u> that this world offers. Following Jesus is the best decision that I (we) can ever make. Take it from me, when I am not in focus on Jesus, all things seem out of place. As soon as I focus back on my Lord, the fog lifts and the sun (Son) shines ever so brightly.

When discouragement comes knocking on your door, imagine that it is like driving through a tunnel: only temporary—a short period in darkness. Holding on to Jesus's Hand makes that discouragement and any other negative thoughts and failures fade away. Coming out of the tunnel, you are able to let go of all those negative thoughts and move forward with Joy (Jesus).

In Word of God (the Bible), I found eight verses (there are many more) that helps me get through this world of darkness and fear. The last one is Psalm 46 that God had planted in my heart to memorize for all the days that I walk through the tunnel of discouragement (many of my 'gray' days are brightened by this Psalm).

"Command those who are rich in this present world not to be arrogant nor to put their hope in wealth, which is so uncertain, but to put their hope in God, who richly provides us with everything for our enjoyment. Commend them to do good, to be rich in good deeds, and to be generous and willing to share. In this way they will lay up treasure for themselves as a firm foundation for the coming age, so that they may take hold of the life that is truly life". (1 Timothy 6:17-19).

"For this reason, I remind you to fan into flame the gift of God, which is in you through the laying on of my hands. For the Spirit of God does not make us timid, but gives us power, love and self-discipline". (2 Timothy 1:6-7).

"And hope does not put us to shame, because God's love has been poured out into our hearts through the Holy Spirit, who has been given to us". (Romans 5:5).

"Love never fails. However, where there are prophecies, they will cease; where there are tongues, they will be stilled; where there is knowledge, it will pass away. For we now in part and we prophesy in part, but when completeness comes, what is in part disappears. When I was a child, I talked like a child; I thought like a child, I reasoned like a child. When I became a man, I put the ways of childhood behind me. For now, we see only a reflection as in a mirror; then we shall see face-to-face. Now I know in part; then I shall know fully, even as I am fully known". (1 Corinthians 13:8-13).

"I am the gate; whoever enters through Me will be saved. They will come in and go out, and find pasture. The thief comes only to steal and kill and destroy; I have come that they may have life, and have it to the full"'. (John 10:9-11).

"Do not let your hearts be troubled. You believe in God; believe also in Me. My Father's House has many rooms; if that were not so, would I have told you that I am going there to prepare a place for you? In addition, if I go and prepare a place for you, I will come back and take you to be with Me so that you also may be where I am. You know the way to the place where I am going"' (John 14:1-4).

"Therefore, get rid of all bitterness, rage and anger, brawling and slander, along with every form of malice. Be kind and compassionate to one another, forgiving each other, just as in Christ God forgave you". (Ephesians 4:31-32).

"God is our refuge and strength, an ever-present help in trouble. Therefore, we will not fear, though the earth gives way and the mountains fall into the heart

of the sea, though its waters roar and foam and the mountains quake with their surging. There is a river whose streams make glad the city of God, the Holy Place where the Most High dwells. God is within her, she will not fall; God will help her at break of day. Nations are in uproar, kingdoms fall; He lifts His voice, the earth melts. The Lord Almighty is with us; the God of Jacob is our fortress. Come and see what the Lord has done, the desolations He has brought on the earth. He makes wars cease to the ends of the earth. He breaks the bow and shatters the spear; He burns the shields with fire. God says, **'Be still and know I am God; I will be exalted among the nations, I will be exalted in the earth'***. The Lord Almighty is with us; the God of Jacob is our fortress". (Psalm 46:1-11).*

The victory over discouragement is to find the source of it and speak God's Truth over it—to dissolve it away. The moment we lift our heads and say, "Father", He steps in and pulls us out of the mud of discouragement. So when discouragement comes creeping into your life, open your Bible to Psalm 42. Read it; meditate on it, and let it teach you how to deal with discouragement, fear, and disappointment.

"As the deer pants for streams of water, so my soul pants for you, my God.

My soul thirsts for God, for the living God. When can I go and meet with God?

My tears have been my food day and night, while people say to me all day long, 'Where is your God?'

These things I remember as I pour out my soul: how I used to go to the house of God under the protection of the Mighty One with shouts of joy and praise among the festive throng.

'Why, my soul, are you downcast'? Why so disturbed within me? Put your hope in God, for I will praise Him, my Savior and my God.

My soul is downcast within me; therefore, I will remember you from the land of the Jordan, the heights of Herman—from Mount Mizar.

Deep calls to deep in the roar of your waterfalls, all your waves and breakers have swept over me.

By day the Lord directs His love, at night His song is with me—a prayer to the God of my life,

I say to God my Rock, 'Why have you forgotten me? Why must I go about mourning, oppressed by the enemy'?

My bones suffer mortal agony as my foes taunt me, saying to me all day long, 'Where is your God'?

Why, my soul, are you downcast? Why so disturbed within me?

Put your hope in God, for I will yet praise Him, my Savior and my God". (Psalm 42:1-11).

As I was writing this Psalm, God showed me His Glory and His smile that just made my heart say, 'Awesome!' and 'Thank You!' Right now, I am feeling so wonderful that my God is pleased with me and refreshing me every moment that I seek to love and know Him. The smile that I just got from Him is the best gift I could have ever received. I will carry this smile wherever I go and forever in my heart. It is the "I love you" from my God, my Father and my rock.

"Walk worthy of the Lord, fully pleasing Him, being fruitful in every good work and increasing in the knowledge of God". (Colossians 1:10).

When I start slipping away from my focus on Jesus, I seem to get a nudge to tell me I am going the wrong way and not seeking His Advice, to increase in His Knowledge of how to live and how to please Him (and only Him), leaving <u>all</u> worldly things and thoughts in the dust. God is the One who is in control of my life, and it is His Son Jesus that walks me through this journey that leads to His Kingdom. These Scripture verses will remind you of the One that is in control:

"Many are the plans in a person's heart, but it is the Lord's Purpose that prevails". (Proverb 19:21).

"And my God will meet all your needs according to the riches of His Glory in Christ Jesus", (Philippians 4:19).

"The fear of the Lord leads to life; then one rests content, untouched by trouble". (Proverb 19:23).

"And we know that in all things God works for the good of those who love

Him, who have been called according to His Purpose". (Romans 8:28).

"'For I know the plans I have for you', *declares the Lord,* **'plans to prosper you and not harm you; plans to give you hope and a future. Then you will call on me, and come and pray to me, and I will listen to you. You will seek me and find me when you seek me with all your heart'".** *(Jeremiah 29:11-13).*

"'Have I not commanded you? Be strong and courageous. Do not be afraid; do not be discouraged, for the Lord you God will be with you wherever you go'" *(Joshua 1:9).*

"In their hearts, humans plan their course, but the Lord establishes their steps". (Proverb 16:9).

"The Lord is my shepherd, I lack nothing. He makes me lie down in green pastures, He leads me beside quiet waters, and He refreshes my soul. He guides me along the right paths for His name's sake. Even though I walk through the darkest valley, I will fear no evil, for You are with me;

Your rod and your staff, they comfort me". (Psalm 23:1-4).

"The Lord is my light and my salvation—whom shall I fear? The Lord is the stronghold of my life—of whom shall I be afraid?". (Psalm 27:1).

"God is our refuge and strength, an ever-present help in trouble". (Psalm 46:1).

"He will cover you with His feathers, and under His wings you will find refuge; His Faithfulness will be your shield and rampart". (Psalm 91:4).

These Scriptures are the ones I refer to when the people of this world keep doubting the works of God. Doubting draws us away from God. God promises us that He will never leave or forsake us. The proof is in His Son Jesus. God sacrificed His Son so we can have a relationship with Him. Therefore, when we doubt any work of His Hands, we doubt His existence and His Love for us. When we seek God first, and then at the right time, He will reveal the answers to our prayers and questions. God's Timing and Perspective are what matters. God always will have time for us; if we could spare time for Him. When He sees that we are faithful to Him and living out His Word and Commands, He will shower us with His Blessings.

One day, I came across this quote that puts all this in perspective:

"A tree is known by its fruit; a man by his deeds; a good deed is never lost; he who sows courtesy reaps friendship; and he who plants kindness gathers love". (Author is unknown).

God Desires that you always look through His Perspective, and to do this is to continually read His Word and always seek deeper to know Him better. As I read God's Word, I receive my hope, faith, and love. Because of my hope in Him, will always strengthen me to keep moving through the dark valleys of the shadows and climb up the mountain to the Glory of my Heavenly Father.

Having Hope that Lasts:

I always wondered what it meant when people said, 'Keep hope alive'. Therefore, I started to research it. The first place I went to was my Bible—where I found all the answers to my questions. Let me tell you the meaning of hope.

Hope is to want something to happen or be true and believe that it could happen. To me hope is to a person as water is to a fish. Hope is essential to our survival on this earth. My hope is my Star Team. When you have no Hope (the Star Team), you fall into depression and despair (not a good place to be). Then all you know is that depression and despair; which by the way are weapons of Satan. Satan can be manipulative in his ways to change our minds to live an unrighteous life—instead of living the Righteous Life that is in the Star Team; and who is the One who teaches us how to live that Righteous Life.

Hope comes from trusting the Star Team who lifts us up out of our hurt and helps us live positively. This is living a life that Jesus lives. So where are you looking for hope if you are not looking at Jesus? Could it be the things of this world (cars, jobs, fame in television and movies)? The things of this world will not last, and you will not be able to take them into Heaven, not to mention have a relationship with God. The things of this world draws us away from God, blocking us from walking the path of righteousness.

Hope is in Jesus. There is no other way to the Father but through His Son. To do this is to seek more of God's Word and thrive to live His Word out. And God's Word says: *"Humble yourselves, therefore, under God's Mighty Hand, that He may lift you up in due time. Cast all anxiety on Him because He cares for you". (1 Peter 5:6-7).*

Here is more of what the Bible says about hope. Read these verses and meditate on them, making them your way of life to live. When you feel depression and despair approaching, God's Word is the best comfort that can push back the weapons of Satan. Do not let Satan have the upper hand in your life. Let it be Jesus who walks every step of the way with you.

"May your unfailing love be with us, Lord, even as we put our hope in you". (Psalm 33:22).

"Many are saying of me, 'God will not deliver him.' However, you, Lord, are a shield around me, my glory, the One who lifts my head high. I call out to the Lord, and He answers me from His holy mountain. I lie down and sleep; I wake again, because the Lord sustains me. I will not fear though tens of thousands assail me on every side". (Psalm 3:2-6).

"Therefore, my heart is glad and my tongue rejoices; my body also will be secure, because you will not abandon me to the realm of the dead, nor will you let your faithful one see decay. You make known to me the path of life; you will fill me with joy in your presence, with eternal pleasures at your right hand". (Psalm 16:9-11).

"Lord, I wait for you; you will answer, Lord my God". (Psalm 38:15).

"Why, my soul, are you downcast? Why so disturbed within me? Put your hope in God, for I will yet praise Him, my Savior and my God". (Psalm 42:11).

"Hope deferred makes the heart sick, but a longing fulfilled is a tree of life". (Proverb 13:12).

"Even youths grow tired and weary, and young men stumble and fall; but those who hope in the Lord will renew their strength; they soar on wings like eagles; they will run and not grow weary, they will walk and not be faint". (Isaiah 40:30-31).

"Blessed is the one who trusts in the Lord, whose confidence is in Him".

(Jeremiah 17:7).

"For I know the plans I have for you,' declares the Lord, 'plans to prosper you and not harm you, plans to give you hope and a future'". *(Jeremiah 29:11).*

"The Lord is good to those whose hope is in Him, to the one who seeks Him; it is good to wait quietly for the salvation of the Lord". (Lamentations 3:25-26).

"Let us hold unswervingly to the hope we profess, for He who promised is faithful". (Hebrews 10:23).

"For by grace you have been saved through faith—and this is not from yourselves, it is the gift of God". (Ephesians 2:8).

"The Lord delights in those who fear Him, who put their hope in His unfailing love" (Psalm 147:11).

"Do not fret because of evildoers or be envious of the wicked, for the evildoer has no future hope, and the lamp of the wicked will be snuffed out". (Proverb 24:19-20).

A Prayer to the Star Team:

Dear Star Team.

I will proclaim always on God's Word all the days and nights that I am on this earth, waiting for my God to take me into His Loving arms and tell me: 'Well done, my faithful child'. There is nowhere I would rather be than in the arms of my loving Star Team. All I do is for His glory, honor, and praise. I will stand in awe of my God, my rock, and my refuge. I love you, Star Team!

I want to thank you for being my Hope, my Love, and Friend; when I can't find no one on this earth to run to. You are the Anchor of my life. Thank you for guiding me safely through the struggles (trials) of this journey. I commit to You that I will tell all about You. I love living out Your Word, so that everyone will see that You are the only Hope in my life.

In Your Glorious Name I pray. Amen.

Preparing Myself to Live Out God's Call for Me (and ALL of His Peoples).

----

*I*t was these three steps that prepared me to understand the Call that God had for me. I was able to step out of the darkness and into the Light. By the way, I found these steps from prayer and reading my Bible. I am very diligent in my devotion to my Star Team.

The first step I took was to open my ears to the Voice of God; and this is what He told me:

*"**My sheep hear My Voice, and I know them, and they will follow Me**". (John 10:27).*

*"**Call to Me and I will answer you, and will tell you great and hidden things that you have not known**". (Jeremiah 33:3). "**I have much more to say to you, more than you can now bear. But when He, the Spirit of Truth, comes, He will guide you into all the Truth. He will not speak on His own; He will speak only what He hears, and He will tell you what is yet to come. He will glorify Me because it is from Me that He will receive what He will make known to you. All that belongs to the Father is Mine. That is why I said the Spirit will receive from Me what He will make known to you**". (John 16:12-15).*

*"And your ears shall hear a word behind you, saying; '**This is the way; walk in it**'. When you turn to the right or when you turn to the left". (Isaiah 30:21).*

For: *"Faith comes from hearing, and hearing through the Word of Christ". (Romans 10:17).*

This first step then lead me to the second step where I took rest in the Truth of who I am; in the arms of the One and only True God (the Star Team):

"Everyone who believes that Jesus Christ is the Christ is born of God, and everyone who loves the Father loves His Child as well. This is how we know that

we love the children of God: by loving God and carrying out His Commands. In fact, this is love for God: to keep His Commands. And His Commands are not burdensome, for everyone born of God overcomes the world. This is the Victory that has overcome the world, even our Faith. Who is it that overcomes the world? Only the one who Believes that Jesus is the Son of God. This is the One who came by water and blood. And it is the Spirit who the Truth. For there are Three that testify: the Spirit, the Water and the Blood; and the Three are in agreement. We accept human testimony, but God's Testimony is Greater because it is the Testimony of the Father, which He has given about His Son. Whoever believes in the Son of God accepts this Testimony. Whoever does not believe the Father has made Him out to be a liar, because they have not believed the Testimony the Father has given about His Son. And this is the Testimony: the Father has given Eternal Life, and this Life is in His Son. Whoever has the Son has Life; whoever does not have the Son of God does not have Life". (1 John 5:1-12).

"I write these things to you who believe in the Name of the Son of God so that you may know that you have Eternal Life. This is the confidence we have in approaching God: that if we ask anything according to His Will; He hears us. And if we know that He hears us – whatever we ask – we know that we have what we asked of Him. If you see any brother or sister commit a sin that does not lead to death, you should pray and God will give them Life. I refer to those whose sin does not lead to death. There is a sin that leads to death. I am not saying that you should pray about that. All wrongdoing is sin, and there is sin that does not lead to death. We know that anyone born of God does not continue to sin; the One who was born of God keeps them safe, and the evil one cannot harm them. We know that we are children of God, and that the whole world is under the control of the evil one. We know also that the Son of God has come and has given us Understanding, so that we may know Him who is True. and we are in Him who is True by being in His Son Jesus Christ. He is the True God and Eternal Life. Dear brothers and sisters, keep yourselves from idols". (1 John 5:13-21).

The third step I took is to delight delight myself in God's Love – so I am able to stand and able to stay focused and ready at all times to serve the Star Team:

"The Lord your God is with you, the Mighty Warrior who saves. He will take great delight in you; in His love He will no longer rebuke you, but will rejoice over you with singing". (Zephaniah 3:17).

The way to Peace, is to rise above your problems, your pains, and the ever-changing world that we live in. Jesus is above all things, and He guarantees that you will always have access to His never-ending Presence so that you can rise above the waves of your situation. All that we need to do is speak out: 'Jesus, help me'; and He will be right there to assist you in any way; bringing you closer to His Father. Therefore, be not discouraged; be not dismayed; for it is the strength of the Lord that makes us strong for the battle that awaits us (and there will always be a battle to fight). For it Satan (who prowls this earth) will always try to turn us away from living the Peaceful Life that God provides for us. Jesus knows that we are weak, so He promises us to walk every step with us on this journey that we are walking for His Father.

When I get discouraged, and things seem to be out of focus (blurry), and I seem to lose sight of Jesus, I remember what happened when Peter lost his focus, because of the storm and the waves were getting bigger and distracting him. This is what Jesus did: *"Immediately Jesus reached out His hand and caught him – **'You of little faith'**, He said, **'why did you doubt?'"**. (Matthew 14:31).*

The moment we doubt, is the moment of distraction; and is the moment we start sinking like quicksand into the ways of evil. By the way quicksand is impossible to get out of, however, *"with God nothing is impossible". (Matthew 19:26).* Therefore, I will always ask God to: *"Show me Your ways, Lord, teach me Your Paths". (Psalm 25:4).* So I don't sink into the quicksand of this angry and cold world.

*To those who do not know God: you think that God has nothing that would appeal to your cold and angry hearts. Why do you think that? Because you are too busy focused on the 'bling' you see dangling in front of you (by no other then Satan himself) that are the things of this world that fills their desires that do not even last. Therefore,

*<u>To those who know God</u>: except the love that God gives to His children who thirst and seek Him for who He really is—the constant companion who is always by your side.

So I say to all of you out there, open the door to the Star Team and be amazed by what He does in your life. I did, and I am never going to let Him go. Oh yeah, I know there will still be troubles lurking around the corners of this world, with false desires that will never last. Satan uses those false desires to turn me away from the ultimate desire—God's Love. As the Bible says: *"I can do all things through Him who strengthens me". (Philippians 4:13).* This Scripture verse means that when Satan starts dangling his desires in front of you, you have the strength to walk away from him, just as Jesus did to him.

Even if the path looks smooth and easy—that is when you need Jesus the most. Because Satan hides himself among those smooth and easy sidelines, just waiting for a weak moment to lure you away from living a wonderful and peaceful life with Star Team. You should never neglect the Glorious Source of strength that Star Team possesses. He is always with us. Without the Star Team, we have no way to the Peace of God. Trusting and thanking Jesus will always bring His awesome Peace He so freely brings into your life.

<u>Here are some Scriptures to prepare yourselves to live out the Calling that God has for you</u>:

"'Do not let your hearts be troubled. You believe in God; believe in Me'". (John 14:1).

"'I am the way and the truth and the life. No one comes to the Father except through me'".

(John 14:6).

"'If you love Me, keep my commands. In addition, I will ask the Father, and He will give you another Advocate to help you and be with you forever—the Spirit of Truth. The world cannot accept Him, because it neither sees Him nor knows Him. However, you know Him for He

lives with you and will be in you. I will not leave you as orphans; I will come to you'". (John 14:15-18).

"But very truly I tell you, it is for your good that I am going away. Unless I go away, the Advocate will not come to you; but if I go, I will send Him to you. When He comes, He will prove the world to be in the wrong about sin and righteousness and judgment: about sin, because people do not believe in Me; about righteousness, because I am going to the Father, where you can see Me no longer; and about judgment, because the prince of this world now stands condemned'". (John 16:7-11).

"Look at me and answer, Lord my God. Give Light to my eyes, or I will sleep in death, and my enemy will say, 'I have overcome him,' and my foes will rejoice when I fall. However, I trust in Your Unfailing Love; my heart rejoices in Your Salvation. I will sing the Lord's Praise, for He has been Good to me". (Psalm 13:3-6).

"Always giving thanks to God the Father for everything, in the Name of our Lord Jesus Christ. Submit to one another out of Reverence for Christ". (Ephesians 5:20-21).

This next two Scripture verses give me a Blessed Assurance, because I have been holding on to these two promises:

"And God says: 'Be still and know I am God. I will be exalted among the nations. I will be exalted among the earth'". (Psalm 46:10).

"My flesh and my heart may fail, but God is the strength of my heart and my portion forever". (Psalm 73:26).

When I say these two verses, I attain a calmness that only God can provide. Bringing strength to my heart, mind, body, and soul to conquer whatever lays ahead of me in my daily journey on this earth. Living a right life and living it with Jesus will always bring the Peace that works Calmness and Assurance (which is in God's Presence) and His Power that saves and keeps you safe from the ways of Satan who is always trying to knock you off the Path of Righteousness.

Let us rest in God's Presence, live in God's Presence, and receive the Calm and Assurance that frees us from the chaos of this world.

Remember that joy is not dependent on your circumstances. True joy is living life in God's Presence, always. Therefore, instead of worrying about your daily difficulties, you need to concentrate on staying in communication with God (through His Son Jesus), trusting in Him that He will help you solve your difficulties in His Time, not your time. Jesus is the Master in problem solving. There is nothing too hard for Jesus to solve. My goal is to live close to Jesus; letting His Father's Glory unfold right in front of me.

Here now is Scriptures revealing the Glory of the Star Team:

"Splendor and majesty are before Him; Strength and Joy are in His Dwelling Place". (1 Chronicles 16:27).

"I will rejoice in the Lord, I will be joyful in God my Savior. The Sovereign Lord is my strength; He makes my feet like the feet of a deer, He enables me to tread on the heights". (Habakkuk 3:18-19).

"Bless the Lord, O my soul! O Lord my God, You are very Great; You are clothed with Splendor and Majesty. The Lord wraps Himself in Light as with a garment; He stretches out the Heavens like a tent and lays the beams of His upper chambers on their waters. He makes the clouds His chariot and rides on the wings of the wind. He makes winds His messengers, flames of fire His servants. He set the earth on its foundations; it can never be moved". (Psalm 104:1-5).

*"After six days Jesus took with Him Peter, James and John the brother of James, and led them up a high mountain by themselves. There, He was transfigured before them. His face shone like the sun, and His clothes became as white as the light. Just then, there appeared before them Moses and Elijah, talking with Jesus. Peter said to Jesus, 'Lord, it is good for us to be here. If you wish, I will put up three shelters—one for you, one for Moses and one for Elijah.' While he was still speaking, a bright cloud covered them, and a voice from the cloud said, **'This is My Son, whom I love; with Him I am well pleased. Listen to Him!'**". (Matthew 17:1-5).*

"The Word became flesh and made His dwelling among us. We have seen His glory, the glory of the one and only Son, who came from the Father, full of grace and truth". (John 1:14).

"The god of this age has blinded the minds of unbelievers, so that they cannot see the Light of the Gospel that displays the Glory of Christ, who is the Image of God. For what we preach is not ourselves as your servants for Jesus' sake. For God, who said, *'Let Light shine out of darkness, make His Light shine in our hearts to give us the Light of the Knowledge of God's Glory displayed in the Face of Christ'*". (2 Corinthians 4:4-6).

"For our light and momentary troubles are achieving for us an Eternal Glory that far outweighs them all. So we fix our eyes not on what is seen, but on what is unseen, since what is seen is temporary, but what is unseen is Eternal". (2 Corinthians 4:17-18).

"For this reason, since the day we heard about you, we have not stopped praying for you. We continually ask God to fill you with the Knowledge of His Will, through all the Wisdom and Understanding that the Spirit gives. So that you may live a life worthy of the Lord, and please

Him in every way. Bearing fruit in every good work; growing in the Knowledge of God, and being strengthened with all power according to His glorious might, so that you may have great endurance and patience, and giving joyful thanks to the Father, who has qualified you to share in the inheritance of His holy people in the kingdom of light". (Colossians 1:9-12).

"You will be a crown of splendor in the Lord's hand, a royal tiara in the hand of your God". (Isaiah 62:3).

"For Great is Your Love, higher than the Heavens; Your Faithfulness reaches to the skies. Be exalted, O God, above the heavens; let Your glory be over all the earth". (Psalm 108:4-5).

"Lord, our Lord, how majestic is Your name in all the earth! You have set Your glory in the heavens". (Psalm 8:1).

"To Him be glory in the church and in Christ Jesus throughout all generations, forever and ever!" (Ephesians 3:21).

There are many times here on this earth when it may seem that the Light of God gets dim a bit, because we tend to focus on our difficulties, our sorrows, and our anger. Yet even in our darkest struggles of this world, we can be sure that God is with us, helping us win the battle.

As you and I walk in God's Light, we are shining His Light through our hearts into this world of darkness. So let us remain Faithful to God and not let Satan slip in any of his poison arrows into our heart, to turn us away from following Jesus. With God's Grace, we can rise above the darkness of this world and live a life that honors Jesus for all He has done for us and will continue to do for us, right into Eternity with His Heavenly Father.

<u>Here are some Scriptures that you can reflect on when you are need the of the Comfort of God</u>:

"Blessed is the one who does not walk in step with the wicked or stand in the way that sinners take or sit in the company of mockers, but whose delight is in the Law of the Lord, and who meditates on His Law day and night. That person is like a tree planted by streams of water, which yields its fruit in season and whose leaf does not wither – whatever they do prospers. Not so the wicked! They are like chaff that the wind blows away. Therefore the wicked will not stand in the judgment, nor sinners in the assembly of the righteous. For the Lord watches over the way of the righteous, but the way of the wicked leads to destruction". (Psalm 1:1-6)

"Grace, Mercy, and Peace, which come from God the Father and from Jesus Christ—the Son of the Father, will continue to be with us who live in Truth and Love". (2 John 1:3).

"For He sets on high those who are lowly, and those who mourn are lifted to safety". (Job 5:11).

"*Do not fear, for I am with you; do not be dismayed, for I am your God. I will strengthen you, I will help you, yes, I will uphold you with My Righteous right hand*". (Isaiah 41:10).

"For those who hope in the Lord, will renew their strength, they will fly on wings like eagles, they will run and not grow weary, they will walk and not faint". (Isaiah 40:31).

"The Lord is my Light and my Salvation – whom shall I fear?

The Lord is the Stronghold of my life – of whom shall I be afraid?

When the wicked advance against me to devour me, it is my enemies and my foes who will stumble and fall. Though an army besiege me my heart will not fear; though war breaks out against me, even then I will be confident. One thing I ask from the Lord, this only do I seek: that I may dwell in the House of the Lord all the days of my life, to gaze on the beauty of the Lord and to seek Him in His Temple. For in the day of trouble He will keep me safe in His Dwelling; He will hide me in the Shelter of His sacred tent and set me high upon a Rock. Then my head will be exalted above the enemies who surround me; at His Sacred tent I will sacrifice with shouts of joy; I will sing and make music to the Lord. Hear my voice when I call, Lord; be merciful to me and answer me. My heart says of You, 'Seek His Face'! Your Face, Lord, I will seek. Do not hide Your Face from me, do not turn Your servant away in anger; You have been my Helper. Do not reject me or forsake me, God my Savior. Though my father and mother forsake me, the Lord will receive me. Teach me Your Way, Lord; lead me in a straight path because of my oppressors. Do not turn me over to the desire of my foes, for false witnesses rise up against me, spouting malicious accusations. I remain confident of this: I will see the Goodness of the Lord in the land of the living. [Therefore, brothers and sisters] *Wait for the Lord; be strong and take heart and wait for the Lord". (Psalm 27:1-14).*

"We know that all things work together for good to those who love God, to those who are called according to His purpose". (Romans 8:28).

"Blessed be God, the Father of our Lord Jesus Christ, the Father of mercies, and the God of all comfort, who comforts us in all our tribulation, that we may be able to comfort those who are in any trouble by the comfort with which we ourselves are comforted by God". (2 Corinthians 1:3-4).

"Do not be anxious about anything, but in everything, by prayer and petition, with thanksgiving, present your requests to God. and the Peace of God, which transcends all understanding, will guard your hearts and your minds in Christ Jesus. Finally, brothers and sisters, whatever is True, whatever is Noble, whatever is Right, whatever is Pure, whatever is Lovely, whatever is Admirable - if anything is Excellent or Praiseworthy - think about such things". (Philippians 4:6-8).

"Let your lives be without love of money, and be content with the things you have. For He has said, **'I will never leave you, nor forsake you'***". (Hebrews*

13:5).

I get out of these Scriptures of Comfort: Strength, Courage, Confidence, and most of all Love; all from the only One that will be with me all this time of my journey-walk.

This is exactly what our Heavenly Father gives us when we surrender it all to Him. But to many people this surrendering sounds impossible, however, when you have God, nothing is impossible (see Matthew 26:19). I was one of those people, holding on to those worldly things that I thought would keep me happy and free. But I was not happy and free. So, I took it to the One who can tell me why I wasn't feeling happy and free. And before I could ask Him what I was holding on to He started revealing what I was still holding on to, so I then stopped talking and started listening to His every word He told me. Since that day, I have been listening to Him and been living in that Freedom that He so gives to His children who love, listen and obey Him.

This is what I did to totally surrender all to God. and keep me on the journey-walk to His Freedom that keeps me happy. First of all, you need to be Star Team-centered; with only Him in your heart and in your mind. With my heart and mind on the Star Team I <u>started</u> saying: 'No matter what I will <u>listen</u> to Your every word Lord'. Then I <u>seeked</u> out all that is in Heaven; not on earthly things. And then I <u>stopped</u> doubting and emerged myself in the Word of God; to <u>overcome</u> the things that blocked my way from pleasing God.

Therefore, pick up your Bible, dust it off (if need be), and seek for the answers that leads to True Freedom (True Happiness). I started with these verses from Ephesians to move me in the right direction:

"Praise be to the God and Father of our Lord Jesus Christ, who has Blessed us in the Heavenly Realms with every Spiritual Blessing in Christ. For He chose us in Him before the Creation of the world to be Holy and Blameless in His Sight. In love He predestined us to be adopted as His sons and daughters, through Jesus Christ, in accordance with His Pleasure and Will – to the Praise of His Glorious Grace, which He has Freely given us in the One He Loves. In Him

we have Redemption through His Blood, the Forgiveness of sins, in accordance with the Riches of God's Grace that He lavished on us with all Wisdom and Understanding. And He made known to us the mystery of His will according to His Good Pleasure, which He purposed in Christ, to be put into effect when the times will have reached their fulfillment – to bring all things in Heaven and on earth together under one head, even Christ. In Him we were also chosen, having been predestined according to the plan of Him who works out everything in conformity with the purpose of His Will, in order that we, who were the first to hope in Christ, might be for the Praise of His Glory". (Ephesians 1:3-12).

It Is All About Forgiveness

What is forgiveness? Forgiveness is a process to cease to feel resentment against an offender. The Bible (God's Word) says about forgiveness that we should, *"Be kind and compassionate to one another, forgiving each other, just as in Christ God forgave you". (Ephesians 4:32).*

"Be completely humble and gentle; be patient, bearing with one another in love. Make every effort to keep the unity of the Spirit through the bond of peace". (Ephesians 4:2-3).

When you ask God for forgiveness, you must do two things: confession of your sin and repentance of that sin, never going there again. In doing these two things, it brings you the compassion and love from our Heavenly Father that we so need in this dark, cold, and corruption of this world that we live in. Forgiveness brings healing to one's soul, enabling you to forgive others as God forgave you. Most all, forgiveness heals you of all the aches you have. Once I learned how to forgive myself, I was free from the shame that my sin brought. It had taken me a while to comprehend this healing/ forgiving process. Until I researched it out in my Bible (God's Word) that what Jesus went through for me, on the cross, was the ransom for many others and me. This is what the Bible says:

"For even the Son of Man did not come to be served, but to serve and to give His life as a ransom for many". (Mark 10:45).

"He [Jesus] was delivered over to death for our sins and was raised to life for our justification". (Romans 4:25).

"No man can redeem the life of another or give to God a ransom for them—the ransom for a life is costly, no payment is ever enough—so that they should live on forever and not see decay". (Psalm 49:7-9).

"This poor man called, and the Lord heard him; He saved him out of all his troubles. The angel of the Lord encamps around those who fear Him, and He delivers them. Taste and see that the Lord is good; blessed is the one who takes refuge in Him. Fear the Lord, you His holy people, for those who fear Him lack nothing. The lions may grow weak and hungry, but those who seek the Lord lack no good thing". (Psalm 34:6-10).

So with this being said, let us fulfill these next Scriptures:

"Get rid of all bitterness, rage and anger, brawling and slander, along with every form of malice. Be kind and compassionate to one another, forgiving each other, just as Christ God forgave you". (Ephesians 4:31-32).

"Make sure that nobody pays back wrong for wrong, but always try to be kind to each other and to everyone else. Be joyful always; pray continually; give thanks in all circumstances—for this is God's Will for you in Christ Jesus". (1 Thessalonians 5:15-18).

"If we confess our sins, He is faithful and just and will forgive us our sins and purify us from all unrighteousness". (1 John 1:9).

"Blessed is the one whose transgressions are forgiven, whose sins are covered. Blessed is the one whose sin the Lord does not count against them and in whose spirit is no deceit. When I kept silent, my bones wasted away through my groaning all day long. For day and night your hand heavy on me, my strength was sapped as in the heat of summer. Then I acknowledged my sin to You and did not cover up my iniquity. I said, 'I will confess my transgressions to the Lord.' And You forgave the guilt of my sin. Therefore, let all the faithful pray to You while You may be found; surely the rising of the mighty waters will not reach them". (Psalm 32:1-6).

Prayer:

"Hear, O Lord, and answer me, for I am poor and needy. Guard my life, for I am devoted to you. You are my God; save Your servant who trusts in You. Have mercy on me, O Lord, for I call to You day long. Bring joy to Your servant, for to You, O Lord, I lift up my soul". (Psalm 86:1-6).

"For You are Great and do marvelous deeds; You alone are God. Teach me your way, Lord, that I may rely on Your Faithfulness; give me an undivided heart, that I may fear Your Name. I will praise you, Lord my God, with all my heart; I will glorify Your Name forever. For Great is Your Love toward me; You have delivered me from the depths, from the realm of the dead". (Psalm 86:10-13).

The Lord tells us:

*"**For if you forgive men when they sin against you, your Heavenly Father will also forgive you. But if you do not forgive men their sins, your Father will not forgive your sins'".** (Matthew 6:14-15). "**So, watch yourselves. If your brother or sister sins against you, rebuke them; and if they repent, forgive them'".** (Luke 17:3).*

*"Peter came to Jesus and asked; 'Lord, how many times shall I forgive my brother when he sins against me? Up to seven times?' Jesus answered; **'I tell you not seven times, but seventy-seven times seven'".** (Matthew 18:21-22).*

"Consequently, just as the result of one trespass resulted in condemnation for all people, so also one righteous act resulted in justification and life for all people". (Romans 5:18).

No matter how sinful and disobedient we have become, we can turn it all around when we go to God (in prayer) and confess and repent (with a humble heart) of our sin of disobedience, and we then will receive God's Forgiveness, Comfort, and Love. Our Heavenly Father is always ready to forgive us, for He is Merciful and Just and will always forgive, redeem, satisfy, cleanse, even though our debt is so great. Our Lord Jesus paid our debt when His Father sent Him to the cross to bring us back to Him.

I know that Jesus will always be walking with me wherever I go. He knows just when to lay His comforting hand upon me. I tell you the truth that when you go to the Father in prayer and confess your sin and repent of your sin, He will forgive you, bless you, protect you, and walk with you all the days of your life. Because God loves to have His children come to Him and desire to know His ways and live His righteous life. This is all because we believe in His Son Jesus and welcome Him into our lives. So join with me, humble your hearts, confess, repent of your sin, and walk in the way of our Lord Jesus Christ.

Here is what the Bible says about God and how He forgives, redeems, satisfies, cleanses and how He knows all the plans for us:

"Who forgives all your sins and heals all your diseases. Who redeems your life from the pit and crowns you with love and compassion. Who satisfies your desires with good things so that your youth is renewed like the eagles". (Psalm 103:3-5).

"I will cleanse them from all sin they have committed against Me and will forgive all their sins of rebellion against Me"'. (Jeremiah 33:8).

"'For I know the plans I have for you', declares the Lord, 'plans to prosper you and not harm you, plans to give you hope and a future'". *(Jeremiah 29:11).*

And here are some Scriptures to tell of God's Forgiveness:

"If we confess our sins, He is faithful and just and will forgive us our sins and purify us from all unrighteousness. If we claim we have not sinned, we make Him out to be a liar and His word is not in us". (1 John 1:9-10).

"In Him we have redemption through His blood, the forgiveness of sins, in accordance with the riches of God's grace that He lavished on us. With all wisdom and understanding, He made known to us the mystery of His will according to His good pleasure, which He proposed in Christ, to be put into effect when the times reach their fulfillment—to bring unity to all things in heaven and on earth under Christ". (Ephesians 1:7-10).

"Then He opened their minds so they could understand the Scriptures. He told them, ***'This what is written: The Messiah will suffer and rise from the dead on the third day, and repentance for the forgiveness of sins will be preached in His name to all nations, beginning at Jerusalem. You are witnesses of these things. I am going to send you what my Father has promised; but stay in the city until you have been clothed with power***

from on high'". (Luke 24:45-49).

"And if a wicked person turns away from all the sins they have committed, and keeps all My Decrees and does what is right that person will surely live; they will not die. None of the offenses they have committed will be remembered against them. Because of the righteous things they have done, they will live'". (Ezekiel 18:21-22).

"Praise the Lord, my soul, and forget not all his benefits—who forgives all your sins and heals all your diseases, who redeems your life from the pit and crowns you with love and compassion, who satisfies your desires with good things so that your youth is renewed like the eagles. The Lord works righteousness and justice for all the oppressed". (Psalm 103:2-6). "You, Lord, are forgiving and good, abounding in love to all who call to you. Hear my prayer, Lord; listen to my cry for mercy. When I am in distress, I call to you, because you answer me". (Psalm 86:5-7). "And everyone who calls on the name of the Lord will be saved; for on Mount Zion and in Jerusalem there will be deliverance, as the Lord has said, even among the survivors whom the Lord calls". (Joel 2:32).

Once God calls your name (and you hear Him), your life will not be the same (as mine was). I heard Him calling my name, and He took me into the shelter of His comforting wings. I saw things more clearly and less confusing. That was ten years ago, and I have never looked back. I will always be thankful for Jesus reaching out His hand and pulling out of the dark and slimy pit of confusion and despair. Forgiveness also brings a new perspective, enabling you to see how

God sees things. As the Bible says: *"From Heaven the Lord looks down and sees all mankind; from His dwelling place He watches all who live on earth—He who forms the hearts of all, who considers everything they do". (Psalm 33:13-15).*

Once God sees that you are living a righteous life and you continually love as He loves, He will search your heart and mind, making sure there is nothing in the world that would tempt you from walking off the righteous path that He so wants you to live. Forgiveness and obedience is what need for God's grace to be flowing in your lives:

"If you love Me, you will keep my commandments". (John 14:15).

"If you are willing and obedient, you shall eat the good of the land". (Isaiah

1:19).

"For the gate is narrow and the way is hard that leads to life, and those who find it are few". (Matthew 7:14).

"And we know that for those who love God all things work together for good, for those who are called according to His purpose". (Romans 8:28).

"To obey is better than sacrifice, and to heed is better than the fat of rams". (1 Samuel 15:22b).

"Therefore, since we have these promises, dear friends, let us purify ourselves from everything that contaminates body and spirit, perfecting holiness out of reverence for God" (2 Corinthians 7:1).

Here are a couple quotes that I found that really explains why we should seek out to obey God and forgive ourselves (and others), all for His Glory, Love, and Respect:

'Give to God what is His; your heart'. (Unknown).

'There are countless reasons to obey God, but a primary reason to remember to obey *His Commandments* and live *His Way*—is because *He* said so!' (Unknown).

I will always trust Jesus and I will refuse to worry, for He is my strength and song who is always with me and empowers me to handle every task that comes my way. My Lord Jesus is the Joy of my heart. I will sing praises about Him (and to Him); to keep Him walking alongside me.

As long as I am walking in *His Light*, I am walking in confidence and hope, that is leading me right into the Gates of Heaven, where His Father is waiting, with open arms. So, while you wait on God to answer your prayers, read these Scriptures and begin freeing yourself from the chains of worrying:

"No one has ever seen God. But if we love each other, God lives in us and His love is brought to full expression in us". (1 John 8:12).

"The Lord is my strength and my defense; He has become my salvation. He is my God, and I will praise Him, my father's God, and I will exalt Him. The Lord is a warrior; the Lord is His Name". (Exodus 15:2-3).

"Let the one who boasts boast in the Lord. For it is not the one who commends himself who is approved, but the one whom the Lord commends". (2 Corinthians

10:17-18).

"The earth is the Lord's, and everything in it, the world, and all who live in it; for He founded it on the seas and established it on the waters. Who may ascend the mountain of the Lord? Who may stand in His Holy Place? It is the one who has clean hands and a pure heart; who does not trust in an idol or swears by a false god. They will receive blessing from the Lord and vindication from God their Savior. Such is the generation of those who seek Him; seek Your Face, God of Jacob. Lift up your heads, you gates; be lifted up, you ancient doors that the King of glory may come in". (Psalm 24:1-7).

"My flesh and my heart may fail, but God is the strength of my heart and my portion forever". (Psalm 73:26).

These are the Scriptures that helped me in my daily battle with the negative voices I hear that are telling me that I am not worthy of any blessings that God has for me. However, God tells me that His Love for me will wash away all the nasty words that people say to me. God tells me:

'I am beautiful and smart, and I can do anything as long as I keep listening to Him'.

We need to remember, therefore, that man's words fade away, but God's Love and Words will last forever, drawing us closer to Him. Therefore: *"Draw near to God and He will draw near to you". (James 4:8).* This is all that God requires for us to do. And for me, this gives me confidence to know that there is no neediness (nothing) that I can do but to turn to Him and walk away from what the world offers. For:

I have no need to grumble to Him. I need to seek Him.

I have no need to plead to Him. I need to know Him.

I have no need to give Him gifts. I need to receive from Him.

I have no need to fear or walk in shame. I need to love Him.

Just a simple turn away from the world brings God's comfort and companionship, which in turn brings His Sweetness, Confidence, and Peace that are so missing on this earth. Just reading God's Word can draw us closer to the One who can transform the conditions of this world into Harmony, Love, Joy, and Peace. Most of all, it brings God's Love that surpasses all.

The Tongue – The Good and the Bad of it.

----

*T*he tongue is a weapon that can heal and can wound. The tongue is guilty of flattery, cursing, lying, gossiping, boasting, and harming others. And all this guilt of the tongue is the result of us giving into the enemy's taunting for us to disappoint God.

Sometimes when we do not realize what our tongue is doing, because of this cold, dark world; it makes us speak words that are very hard to erase. However, you need not worry, for when you accept Jesus as your Lord and Savior, He takes those hurtful words and turns them into encouraging, comforting, and loving words, words that melt a cold, hard heart.

The Bible is our manual to train yourself to speak like Jesus speaks. Let me start you off with some of the Scriptures I found that helped me melt away the harsh words of this world:

"A gentle answer turns away wrath, but a harsh word stirs up anger. The tongue of the wise adorns knowledge, but the mouth of the fool gushes folly. The eyes of the Lord are everywhere, keeping watch on the wicked and the good. The soothing tongue is a tree of life, but a perverse tongue crushes the spirit". (Proverbs 15:1-4).

"The discerning heart seeks knowledge, but the mouth of a fool feeds on folly". (Proverb 15:14).

"A hot-tempered person stirs up conflict, but the one who is patient calms a quarrel". (Proverb 15:18).

"Through patience a ruler can be persuaded, and a gentle tongue can break a bone". (Proverb 25:15).

"The mouth of the righteous is a fountain of life, but the mouth of the wicked conceals violence. Hatred stirs up conflict, but love covers over all wrongs. Wisdom is found on the lips of the discerning, but a rod is for the back of one who

has no sense. The wise store up knowledge, but the mouth of a fool invites ruin."
(Proverbs 10:11-14).

"*Evildoers do not understand what is right, but those who seek the Lord understand it fully. Better the poor whose walk is blameless than the rich whose ways are perverse". (Proverbs 28:15-16).*

"*The one whose walk is blameless is kept safe, but the one whose ways are perverse will fall into the pit". (Proverb 28:18).*

"*The greedy stir up conflict, but those who trust in the Lord will prosper. Those who trust in themselves are fools, but those who walk in wisdom are kept safe". (Proverbs 28:25-26).*

"*Pride goes before destruction, a haughty spirit before a fall". (Proverb 16:18).*

"*To humans belong the plans of the heart, but from the Lord comes the proper answer of the tongue. All a person's ways seem pure to them, but motives are weighed by the Lord. Commit to the Lord whatever you do, and He will establish your plans". (Proverb 16:1-3).*

"*Humble yourselves before the Lord, and He will lift you up". (James 4:10).*

"*Be completely humble and gentle; be patient, bearing with one another in love. Make every effort to keep the unity of the Spirit through the bond of peace". (Ephesians 4:2-3).*

"*Get rid of bitterness, rage and anger, brawling and slander, along with every form of malice. Be kind and compassionate to one another, forgiving each other, just as in Christ God forgave you". (Ephesians 4:31-32).*

"*Therefore, confess your sins to each other and pray for each other, so that you may be healed. The prayer of a righteous person is powerful and effective". (James 5:16).*

"*The righteous person is rescued from trouble, and it falls on the wicked instead. With their mouths, the godless destroy their neighbors, but through knowledge, the righteous escape. When the righteous prosper, the city rejoices; when the wicked perish, there are shouts of joy. Through the blessing of the upright, a city is exalted, but the mouth of the wicked destroys it. Whoever derides their neighbor has no sense, but the one who has understanding holds their tongue. Gossip betrays confidence, but a trustworthy person keeps a secret. For lack of guidance a nation falls, but victory is won through many advisers". (Proverbs*

11:8-14).

"A kindhearted woman gains honor, but ruthless men gain only wealth. Those who are kind benefit themselves, but the cruel bring ruin on themselves". (Proverbs 11:16-17).

"Do not judge or you will be judged. For in the same way you judge others, you will be judged, and with the measure you use, it will be measured to you". (Matthew 7:1-2).

"Everyone who calls on the name of the Lord will be saved". (Romans 10:13).

"Therefore, I urge you, brothers and sisters, in view of God's mercy, to offer your bodies as a living sacrifice, holy and pleasing to God—this is your true and proper worship. Do not conform to the pattern of this world, but be transformed by the renewing of your mind. Then you will be able to test and approve what God's will is—His Good, Pleasing and Perfect Will". (Romans 12:1-2).

"For God so loved the world that He gave His one and only Son, that whoever believes in Him shall not perish, but have eternal life. For God did not send His Son in the world to condemn the world, but to save the world through Him. Whoever believes in Him is not condemned, but whoever does not believe stands condemned already, because they have not believed in the name of God' one and only Son. This is the verdict: Light has come into the world, but people loved darkness instead of light, because their deeds were evil. Everyone who does evil hates the Light, and will not come into the Light for fear that their deeds will be exposed. But whoever lives by the Truth comes into the Light, so that it may be seen plainly that what they have done has been done in the sight of God". (John 3:16-21).

"He will wipe every tear from their eyes. There will be no more death, mourning, crying, or pain, for the old order of things has passed away. He who seats on the throne says, 'I am making everything new!'". (Revelation 21:4-5a).

"My tongue will proclaim your righteousness, your praises all day long". (Psalm 35:28).

"The mouths of the righteous utter wisdom, and their tongues speak what is just. The law of their God is in their hearts; their feet do not slip". (Psalm 37:30-31).

When your tongue speaks God's Words (without doubting), those words will calm the strongest storm that you thought would never go away. God spoke this world into existence. So use the words that will bring the most down person to the throne of our Heavenly Father, and they will rise from the ashes of despair and be healed.

The Bible as a sword – *"The Sword of the Spirit, which is the Word of God". (Ephesians 6:17b).*

If you notice, if you take the letter 's' from the sword, you are left with 'word', confirming that the Word of God is the Sword of the Spirit which will heal – when you are wounded; and it will defend – when you are too weak to fight. This proves that the Spirit sees all that is going on in our lives and will take action when Satan is displaying his evil tricks upon us; so he can steal the Word of God from you (that is if you are not totally into God's Word). Here is how the Bible explains how some people are with the Word of God:

"Then Jesus said to them [explaining the parable about the farmer]: The farmer sows the word. Some people are like seeds along the path, where the word is sown. As soon as they hear it, Satan comes and takes away the word that was sown in them. Others are like seed sown on rocky places, hear the word and at once receive it with joy. However, since they have no root, they last only a short time—when trouble or persecution comes—because of the word, they quickly fall away. Still others are like seeds sown among thorns, hear the word—but the worries of this life, the deceitfulness of wealth and the desires for other things come in and choke the word, making it unfruitful. Others are like seeds sown on good soil, hear the word, accept it, and produce a crop—some thirty, some sixty, some a hundred times what was sown". (Mark 4:13-20).

Most of us try to be the seed that falls on good soil. However, the things of this world distract us. That is why you need to keep your eyes fixed on Jesus and do what He does to resist Satan. You cannot do it alone. You will fail every time. Read Ephesians 6:10-18 to get the full understanding of the armor of God and how the Word of God can help you resist all what Satan throws at you daily. Never get tired of reading the Word of God (the Bible); you will be stronger for it.

Knowing and Resisting the Enemy (Satan)

W all know that we have an enemy (Satan) who prowls around this earth just looking for someone to deceive and devour. Satan will deceive you in many ways; he can take something that seems wonderful and drag it and you, right into the ground. As we all know, Satan was the one that deceived humankind (see chapter 3 of Genesis - The Fall), and he has not stopped. Even though Jesus defeated him, it just made him more determined to destroy Jesus's followers. Therefore, we must keep our eyes open, and alert, to know just how Satan is prowling around here on this earth.

Therefore, let me tell you about the tools (weapons) that Satan just might be using to deceive you and me. The Bible says that Satan has many disguises and tricks up his sleeve; and his tricks involve people deceiving their friends and family, turning them away from following Jesus and in turn becoming one of his deceitful workers masquerading as followers of Jesus.

"For such people are false apostles, deceitful workers, masquerading as apostles of Christ. Moreover, it is no wonder—for Satan himself masquerades as an angel of light. It is not surprising, then, if his servants also masquerade as servants of righteousness. Their end will be what their actions deserve". (2 Corinthians 11:13-15).

Temptation is the biggest tool that Satan gets us into his cave of deceit. What is temptation, you ask? Temptation is all the tools that Satan uses and is against God.Temptation does not come from God but within the cold heart of a person who does not know God. God does not tempt us, but like I said before, it is Satan who tempts us away from living as our Lord Jesus lives. Our God does delight in helping us grow stronger through the temptation that Satan uses.

Temptation is one of Satan's favorite tools to use. Satan used temptation on Adam and Eve in the Garden of Eden (see chapter 3 in Genesis). Satan even used temptation on Jesus, and if Jesus can be strong against Satan's temptations, we must not give into Satan's foolishness either. Sin is the result of temptation.

Often temptation may seem alluring and beautiful, shiny and appealing, and then, bam! We give into it ('cause we are weak), and the pain starts brewing like a coffee pot (the more it brews, the stronger it gets). Satan thinks he knows everything, but he only knows our weaknesses (that he uses against us). However, when we are strong in Jesus, we are able to resist Satan. The Word of God (the Bible) says: *"For I am weak then He is strong".* *(2 Corinthians 12:10b).* And God knows every single heart of man—past, present, and future. And once again from the Word of God: *"This is what the Lord says—your Redeemer, the Holy One of Israel:*

'I am the Lord your God, who teaches you what is best for you, who directs you in the way you should go'". *(Isaiah 48:17).*

Satan's many names are the weapons that he uses toward us; and they are negative and harmful. Jesus's names are positive, encouraging, comforting, and healing to our souls. I put together a list of the names of both Jesus' Names and Satan's names. I know you might recognize some of the weapons of Satan's (I sure have) that you just might be harvesting in your heart (a place where they do not belong). I also put Scripture next to Satan's negative names so you can read them and get to know Satan (the maker of temptations) and resist him with the strength of Jesus' Names. To know that you have Jesus by your side is the best way to fight off Satan who prowls around looking for a 'weak link' to pounce on.

Names of Jesus: – *Positive* **encouragement to keep us living for the Glory of God:**

[These 31 Names of Jesus are what I will call the Goodness of God.]
Almighty:

"'I am the Alpha and the Omega', says the Lord God, 'who is, who was, and who is to come, <u>The Almighty</u>'". (Revelation 1:8).

"For in Christ all the Fullness of the Deity lives in bodily form, and in Christ you have been brought to Fullness – He is the Head over every power and authority". (Colossians 2:9-10).

"In your relationships with one another, have the same mindset as Christ Jesus: Who, being in very nature God, did not consider equality with God something to be used to His own advantage; rather, He made Himself nothing by taking the very nature of a servant, being made in human likeness. And being found in appearance as a man, He humbled Himself by becoming obedient to death – even death on a cross!" (Philippians 2:5-8).

Let us then brothers and sisters *"sing the song of God's servant Moses and of the Lamb: 'Great and marvelous are Your Deeds, <u>Lord God Almighty</u>. Just and True are Your Ways, King of the nations. Who will not fear You, Lord, and bring glory to You Name? For You alone are Holy. all nations will come and worship before You, for Your Righteous Acts have been revealed'". (Revelation 15:3).*

<u>Son of God</u>:

"For God loved the world that He gave <u>His one and only Son</u>, that whoever believes in Him shall not perish, but have eternal life". (John 3:16).

"My sheep listen to My Voice; I know them, and they follow Me. I give them Eternal Life, and they shall never perish; no one will snatch them out of My Hand. My Father, who has given them to Me, is greater than all; no one can snatch them out of My Father's Hand. I and the Father are one'". *(John 10:27-30,).*

<u>Savior</u>:

"It is a trustworthy statement, deserving full acceptance, that Christ Jesus came into the world to save sinners, among whom I am foremost of all". (1 Timothy 1:15).

"At one time, we too were foolish, disobedient, deceived and enslaved by all kinds of passions and pleasures. We lived in malice and envy, being hated and hating one another. However, when the kindness and love of God our Savior

appeared, He saved us, not because of righteous things we had done, but because of His mercy. He saved through the washing of rebirth and renewal by the Holy Spirit, whom He poured out on us generously through Jesus Christ our Savior, so that, having been justified by His Grace, we might become heirs having the Hope of Eternal Life". (Titus 3:3-7).

"For our citizenship is in Heaven, from which also we eagerly wait for a Savior, the Lord Jesus Christ". (Philippians 3:20).

Fellowship:

"Therefore, you do not lack any spiritual gift as you eagerly wait for our Lord Jesus Christ to be revealed. He will also keep you firm to the end, so that you will be blameless on the day of our Lord Jesus Christ. God is faithful, who has called you into fellowship with His Son, Jesus Christ our Lord". (1 Corinthians 1:7-9).

"Here I am! I stand at the door and knock. If anyone hears My Voice and opens the door, I will come in and eat with that person, and they with Me. To the one who is victorious, I will give the right to sit with Me on My throne, just as I was victorious and sat down with My Father on His throne". (Revelation 3:20-21).

"Truly I tell you, whatever you bind on earth will be bound in Heaven, and whatever you loose on earth will be lost in Heaven. Again, truly I tell you that if two of you on earth agree about anything they ask for, it will be done for them by My Father in Heaven. For where two or three gather in My Name, there am I with them". (Matthew 18:18-20).

"Sitting down, Jesus called His Twelve disciples and said, **'Anyone who wants to be first must be the very last, and the servant of all'"**. (Mark 9:37).

"I say to you, My brothers and sisters are those who hear God's Word and put it into practice'". (Luke 8:21).

Friend:

"One who has unreliable friends soon comes to ruin, but there is a friend who sticks closer than a brother". (Proverb 18:24).

"If you keep My commands, you will remain in My love, just as I

have kept My Father's Commands and remain in His Love. I have told you this so that My Joy may be in you and that your joy may be complete. My Command is this: Love each other as I have loved you. Greater Love has no one than this: to lay down One's life for One's friends. You are My friends, if you do what I command". *(John 15:10-14)*.

<u>Companion</u>:

"Keep your lives free from the love of money and be content with what you have, because God has said, **'Never will I leave you; never will I forsake you'**". *(Hebrews 13:5)*.

"Though my father and mother forsake me, the Lord will receive me". *(Psalm 27:10)*.

<u>Deliverer</u>:

"Our God is a God who saves; from the Sovereign Lord comes escape from death". *(Psalm 68:20)*.

"Defend the weak and the fatherless; uphold the cause of the poor and the oppressed. Rescue the weak and the needy; deliver them from the hand of the wicked". *(Psalm 82:3-4)*.

"If we are thrown into the blazing furnace, the God we serve is able to deliver us from it, and He will deliver us with His Majesty's hand". *(Daniel 3:17)*.

"In God, whose word I praise, in the Lord, whose word I praise—in God I trust and am not afraid. What can man do to me? I am under vows to You, my God; I will present my thank offerings to You. For You have delivered me from death and my feet from stumbling, that I may walk before God in the light of life". *(Psalm 56:10-13)*.

"Whoever dwells in the shelter of the Most High will rest in the shadow of the Almighty. I will say of the Lord, 'He is my refuge and my fortress, my God, in whom I trust.' Surely, He will save you from the fowler's snare and from the deadly pestilence. He will cover you with His feathers, and under His wings you will find refuge; His faithfulness will be your shield and rampart". *(Psalm 91:1-4)*.

"Then you will know the truth and the truth will set you free". *(John 8:32)*.

"So if the Son sets you free, you will be free indeed". (John 8:36).

Redeemer:

"This is what the Lord says: 'Yes, captives will be taken from warriors, and plunder retrieved from the fierce; I will contend with those who contend with you, and your children I will save. I will make you oppressors eat their own flesh; they will be drunk on their own blood, as with wine. Then all mankind will know that I, the Lord, am you Savior, your Redeemer, and the Mighty One of Jacob'". (Isaiah 49:25-26).

"Praise be the Lord, the God of Israel, because He has come to His people and redeemed them". (Luke 1:68).

"By the grace of God I am what I am, and His grace to me was not without effect. No, I worked harder than all of them—yet not I, but the Grace of God that was with me" (1 Corinthians 15:10).

"May the words of my mouth and this meditation of my heart be pleasing in your sight, Lord, my Rock and my Redeemer". (Psalm 19:14).

Forgiver:

"To the praise of His Glorious Grace, which He has freely given us in the One He loves. In Him, we have Redemption through His Blood, the forgiveness of sins, in accordance with the riches of God's Grace that He lavished on us. With all wisdom and understanding, He made known to us the mystery of His will according to His good pleasure; which He Purposed in Christ, to be put into effect when the times reach their fulfillment—to bring unity to all things in heaven and on earth under Christ". (Ephesians 1:6-10).

"You Lord, showed favor to Your land; You restored the fortunes of Jacob. You forgave the iniquity of Your people and covered all their sins. You set aside all Your wrath and turned from your fierce anger. Restore us again, God our Savior, and put away Your displeasure toward us".

(Psalm 85:1-4).

Helper:

"God is our Refuge and Strength, an ever-present help in trouble. Therefore, we will not fear, though the earth gives way and the mountains fall into the heart

of the sea, though its waters roar and foam and the mountains quake with their surging". (Psalm 46:1-3).

"Trust in the Lord with all your heart and lean not on your own understanding; in all you ways submit to Him, and He will make your paths straight. Do not be wise in your own eyes; fear the Lord and shun evil. This will bring health to your body and nourishment to your bones". (Proverb 3:5-8).

"We say with confidence; 'The Lord is my Helper; I will not be afraid. What can mere mortals do to me'?". (Hebrews 13:6).

<u>Love</u>**:**

"Dear friends, let us love one another, for Love comes from God. Everyone who loves has been born of God and knows God. Whoever does not love does not know God, because <u>God is Love</u>". (1 John 4:7-8). And: *"This is how we know that we live in Him and He in us: He has given us of His Spirit". (1 John 4:13).*

"If anyone acknowledges that Jesus is the Son of God, God lives in them and they in God. And so we know and rely on the Love God has for us ". (1 John 4:15-16).

"For God so loved the world that He gave His One and only Son, that whoever believes in Him shall not perish but have Eternal Life. For God did not send His Son into the world to condemn the world, but save the world through Him". (John 3:16-17).

*"**Greater Love has no one than this: to lay down One's Life for one's friends**"". (John 15:13).*

"Because of His Great Love for us, God, who is rich in Mercy, made us alive with Christ even when we were dead in transgressions – it is by Grace you have been saved". (Ephesians 2:4-5).

*" This is how Love is made complete among us so that we will have confidence on the Day of Judgment: In this world we are like Jesus. There is no fear in Love. but Perfect Love drives out fear, because fear has to do with punishment. The one who fears is not made perfect in Love. We love because He first loved us. Whoever claims to love God yet hates a brother or sister is a liar. For whoever does not love their brother and sister, whom they have seen, cannot love God, whom they have not seen. And He has given us this Command: '**Anyone who loves God must***

also love their brother and sister'". (1 John 4:17-21).

<u>Joy</u>:

"As the Father has loved Me, so have I loved you. Now remain in My Love, If you keep My Commands, you will remain in My Love, just as I have kept My Father's Commands and remain in His Love. I have told you this so that My Joy may be in you and that your joy may be complete. My Command is this: Love each other as I have loved you'". (John 15:9-12).

<u>Peace</u>:

"Glory to God in the Highest Heaven, and on earth Peace to those whom His Favor rests". (Luke 2:14).

"For to us a child is born, to us a Son is given, and the government will be on His Shoulders. And He will be called Wonderful Counselor, Mighty God, Everlasting Father, Prince of Peace". (Isaiah 9:6).

"Peace I leave with you; My Peace I give you. I do not give to you as the world gives. Do not let your hearts be troubled and do not be afraid'". (John 14:27).

"Therefore, since we have been justified through Faith, we have Peace with God through our Lord Jesus Christ, through whom we have gained access by Faith into this Grace in which we now stand. And we boast in the Hope of the Glory of God". (Romans 5:1).

<u>Kindness</u>:

"Do not let any unwholesome talk come out of your mouths, but only what is helpful for building others up according to their needs, that it may benefit those who listen. And do not grieve the Holy Spirit of God, with whom you were sealed for the Day of Redemption. Get rid of all betterness, rage and anger, brawling and slander, along with every form of malice. Be kind and compassionate to one another, forgiving each other, just as in Christ God forgave you". (Ephesians 4:29-32).

"He has shown you, O mortal, what is Good. and what does the Lord require

of you? To act justly and to love mercy and to walk humbly with your God". (Micah 6:8).

"Therefore, as God's chosen people, holy and dearly loved, clothe yourselves with Compassion, Kindness, Humility, Gentleness and Patience". (Colossians 3:12).

Gentleness:

"Let your gentleness be evident to all. The Lord is near. Do not be anxious about anything, but in every situation, by prayer and petition, with thanksgiving, present your requests to God. In addition, the peace of God, which transcends all understanding, will guard your hearts and your minds in Christ Jesus. Finally, brothers and sisters, whatever is true, whatever is noble, whatever is right, whatever is pure, whatever is lovely, whatever is admirable – if anything is excellent or praiseworthy – think about such things. Whatever you have learned or received or heard from me, or seen in me—put it into practice. And the God of peace will be with you". (Philippians 4:5-9).

Goodness:

"The Lord is Gracious and Compassionate, slow to anger and rich in Love. The Lord is Good to all; He has compassion on all He has made. All Your works praise You, Lord; Your faithful people extol You ". (Psalm 145:8-10).

"The Lord is Good to those who wait for Him, to the soul who seeks Him. It is good that one should wait quietly for the Salvation of the Lord". (Lamentations 3:25-26).

"He who searches our hearts knows the mind of the Spirit, because the Spirit intercedes for God's people in accordance with the Will of God. and we know that in all things God works for the Good of those who love Him, who have been called according to His Purpose". (Romans 8:27-28).

Patience:

"Love is Patient and Kind; Love is not jealous or conceited or proud; Love is not arrogant". (1 Corinthians 13:4).

"You also must be patient. Keep your hopes high, for the Day of the Lord's *coming is near". (James 5:8).*

"*Therefore, do not be anxious about anything, but in everything by prayer and supplication with thanksgiving let your requests be made known to God". (Philippians 4:6).*

"*Rejoice in Hope, be patient in tribulation, be constant in prayer". (Romans 12:12).*

Faithfulness:

"*May the God of Hope fill you with all Joy and Peace as you trust in Him, so that you may overflow with Hope by the Power of the Holy Spirit". (Romans 15:13).*

Let us draw Faith from our Lord in what He tells us: "***Do not fear, for I am with you; do not be dismayed, for I am your God. I will strengthen you and help you; I will uphold you with My Righteous right hand"***. *(Isaiah 41:10).*

"*I can do all this through Him who gives me strength". (Philippians 4:13).*

Self-control:

"*The Lord sits enthroned over the flood; the Lord is enthroned as King forever. The Lord gives strength to His people; the Lord blesses His people with peace". (Psalm 29:10-11).*

"*Let love and faithfulness never leave you; bind them around your neck, write them on the tablet of your heart. Then you will win favor and a good name in the sight of God and man". (Proverbs 3:3-4).*

Hope and Fulfillment:

"*Do not fret because of those who are evil or be envious of those who do wrong; for like grass they will soon wither, like green plants they will soon die away. Trust in the Lord and do good; dwell in the land and enjoy safe pasture. Take delight in the Lord, and He will give you the desires of your heart. Commit your way to the Lord; trust in Him and He will do this: He will make your righteous reward shine like the dawn, your vindication like the noonday sun. Be still before the Lord and wait patiently for Him; do not fret when people succeed in their ways, when they carry out their wicked schemes. Refrain from anger and turn from wrath; do not fret – it leads only to evil. For those who are evil will be destroyed, but those who hope in the Lord will inherit the land". (Psalm 37:1-9).*

"Give thanks to the Lord, for He is Good; His Love endures forever. For He satisfies the thirsty and fills the hungry with Good Things". (Psalm 107:1,9).

"The poor will eat and be satisfied; those who seek the Lord will praise Him – may your hearts live forever". (Psalm 22:26).

"Jesus has said: **'Everyone who drinks this water [of evil] will be thirsty again, but whoever drinks the water I give will never thirst. Indeed, the Water I give you will become in you a spring of water welling up to Eternal Life'".** *(John 4:13-14).*

"'Then, you will know that I am the Lord; and those who hope in Me will not be disappointed'". *(Isaiah 49:23b).*

"Hope does not put us to shame, because God's love has been poured out into our hearts through the Holy Spirit, who has been given to us". (Romans 5:5).

Counselor:

"For to us a child is born, to us a Son is given, and the government will be on His shoulders, and He will be called; Wonderful Counselor, Mighty God, Everlasting Father, Prince of Peace". (Isaiah 9:6).

"My dear children, I write this to you so that you will not sin, but if anybody does sin, we have an advocate with the Father – Jesus Christ, the Righteous One – He is the Atoning Sacrifice for our sins, and not only for ours, also for the sins of the whole world". (1 John 2:1-2).

"'If you love Me, keep My commands, and I will ask the Father, and He will give you another advocate to help you and be with you forever – the Spirit of Truth. The world cannot accept Him, because it neither sees Him nor knows Him, but you know Him, for He lives with you and will be in you. I will not leave you as orphans; I will come to you'". *(John 14:15-18).*

Righteousness:

"Seek first His kingdom and His righteousness, and all these things will be

given to you as well". (Matthew 6:33).

"God made Him who had no sin to be sin for us, so that in Him we might become the Righteousness of God". (2 Corinthians 5:21).

Sufficiency:

"To keep me from becoming conceited, I was given a thorn in my flesh, a messenger of Satan, to torment me. Three times I pleaded with the Lord to take it away from me. But He said to me: **'My grace is sufficient for you, for My power is made perfect in weakness'.** *Therefore, I will boast all the more gladly about my weaknesses, so that Christ's Power may rest on me. That is why, for Christ's sake, I delight in weaknesses, in insults, in hardships, in persecutions, in difficulties. For when I am weak, then I am strong". (2 Corinthians 12:7-10).*

"As it is written: For Your sake we face death all day long; we are considered as sheep to be slaughtered. No, in all these things we are more than conquerors through Him who loved us". (Romans 8:36-37).

Guardian:

"'Do not fear, for I have redeemed you; I have summoned you by name; you are Mine. When you pass through the waters, I will be with you, and when you pass through the rivers, they will not sweep over you. When you walk through the fire, you will not be burned; the flames will not set you ablaze'". *(Isaiah 43:1b-2).*

"You, Lord, are a shield around me, my glory, the One who lifts my head high. I call out to the Lord, and He answers me from His holy mountain". (Psalm 3:3-4).

"He raises the poor from the dust and lifts the needy from the ash heap; He seats them with princes and has them inherit a throne of honor. For the foundations of the earth are the Lord's; on them He has set the world. He will guard the feet of His faithful servants, but the wicked will be silenced in the place of darkness". (1 Samuel 2:8-9).

"A thousand may fall at your side, ten thousand at your right hand, but it will not come near you. You will only observe with your eyes and see the punishment of the wicked". (Psalm 91:7-8).

Light:

"When Jesus spoke again to the people, He said, '**I am the <u>Light</u> of the world. Whoever follows Me will never walk in darkness, but will have the light of life**'". *(John 8:12).*

"*Your word is a lam for my feet, a light on my path*". *(Psalm 119:105).*

"*In Him was life, and that life was the light of all mankind. The light shines in the darkness, and the darkness has not overcome it*". *(John 1:4-5).*

"*Then Jesus told them, '**You are going to have the light just a little while longer. Walk while you have the <u>Light</u>, before darkness overtakes you. Whoever walks in the dark does not know where they are going. Believe in the Light while you have the Light, so that you may become children of Light**'". (John 12:35-36a).*

"*This is the Message we have heard from Him and declare to you: God is Light; in Him there is no darkness at all. If we claim to have fellowship with Him and yet walk in the darkness, we lie and do not live out the Truth. But if we walk in the Light, as He is in the light, we have fellowship with one another, and the blood of Jesus, His Son, purifies us from all sin*". *(1 John 1:5-7).*

Living Water:

"*Jesus explains how He is the <u>Living Water</u>: '**Everyone who drinks this water will be thirsty again, but whoever drinks this water will be thirsty again, but whoever drinks the water I give them will never thirst. Indeed, the water I give them will become in them a spring of water welling up to eternal life.**'". (John 4:13-14).*

"*On the last and greatest day of the festival, Jesus stood and said in a loud voice, '**Let anyone who is thirsty come to Me and drink. Whoever believes in Me, as Scripture has said, rivers of Living Water will flow from within them**'". (John 7:37-38).*

"*With joy you will draw water from the wells of salvation*". *(Isaiah 12:3).*

Lord:

"*If you declare with your mouth, '<u>Jesus is Lord</u>,' and believe in your heart that God raised Him from the dead, you will be saved. For it is with your heart* *that you believe and are justified, and it is with your mouth that you profess your faith and are saved. As Scripture says, anyone who believes in Him will never be put to shame". (Romans 10:9-11).*

"Praise be to the Lord, to God our Savior, who daily bears our burdens". (Psalm 68:19).

"As for me, it is good to be near God. I have made the Sovereign Lord my refuge; I will tell of all your deeds". (Psalm 73:28).

"You, Lord, are forgiving and good, abounding in love to all who call to You. Hear my prayer, Lord; listen to my cry for mercy. When I am in distress, I call to You, because You answer me".

(Psalm 86:5-7).

"Because the Sovereign Lord helps me, I will not be disgraced. Therefore, have I set my face like a flint, and I know I will not be put to shame". (Isaiah 50:7).

Bread of Life:

"Our ancestors ate manna in the wilderness; as it is written: 'He [gave them bread from Heaven to eat'. Jesus said to them: **'Very truly I tell you, it is not Moses who has given you the bread of Heaven, but it is my Father who gives you the True Bread from Heaven. For the Bread of God is the Bread that comes down from Heaven and gives Life to the world'.** *'Sir', they said, 'always give us this Bread'. Then Jesus declared,* **'I am the <u>Bread of Life</u>. Whoever comes to Me will never go hungry, and whoever believes in Me will never be thirsty'".** *(John 6:31-35).*

"Then Jesus said to them, **'Very truly I tell you, unless you eat the flesh of the Son of Man and drink His Blood, you have no life in you. Whoever eats My Flesh and drinks My Blood has Eternal Life, and I will raise them up at the last day. For My Flesh is real food and My Blood is real drink. Whoever eats My Flesh and drinks My Blood remains in Me, and I in them. Just as the Living Father sent Me and I live because of the Father, so the one who feeds on me will live because of Me. This is the Bread that came down from Heaven. Your ancestors ate manna and died, but whoever feeds on this Bread will live forever'".** *(John 6:53-58).*

Anchor:

"We have this Hope as an <u>Anchor</u> for the soul, firm and secure. It [He] enters the inner sanctuary behind the curtain, where our forerunner, Jesus, has entered on our behalf. He has become a High Priest forever, in the order of Melchizedek". (Hebrews 6:19-20).

"So then, just as you received Christ Jesus as Lord, continue to live your lives in Him, rooted and built up in Him, strengthened in the Faith as you were taught, and overflowing with thankfulness. See to it that no one takes you captive through hollow and deceptive philosophy, which depends on human tradition and the elemental spiritual forces of this world rather than on Christ". (Colossians 2:6-8).

Comforter:

"I know, Lord, that Your Laws are Righteous, and that in Faithfulness You have afflicted me, May Your Unfailing Love be my <u>Comfort</u>, according to Your Promise to Your servant. Let Your Compassion come to me that I may live, for Your Law is my delight". (Psalm 119:75-77).

"Praise be to the God and Father of our Lord Jesus Christ, the Father of Compassion and the God of all Comfort, who comforts us in all our troubles, so that we can comfort those in any trouble with the Comfort we ourselves receive from God". (2 Corinthians 1:3-4).

"Do not be anxious about anything, but in every situation, by prayer and petition, with thanksgiving, present your requests to God. and the Peace of God, which transcends all understanding, will guard your hearts and your minds in Christ Jesus". (Philippians 4:6-7).

"Because the Lord has said: 'Never will I leave you; never will I forsake you'". (Hebrews 13:5b).

"May the God of Hope fill you with all joy and peace as you trust in Him, so that you may overflow with Hope by the Power of the Holy Spirit". (Romans 15:13).

Example:

"To this you are called, because Christ suffered for you, leaving you an *example that you should follow in His steps. He committed no sin, and no deceit was found in His mouth". (1 Peter 2:21-22).*

"Whoever claims to live in Him must live as Jesus did". (1 John 2:6).

"Follow God's example, therefore, as dearly loved children and walk in the way of love, just as Christ loved us and gave Himself up for us as a fragrant offering and sacrifice to God". (Ephesians 5:1-2).

Next up the Names of Satan – Negative – that drags us down into a slippery pit:

[These 24 names of Satan are what I call the badness of Satan.]

All of these names will block your way to a Life with the Star Team – the Father, the Son and Holy Spirit. Which is the Life of Love, Compassion and Grace. And who does the Word of God say these names belong to? They belong to: *"The great dragon was hurled down – that ancient serpent called the devil, Satan, who leads the whole world astray – was hurled to the earth, along with his demon angels". (Revelation 12:9).* And the Word of God also says these names will produce this: *"The acts of the flesh are obvious: sexual immorality, impurity and debauchery; idolatry and witchcraft; hatred, discord, jealousy, fits of rage, selfish ambitions, dissensions, factions and envy; drunkenness, orgies, and the like. I warn you, as I did before, that those who live like this will not inherit the kingdom of God". (Galatians 5:19-21). "And that is what some of you were. But you were washed, you were sanctified, you were justified in the Name of the Lord Jesus Chriat and by the Spirit of our God". (1 Corinthians 6:11).*

Let us now see what the Word of God says about these names and other names of Satan:

Lust (sexual immorality):

"The body however, is not meant for sexual immorality but for the Lord, and the for the body".

(1 Corinthians 6:13b).

"Do you not know that your bodies are members of Christ Himself? Shall I then take the members of Christ and unite them with a prostitute? Never!". (1 Corinthians 6:15).

"But whoever is united with the Lord is one with Him in Spirit. Therefore, flee from sexual immorality. All other sins a person commits are outside the body, but whoever sins sexually, sins against their own body. Do you not know that your bodies are temples of the Holy Spirit, who is in you, whom you have received from God? You are not your own; you were bought at a price. Therefore, honor God with your bodies". (1 Corinthians 6:17-20).

"Marriage should be honored by all, and the marriage bed kept pre, for God will judge the adulterer and all the sexually immoral. Keep your lives free from the love of money and be content with what you have, because God has said, 'Never will I leave you; never will I forsake you'". (Hebrews 13:4-5).

"It is God's Will that you should be sanctified; that you should avoid sexual immorality; that each of you should learn to control your own body in a way that is holy and honorable, not in passionate lust like the pagans, who do not know God; and that in this matter no one should wrong or take advantage of a brother or sister. The Lord <u>will</u> punish <u>all</u> those who commit such sins, as we told you and warned you before. For God did not call us to be impure, but to live a holy life. Therefore, anyone who rejects this instruction does not reject a human being but God, the very God who gives you his Holy Spirit". (1 Thessalonians 4:3-8).

The Lord says: ***"Among you there must not be even a hint of sexual immorality, or of any kind of impurity, or of greed, because these are improper for God's holy people. Nor should there be obscenity, foolish talk or coarse joking, which are out of place, but rather thanksgiving. For, of this you can be sure: No immoral, impure or greedy person – such a person is an idolater – has any inheritance in the Kingdom of Christ and of God. Let no one deceive you with empty words, for because of such things God's Wrath comes on those who are disobedient. Therefore, do not be partners with them'".*** *(Matthew 5:3-7).*

Idolatry:

"You shall have no other gods before Me. You shall not make for yourself an image in the form of anything in Heaven above or on the

earth beneath or in the waters below. You shall not bow down to them or worship them; for I, the Lord your God, am a jealous God, punishing the children for the sin of the parents to the third and fourth generation of those who hate Me, but showing Love to the thousand generations of those who love Me and keep My Commandments'''. *(Exodus 20:3-6).*

"'It is written: 'Worship the Lord your God and serve Him only'''. *(Luke 4:8).*

"Those who run after other gods will suffer more and more. I will not pour out libations of blood to such gods or take up their names on my lips. Lord, You alone are my portion and my cup; You make my lot secure. The boundary lines have fallen for me in pleasant places; surely I have a delightful inheritance. I will praise the Lord, who counsels me; even at night my heart instructs me. I keep my eyes always on the Lord. With Him at my right hand, I will not be shaken. Therefore, my heart is glad and my tongue rejoices; my body also will rest secure, because you will not abandon me to the realm of the dead, nor will You let Your faithful one see decay. You make known to me the Path of Life; You will fill me with Joy in Your Presence, with Eternal Pleasures at Your Right Hand". *(Psalm 16:4-11).*

As I have told you earlier: *"The acts of the flesh* [Satan] *are obvious: sexual immorality, impurity and debauchery; idolatry and witchcraft; hatred, discord, jealousy, fits of rage, selfish ambition, dissensions, factions and envy; drunkenness, orgies, and the like. I warn you, as I did before, that those who live like this will not inherit the Kingdom of God"*. *(Galatians 5:19-21).*

"Therefore, my dear friends, flee from idolatry". *(1 Corinthians 10:14).*

Hatred:

"What causes fights and quarrels among you? Don't they come from your desires that battle within you? You desire but do not have, so you kill. You covet but you cannot get what you want, so you quarrel and fight. You do not have because you do not ask God. When you ask, you do not receive, because you ask with wrong motives, that you may spend what you get on your pleasures. You adulterous people, don't you know that friendship with the world means enmity against God? Therefore, anyone who chooses to be a friend of the world

becomes an enemy of God. Or do you think Scripture says without reason that He jealously longs for the Spirit He has caused to dwell in? But He gives us more Grace. That is why Scripture says:

'God opposes the proud but shows favor to the humble'

Submit yourselves, then, to God. Resist the devil, and he will flee from you. Come near to God and He will come near to you. Wash your hand, you sinners, and purify your hearts, you double-minded. Grieve, mourn and wail. Change your laughter to mourning and your joy to gloom. Humble yourselves before the Lord, and He will lift you up. Brothers and sisters, do not slander one another. Anyone who speaks against a brother or sister or judges them speaks against the Law and judges it. When you judge the Law, you are not keeping it, but sitting in judgment on it. There is only one Lawgiver and Judge, the One who is able to save and destroy. But you – who are you to judge your neighbor?" (James 4:1-12).

"For this is the message you heard from the beginning: We should love one another. Do not be like Cain, who belonged to the evil one and murdered his brother. And why did he murder him? Because his own actions were evil and his brother's were righteous. Cannot be surprised, my brothers and sisters, if the world hates you. We know that we have passed from death to Life, because we love each other. Anyone who does not love remains in death. Anyone who hates a brother or sister is a murderer, and you know that no murderer has Eternal Life residing in him. This is how we know what love is: Jesus Christ laid down His Life for us. And we ought to lay down our lives for our brothers and sisters. If anyone has material possessions and sees a brother or sister in need but has no pity on them, how can the Love of God be in that person?

Dear children, let us not love with words or speech but with actions and truth". (1 John 3:11-18). Therefore: *"Receive from Him anything we ask, because we keep His Commands and do what pleases Him. And this is His Command: to believe in the Name of His Son, Jesus Christ, and to love one another as He Commanded us. The one who keeps God's Commands lives in Him, and He in them. And this is how we know that He lives in us: We know it by the Spirit He gave us". (1 John 3:22-24).*

"You love righteousness and hate wickedness; therefore God, your God, has set you above your companions by anointing you with the Oil of Joy". (Psalm

45:7).

"For God so loved the world that He gave His one and only Son, that whoever believes in Him shall not perish but have Eternal Life. For God did not send His Son into the world to condemn the world, but to save the world through Him. Whoever believes in Him is not condemned, but whoever does not believe stands condemned already because they have not believed in the Name of God's one and only Son. This is the verdict: Light has come into the world, but people loved darkness instead of Light because their deeds were evil. Everyone who does evil hates the Light, and will not come into the Light for fear that their deeds will be exposed. But whoever lives by the Truth comes into the Light, so that it may be seen plainly that what they have done has been done in the Sight of God". (John 3:16-21)

Jealousy:

"If you harbor bitter envy and selfish ambition in your hearts, do not boast about it or deny the Truth". (James 3:14). "For where you have envy and selfish ambition, there you find disorder and every evil practice". (James 3:16).

"The god of this age has blinded the minds of unbelievers, so that they cannot see the Light of the Gospel that displays the Glory of Christ, who is the image of God". (2 Corinthians 4:4).

"Satan himself masquerades as an angel of light". (2 Corinthians 11:14)

"Submit yourselves, then, to God. Resist the devil, and he will flee from you. Come near to God and He will come near to you. Wash your hands, you sinners, and purify your hearts, you double-minded". (James 4:7-8).

"These people are grumblers and fault-finders; they follow their own evil desires; they boast about themselves and flatter others for their own advantage". (Jude 1:16).

"Be alert and of sober mind. Your enemy the devil prowls around like a roaring lion looking for someone to devour. Resist him, standing firm in the Faith, because you know that the family of believers throughout the world is undergoing the same kind of sufferings". (1 Peter 5:8-9).

Rage and Anger:

"Fools give full vent to their rage, but the wise bring calm in the end". (Proverb 29:11).

"Do not be quickly provoked in your spirit, for anger resides in the lap of fools". (Ecclesiastes 7:9).

"My dear brothers and sisters, take note of this: Everyone should be quick to listen, slow to speak and slow to become angry, because human anger does not produce the righteousness that God desires. Therefore, get rid of all moral filth and the evil that is so prevalent and humbly accept the word planted in you, which can save you". (James 1:19-21).

"Your enemies will be clothed in shame, and the tents of the wicked will be no more" (Job 8:22).

"I trust in You; do not let me be put to shame, nor let my enemies triumph over me". (Psalm 25:2).

Selfishness:

"Those who want to get rich fall into temptation and a trap and into many foolish and harmful desires that plunge people into ruin and destruction. For the love of money is a root of all kinds of evil. Some people, eager for money, have wandered from the Faith and pierced themselves with many griefs". (1 Timothy 6:10).

"Each person is tempted when they are dragged away by their own evil desire and enticed. Then, after desire has conceived, it gives birth to sin; and sin, when it is full-grown, gives birth to death. Don't be deceived, my dear brothers and sisters. Every good and perfect gift is from above, coming down from the Father of the Heavenly Lights, who does not change like shifting shadows. He chose to give us birth through the Word of Truth, that we might be a kind of firstfruits of all He created". (James 1:14-18).

"You were blameless in your ways from the day you were created till wickedness was found in you". (Ezekiel 28:15).

"Then Jesus said to His disciples (and all of us): **'Whoever wants to be My disciple must deny themselves and take up their cross and follow Me'".** *(Matthew 16:24).*

Envy:

"If you harbor <u>bitter envy</u> and selfish ambition in your hearts, do not boast about it or deny the truth. Such 'wisdom' does not come down from heaven, but is earthly, unspiritual, and demonic. For where you have envy and selfish ambition, there you find disorder and every evil practice".

(James 3:14-16).

"Do not fret because of those who are evil or be <u>envious</u> of those who do wrong; for like the grass they will soon wither, like green plants they will soon die away. Trust in the Lord and do good; dwell in the land and enjoy safe pastures. Take delight in the Lord, and He will give you the desires of your heart". (Psalm 37:1-4).

"A heart at peace gives life to the body, but <u>envy</u> rots the bones". (Proverb 14:30).

Foolishness:

"The one who does what is sinful is of the devil, because the devil has been sinning from the beginning. The reason the Son of God appeared was to destroy the devil's work". (1 John 3:8).

"Submit yourselves, then, to God [the Star Team]. Resist the devil; and he will flee from you". (James 4:7).

"The thief comes only to steal and kill and destroy; I have come that they may Life, and have it to the full". (John 10:10).

"The God of Peace will soon crush Satan under your feet. The Grace of our Lord Jesus be with you". (Romans 16:20).

Liar:

*"Jesus said to them, **'If God were your Father, you would love Me, for I have come here from Him. I have not come on My own; God sent Me. Why is My language not clear to you? Because you are unable to hear what I say. You belong to your father, the devil, and you want to carry out your father's desires. He was a murderer from the beginning, not holding to the truth, for there is no truth in him. When he lies, he speaks his native language, for he is a liar and the father of lies'"** (John 8:42-44).*

Devil:

*"One day the angels came to present themselves before the Lord, and Satan also came with them. The Lord said to Satan, **'Where have you come from'?** Satan answered the Lord, 'From roaming throughout the earth, going back and forth on it'"" (Job 1:6-7).*

"Humble yourselves, therefore, under God's Mighty Hand, that He may lift you up in due time. Cast all your anxiety on Him because He cares for you. Be alert and of sober mind. Your enemy the devil prowls around lie a roaring lion looking for someone to devour". (1 Peter 5:6-8).

"Submit yourselves, then, to God. resist the devil, and he will flee from you. Come near to God and He will come near to you. Wash your hands, you sinners, and purify your hearts, you double-minded. Grieve, mourn and wail. Change your laughter to mourning and your joy to gloom. Humble yourselves before the Lord, and He will lift you up". (James 4:7-10).

Be aware that: *"Satan himself masquerades as an angel of light. It is not surprising, then, if his servants also masquerade as servants of righteousness. Their end will be what their actions deserve". (2 Corinthians 11:14-15).*

"Everyone who sins breaks the Law; in fact, sin is lawlessness. But you know that He appeared so that He might take away our sins. And in Him is no sin. No one who lives in Him keeps on sinning. No one who continues to sin has either seen Him or known Him. Dear brothers and sisters, do not let anyone lead you astray. The one who does what is right is righteous, just as He is Righteous. The one who does what is sinful is of the devil, because the devil has been sinning from the beginning. The reason the Son of God appeared was to destroy the devil's work. No one who is born of God will continue to sin, because God's seed remains in them; they cannot go on sinning, because they have been born of God. this is how we know who the children of God are and who the children of the devil are: Anyone who does not do what is right is not God's child, nor is anyone who does not love their brother and sister ". (1 John 3:4-10).

Enemy:

"Jesus answered, 'The one who sowed the hood seed is the Son of Man. The field is the world, and the good seed stands for the people of the kingdom. The

weeds are the people of the evil one, and the enemy who sows them is the devil. The harvest is the end of the age, and the harvesters are angels. As the weeds are pulled up and burned, in the fire, so it will be at the end of the age. The Son of Man will send out His angels, and they will weed out of His kingdom everything that causes sin and all who are so evil. They will throw them into the blazing furnace, where there will be weeping and gnashing of teeth. Then the righteous will shine like the sun in the kingdom of their Father. Whoever has ears, let them hear". *(Matthew 13:37-43)*.

Beast:

"A third angel followed them and said in a loud voice: 'If anyone worships the beast and its image and receives its mark on their forehead or on their hand, they, too, will drink the wine of God's fury, which has been poured full strength in the cup of His wrath. They will be in torment with burning sulfur, in the presence of the holy angels and of the Lamb. In addition, the smoke of their torment will rise forever and ever. There will be no rest day or night for those who worship the beast and its image or for anyone who receives the mark of its name.' This calls for patient endurance on the part of the people of God who keep His commands and remain faithful to Jesus". *(Revelation 14:9-12)*.

Forces of evil:

"Put on the full armor of God, so that you can take your stand against the devil's schemes. For our struggle is not against flesh and blood, but against the rulers, against the authorizes, against the powers of this dark world, and against the spiritual forces of evil in the heavenly realms". *(Ephesians 6:11-12)*.

Antichrist:

"But, every spirit that does not acknowledge Jesus is not from God. This is the spirit of the antichrist, which you have heard is coming and even now is already in the world". *(1 John 4:3)*.

Evil one: "My prayer is not that you take them out of the world but that you protect them from the evil one". *(John 17:15)*.

"In addition to all this, take up the shield of faith, with which you can extinguish all the arrows of the evil one". *(Ephesians 6:16)*.

Deceiver:

"For such people are false apostles, deceitful workers, masquerading as apostles of Christ. In addition, no wonder, for Satan himself masquerades as an angel of light. It is not surprising, then, if his servants also masquerade as servants of righteousness. Their end will be what their actions deserve". (2 Corinthians 11:13-15).

"Watch out for false prophets. They come to you in sheep's clothing, but inwardly they are ferocious wolves. By their fruit, you will recognize them. Do people pick grapes from thorn-bushes, or figs from thistles?(Matthew 7:15-16).

Murderer:

"You belong to your father, the devil, and you want to carry out your father's desires. He was a murderer from the beginning, not holding to the truth, for there is no truth in him. When he lies, he speaks his native language, for he is a liar and the father of lies". (John 8:44).

Thief:

"The thief comes only to steal and kill and destroy; I have come that they may have life, and have it to the full". (John 10:10).

Complainers and Grumblers:

"These people are grumblers and fault-finders; they follow their own evil desires; they boast about themselves and flatter others for their own advantage". (Jude 1:16).

Slander:

"Whoever conceals hatred with lying lips and spreads slander is a fool". (Proverb 10:18).

Destroyer:

"Watch out for these Names of Satan that he will use as Weapons (bringing us down into his slimy pit)". (Isaiah 33:1).

Pride:

"When pride comes, then comes disgrace, but with humility comes wisdom". (Proverb 11:2).

"Where there is strife, there is pride, but wisdom is found in those who take advice". (Proverb 13:10).

"The Lord detests all the proud of heart. Be sure of this: They will not go unpunished". (Proverb 16:5).

Worried:

"Cast your burden on the Lord, and He will sustain you; He will never permit the righteous to be moved". (Psalm 55:22).

"To be carnally minded is death, but to be spiritually minded is life and peace". (Romans 8:6).

Confused:

"For God is not the author of confusion, but of peace, as in all churches of the saints". (1 Corinthians 14:33).

"For God has not given us a spirit of fear, but of power and of love and of a sound mind". (2 Timothy 1:7).

Shame:

"Lord, you are the hope of Israel; all who forsake you will be put to shame. Those who turn away from you will be written in the dust, because they have forsaken the Lord, the spring of living water". (Jeremiah 17:13).

Regret:

"Be sober-minded; be watchful. Your adversary, the devil, prowls around like a roaring lion, seeking to devour". (1 Peter 5:8).

"For godly grief produces a repentance that leads to salvation without regret, whereas worldly grief produces death". (2 Corinthians 7:10).

"A glad heart makes a cheerful face, but by sorrow of heart the spirit is crushed" (Proverb 15:13).

Doubt:

"Trust in the Lord with all your heart and lean not on your own understanding; in all your ways submit to Him, and He will make your paths straight. Do not be wise in your own eyes; fear the Lord and shun evil. This will bring health to your body and nourishment to your bones". (Proverb 3:5-8).

"I remain confident of this: I will see the goodness of the Lord in the land of the living. Wait for the Lord; be strong and take heart and wait for the Lord". (Psalm 27:13-14).

Gossip:

"The mouth of the righteous is a fountain of life, but the mouth of the wicked conceals violence". (Proverb 10:11).

Notice, Jesus's names are names of life, and every name of Satan's are names of death. When our Heavenly Father sees that Satan is trying to drag us down into his slimy pit, He reaches down and gives us that helping hand. For every hurtful name of Satan's, Jesus' names crush them into dust. I know this is true, because I do not feel any of those hurtful words for no longer than one minute. That is as long as it takes for Jesus to crush Satan—one minute! Just call out, "Jesus, help me!" and your troubles become dust. I am constantly telling Satan, "Jesus is Lord! Flee from me!" and Satan goes running away with his tail between his legs.

Satan works hard at making the children of God fall from grace. In addition, when he gets us to fall from grace, he leaves us alone caged in his darkness. This is Satan's biggest focus—getting us away from following Jesus. This is our daily battle to go through with these temptations, regrets, doubts, angers, shames, and stresses. Satan starts using the "weapons" of his when he sees that we are ignoring him and staying close to Jesus. All temptations are what Satan mostly uses as weapons of attack. That is why you must put on the whole armor of

God and guard your heart always! The Armor of God is the best weapon against Satan along with the Word of God (the Bible). If you do not have one (a Bible), get one. It is the best investment that you will ever make. There is one more name of Satan that the Bible will help you resist Satan from your life; and that is: Tempter.

Tempter:

"The tempter came to Him and said, 'If you are the Son of God, tell these stones to become bread'". (Matthew 4:3).

"For this reason, when I could no longer stand it, I sent to find out about your faith. I was afraid that in some way the tempter had tempted you and that our labors might have been in vain". (1 Thessalonian 3:5).

Temptation is what made Adam and Eve fall from grace (see Genesis 3:1-24). Temptation can make you fall too. You might be asking yourself (as I did), "How can I avoid falling into temptation?" Well, it is difficult, when living in a world of so many temptations surrounding us. The best thing to do is to walk away from that tempting thing and cling on to Jesus's side, and the only way to do this is to meditate on God's Word day and night. This means, every chance you have, open your Bible and let God speak to you. I only realized this ten years ago when I finally opened the door for Jesus. I saw many tempting things. Some I gave into, and some I just walked away. The moments that made me feel shameful were the moments I fell for. It is not that easy to walk away when you look around in this world of many temptations. However, once my Lord Jesus talked with me and told me that He will never leave me, I have the strength to walk away. Now, I do not have those empty feelings. Those empty feelings are full of the wonders of my Star Team—Heavenly Father and His Son Jesus and the Holy Spirit. Temptations will always be a part of this world. We must stay focused and trust in Jesus to fight off those burning arrows (tactics) of Satan. When the temptations of this world starts invading your space and attention, pick up your Bible and find the Scriptures matching your situation, and you will be able to walk away from that bad situation.

Here are some Scriptures that will help you walk away from the temptations of this world:

"Blessed is the one who perseveres under trial, because having stood the test, that person will receive the crown of life that the Lord has promised to those who *love Him". (James 1:12).*

"*Every good and perfect gift is from above, coming down from the Father of the heavenly lights, who does not change like shifting shadows. He chose to give us birth through the word of truth that we might be a kind of first-fruits of all He created" (James 1:17-18).*

"*Submit yourselves, then, to God. Resist the devil, and he will flee from you. Come near to God and He will come near to you. Wash your hands, you sinners, and purify your hearts, you double-minded". (James 4:7-8).*

"*No temptation has overtaken you except what is common to mankind. In addition, God is faithful; He will not let you be tempted beyond what you can bear. But when you are tempted, He will also provide a way out, so that you can endure it" (1 Corinthians 10:13).*

The Word of God (the Bible) is the best weapon that we have to resist the temptations of this world and to walk in the light of God.

Here I give you four ways to resist the enemy (Satan):

The first way is to come at Satan with (you guessed it) the Word of God:

"*Jesus answered;* **'It is written: Man shall not live on bread alone, but on every word that comes from the mouth of God'**". *(Matthew 4:8).*

"*In your anger do not sin: Do not let the sun go down while you are still angry, and do not give the devil a foothold". (Ephesians 4:26-27).*

"*Finally, be strong in the Lord and in His mighty power. Put on the full armor of God; so that you can take your stand against the devil's schemes". (Ephesians 6:10-11).*

"*Finally, brothers and sisters, whatever is true, whatever is noble, whatever is right, whatever is pure, whatever is lovely, whatever is admirable—think about such things". (Philippians 4:8)*

"*And that they will come to their senses and escape from the trap of the devil, who has taken them captive to do his will". (2 Timothy 2:26)*

"*Submit yourselves, then to God. Resist the devil, and he will flee from you". (James 4:7)*

"*You too, be patient and stand firm, because the Lord's coming is near". (1*

Peter 5:8)

"This then is how you should pray: 'Our Father in Heaven, hallowed be your name, your kingdom come, your will be done, on earth as it is in Heaven. Give us today our daily bread. And forgive us our debts, as we also have forgiven our debtors. And lead us not into temptation, but deliver us from the evil one'". (Matthew 6:9-13)

"The Lord is my light and my salvation—whom shall I fear? The Lord is the stronghold of my life—of whom shall I be afraid?" (Psalm 27:1).

"Whoever dwells in the shelter of the Most High will rest in the shadow of the Almighty".

(Psalm 91:1-2)

"So do not fear, for I am with you; do not be dismayed, for I am your God. I will strengthen you and help you; I will uphold you with my righteous right hand". *(Isaiah 41:10).*

"In addition to all this, take up the shield of faith, with which you can extinguish all the flaming arrows of the evil one. Take the helmet of salvation and the sword of the Spirit, which is the Word of God". (Ephesians 6:16-17)

The second way is to always add prayer when you are putting on the whole armor of God:

"Give thanks to the Lord, for He is good; His love endures forever. Let the redeemed of the Lord tell their story—those He redeemed from the hand of the foe". (Psalm 107:1-2).

"But as for me, I watch in hope for the Lord, I wait for God my Savior; my God will hear me. Do not gloat over me, my enemy! Though I have fallen, I will rise. Though I sit in darkness, the Lord will be my Light". (Micah 7:7-8).

The third way is to worship God until it drowns out Satan's deceitful words and he goes fleeing from your sight:

"Jesus said to him; ***'Away from me, Satan! For it is written: Worship the Lord your God, and serve Him only. Then the devil left Him, and angels came and attended Him'"***. *(Matthew 4:10-11).*

"I will praise you, Lord, with all my heart; before the 'gods' I will sing Your praise. I will bow down toward Your holy temple and will praise Your name

for Your unfailing love and Your faithfulness, for you have exalted your solemn decree that it surpasses your fame. When I called, you answered me; you greatly emboldened me. May all the kings of the earth praise you, Lord, when they hear what you have decreed. May they sing of the Lord, for the glory of the Lord is great. Though the Lord is exalted, He looks kindly on the lowly; though lofty, He sees them from afar. Though I walk in the midst of trouble, you stretch out your hand against the anger of my foes; with your right hand, you save me. The Lord will vindicate me; your love, Lord, endures forever—do not abandon the works of your hands". (Psalm 138:1-8).

"For you, Lord, are the Most High over all the earth; you are exalted far above all gods. Let those who love the Lord, hate evil, for He guards the lives of His faithful ones and delivers them from the hand of the wicked. Light shines on the righteous and joy on the upright in heart.

Rejoice in the Lord, you who are righteous, and praise His holy name". (Psalm 97:9-12).

Fourth way is to always meditate and speak the words of God, keeping them in your heart, so that you are always ready to defeat Satan and his ways:

"May these words of my mouth and this meditation of my heart, be pleasing in your sight, Lord, my Rock and my Redeemer" (Psalm 19:9).

Remember when walking with Jesus and living the way His Father intended is the best defense against Satan (who has no power against Jesus). Because it is said, "For the wages of sin is death, but the gift of God is eternal life in Christ Jesus our Lord". (Romans 6:23).

Here are some words that our Lord Jesus would like to share with you who believe in Him:

*"Jesus declared, **'I am the Bread of life. Whoever comes to Me will never go hungry, and whoever believes in Me will never be thirsty'".** (John 6:35).*

"'All those the Father gives Me will come to Me, and whoever comes to Me, I will never drive away. For I have come down from Heaven not to do My will but to do the will of Him who sent Me, and this is the will of Him who sent Me, that I shall lose none of all those He has given Me, but raise them on the last day. For My Father's will is that everyone who

looks to the Son and believes in Him shall have eternal life, and I will raise them up at the last day'". (John 6:37-40).

"'Very truly, I tell you, the one who believes has eternal life. I am the Bread of life'". (John 6:47-48).

"I am the living Bread that came down from Heaven. Whoever eats this Bread will live forever. This Bread is my flesh, which I will give for the life of the world". (John 6:51).

"Jesus said to them, 'Very truly I tell you, unless you eat the flesh of the Son of Man and drink His blood, you have no life in you. Whoever eats My flesh and drinks My blood has eternal life, and I will raise them up at the last day. For My flesh is real food and My blood is real drink. Whoever eats My flesh and drinks My blood remains in Me, and I in them. Just as the living Father sent Me and I live because of the Father, so the one who feeds on Me will live because of Me. This is the Bread that came down from Heaven. Your ancestors ate manna and died, but whoever feeds on this Bread will live forever'. He said this while teaching in the synagogue in Capernaum". (John 6:53-59).

"'Very truly, I tell you, whoever believes in Me will do the works I have been doing, and they will do even greater things than these, because I am going to the Father. And I will do whatever you ask in My Name, so that the Father may be Glorified in the Son. You may ask Me for anything in My name, and I will do it'". (John 14:12-14).

As you can see, in these few verses, it has been repeated many times that Jesus is the Bread of Life. Without Jesus, we die; without Jesus, we have no strength; and without Jesus, we have no relationship with His Father (our Creator and source of Love). Read these Scripture words to defeat the enemy (Satan):

"Dear children, do not let anyone lead you astray. The one who does what is right is righteous, just as He is righteous. The one who does what is sinful is of the devil, because the devil has been sinning from the beginning. The reason the Son of God appeared was to destroy the devil's work. No one who is born of God will continue to sin, because God's Seed remains in them; they cannot go on sinning, because they have been born of God. This is how we know who the children of God are and who the children of the devil are: Anyone who does not

do what is right is not God's child, nor is anyone who does not love their brother and sister. For this is the message you heard from the beginning: We should love one another". (1 John 3:7-11).

"Do not be surprised, my brothers and sisters, if the world hates you. We know that we have passed from death to life, because we love each other. Anyone who does not love remains in death. Anyone who hates a brother or sister is a murderer, and you know that no murderer has eternal life residing in him. This is how we know what love is: Jesus Christ laid down His life for us. And we ought to lay down our lives for our brothers and sisters". (1 John 3:13-16).

"The God of peace will soon crush Satan under your feet. The grace of our Lord Jesus be with you". (Romans 16:20).

"Therefore, put on the full Armor of God, so that when the day of evil comes, you may be able to stand your ground, and after you have done everything, to stand. Stand firm then, with the Belt of Truth buckled around your waist, with the Breastplate of Righteousness in place, and with your feet fitted with the Readiness that comes from the Gospel of Peace. In addition to all this, take up the shield of faith, with which you can extinguish all the flaming arrows of the evil one. Take the Helmet of Salvation and the Sword of the Spirit, which is the Word of God, and pray in the Spirit on all occasions with all kinds of prayers and requests. With this in mind, be alert and always keep on praying for all the Lord's people". (Ephesians 6:13-18).

"Get rid of all bitterness, rage and anger, brawling and slander, along with every form of malice. Be kind and compassionate to one another, forgiving each other, just as in Christ God forgave you". (Ephesians 4:31-32).

"And do not give the devil a foothold". (Ephesians 4:27).

"Submit yourselves, then, to God. Resist the devil, and he will flee from you. Come near to God and He will come near to you. Wash your hands, you sinners, and purify your hearts, you double-minded". (James 4:7-8).

"Cast all your anxiety on Him because He cares for you. Be alert and of sober mind. Your enemy the devil prowls around like a roaring lion looking for someone to devour. Resist him, standing firm in the faith, because you know that the family of believers throughout the world is undergoing the same kind of sufferings. In addition, the God of all grace, who called you to His Eternal Glory in Christ, after you have suffered a little while, will Himself restore you *and make you strong, firm and steadfast. To Him be the power forever and ever. Amen" (1 Peter 5:7-11).*

"Do not gloat over me, my enemy! Though I have fallen, I will rise. Though I sit in darkness, the Lord will be my light". (Micah 7:8).

"Give thanks to the Lord, for He is good; His love endures forever. Let the redeemed of the Lord tell their story—those He redeemed from the hand of the foe". (Psalm 107:1-2).

Just knowing that the Lord God Almighty equips us with Words that sends Satan fleeing from our sight is enough to walk with confidence through the shadows of this cold and cruel world. I know for sure that my Lord Jesus has been fighting my battles for me all my life. I know I would have been dead a long, long time ago. When the protection of the Star Team is with you (even though you cannot see Him), life is like a walk in the park, with the birds singing, and the ways of this world cannot phase you. We are so weighed down by all kinds of deadwood, such as disobedience and idolatry that accumulates over the years that these deadwoods break God's heart. When God sees that we are not listening to Him, He sends a message to our hearts, cleansing our hearts of any decay that Satan placed there. The message may come in harsh words, through someone that God uses to bring His message or the message may come through an illness that brings you to your knees, asking for healing and forgiveness. No matter what the message, God will shine the His Light of Repentance to get you back on the path to His Kingdom. The Holy Spirit will always alert you that something is wrong. We just need to understand the message that He is sending. We must seek God and repent of our sins.

When God chooses to burn out the deadwood in your life, you may feel a lot of pain in the process. Do not fight it or turn away from it. Learn from it. Get on your knees and ask God to give you strength and patiently wait for the renewed strength and the healing.

When I feel any kind of pain dwelling up inside, I pick up my Bible, opening it to the Book of Psalms. There, is where I find my healing and strength. King David did, but he did not have a Bible as we have to open up to. David went to the source—God Himself, the One who restores hurt and bruised hearts. When David went through the shadows, God was with him; he was never alone. You too can have that closeness, just keep on holding on to Jesus's Hand, and you will never walk alone.

Here is one of my favorite verses from the Book of Psalms:

"For you are great and do marvelous deeds; you alone are God. Teach me your way, O Lord, and I will walk in your truth. Give me an undivided heart, that I may fear your name. I will praise you, O Lord, my God, with all my heart; I will glorify your name forever. For great is your love toward me; You have delivered me from the depths of the grave". (Psalms 86:10-13).

I will learn from no one else but the Star Team, learning of who Jesus is and how He overcame this cruel and angry world. Christians are only to point to the way to Eternal Life; and let Jesus (the Way) teach them how to walk through the journey that is before us.

The words 'Eternal Life' are words that explain how we will live with God. Abiding and Accepting Jesus's Teaching of His Wisdom and Knowledge to stay firm on the Path of Righteous Living. I get so full of gratitude and praise when I pray in the Presence of my Heavenly Father that many times I am speechless, only to say thank you.

With all that is happening on this earth, God's Plan is for His children to turn away from their sin and turn to Him and His Loving Embrace of Love, Hope, and Peace. It is His Glory and Victory, even if just one person turns to His Life Eternal!

"Strengthen the feeble hands, steady the knees that give way; say to those with fearful hearts, 'Be strong, do not fear; your God will come, He will come with vengeance; with divine retribution He will come to save you'". (Isaiah 35:3-4).

"And a highway will be there; it will be called the Way of Holiness; it will be for those who walk on that Way. The unclean will not journey on it; wicked fools will not go about it". (Isaiah 35:8).

Live first in God's Presence. This awareness will increase your ability to give love and encouragement, making your relationships with your loved ones much stronger. God's Peace will ease the pains of this world and keep you from being overwhelmed. The Narrow Path that is right before you, it is the way to follow, wholeheartedly. In addition, you will experience that Abundant Life of Peace that Jesus teaches us, as He leads us down that Path.

"Blessed are those who have learned to acclaim you, and who walk in the light of your presence, Lord. They rejoice in your name all day long; they celebrate your righteousness. For you are their glory and strength, and by your favor you exalt our horn". (Psalm 89:15-16, 17).

"I keep my eyes always on the Lord. With Him at my right hand, I will not be shaken. Therefore my heart is glad and my tongue rejoices; my body also will rest secure". (Psalm 16:8, 9).

"Grace to you and peace be multiplied in the knowledge of God and of Jesus our Lord". (2 Peter 1:2).

To draw closer to God, you must study and apply His Word, giving God your undivided attention. To do this, you have to read God's instruction book—the Bible—all sixty-six books. It will nurture your relationship with Him and teach you how to live a godly life that pleases God and not man.

Six Personality Traits of God

Who is God?

God is Knowledgeable. Not only can we know about Him, but also we can know Him intimately.

"This is what the Lord says: 'Let not the wise boast of their wisdom, or the strong boast of their strength, or the rich boast of their riches. But let the one who boasts boast about this: that they have the understanding to know Me, that I am the Lord, who exercises kindness, justice and righteousness on earth,' declares the Lord".(Jeremiah 9:23-24).

Who is God?

God is Approachable. God invites us Himself to talk with Him on what concerns us. We do not need to become organized first. It is His Nature to be Loving and Accepting when we call on Him. As long as we go to Him and call on Him in truth and love.

"The Lord is near to all who call on Him, to all who call on Him in truth. He fulfills the desires of those who fear Him; He hears their cry and saves them". (Psalm 145:18-19).

Who is God?

God is Creative. God can use His Mighty Power to create ways to make us understand what He wants us to do. This Power has no limit. Only God can create the way He creates.

"Great is our Lord and mighty in power; His understanding has no limit. The Lord sustains the humble but casts the wicked to the ground". (Psalm 147:5-6).

"I lift up my eyes to the mountains—where does my help come from? My help comes from the Lord, the Maker of heaven and earth". (Psalm 121:1-2).

Who is God?

<u>God is Forgiveness</u>. God forgives us the moment we confess and repent of our sins to Him.

"Who forgives all your iniquity, who heals all your diseases". (Psalm 103:3).

"I, I am He who blots out your transgressions for my own sake, and I will not remember your sins". (Isaiah 43:25)

"But with You there is forgiveness, that You may be feared". (Psalms 130:4).

"I acknowledged my sin to You, and I did not cover my iniquity; I said, 'I will confess my transgressions to the Lord,' and you forgave the iniquity of my sin. Selah". (Psalm 32:5).

"For You, O Lord, are good and forgiving, abounding in steadfast love to all who call upon you". (Psalm 86:5).

"I will cleanse them from all the guilt of their sin against Me, and I will forgive all the guilt of their sin and rebellion against Me". (Jeremiah 33:8).

"If we confess our sins, He is faithful and just to forgive us our sins and to cleanse us from all unrighteousness". (1 John 1:9).

Who is God?

<u>God is Honest</u>. God clearly talks to us about Himself. He always speaks honestly in everything He does. Every promise, thought, perception, and mercy are true and can be fully trusted.

"Your Word is a Lamp for my feet, a Light on my path". (Psalm 119:105).

"The unfolding of your words gives light; it gives understanding to the simple" (Psalm 119:130).

"Turn to me and have mercy on me, as you always do to those who love your name. Direct my footsteps according to your word; let no sin rule over me. Redeem me from human oppression, that I may obey your precepts". (Psalm 119:132-134).

"You are Righteous, Lord, and your laws are right". (Psalm 119:137).

Who is God?

<u>God is Capable</u>. God is always and 100 percent right about everything. His wisdom is unlimited, in all situations, including the future that is to come. God is capable of doing everything that He does. God's motives are pure, and He never makes a mistake. God will never deceive us. God is capable to do the right thing all the time and every time. God can be trusted for all that He does.

"Show me your ways, Lord, teach me your path". (Psalm 25:4).

"He guides the humble in what is right and teaches them His way. All the ways of the Lord are Loving and Faithful toward those who keep the demands of His covenant" (Psalm 25:9-10).

I know that Jesus is right beside me right now taking my fears away and replacing the fears with strength to get me through what I need to do. All for His Father's glory. God is mightier than any man on this earth is. I can face anything with the help of my Lord Jesus. As the Bible says:

"With God all things are possible". (Matthew 19:20).

And

"When I am weak, He is strong". (2 Corinthians 12:10b).

Keeping these Scriptures in my heart will keep me strong and courageous, ready for anything that Satan throws at me. For Jesus will never leave me or forsake me. This I know is the truth. Jesus has always been there for me, even when I did not feel Him. Jesus loves me, this I know, because He told me so.

I thank my Heavenly Father for creating me the way He desires me to be. I am forever grateful! I am forever His!

Complaining: The Dangers and the Solutions

*T*here is one thing that really displeases God—our tendency to complain about how others are acting. Complaining about others is indirectly complaining about how God is acting. When you keep on complaining and complaining about others, you fail to keep God's Laws and Commands.

"Brothers and sisters do not slander one another. Anyone who speaks against a brother or sister or judges them speaks against the law and judges it. When you judge the law, you are not keeping it, but sitting in judgment on it. There is only one Lawgiver and Judge, the One who is able to save and destroy. But you, who are you to judge your neighbor?" (James 4:11-12).

"Do not grumble against one another, brothers and sisters, or you will be judged. The Judge is standing at the door!" (James 5:9).

Doing this (complaining) just opens the door to a deadly sin called self-pity and rage. Yeah, complaining leads to the sin of selfish behavior and anger. Because we live in a world that is full of anger and selfishness—where everyone is out to number one. The Scriptures on grumbling makes it clear that God despises complaining (along with many others). Read Proverbs 6:16-19, it says:

"There are six things the Lord hates, seven that are detestable to Him: haughty eyes, a lying tongue, hands that shed innocent blood, a heart that devises wicked schemes, feet that are quick to rush into evil, a false witness who pours out lies and a person who stirs up conflict in the community". (Proverbs 6:16-19).

Place these words in your heart and mind, and you will be able to live the life God desires us to live. Also, make sure you add Faith, Hope, Trust, and (most important) Love. As we trust Jesus with the things that are happening on this earth, He will refresh us in His light of everlasting love and walk

246

(or carry) us through the fire without us getting consumed in the fires of this angry and selfish world. Trying to be self-sufficient and living without Jesus's help is the beginning for Satan to slip in unnoticed. I myself will continue to be dependent on Jesus for everything and every moment. Jesus will always be with me, teaching me how to handle any problem that arises. I just have to continually believe and trust in Him and always seek His help to face each day I walk at His side.

Here are some Scriptures to meditate on, hold on to, and keep you on the Righteous Path:

"I will refresh the weary and satisfy the faint". (Jeremiah 31:25).

"Do everything without grumbling or arguing, so that you may become blameless and pure, 'children of God without fault in a warped and crooked generation.' Then you will shine among them like stars in the sky as you hold firmly to the word of life. And then I will be able to boast on the day of Christ that I did not run or labor in vain". (Philippians 2:14-16).

"Do not fret because of those who are evil or be envious of those who do wrong; for like the grass they will soon wither, like green plants they will soon die away. Trust in the Lord and do good; dwell in the land and enjoy safe pastures. Take delight in the Lord, and he will give you the desires of your heart. Commit your way to the Lord; trust in him and he will do this: He will make your righteous reward shine like the dawn, your vindication like the noonday sun. Be still before the Lord and wait patiently for him; do not fret when people succeed in their ways, when they carry out their wicked schemes. Refrain from anger and turn from wrath; do not fret—it leads only to evil. For those who are evil will be destroyed, but those who hope in the Lord will inherit the land". (Psalm 37:1-9).

"And my God will meet all your needs according to the riches of His glory in Christ Jesus".(Philippians 4:19).

Jesus has lifted me up out of the dark, lonely, slimy pit that I was in and brought me into His marvelous light. I rest assured in the knowledge that I am complete in Him (and only Him)—the giver of life. I will never lose sight of His presence, no matter what goes on in this crazy world. However, I have to continually not see myself through the eyes of other people because this dampens any desire to please God. Only the eyes of God is the eyes I should be looking through, for He sees me as His creation of love. Every day I struggle with this to stay focused on how God sees me and not the way others see me. All my life I had other people telling me how I should be, not realizing how God sees me and wants me to be for Him and only Him. God is the one who designed me. God is the one who tells (teaches) me how to live this life on this earth. When I finally opened the door to Jesus to come into my life, He sat down with me and told me what I was doing wrong. Jesus is teaching me that to see myself through His Father's eyes brings joy and peace to me. I now know (when others try to change me), I remember how my Heavenly Father sees me and how He loves me just how He designed me. I also take time to be still in God's presence and let Him be whom He is, letting Him work His fruits into me, enabling me to face the challenges of my daily life on this earth. I enjoy sitting with my Star Team, talking out all that concerns me.

Some Scriptures that God tells me to read to keep me focused on Him and the treasures in heaven:

"Yes, my soul, find rest in God; my hope comes from Him. Truly, He is my rock and my salvation; He is my fortress, I will not be shaken. My salvation and my honor depend on God; He is my mighty rock, my refuge. Trust in Him at all times, you people; pour out your hearts to

Him, for God is our refuge". (Psalm 62:5-8).

"Dear friends, I urge you, as foreigners and exiles, to abstain from sinful desires, which wage war against your soul. Live such good lives among the pagans that, though they accuse you of doing wrong, they may see your good deeds and glorify God on the day He visits us". (1 Peter 2:11-12).

"Don't be deceived, my dear brothers and sisters. Every good and perfect gift is from above, coming down from the Father of the Heavenly Lights, who does not change like shifting shadows. He chose to give us birth through the word of truth that we are a kind of first-fruits of all He created. My dear brothers and sisters, take note of this: Everyone should be quick to listen, slow to speak and slow to become angry, because human anger does not produce the righteousness that God desires. Therefore, get rid of all moral filth and the evil that is so prevalent and humbly accept the word planted in you, which can save you. Do not merely

listen to the word, and so deceive yourselves. Do what it says". (James 1:16-22).

*"**I am the Alpha and the Omega'**, says the Lord God, **'who is, and who was, and who is to come, the Almighty'**". (Revelation 1:8).*

"Now faith is confidence in what we hope for and assurance about what we do not see. This is what the ancients were commended for". (Hebrews 11:1-2).

"Without faith it is impossible to please God, because anyone who comes to Him must believe that He exists and that He rewards those who earnestly seek Him". (Hebrews 11:6).

"Yet a time is coming and has now come when the true worshipers will worship the Father in the Spirit and in truth, for they are the kind of worshipers the Father seeks. God is spirit, and His worshipers must worship in the Spirit and in truth". (John 4:23-24).

*"Come and see what the Lord has done, the desolations He has brought on the earth. He makes wars cease to the ends of the earth. He breaks the bow and shatters the spear; He burns the shields with fire. He says, **'Be still and know I am God; I will be exalted among the nations,***

***I will be exalted on the earth. The Lord Almighty is with us; the God of Jacob is our fortress'**". (Psalm 46:8-11).*

"The Lord bless you and keep you; the Lord make his face shine on you and be gracious to you and give you peace". (Numbers 6:24-26).

"May the Lord make your love increase and overflow for each other and for everyone else, just as ours does for you. May He strengthen your hearts so that you will be blameless and holy in the presence of our God and Father when our Lord Jesus comes with all His holy ones". (1 Thessalonians 3:12-13).

"Your word is a lamp for my feet, a light on my path". (Psalm 119:105).

The sacrifice of suffering patiently brings good to all. Do not run from the pain of your circumstances or even try to hide from your circumstances. God's Purpose for suffering is to draw us closer to Him, because when we enter into God's presence, we will find the comfort that surpasses all suffering. Jesus always went away from the crowds to get His Father's comfort.

"Consider it pure joy, my brothers and sisters, whenever you face trials of many kinds, because you know that the testing of your faith produces perseverance. Let

perseverance finish its work so that you may be mature and complete, not lacking anything". (James 1:2-4).

"Let them give thanks to the Lord for His unfailing love and His wonderful deeds for mankind. Let them sacrifice thank offerings and tell of His works with songs of joy". (Psalm 107:21-22).

A rest for the weary: *"Come to me, all you who are weary and burdened, and I will give you rest. Take my yoke upon you and learn from me, for I am gentle and humble in heart, and you will find rest for your souls. For my yoke is easy and my burden is light". (Matthew 11:28-30).*

I accept each day as God gives me as a gift from Him, exactly as the day is presented to me, trusting Him to be faithful to walk with me through all my trials (good and bad). Relaying on God is the best choice I could have ever made. God's empowering presence is all I need to keep me strong enough to face the battle, especially on the days that I feel too weak to even get up and out of bed.

When discouragement creeps in and tries to run me off the path to a righteous living with Jesus, I hold on to this statement: "For when I am weak, Jesus is strong." Lately, I have been saying this statement a lot. However, as soon as I say it, discouragement flees from me.

Here are some more Scripture verses that make discouragement flee:

"Deep calls to deep in the roar of your waterfalls; all your waves and breakers have swept over me. By day the Lord directs His love, at night His song is with me—a prayer to the God of my life". (Psalm 42:7-8).

"For we cannot do anything against the Truth, but only for the Truth. We are glad whenever we are weak but you are strong; and our prayer is that you may be fully restored". (2 Corinthians 13:8-9).

*"**This is the covenant I will make with the people of Israel after that time**', declares the Lord. '**I will put my Laws in their minds and write it in their hearts. I will be their God, and they will be my people. No longer will they teach their neighbor, or say to one another, 'Know the Lord',** because they will all know me, from the greatest',* declares the Lord. '**For I will forgive their wickedness and will remember their sins no more**'".

(Jeremiah 31:33-34).

Every morning that I wake up, I am like the early bird at dawn (to catch the best worm), to be ready and fully awake and alert, to receive the skills that God gives me, to slice through the evil that approaches me, throughout my day. I am never alone in facing the evils of this world. I always will have my Lord Jesus by my side.

Living in the Presence of God

I always wondered what it takes to live in God's presence. Therefore, I went to the Bible to see what God's Word says about it:

"Ask, and it will be given to you. Seek, and you will find. Knock and it will be opened for you. For everyone who asks, He who seeks finds. To him who knocks it will be opened". (Matthew 7:7-8).

"If you remain in me, and my words remain in you, you will ask whatever you desire, and it will be done for you". (John 15:7).

"Humble yourselves in the sight of the Lord, and he will exalt you". (James 4:10).

"You make known to me the Path of Life; You will fill me with Joy in Your Presence, with Eternal Pleasures at Your Right Hand". (Psalm 16:11).

"As a deer pants for streams of water, so my soul pants for you, my God. My soul thirsts for God, for the living God. When can I go and meet with God?" (Psalm 42:1-2).

"In Him and through faith in Him, we may approach God with freedom and confidence". (Ephesians 3:12).

"Let us then approach God's throne of grace with confidence, so that we may receive mercy and find grace to help us in our time of need". (Hebrews 4:16).

"Seek the Lord while He may be found; call on Him while He is near". (Isaiah 55:6).

"Come near to God and He will come near to you. Wash your hands, you sinners, and purify your hearts, you double-minded". (James 4:8).

"My flesh and heart may fail, but God is the strength of my heart and my portion forever. Those who are far from You will perish; You destroy all who

are unfaithful to you. But as for me, it is good to be near God. I have made the Sovereign Lord my refuge; I will tell of all your deeds". (Psalm 73:26-28).

"Surely Your Goodness and Love will follow me all the days of my life, and I will dwell in the House of the Lord forever". (Psalm 23:6).

"Repent, then, and turn to God, so that your sins may be wiped out, that times of refreshing may come from the Lord". (Acts 3:19).

"And God says: Be still and know I am God. I will be exalted among the nations. I will be exalted among the earth". (Psalm 46:10).

Rebellious and resentment tendencies bring the gray clouds that hang over my head, hindering any joy and blessings that God has for me. However, when I take those rebellious and resentment tendencies to God and talk them over with Him, the gray clouds suddenly fade away. This is what happens when you and I spend time in God's Presence.

I know that Jesus loves me and abides in me. The proof is when He died on the cross for me. Jesus will always be at my side whenever I want Him to help me fight the arrows that Satan throws my way. All I need to do is reach out for His hand and whisper His name. The moment I do that, the arrows go flying away from me.

Lately, I found out that I was holding in resentment and feelings that have been weighing me down with a heaviness that I was unable to even move or even see the joy that God was revealing to me. God did not create me to live in resentment and regret; He created me (us) to live in His Joy. Jesus did not die for me (us) to turn away from Him, leaving Him to stand alone, without a place to live. I (we) have to stop holding onto resentment and regret and start holding on to Jesus's Hand (holding on tightly) and walk along this journey with Him and never feel lonely again. No matter what I go through, I can always count on Jesus for His companionship, to be willing and ready to give me comfort, advice, and most of all His love. Those gray clouds might hang around, but they do not have to affect me. For I walk in the light of Jesus, to change that gray into bright yellow, making me walk with a smile on my face and love in my heart.

Resentment is a feeling of anger or displeasure about someone or something unfair. After reading this about resentment, I had to go to my source for advice, that source is my Star Team (the Father, the Son, Jesus, and the Holy Spirit) if I had any resentment in me. It did not take long until God revealed to me that my resentment was when other people spoke to me as if I was a small child who does not know how to solve a problem. He also taught me how to get rid of that resentment from my inner being and get on with my walk with Him. Since then, I started to pull out that root of resentment that was causing the problems. I found out how to let go of the problem and walk with confidence alongside my Star Team.

I was then led to open my Bible, and start reading all the Scriptures about resentment and its cause. I sure found many causes of resentment.

Here are some of what I found:

Disagreement—

"Live such good lives among the pagans that, though they accuse you of doing wrong, they may see your good deeds and glorify God on the day He visits us". (1 Peter 2:12).

"Brothers and sisters do not slander one another. Anyone who speaks against a brother or sister or judges them speaks against the law and judges it. When you judge the law, you are not keeping it, but sitting in judgment on it" (James 4:11-12).

Being Deceived—

"Do not believe every spirit, but test the spirits to see whether they are from God, because many false prophets have gone out into the world". (1 John 4:1).

"See to it that no one takes you captive through hollow and deceptive philosophy, which depends on human tradition and the basic principles of this world rather than on Christ". (Colossians 2:8).

"If we claim to be without sin, we deceive ourselves and the truth is not in us". (1 John 8).

Feeling of being left out—

"I am forgotten by them as though I were dead; I have become like broken

pottery. For I hear the slander of many; there is terror on every side; they conspire against me and plot to take my life". (Psalm 31:12-13).

"Look to my right and see; no one is concerned for me. I have no refuge; no one cares for my life". (Psalm 142:4).

*"**'You believe at last'.** Jesus answered. **'But a time is coming, and has come, when you will be scattered, each to his own home. You will leave Me all alone. Yet I am not alone, for My Father is with Me'**". (John 16:31-32).*

Favoritism (God forbids favoritism)—

"My brothers and sisters, believers in our glorious Lord Jesus Christ must not show favoritism". (James 2:1).

"Listen, my dear brothers and sisters; has not God chosen those who are poor in the eyes of the world to be rich in faith and to inherit the kingdom He promised those who love Him?" (James 2:5).

"If you really keep the royal law found in Scripture, 'Love your neighbor as yourself',you are doing right" (James 2:8).

"Speak and act as those who are going to be judged by the law that gives freedom, because judgment without mercy will be shown to anyone who has not been merciful. Mercy triumphs over judgment". (James 2:12-13).

"Then Peter began to speak: 'I now realize how true it is that God does not show favoritism but accepts from every nation the one who fears Him and does what is right'" (Acts 10:34-35).

"Serve wholeheartedly, as if you were serving the Lord, not people, because you know that the Lord will reward each one for whatever good they do, whether they are slave or free". (Ephesians 6:7-8).

Envy or Jealousy—

"Do not fret because of those who are evil or be envious of those who do wrong; for like the grass they will soon wither, like green plants they will soon die away". (Psalm 37:1-2).

"Commit your way to the Lord; trust in Him and He will do this: He will make your righteous reward shine like the dawn, your vindication like the noonday sun. Be still before the Lord and wait patiently for Him; do not fret

when people succeed in their ways, when they carry out their wicked schemes. Refrain from anger and turn from wrath; do not fret—it leads to evil. For those who are evil will be destroyed, but those who hope in the Lord will inherit the land". (Psalm 37:5-9).

"Do not envy the violent or choose any of their ways. For the Lord detests the perverse but takes the upright in His confidence". (Proverb 31:31-32).

"Do not let your heart envy sinners, but always be zealous for the fear of the Lord. There is surely a future hope for you, and you hope will not be cut off ". (Proverbs 17-18).

These are just some of the causes of resentment. The Bible speaks of much, much more.

Once I started reading all these causes, I turned to Jesus and asked Him, How do I handle this resentment that is in me? And He answered with one word, 'Love' You see, you build up love and forgiveness in your life until the feeling of resentment and regret can no longer stand; they will flee from your side. This is what love (God) does in your life. We must remember this: God's love is the only shield that wards off Satan's tactics of destruction. So when Satan starts approaching you with those burning arrows, just throw back at him God's words from the Bible. Satan hates it when you speak God's Words. Here are some verses that you can start with. Once you start searching the Bible on your own, you will find more that will fit your circumstances. Just like I did.

The Power of the Word of God

"The mouth of the righteous is a fountain of life, but the mouth of the wicked conceals violence. Hatred stirs up conflict, but love covers over all wrongs. Wisdom is found, on the lips of the discerning, but a rod is for the back of one who has no sense. The wise store up knowledge, but the mouth of a fool invites ruin.". (Proverbs 10:11-14).

"In the morning, as they went along, they saw the fig tree withered from the roots. Peter remembered and said to Jesus, 'Rabbi, look! The fig tree you cursed has withered!' 'Have faith in God,' Jesus answered. 'Truly, I tell you, if anyone says to this mountain, "Go, throw yourself in the sea," and does not doubt in their heart but believes that what they say will happen, it will be done for

them. Therefore, I tell you, whatever you ask for in prayer, believe that you have received it, and it will be yours'". (Mark 11:20-24).

"When you heard about Christ and were taught in Him in accordance with the truth that is in Jesus. You were taught, with regard to your former way of life, to put off your old self, which is being corrupted by its deceitful desires; to be made new in the attitude of your minds; and to put on the new self, created to be like God in true righteousness and holiness. Therefore, each of you must put off falsehood and speak truthfully to your neighbor, for we are all members of one body. In your anger do not sin: Do not let the sun go down while you are still angry, and do not give the devil a foothold" (Ephesians 4:20-27).

"Do not let any unwholesome talk come out of your mouths, but only what is helpful for building up according to their needs, that it may benefit those who listen. In addition, do not grieve the Holy Spirit of God, with whom you were sealed, for the day of redemption. Get rid of all bitterness, rage and anger, brawling and slander, along with every form of malice. Be kind and compassionate to one another, forgiving each other, just as in Christ God forgave you". (Ephesians 4:29-32).

"Make sure that nobody pays back wrong for wrong, but always strive to do what is good for each other and for everyone else. Rejoice always; pray continually; give thanks in all circumstances; for this is God's will for you in Christ Jesus". (1 Thessalonians 5:15-18).

"You too, be patient and stand firm, because the Lord's coming is near. Do not grumble against one another, brothers and sisters, or you will be judged. The judge is standing at the door! Above all, my brothers and sisters do not swear— not by heaven or by earth or by anything else. All you need to say is a simple 'Yes' or 'No.' Otherwise, you will be condemned. Is anyone among you in trouble? Let them pray. Is anyone happy? Let them sing songs of praise" (James 4:8-9, 12-13).

Negative Emotions

S truggling with negative emotions is a lifelong battle. For they are weapons of Satan, where he will use them. I know this because Satan has been using them to trip me up and bring me down all my life. Even now, Satan is trying to discourage me from finishing this book with his web of lies. However, I am confident that I have the best weapon to fight Satan with, and that is God's Word and His Son Jesus Christ. We all know that Jesus defeated Satan. For this reason, Satan does not like it when we ask Jesus for help, because Satan knows the power of Jesus, and nothing can break Him. Start today and begin to let God free you from all negative emotions so you can walk every step of this journey with Jesus. Taking that first step is not as hard as it seems. When you keep your eyes fixed on Jesus, your brokenness turns to wholeness, and failure turns to true success. Only Jesus can help you with this battle of negative emotions, for He defeated Satan who hurls those arrows of negative emotions.

The battle that we have against Satan is one that we have to accept while we are on this earth that Satan prowls around on, thinking that he is powerful, but we know that he is powerless against the Star Team. We can feel strong and courageous with Jesus by our side. I just keep on telling myself these two truths from the Bible:

> "The Lord restores my soul and leads me on the right path". (Psalm 23:3).
>
> "When I am weak He is strong". (2 Corinthians 12:10b).

There is no one else that can make you strong enough to walk this journey. Walking down any other path takes you in the wrong direction and makes the journey to wholeness a very, very, very long journey.

Here are three important steps to free you of negative emotions:

Step 1—Put God first in everything. Say, "Lord, I will serve you and not my emotions".

Step 2—Fortify yourself with the Word of God. Say, "Lord, you say your word has greater influence in my heart than my own feelings and words".

Step 3—Pray about everything. Say, "Lord, I refuse to give place to negative emotions, so I pray you will help me in fading them away. Thank you for protecting my heart and mind and giving me peace in the process".

Saying these three steps (as I did) might seem uncomfortable but it took a lot of courage to remove those negative words and receive the comfort of our Lord God and Savior that lasts forever. I never again felt uncomfortable for doing what my Lord God tells me to do. I was tired of feeling shameful and degraded and uneasy. However, Jesus changed all that, and now, I can walk confidently, pushing through those hurtful words and singing praise to my Lord God.

I will end this section with a prayer of power that helped me through my difficult times of negative emotions:

Father, today I refuse all depression, anxiety, fear, dread, anger, and sadness. For I know that they are not from You. With Your Help, Lord, I can resist any negative emotions and temptations that are in my life, as You open my eyes to all the Good that is in You. Keep me in Your Presence at all times, no matter what is going on in my life. I place my life in Your Hands and trust You that You will carry me through this wall of negative emotions. Your Mercy and Joy fills up within my heart and strengthens me to fight this battle of negative emotions. I look to You and not to my problems. Help me see that this battle will deepen my roots in You. Bring me closer to You, and keep me strong. Thank You, Lord, ever so much for letting me live in Your Light and Strength instead of the pit of darkness that the negative emotions had me in. I feel assured that I can call on You at any time, to save me out of my sea of negative emotions. Thank you for giving me the Garment of Praise to take away the spirit of heaviness. In Your Presence, I rest. In Your Joy, I delight. In Jesus's Name, I pray. Amen

Here are some Words of Power that helped me with my negative emotions:

"The lions may grow weak and hungry, but those who seek the Lord lack no

good thing". (Psalm 34:10).

"Whoever of you loves life and desires to see many good days, keep your tongue from evil and your lips from speaking lies. Turn from evil and do good; seek peace and pursue it". (Psalm 34:12-14).

"The Lord is close to the brokenhearted and saves those who are crushed in spirit. A righteous person may have many troubles, but the Lord delivers him from them all; He protects all his bones, not one of them will be broken". (Psalm 34:18-20).

"Evil will slay the wicked; the foes of the righteous will be condemned. The Lord will rescue His servants; no one who takes refuge in Him will be condemned". (Psalm 34:21-22).

"**Those who plunder you will be plundered; all who make spoil of you, I will despoil. But I will restore you to health and heal your wounds'**, declares the Lord, '**because you are called an outcast, Zion for whom no one cares'**". (Jeremiah 30:16b, 17).

"When I called, you answered me: you made me bold and stouthearted". (Psalm 138:3).

"Though I walk in the midst of trouble, You preserve my life; You stretch out Your Hand against the anger of my foes, with Your Right Hand You save me. The Lord will fulfill His Purpose for me; Your Love, O Lord, endures forever—do not abandon the works of Your Hands". (Psalm 138:7-8).

"The Lord is my shepherd; I lack nothing. He makes me lie down in green pastures, He leads me beside quiet waters, He refreshes my soul. He Guides me along the Paths of Righteousness for His Name's sake. Even though I walk through the darkest valley, I will fear no evil, for You are with me; Your Rod and Your Staff, they comfort me. You prepare a table before me in the presence of my enemies. You anoint my head with oil ; my cup overflows. Surely Your Goodness and Love will follow me all the days of my life, and will dwell in the House of the Lord forever".

(Psalm 23: 1-6).

"I love those who love Me, and those who seek Me find Me. With Me are riches and honor, enduring wealth and prosperity. My fruit is better than fine gold; what I yield surpasses choice silver". (Proverbs 8:17-19).

"Light shines on the godly, and joy on those whose hearts are right". (Psalm 97:11).

The Passion to Know God (to Seek Wholeheartedly)

What does it take to have a strong passion to know God?

First, you have to have an eagerness and a desire to want to know God, the Father and His Son Jesus Christ. To do this, you must seek deeper and deeper into the Bible (God's Word)—where you will find all you need to know about the God that we serve. In addition, you must answer that knocking at your heart's door, to let Jesus into your life and walk with you through the shadows of this world.

Second, you have to demonstrate a steadfast commitment to God, building an intimate relationship with Him.

Third, you have to make it a top priority to know God and to love Him with your whole heart and soul, making quiet time with Him, number 1 above anything else in this world, letting you receive all instructions of how to stay in obedience to Him. Make prayer a place of listening to God rather than complaining to Him. Bring your requests to the Father and then listen for His response. Speaking too many words in prayer sometimes blocks out the words that God is trying to speak to you. As the Bible says:

"Sin is not ended by multiplying words, but the prudent hold their tongues". (Proverbs 10:19).

"Those who guard their lips preserve their lives, but those who speak rashly will come to ruin". (Proverbs 13:3).

Fourth, you have to push aside all the desires of this world and walk with Jesus wholeheartedly, with no looking back on old failures. Exchange your sorrows for joy, your failures for success, your wounds for healing. Trust and Believe that God will change your mistakes and flaws into good. He is your sculptor, and He is always going to fix those flaws. As long as you go to Him and ask Him to change you, God will never cast you aside for trash. He takes you into His arms and wipes your tears, cleaning away those flaws and faults, exchanging them to resemble His image. There may be some aches while He does this exchanging, but in the end, you will shine in His glory. Our Heavenly Father is a loving Father and knows just how to "fix" us.

All we have to do is to walk with Him and His Son Jesus down the path of righteousness. This simple action shows that you want to get to know Him and have a relationship with Him. Staying close with

Jesus is an act of spiritual worship that is pleasing to His Father.

Resting in God's presence with joy and confidence gives us the assurance of God's unconditional love, which is never forced upon us. I cannot wait for the day when all I will be doing is sitting at Jesus's feet and listening to all He has to say. Praise be to my Heavenly

Father God and Lord Jesus Christ and the Holy Spirit.

"Greater love has no one than this: to lay down one's life for one's friends. You are my friends if you do what I command". (John 15:13-14).

"For everything that I learned from my Father I have made known to you. You did not choose me, but I chose you and appointed you so that you might go and bear fruit—fruit that will last—and so that whatever you ask in my name the Father will give you. This is my command: Love each other" (John 15:15-17).

"The Lord your God is with you, the Mighty Warrior who saves. He will take great delight in you; in His love He will no longer rebuke you, but will rejoice over you with singing". (Zephaniah 3:17).

I will always seek to know more about my God and Savior Jesus Christ, for He is my strength when I am weak and He always answers my cry for help. There is no one on this earth that is a better friend than Jesus Christ.

Timely Words—To Speak or Not To Speak

*T*iming is everything, according to the Bible; a word can refresh when you need that good word. However, the timing might not be good, so then, you would be wiser to remain silent. This is called having self-control. The Bible says:

"Like a city whose walls are broken through, is a person who lacks self-control". (Proverbs 25:28).

"Set a guard over my mouth, Lord; keep watch over the door of my lips. Do not let my heart be drawn to what is evil". (Psalm 141:3-4a).

"My dear brothers and sisters, take note of this: Everyone should be quick to listen, slow to speak and slow to become angry, because human anger does not produce the righteousness that God desires. Therefore, get rid of all moral filth and the evil that is so prevalent and humbly accept the word planted in you, which can save you". (James 1:19-21).

"Those who guard their mouths and their tongues keep themselves from calamity". (Proverbs 21:23).

There are always going to be times in our lives when we will need those encouraging, comforting, and truthful words. Here are some words from the Bible (God's Words) that will help us to lift a hurtful person.

To Comfort

"The Lord Himself goes before you and will be with you; He will never leave you nor forsake you. Do not be afraid; do not be discouraged". (Deuteronomy 31:8).

"The Lord is a refuge for the oppressed, a stronghold in times of trouble. Those who know your name trust in you, for you, Lord, have never forsaken those who seek you". (Psalm 9:9-10).

"The Lord is my shepherd, I lack nothing. He makes me lie down in green pastures, He leads me beside quiet waters, and He refreshes my soul. He guides me along the right paths for His name's sake. Even though I walk through the darkest valley, I will fear no evil, for you are with me; your rod and your staff, they comfort me". (Psalm 23:1-4).

"Cast your cares on the Lord and He will sustain you; He will never let the righteous be shaken". (Psalm 55:22).

"Come to me, all you who are weary and burdened, and I will give you rest. Take my yoke upon you and learn from me, for you will find rest for your souls. For my yoke is easy and my burden is light". (Matthew 11:28-30).

To Encourage

"Peace I leave with you; my peace I give you. I do not give to you as the world gives. Do not let your hearts be troubled and do not be afraid". (John 14:27).

"I have told you these things, so that in me you may have peace. In this world, you will have trouble. However, take heart! I have overcome the world". (John 16:33).

"The mind governed by the flesh is death, but the mind governed by the Spirit is life and peace".

(Romans 8:6).

"Let your gentleness be evident to all. The Lord is near. Do not be anxious about anything, but in every situation, by prayer and petition, with thanksgiving, present your requests to God. And the Peace of God, which transcends all understanding, will guard your hearts and your minds in Christ Jesus". (Philippians 4:5-7).

"Let the peace of Christ rule in your hearts, since as members of one body you were called to peace. And be thankful". (Colossians 3:15).

To Walk In and Speak Truthful Words

"Lord, who may dwell in your sacred tent? Who may live on Your Holy Mountain? The one whose walk is blameless, who does what is righteous; who speaks the truth from their heart; whose tongue utters no slander, who does no wrong to a neighbor, and casts no slur on others; who despises a vile person but

honors those who fear the Lord; who keeps an oath even when it hurts, and does not change their mind; who lends money to the poor without interest; who does not accept a bribe against the innocent. Whoever does these things will never be shaken". (Psalm 15:1-5).

"These are the things you are to do: Speak the truth to each other, and render true and sound judgment in your courts; do not plot evil against each other, and do not love to swear falsely. I hate all this", declares the Lord". (Zechariah 8:16).

"Therefore, each of you must put off falsehood and speak truthfully to your neighbor, for we are all members of one body. In your anger do not sin: Do not let the sun go down while you are still angry, and do not give the devil a foothold". (Ephesians 4:25-27).

"If we claim to be without sin, we deceive ourselves and the truth is not in us. If we confess our sins, He is faithful and just and will forgive us our sins and purify us from all unrighteousness. If we claim we have not sinned, we make Him out to be a liar and His word is not in us". (1 John 1:8-10).

"Dear children, let us not love with words or speech but with actions and in truth". (1 John 3:18).

These words are only from God's awesome and pure heart, for these are the only words that He speaks. Satan, on the other hand, is the one who speaks those nasty and negative words, for this is why we feel so horrible when we speak those nasty and negative words. Sometimes, I feel like asking those people who speak negative words if they like feeling horrible for speaking so many nasty and negative words. I myself cannot even say one letter of a nasty word, without feeling dark and ugly. I know when I start feeling dark and ugly, I remember that Satan makes me feel that way, to shake me from speaking the positive and encouraging words of my Lord Jesus Christ. When speaking positive, loving, and encouraging words, you can definitely defeat the enemy, just as Jesus did.

There are many times when I would be speaking to someone, trying to help him or her with his or her problem, and as I would be in the middle of saying something to them, suddenly a word would catch my attention, a word that God would be saying to me. I would suddenly stop speaking (for a moment), changing my whole response to their problem. This is where I had to discern (very quickly and in my head). I had to see if the word was from God (encouraging and beautiful) or from Satan (negative and ugly). This was my moment of silence to ask for Jesus's help. When I was in school, my classmates said words that should not be said to me. The words were very hurtful, belittling, and demeaning. They were not holding their tongues and thinking before they spoke. They were listening to the enemy's voice, telling them to use mean (negative) words instead of nice (positive) words; they were lacking the self-control the Bible (God's Words) says for us to have.

"A man without self-control is like a city broken into and left without walls". (Proverbs 25:28).

In today's world, timing is everything, and everything has timing. When spoken hurtful words, they lead to gossip, and gossip leads to anger, and anger leads to sinning against God. Hurtful words, gossip, slander, and anger are sin in the eyes of God. We must restrain ourselves from hurtful words, gossip, slander, and anger; they only lead to destruction, which breaks God's heart when He hears His children acting and speaking in this way (the way of Satan). We should definitely live out what the Bible says to do:

"Everyone should be quick to listen, slow to become angry, for man's anger does not bring about the righteous life that God desires. Therefore, get rid of all moral filth and the evil that is so prevalent and humbly accept the Word planted in you, which can save you. Do not merely listen to the Word, and so deceive yourselves. Do what it says". (James 1:19-22).

When my classmates were saying all those nasty words, I would just stay quiet and walk away. I never did "get back" at them. I knew it was not my battle to fight; it was God's battle, and He did fight the battle and won. God took me out of the situation and gave me peace. There are three Scripture verses (from the Bible) that always play in my head at the times of the arrows of hurtful words that Satan throws my way:

"My flesh and my heart may fail, but God is the Strength of my heart and my Portion forever". (Psalm 73:26).

"Have I not commanded you? Be strong and courageous. Do not be

terrified; do not be discouraged, for the Lord your God will be with you wherever you go'". (Joshua 1:9).

"'Be still and know I am God. I will be exalted among the nations. I will be exalted in the earth'". (Psalm 46:10.

God has been speaking these words of truth, love, and encouragement to me all my life. The verses got me out of a lot of anguish and pain. When God revealed to me these words it made me realize that He sees, knows, and hears all that is happening to me. God calms the storm at the right time (His time) so I can praise Him in the storm and proclaim His love to others, giving Him the glory and victory.

Truths for the days you need to focus on instead of your problems.

*Truth—Remembering what Jesus did for you in your life.

"Therefore, there is now no condemnation for those who are in Christ Jesus, because through Christ Jesus the law of the Spirit of life set me free from the law of sin and death. For what the law was powerless to do in that it was weakened by the sinful nature, God did by sending His own Son in the likeness of sinful man to be a sin offering. And so He condemned sin in sinful man, in order that the righteous requirements of the law might be fully met in us, who do not live according to the sinful nature but according to the Spirit".(Romans 8:1-4).

Truths for the days you need to focus on instead of those negative emotions:

*Truth—The Holy Spirit gives you positive thoughts that lift you up not put you down.

"So letting your sinful nature control your mind leads to death. But letting the Spirit control your mind leads to life and peace". (Romans 8:6).

"When the Holy Spirit controls our lives, He will produce this kind of fruit in us: Love, Joy, Peace, Patience, Kindness, Goodness, Faithfulness, Gentleness, and Self-control. Against such things there is no law". (Galatians 5:22-23).

Truth—Having the ability to say no to those negative emotions and move forward and upward and not backward and downward into the pit of emptiness and darkness.

"Having the appearance of godliness, but denying its power. Avoid such people". (2 Timothy 3:5).

"Do you not know that you are God's temple and that God's Spirit dwells in you?". (1 Corinthians 3:16).

"Do not love the world or the things in the world. If anyone loves the world, the love of the Father is not in him". (1 John 2:15).

"I have seen you in the sanctuary and beheld your power and your glory. Because your love is better than life, my lips will glorify you. My soul clings to you; your right hand upholds me. They who seek my life will be destroyed; they will go down to the depths of the earth". (Psalm 63:2-3, 8-9).

Truth—Turning your thoughts to God's thoughts when negative emotions are all up in your face.

"Clothe yourselves with the Lord Jesus Christ, and do not think about how to gratify the desires of the sinful nature". (Romans 13:14).

"'For my thoughts are not your thoughts, neither are your thoughts my ways,' declares the Lord". (Isaiah 55:8).

*Truth—Focus on the reward that is waiting for us at the end of this journey that we are on.

"Blessed is the man who remains steadfast under trial, for when he has stood the test he will receive the crown of life, which God has promised to those who love Him" (James 1:12).

"For the Son of Man is going to come with His angels in the glory of His Father, and then He will repay each person according to what he has done". (Matthew 16:27).

"His master said to him, 'Well done, good and faithful servant. You have been faithful over a little; I will set you over much. Enter into the joy of your master". (Matthew 25:21).

*Truth—Remind yourself that God is good, loving, and with you always.

"But you, O Lord, are a compassionate and gracious God, slow to anger, abounding in love and faithfulness". (Psalm 86:15).

"See what kind of love the Father has given to us that we should be called children of God; and so we are. The reason why the world does not know us is that it did not know Him". (1 John 3:1).

"I love those who love me, and those who seek me diligently find me". (Proverbs 8:17).

*Truth—Trust that God will never stop loving you, no matter what the world says about you.

"Give thanks to the God of Heaven, for His steadfast love endures forever". (Psalm 136:26).

When you focus on God's Truth in the midst of trouble and despair, you are clinging to Hope (Jesus). And clinging to Jesus is the Anchor that you need to stay on the Righteous Path that leads to a place of refuge in the presence of God, where He lifts you up, refreshing you to the likeness of Him. Here are some Scriptures to lift you up and clear away those troubles and despairs that you are facing right now in this world. Our enemy, Satan, hates it when we use God's Word against him. There is nothing more satisfying than to have hope and a place of refuge that makes Satan flee from sight.

Hope in God is the weapon against the destruction and despair in this cold and angry world.

"Though I walk in the midst of trouble, you preserve my life; you stretch out your hand against the anger of my foes, with your right hand you save me. The Lord will fulfill His purpose for me; your love, O Lord, endures forever—do not abandon the works of your hands". (Psalm 138:7-8).

"The Lord your God is with you, He is mighty to save. He will take great delight in you, He will quiet you with His Love, He will rejoice over you with singing". (Zephaniah 3:17).

"Do not repay evil with evil or insult with insult. On the contrary, repay evil with blessing, because to this, you were called, so that you may inherit a blessing. For whoever would love life, and see good days must keep their tongue from evil, and their lips from deceitful speech. They must turn from evil and do good; they must seek peace, and pursue it. For the eyes of the Lord are on the righteous, and His ears are attentive to their prayer, but the face of the Lord is against those who

do evil". (1 Peter 3:9-12).

"The Voice of the Lord is over the waters; the God of Glory thunders, the Lord thunders over the mighty waters. The Voice of the Lord is Powerful; the Voice of the Lord is Majestic". (Psalm 29:3-4).

"The Voice of the Lord strikes with flashes of lighting". (Psalm 29:7).

"I waited patiently for the Lord; He turned to me and heard my cry. He lifted me out of the slimy pit, out of the mud and mire; He set my feet on a rock and gave me a firm place to stand. He put a new song in my mouth, a hymn of praise to our God. Many will see and fear the Lord and put their trust in Him. Blessed is the one who trusts in the Lord, who does not look to the proud, to those who turn aside to false gods. Many, Lord my God, are the wonders you have done, the things you planned for us. None can compare with you; were I to speak and tell of your deeds, they would be too many to declare". (Psalm 40:1-5).

"The Light of the righteous shines brightly, but the lamp of the wicked is snuffed out. Where there is strife, there is pride, but wisdom is found in those who take advice". (Proverbs 13:9-10).

"Whoever scorns instruction will pay for it, but whoever respects a command is rewarded. The teaching of the wise is a fountain of life, turning a person from the snares of death. Good judgment wins favor, but the way of the unfaithful leads to their destruction. All who are prudent act with knowledge, but fools expose their folly" (Proverbs 13:13-16).

"He hides me in His shelter when there is trouble. He keeps me hidden in His tent. He sets me high on a rock". (Psalm 27:5).

This is why we must stop worrying about the things of this world and start listening to the Voice of Truth. To live the Life of God's Love is to trust and obey, clinging to His Son Jesus and to His every Word that comes out of His mouth. Our God knows what is going on in this world, and He would never let anything harm us. I am continually running through my mind and heart these verses from Psalm 23:

"Even though I walk through the darkest valley, I will fear no evil, for you are with me; your rod and your staff, they comfort me....Surely your goodness and love will follow me all the days of my life, and I will dwell in the house of the Lord forever". (Psalm 23:4, 6).

I will always greatly admire God all the days of my life, for I trust and believe that He will protect me and go before me to clear any obstacles that Satan has placed in front of me that just might trip me up. There is no one like God. His glory shines throughout all of creation. From the moment I wake up to the moment I lay down to sleep, I feel Him with me.

The Creator of Heaven and Earth and Savior for Everyone

"This is what the Lord says: your Redeemer, who formed you in the womb: ***'I am the Lord, the Maker of all things, who stretches out the Heavens, who spreads out the earth by myself'"***.

(Isaiah 44:24).

"Listen to me, Jacob, Israel, whom I have called: I am He; I am the first and I am the last. My own hand laid the foundations of the earth, and my right hand spread out the Heavens; when I summoned them, they all stood up together. Come together, all of you, and listen". (Isaiah 48:12-13a).

"I am the Lord you God, I am the Lord you God, who teaches you what is best for you, who directs you in the way you should go". (Isaiah 48:17).

"To restore the tribes of Jacob and bring back those of Israel I have kept. I will also make you a light for the Gentiles that my salvation may reach to the ends of the earth". (Isaiah 49:6b).

Our Obedience to Serve the Lord

This is what the Bible has taught me about being an obedient servant of God. I would use my words to explain, but God's Words says it the best:

"The Sovereign Lord has taught me what to say, so I can strengthen the weary. Every morning He makes me eager to hear what He is going to teach me. The Lord has given me understanding, and I have not rebelled or turned away from Him". (Isaiah 50:1-5).

When people insulted me; *"I did not stop them when they insulted me". (Isaiah 50:6).*

"But their insults cannot hurt me, because the Sovereign Lord gives me help. I brace myself to endure them. I know that I will not be disgraced, for God is

near, and He will prove me innocent. The Sovereign Lord Himself defends me. All my accusers will disappear they will vanish like moth-eaten cloth. All of you that have reverence for the Lord and obey the words of His servant—the path you walk may be dark indeed, but trust in the Lord, rely on your God. Your own plots will destroy all of you that plot to destroy others. The Lord Himself will make this happen—you will suffer miserable fate" (Isaiah 50:7-11).

Now, here are Words of comfort from the Word of God:

"The Lord says; **'Listen to me, you that want to be saved, you that come to me for help. Think of the rock from which you came, the quarry from which you were cut'".** *(Isaiah 51:1).*

"I will come quickly and save them; the time of my victory is near. I myself will rule over the nations. Distant lands wait for me to come; they wait with hope for me to save them. Look up at the heavens; look at the earth! The deliverance I bring will last forever; my victory will be final. Listen to me, you that know what is right, who have my teaching fixed in your hearts. Do not be afraid when people taunt and insult you; they will vanish like moth-eaten clothing! But the deliverance I bring will last forever—my victory will endure for all time'". *(Isaiah 51:5-8).*

Being a servant of the Lord God requires four actions:

First, you must put yourselves under His Authority.

Second, open your ears to His Instructions.

Third, be willing to carry out His Instructions.

Fourth, be obedient to His every Word.

My Star Team—the Father, His Son and His Holy Spirit.

When God assigns a task to me, I do not have to worry about how I am going to handle the task. For my Star Team is right at my side, talking me through it and teaching me all the ways to accomplish the task. It is very assuring to have such support at my side anytime that I need it.

Once I accepted the task that God gave me, He started refining my heart and mind and taking out any uncleanliness that was there, transforming my self-centered heart into a heart that delights Him, humbling me to serve Him and lead others to Him. How God did this, you ask. Well, He used the hard times that I was going through to prepare me and strengthen me into becoming like His Son Jesus, who did not have any kind of negative words or attitude in Him. Jesus never told His Father no, knowing that doing His Father's Will was enough for Him. Doing God's will is the whole purpose for living a loving and peaceful life. Once that you are in the will of God, all goes well for you.

There are two reasons why a positive attitude is the best way to go in a negative situation:

(1) To <u>teach</u> you endurance.

(2) To <u>refine</u> you to purity and bring us to a greater spiritual maturity.

These two words 'teach' and 'refine', God speaks to me a lot. When He told me to write this book, I was unsure that I would be able to do it, but God said to me that He would teach me how to write by refining my words into His words.

God looks for people (believers) who are teachable and willing to walk away from the ways of this world. Confessing, repenting, and walking away from sin is what God requires in total surrender to Him. God does not choose solid rock that is without cracks or crevices. If God finds any cracks or crevices in someone that He wants to use, He then takes those cracks and crevices (our weaknesses and failures) and works them to fit His desire of who He wants us to be. God wants His followers to echo Isaiah's call: *"Here I am. Send me!"*. *(Isaiah 6:8)*. Once I did say those words, submitted to God, and turned away from the ways of this world, I found the Mercy and Grace that surrounds me to be strong enough to walk in God's Steps and Ways.

Read these Scriptures and follow every word, for this is what our Father in heaven wants us to do:

"Blessed are they whose ways are blameless, who walk according to the law of the Lord. Blessed are they who keep His statutes and seek Him with all their heart. They do no wrong; they walk His ways". (Psalm 119:1-3).

"I seek you with all my heart; do not let me stray from your commands. I have hidden your word in my heart that I might not sin against you. Praise be to you, Lord; teach me your decrees. With my lips, I recount all the laws that come from your mouth. I rejoice in following your statutes as one rejoices in great riches. I meditate on your precepts and consider your ways. I delight in your decrees; I will not neglect your word" (Psalm 119:10-16).

"To them God has chosen to make known among the Gentiles the Glorious Riches of this mystery, which is Christ in you, the Hope of Glory. He is the One we proclaim, admonishing and teaching everyone with all Wisdom, so that we may present everyone fully mature in Christ. To this end I strenuously contend with all the energy Christ so powerfully works in me". (Colossians 1:27-29).

"This is the message we have heard from Him and declare to you: God is Light; in Him there is no darkness at all. If we claim to have fellowship with Him and yet in the darkness, we lie and do not live out the truth. However, if we walk in the light, as He is in the light, we have fellowship with one another, and the blood of Jesus, His Son, purifies us from all sin. If we claim to be without sin, we deceive ourselves and the truth is not in us. If we confess our sins, He is faithful and just and will forgive us our sins and purify us from all unrighteousness. If we claim we have not sinned, we make Him out to be a liar and His word is not in us". (1 John 1:5-10).

One part of being a servant of God is to let go of the past that dragged you down into that pit of despair. There are three steps that found in letting go of my past and living like God intends me to live:

Step 1: I came face to face with my sin. It is very important to face, confess, and repent of your sin and drop all guilt of burden at the throne of our Almighty God. Therefore, He can transform you into whom He designed you to be. This can be difficult if you do not have your grip onto Jesus's hand who can lead you to the new you.

Step 2: Accept forgiveness and salvation as a gift from the Almighty God. Therefore, you can live close to Him and be the vessel that He uses to bring more people to (or back) to Him.

Step 3: Believe you have a new life with the Almighty God. So that you are not downcast any longer by your wrongs of the past and you can live in freedom with your Lord and Savior Jesus Christ.

God knows that it is necessary to break your selfish ways in order to make you useful to serve Him. Therefore, He can transform the parts of you that need to be removed to make room for the parts of Him, which would reflect His Son Jesus. The parts of you that hinders your spiritual growth are attitudes of pride, jealousy, anger, selfishness, and unforgiveness. All these (and more) need to be dealt with, before God can use you in His plan. The moment you surrender all the negative words and attitudes in cooperation and obedience to God is the moment of your transformation. Yielding to God makes you valuable to Him.

Remembering this key advice for surviving the tough times is easier than we all think. To endure the trouble not with your own strength but to endure the trouble with the Strength of the Lord. For when you endure with your own strength, you tend to choose the wrong thing or path to do or go. Always remember the Lord overcame the troubles of this troublesome world. As this our Lord tells us: ***"I have told you these things, so that in Me you may have Peace. In this world you will have trouble. But take heart! I have overcome the world"***. *(John 16:33).*

With the help of my Star Team (the Father, Son, and Holy Spirit), I learned to live with the continuing awareness of them in my life. Therefore, they gave me Peace in my heart that led me down the Right Path. All I had to do was to be aware of Their Presence in my daily life.

God designed you and me to function under the Power of His Son, Jesus. As the Bible (God's Word) says, *"I can do all things through Christ who strengthens me". (Philippians 4:13).* Also the Word of God says, *"With God all things are possible" (Mathew 26:19),* and let us not forget this one, *"When I am weak, He is strong". (2 Corinthians 12:10).*

Since I grabbed onto Jesus's hand, He has been always with me, walking, talking, and protecting me. Nothing can defeat Jesus. I can be strong and brave and have confidence that He will be carrying me on His Shoulders to get me through the troubles of this world. For the Glory and Victory is His and His alone. Any kind of apprehension can halt and freeze God's Plan for me (and you), but having Faith in His Direction unleashes His Power and sets His work into motion, the motion to step out of the boat of troubles and walk with Jesus through those troubles of this troublesome world.

The Bible has every answer for every issue that we will face daily. We have no need to worry where to go for help in our times of trouble. In God's Word, He Teaches us how to stand strong and endure the troubles that we are going through in this world, lifting us up to a place of Love and Peace. In these challenging times, the Bible shows us that we are never alone. In addition, it is not just challenging times that Jesus is with us, He is with us also in the good times, giving us

Love, Joy, and Peace to live strong and courageous.

This next section are Scriptures to stand strong in the Knowledge of God, the Word of God, Obedience to God, the Will of God, and most important Faith, Hope, and Wisdom in God. Also, stand strong in what you have learned of God's Ways and Actions in your youth. In addition, stand strong in the Presence of God, who is our Refuge and Strength. Finally yet importantly, stand strong in victory and thankfulness to the Star Team (the Father, the Son and Holy Spirit).

<u>Stand strong in the Knowledge of God:</u>

"Therefore, dear friends, since you have been forewarned, be on your guard so that you may not be carried away by the error of the lawless and fall from your secure position. However, grow in the Grace and Knowledge of our Lord and Savior Jesus Christ. To Him be glory now and forever! Amen". (2 Peter 3:17-18).

"Be strong in the Lord and in His mighty power". (Ephesians 6:10).

"My son, if you accept My words and store up My commands within you, turning your ear to Wisdom and applying you heart to understanding—indeed, if you call out for insight and cry aloud for understanding, and if you look for it as for silver and search for it as for hidden treasure, then you will understand the fear of the Lord and find the Knowledge of God. For the Lord gives Wisdom; from His Mouth comes Knowledge and Understanding". (Proverb 2:1-6).

"What we have received is not the spirit of the world, but the Spirit who is from God; so that we may understand what God has freely given us". (1 Corinthians 2:12).

Stand strong in the Word of God:

"Keep your lives free from the love of money and be content with what you have, because God has said, 'Never will I leave you; never will I forsake you.' So we say with confidence, 'The Lord is my helper; I will not be afraid. What can mere mortals do to me?"(Hebrew 13:5- 6).

"A truthful witness saves lives, but a false witness is deceitful. Whoever fears the Lord has a secure fortress, and for their children it will be a refuge. The fear of the Lord is a fountain of life, turning a person from the snares of death". (Proverb 14:25-27).

"I rejoice in Your promise, like one who finds great spoils. I hate and detest falsehood, but I love Your Law. Seven times a day I praise You, for Your righteous laws. Great Peace has those who love Your Law, and nothing can make them stumble. I wait for Your salvation, Lord, and I follow Your commands. I obey Your statutes, for I love them greatly. I obey Your precepts and Your statutes, for all my ways are known to You". (Psalm 119:162-168).

"Hear my cry, O God; listen to my prayer. From the ends of the earth I call to you, I call, as my heart grows faint; lead me to the roc that is higher than I am. For You have been my Refuge, a Strong Tower against the foe. I long to dwell in Your tent forever and take refuge in the shelter of Your wings. For You, God, have heard my vows; You have given me the heritage of those who fear Your name". (Psalm 61:1-5).

Stand strong in the obedience to God:

*"Jesus replied, **'Anyone who loves Me will obey My teaching. MyFather will love them, and we will come to them and make our home with them. Anyone who does not love Me will not obey My Teaching. These words you hear are not My own; they belong to the Father who sent Me'".** (John 14:23-24).*

"Do not merely listen to the word, and so deceive yourselves. Do what it says". (James 1:22).

"Keep this Book of the Law always on your lips; meditate on it day and night, so that you may be careful to do everything written in it. Then you will be prosperous and successful. Have I not commanded you? Be Strong and courageous. Do not be afraid; do not be discouraged, for theLord your God will be with you wherever you go'" (Joshua 1:8-9).

"The wicked desire the stronghold of evildoers, but the root of the righteous endures. Evildoers are trapped by their sinful talk, and so the innocent escape trouble. From the fruit of their lips, people are filled with good things, and the work of their hands brings them reward. The way of fools seems right to them, but the wise listen to advice". (Proverb 12:13).

Standing strong in God's Will:

"Give thanks in all circumstances; for this is the will of God in Christ Jesus for you". (1 Thessalonians 5:18).

"Do not be conformed to this world, but be transformed by the renewal of your mind, that by testing you may discern what is the will of God, what is good and acceptable and perfect". (Romans 12:2).

"For all that is in the world—the desires of the flesh and the desires of the eyes and pride in possessions—is not from the Father but is from the world. And the world is passing away along with its desires, but whoever does the will of God abides forever". (1 John 2:16-17).

"It is God's Will that you should be sanctified: that you should avoid sexual immorality; that each of you should learn to control your own body in a way that is holy and honorable, not in passionate lust like the pagans, who do not know God; and that in this matter no one should wrong or take advantage of a brother or sister. The Lord will punish all those who commit such sins, as we told you and warned you before. For God did not call us to be impure, but to live a holy life. Therefore, anyone who rejects this instruction does not reject a human being but God, the very God who gives you His Holy Spirit". (1 Thessalonians 4:3-8).

"Therefore, be on your guard; stand firm in the Faith; be courageous; be strong. Do everything in Love". (1 Corinthians 16:13-14).

"Do not throw away your confidence; it will be richly rewarded. You need to persevere so that when you have done the will of God, you will receive what He has promised. For, 'In just a little while, He who is coming will come and will *not delay.' In addition, 'But my righteous one will live by Faith. And I take no pleasure in the one who shrinks back'. But we do not belong to those who shrink back and are destroyed, but to those who have faith and are saved". (Hebrews 10:35-39).*

"What the wicked dread will overtake them; what the righteous desire will be granted. When the storm has swept by, the wicked are gone, but the righteous stand firm forever". (Proverbs 10:24-25).

"The fear of the Lord adds length to life, but the years of the wicked are cut short. The prospect of the righteous is joy, but the hopes of the wicked come to nothing. The way of the Lord is a refuge for the blameless, but it is the ruin of those who do evil". (Proverb 10:27-29).

"From the mouth of the righteous comes the fruit of wisdom, but a perverse tongue will be silenced. The lips of the righteous know what finds favor, but the mouth of the wicked only what is perverse". (Proverbs 10:31-32).

Stand strong in the Ways of God:

"He called you to this through our gospel that you might share in the glory of our Lord Jesus Christ. So then, brothers and sisters stand firm and hold fast to the teachings we passed on to you, whether by word of mouth or by letter. May our Lord Jesus Christ Himself and God our

Father, who loved us and by His grace gave us eternal encouragement and good hope, encouraged your hearts and strengthened you in every good deed and word". (2 Thessalonians 2:14-17).

"Be on your guard; stand firm in the faith; be courageous; be strong. Do everything in love". (1 Corinthians 16:13-14).

Stand strong in the Presence of God who is our refuge and strength in times of fear and trouble.

"God is our refuge and strength, an ever-present help in trouble. Therefore we will not fear, though the earth gives way and the mountains fall into the heart of the sea, though its waters roar and foam and the mountains quake with their surging". (Psalm 46:1-3).

"Come and see what the Lord has done, the desolations He has brought on

the earth. He makes wars cease to the ends of the earth. He breaks the bow and shatters the spear; He burns the shields with fire. He says, **'Be still, and know that I am God; I will be exalted among the nations, I will be exalted in the earth'.** *The Lord Almighty is with us; the God of Jacob is our fortress".* *(Psalm 46: 8-11).*

Finally, you must stand strong in your weakness so that His Power can make you perfect and strong. Also, stand strong in victory and thankfulness to God.

"But He said to me, 'My Grace is sufficient for you, for My power is made perfect in weakness.' Therefore, I will boast all the more gladly about my weaknesses, so that Christ's power may rest on me. That is why, for Christ's sake, I delight in weaknesses, in insults, in hardships, in persecutions, in difficulties. For when I am weak, then I am strong". *(2 Corinthians 12:9-10).*

"My flesh and my heart may fail, but God is the strength of my heart and my portion forever". *(Psalm 73:26).*

"The sting of death is sin, and the power of sin is the law. However, thanks be to God! He gives us victory through our Lord Jesus Christ. Therefore, my dear brothers and sisters, stand firm. Let nothing move you. Always give yourselves fully to the work of the Lord, because you know that your labor in the Lord is not in vain". *(1 Corinthians 15:56-58).*

Grace is a gift from our Father in heaven. Grace draws us closer to Him. Grace can refine a heart that is dirty with corruption and make it as pure as a new fallen snow. Having grace is never a license to sin. As we are in meditation, grace happens. As we are receiving Jesus, salvation happens. As we trust, God, mercy and grace will carry us. God knows most of the issues that we encounter. As the Bible says: "And let the peace that comes from Christ rule in your hearts. For as members of one body you are called to live in peace. And always be thankful". (Colossians 3:15).

"This righteousness is given through faith in Jesus Christ to all who believe. There is no difference between Jew and Gentile, for all have sinned and fall short of the glory of God, and all are justified freely by His grace through the redemption that came by Christ Jesus". *(Romans 3:22-24).*

Many times when I encountered a situation that made me feel hurt and confused, I would wonder why I am feeling this way, and I would ask God for help in my confusion. I would also ask Him to show me what I needed to learn from this hurtful situation. It was then when I felt like a turtle on a fence post (turtles cannot climb; someone put him there, so the turtle waits there for someone to help). Well, that is what God does with me, placing me on that 'fence post', teaching me patience and a lesson in the situation I was about to go through.

Most of my life (and even now), God puts me on that fence post, observing all the wrongs and rights that are in this world. Each time I would learn that lesson I needed to learn, God would take me off that fencepost and move me to another fencepost, somewhere else, for another lesson. Right now, I am on this fence post for a while, observing all I need to learn. It gets difficult at times to understand the lesson. However, God tells me every day that this is the reason why He has me writing this book (the fence post) to take in the view and walk with Him as He shows me the instructions of each lesson. So I could relay to all who need to hear the lesson. The Scriptures that God brings to my attention are on how He places His servants in the places where His Purpose is to be fulfilled. Each day I would read His Word (the Bible) and learn the His Instructions that He has for me for that day.

Here now are some of the Scriptures that God has revealed to me reminding me how to live the life that He designed for me to live (and share with others) on this earth.

Reminder 1:

That nothing can separate me from my Heavenly Father and just hold of His Son's hand and walk with Him in this journey.

"No one will be able to stand up against you all the days of your life. As I was with Moses, so I will be with you; I will never leave you nor forsake you. Be strong and very courageous. Be careful to obey all the law my servant Moses gave you; do not turn from it to the right or to the left, that you may be successful wherever you go. Do not let this Book of the Law depart from your mouth; meditate on it day and night, so

that you may be careful to do everything written in it. Then you will be prosperous and successful'" (Joshua 1:5, 7-8).

*"**See, I have engraved you on the palms of my hands; your walls are ever before me'".** (Isaiah 49:16).*

"For I am convinced that neither death nor life, neither angels nor demons, neither the present nor the future, nor any powers, neither height nor depth, nor anything else in all creation, will be able to separate us from the love of God that is in Christ Jesus our Lord". (Romans 8:38-39).

Reminder 2:

To sacrifice my time to sit quietly in God's Presence, letting the streams of living water flow freely through me. Strengthening me and glorifying Him.

"Surely, You have granted him Eternal Blessings and made him glad with the Joy of Your Presence. For the king trusts in the Lord; through the Unfailing Love of the Most High he will not be shaken". (Psalm 21:6-7).

"Whoever believes in me, as the Scriptures have said, a stream of Living Water will flow from within him". (John 7:38).

"For as high as the heavens are above the earth, so great is His love for those who fear Him; as far as the east is from the west, so far has He removed our transgressions from us". (Psalm 103:11-12).

"The Sovereign Lord is my strength; He makes my feet like the feet of a deer, He enables me to go on the heights". (Habakkuk 3:19).

"I can do everything through Him who gives me strength". (Philippians 4:13).

"For all the gods of the nations are idols, but the Lord made the Heavens. Splendor and Majesty are before Him; Strength and Glory are in His Sanctuary". (Psalm 96:5-6).

Reminder 3:

To watch the words I speak, they can bless and they can wound. To speak the Words of God at all times with no anger or malice.

"A fool shows his annoyance at once, but a prudent man overlooks an insult. A truthful witness gives honest testimony, but a false witness tells lies. Reckless words pierce like a sword, but the tongue of the wise brings healing. Truthful lips

endure forever, but a lying tongue lasts only a moment". (Proverbs 12:16-19).

"My dear brothers and sisters, take note of this: Everyone should be quick to listen, slow to speak and slow to become angry, for a man's anger does not bring about the righteous life that God desires". (James 1:19-20).

"Do not let any unwholesome talk come out of your mouths, but only what is helpful for building others up according to their needs, that it may benefit those who listen. In addition, do not grieve the Holy Spirit of God, with whom you were sealed for the day of redemption. Get rid of all bitterness, rage and anger, brawling and slander, along with every form of malice. Be kind and compassionate to one another, forgiving each other, just as in Christ God forgave you". (Ephesians 4:29-32).

Reminder 4:

To hold on to Jesus's hand and walk joyously through my day, taking in the pleasures and difficulties together. Worry not for what is around the bend, letting Jesus guide me through the journey and never letting me get hurt.

*"**Do not let your hearts be troubled. Trust in God; trust also in Me. In my Father's House there are many rooms; if it were not so, I would have told you. I am going there to prepare a place for you. In addition, if I go and prepare a place for you, I will come back and take you to be with Me so that you also may be where I am. You know the Way to the Place where I am going**'. Thomas said to Him, 'Lord, we don't know where you are going, so how can we know the way?' Jesus answered, '**I am the Way and the Truth and the Life. No one comes to the Father except through Me. If you really knew Me, you would know My Father as well. From now on, you do know Him and have seen Him**'". (John 14:1-7).*

"Devote yourselves to prayer, being watchful and thankful". (Colossians 4:2).

*"But now, this is what the Lord says—He who created you, O Jacob, He who formed you, O Israel: '**Fear not, for I have redeemed you; I have summoned you by name; you are Mine**'". (Isaiah 43:1).*

*"**See, I have engraved you on the palms of my hands; your walls are ever before me. Lift up your eyes and look around; all your sons gather***

and come to you. As surely as I live', *declares the Lord,* ***'you will wear them all as ornaments; you will put them on, like a bride'".*** *(Isaiah 49:16, 18).*

"For I am convinced that neither death nor life, neither angels nor demons, neither the present nor the future, nor any powers, neither height nor depth, nor anything else in all creation, will be able to separate us from the love of God that is in Christ Jesus our Lord". (Romans 8:38-39).

Reminder 5:

To take time to sit quietly in the presence of God, while He blesses me with His love and grace. As I consider the challenges of the day, I will talk them over with Jesus (who is by side) and trust Him that He will walk me through the pressures without hurting too bad. Talking with God about all that concerns me will always bring me strength to face those challenges. A slow pace accomplishes more than a fast rushed striving. I always remember who I am and who I belong to. I belong to the Royal Family of Heaven, my Star Team.

"Do not fret because of evil men or be envious of those who do wrong; for like the grass they will soon wither, like green plants they will soon die away. Trust in the Lord and do good; dwell in the land and enjoy safe pastures. Delight yourself in the Lord and He will give you the desires of your heart. Commit your way to the Lord; trust in Him and He will do this: He will make your righteousness shine like the dawn, the justice of your cause like the noonday sun. BE STILL BEFORE THE LORD AND WAIT PATIENTLY FOR HIM; do not fret when men succeed in their ways, when they carry out their wicked schemes. Refrain from anger and turn from wrath; do not fret—it leads only to evil". (Psalm 37:1-8).

"For you did not receive a spirit that makes you a slave again to fear, but you received the Spirit Of son-ship. And by Him we cry, 'Abba, Father.' The Spirit Himself testifies with our spirit that we are God's children. Now if we are children, then we are heirs—heirs of God and co-heirs with Christ, if indeed we share in His sufferings in order that we may also share in His glory". (Romans 8:15-17).

"Dear friends, I urge you, as aliens and strangers in the world, to abstain from sinful desires, which war against your soul. Live such good lives among the

pagans that, though they accuse you of doing wrong, they may see your good deeds and glorify God on the day He visits us". (1 Peter 2:11-12).

"And we urge you, brothers, warn those who are idle, encourage the timid, help the weak; be patient with everyone. Make sure that nobody pays back wrong for wrong, but always try to be kind to each other and to everyone else. Be joyful always; pray continually; give thanks in all circumstances, for this is God's will for you in Christ Jesus. Do not put out the Spirit's fire; do not treat prophecies with contempt. Test everything. Hold on to the good. Avoid every kind of evil. May God Himself, the God of peace, sanctify you through and through. May your whole spirit, soul and body, be kept blameless at the coming of our Lord Jesus Christ. The one who calls you is faithful and He will do it". (1 Thessalonians 5:14-24).

Reminder 6:

To learn of the things that seem to be going wrong and to be still, trust, and know that He is God. To thank God for taking control of my life and to continue to stay in touch with Him. For God works all things out for my good. God will enable me to walk through the troubles and responsibilities, making progress all the way. I should continue to rejoice always in Him and never give in to Satan's temptations and words of doubt and destruction.

*"**Listen carefully to my words; let your ears take in what I say**". (Job 13:17).*

"The Lord is my rock, my fortress and my deliverer; my God is my rock, in whom I take refuge. He is my Shield and the horn of my Salvation, my Stronghold....He makes my feet like the feet of a deer; He enables me to stand on the heights. He trains my hands for battle; my arms can bend a bow of bronze. You give me your shield of victory, and your right hand sustains me; you stood down to make me great" (Psalm 18:2, 33-35).

"As for God, His Way is Perfect; the Word of the Lord is flawless. He is a Shield for all who take refuge in Him. For who is God besides the Lord? And who is the Rock except our God? It is God, who arms me with Strength and makes my way perfect. He makes my feet like the feet of a deer; He enables me to stand on the heights. He trains my hands for battle; my arms can bend a bow of bronze. You give me your shield of victory; you stoop down to make me great". (2 Samuel

22:31-36).

"The Lord is my shepherd I shall not be in want. He makes me lay down in green pastures, He leads me beside quiet waters, and He restores my soul. He guides me in paths of righteousness for His name's sake. Even though I walk through the valley of the shadow of death, I will fear no evil, for You are with me; Your Rod and Your Staff, they comfort me". (Psalm 23:1-4).

The best reminder that God reveals to me is found (of course) in His Word (the Bible) in the Book of Second Peter. Here, Peter reminds us to add these things to our Faith so we never stumble and have entrance into the Kingdom of our Lord Jesus Christ:

"Giving all diligence, add to your Faith Virtue, to Virtue Knowledge, to Knowledge Self-control, to self-control Perseverance, to Perseverance Godliness, to Godliness brotherly kindness, and to brotherly kindness Love. For if these things are yours and abound, you will be neither barren nor unfruitful in the Knowledge of our Lord Jesus Christ". (2 Peter 1:5-8). "For if you do these things you will never stumble; for so an entrance will be supplied to you abundantly into the everlasting kingdom of our Lord and Savior Jesus Christ". (2 Peter 1:10b, 11).

As I sit quietly in God's Presence and meditate on these reminders; He reveals to me daily, I am being full of Thankfulness, Love, Wisdom, and Grace. God fills me with these things to become stronger and become closer to the likeness of His Son, Jesus. This act of obedience (Spiritual) is what God has designed you and me to do. My circumstances may not go totally away, but I have the best assurance that I will never be alone to walk this world of chaos. For

Jesus is, and always will be, holding my hand and leading me through the chaos and into the joy and peace that surpasses all chaos. I thank Jesus every day for His light that removes the sting that the enemy (Satan) throws my way. Jesus has been, and always will be, my shield. This assurance of Jesus's presence with me releases all that, is troubling me and keeps my focus and attention on the goal at the end of this journey—a life without chaos, and a life with my Star Team. I (we) are blessed to have Jesus walk alongside us. There is nothing that can separate us from Him. Jesus loves you and me too much to leave us to walk this journey alone.

"Humble yourselves, therefore, under God's mighty hand, that He may lift you up in due time. Cast all your anxiety on Him because He cares for you. Be self-controlled and alert. Your enemy the devil prowls around like a roaring lion looking for someone to devour". (1 Peter 5:6-8).

"Let them give thanks to the Lord for His Unfailing Love and His Wonderful Deeds for men. Let them sacrifice thank offerings and tell of His works with songs of joy". (Psalm 107:21-22).

"The Lord will guide you always; He will satisfy your needs in a sun-scorched land and will strengthen your frame. You will be like a well-watered garden, like a spring whose waters never fail". (Isaiah 58:11).

"He tends his flock like a shepherd: He gathers the lambs in His arms and carries them close to His heart; He gently leads those that are young" . (Isaiah 40:11).

I always talk over my problems with my Star Team, seeking their advice and their perspectives on all situations. Those problems seem to fade away; while my mind is filling up with the thoughts of how beautiful it is living and breathing the Life of God. Nothing else, or no one else, can love me more than Jesus can. I am forever grateful for His friendship, peace, and most of all His Love.

"*I will instruct you and teach you in the Way you should go; I will counsel you and watch over you*" *(Psalm 32:8).*

Dwelling and Waiting

There is no difference between dwelling and waiting. Dwelling means to remain for a time; and waiting means to remain for a time. All through the Bible, it speaks a lot about 'dwelling in the Lord' and 'waiting on the Lord'. Each statement comes with instructions, because there are ways that dwelling can be bad for us. One way is when we dwell in our past. Dwelling in our past keeps us in our sin and from moving forward into the Blessings that God has for us. I found out that when I find myself dwelling in the past, I start feeling ugly inside. Therefore, when those feelings start approaching my mind, I immediately reach out to the Star Team to help me shield those negative thoughts off. This is the Dwelling that is the Best Choice: To sit with the Star Team (the Father, the Son and the Holy Spirit) reading Scriptures that will help me come back to feeling beautiful again.

God is our Dwelling Place (the Star Team):

"For God so loved the world that He gave His one and only Son, that whoever Believes in Him shall not perish but have Eternal Life. For God did not send His Son into the world to condemn the world, but to save the world through Him". (John 3:16-17).

"Blessed is the one who does not walk in step with the wicked or stand in the way that sinners take or sit in the company of mockers, but whose delight is in the Law of the Lord, and who meditates on His Law day and night. That person is like a tree planted by streams of water, which yields its fruit in season and whose leaf does not wither – whatever they do prospers. Not so, the wicked! They are like chaff that the wind blows away. Therefore, the wicked will not stand in the Judgment, nor sinners in the Assembly of the Righteous. For the Lord watches over the way of the righteous, but the way of the wicked leads to destruction". (Psalm 1:1-6).

And the Lord says: ***"And I will put my Spirit in you, and move you to follow my decrees, and be careful to keep my laws. Then you will live in the land I gave your ancestors; you will be My people, and I will be your God. I will save you from all your uncleanness. I will call for the grain and make it plentiful and will not bring famine upon you. I will increase the fruit of the trees and the crops of the field, so that you will no longer suffer disgrace among the nations because of famine"***. *(Ezekiel 36:27-30).*

"We know that in all things God works for the good of those who love Him, who have been called according to His Purpose. For those God foreknew He also predestined to be conformed to the image of His Son, that He might be the firstborn among many brothers and sisters. And those He predestined, He also called; those He called, He also justified; those He justified, He also glorified". *(Romans 8:28-30).*

"Do not get drunk on wine, which leads to debauchery. Instead, be filled with the Spirit, speaking to one another with psalms, hymns, and songs, from the Spirit. Sing and make music from your heart to the Lord, always giving thanks to God the Father for everything, in the name of our Lord Jesus Christ. Submit to one another out of reverence for Christ". *(Ephesians 5:18-21).*

"I have much more to say to you, more than you can now bear. However, when He, the Spirit of Truth, comes, He will guide you into all the truth. He will not speak on His own; He will speak only what He hears, and He will tell you what is yet to come. He will glorify Me, because it is from Me that He will receive what He will make known to you. All that belongs to the Father is Mine. That is why I said the Spirit will receive from Me what He will make known to you" *(John 16:12-15).*

"You, my brothers and sisters, were called to be free. However, do not use your freedom to indulge the flesh; rather, serve one another humbly in love. For the entire Law is fulfilled in keeping this on command: 'Love your neighbor as yourself.' If you bite and devour each other, watch out or you will be destroyed by each other. So I say, walk by the Spirit, and you will not gratify the desires of the flesh. For the flesh desires what is contrary to the Spirit and the Spirit what is contrary to the flesh. They are in conflict with each other, so that you are not able to do whatever you want. However, if you are led by the Spirit,

you are not under the law. The acts of the flesh are obvious: sexual immorality, impurity and debauchery; idolatry and witchcraft; hatred, discord, jealousy, fits of rage, selfish ambition, dissensions, factions and envy; drunkenness, orgies, and the like. I warn you, as I did before, that those who live like this will not inherit the kingdom of God. However, the Fruit of the Spirit is Love, Joy, Peace, Forbearance (Patience), Kindness, Goodness, Faithfulness, Gentleness and Self-control. Against such things, there is no law. Those who belong to Christ Jesus have crucified the flesh with its passions and desires. Since we live by the Spirit, let us keep in step with the Spirit. Let us not become conceited, provoking and envying each other". (Galatians 5:13-26).

"Because you are His sons, God sent the Spirit of His Son into our hearts, the Spirit who calls out; 'Abba, Father'. So you are no longer a slave, but God's child; and since you are His child, God has made you also an heir". (Galatians 4:6-7).

"How lovely is your dwelling place, O Lord, Almighty! My soul yearns, even faints, for the courts of the Lord; my heart and flesh cry out for the living God". (Psalm 84:1-2).

"Better is one day in Your courts, than a thousand elsewhere; I would rather be a doorkeeper in the house of my God than dwell in the tents of the wicked. For the Lord God is a sun and shield; the Lord bestows favor and honor; no good thing does He withhold from those whose walk is blameless. Lord Almighty, blessed is the man who trusts in You". (Psalm 84:10-12).

"Don't you know that you yourselves are God's temple and that God's Spirit lives in your midst? If anyone destroys God's temple, God will destroy him; for God's temple is sacred and you are that temple". (1 Corinthians 3:16-17).

"Whoever dwells in the Shelter of the Most High will rest in the Shadow of the Almighty". (Psalm 91:1).

As we dwell in God's Presence, we have the Power to forgive others. This is what God wants us to do: *"Be kind and compassionate to one another, forgiving each other, just as in Christ God forgave you". (Ephesians 4:32).* The more you forgive and forget, the faster you can get it together and move forward. It is not right to keep in front of you, what God has already placed behind Him. In other words, God has forgotten your past sin when you accepted His Son Jesus into your life. So let us let go, forgive, forget, and move on! The Bible says:

"Therefore, as God's chosen people, holy and dearly loved, clothe yourselves with compassion, kindness, humility, gentleness and patience. Bear with each other and forgive one another, if any of you has a grievance against someone. Forgive as the Lord forgave you. And over all these virtues, put on love, which binds them all together in perfect unity". (Colossians 3:12-14).

Keeping close to Jesus is to read the Scriptures every day, by being quick to confess any sin that might be hindering your walk with Him; keep a tender heart that grows warmer, not colder. And most of all stay in communication with the Father; through His Son Jesus, to have a good conscience and walk humbly with Him.

Everyone wants things to happen right away, and God says to just trust Him and wait for Him patiently. When we continually wait on God, He will clearly give directions of how to reap major rewards, for our patience. As the Lord tells us: ***"I will instruct you and teach you in the way you should go; I will guide you with my eye'"***. *(Psalm 32:8).*

The Five Major Rewards for Waiting on God:

The first major reward is that we discover God's Will. Keeping our eyes fixed on Him at all times and listening to His instructions makes our relationship with Him grow deeper.

"The Lord is good to those who wait for Him; to the person who seeks Him". (Lamentations 3:25).

The second major reward is that we receive His Energy and Strength. As our energy increases, so does our endurance to stand firm in our faith. We also grow into the likeness of Jesus, which includes possessing:*"Love, Joy, Peace, Patience, Kindness, Goodness, Faithfulness, Gentleness,and Self-control". (Galatians 5:22-23).* Waiting on God is never wasted time, for I have said it before, 'God waits for us, so we can wait for Him'. *"He gives strength to the weary and increases the power of the weak. Even youths grow tired and weary, and young men stumble and fall; but those who hope in the Lord will renew their strength. They will soar on wings like eagles; they will run and not grow weary, they will walk and not faint". (Isaiah 40:29-31).*

The third major reward is that we win in the battles of this world. Doing things our way quickly, we end up defeated. However, when we wait on God's help and obey His instructions, He ensures our victory in every battle we fight with Him by our side.

"The Lord will fight for you; you need only to be still". (Exodus 14:14).

The fourth major reward is that we see the fulfillment in our faith. Putting hope in Jesus and waiting on Him is the smartest move you can make. I know there will be people telling you to forge ahead instead of waiting on Jesus. However, you must remember that Jesus is the only One who can truly help you through your troubles; He will never let you down. Because Jesus has overcome all the troubles that you and I go through. In addition, Jesus went to the cross to fulfill His Father's Command for us to live with Him in His glorious presence.

"There is surely a future hope for you, and your hope will not be cut off ". (Proverbs 23:18).

The fifth major reward is that we see God working on our behalf. Everyday God is actively working on our behalf to make sure that all things that happen in our lives are going according to His Purpose. In addition, God does give instructions in the periods of waiting. While we are waiting patiently for Him, He is Blessing us. God knows how long we need to wait, to mature us in producing the most precious and wonderful fruit, for His Glory. Therefore, I will wait on the Lord as long as it takes, to live forever with Him. I will trust in Jesus to bring me home to the Glory that awaits me. *"God acts on behalf of the one who waits for Him". (Isaiah 64:4).*

These five major rewards are not the only rewards that you will receive. Yet at the end of your journey here on this earth, you will receive all the treasures that are piled up for you in Heaven, all because you lived, waited, trusted, obeyed, and loved God's Way (His Son).

Faith does not come by seeing results. Faith comes by Believing in the Power of the Lord. Faith also comes by waiting patiently to hear what God has to tell you what to do. Waiting gives us guidance to take every step alongside Jesus, to show the way to walk, to worry less and place the worries on His Shoulders, to give us the freedom to walk a God-guided Life in every moment we live. Therefore, the next time you become inpatient to unanswered prayers, let this little reminder strengthen you to wait on God's Guidance. Because we all know that Jesus is the Guide to the Kingdom of His Almighty Father.

Sometimes in our waiting, we are waiting because of something we did wrong. Kind of a way when parents give their child a time-out when they do something wrong. Nobody likes discipline, but if we do something wrong, we have to endure the consequences of our wrong doings. In addition, we must learn from both our mistakes and the consequences (discipline) that we face. In a time-out, we are silent, so we can think of what we did wrong. In addition, in our silence, we are able to hear what our Heavenly Father has to say, and we must listen to Him.

Here is what the Word of God says:

"The mouth of the righteous is a fountain of life, but the mouth of the wicked conceals violence. Hatred stirs up conflict, but Love covers over all wrongs. Wisdom is found on the lips of the discerning, but a rod is for the back of one who has no sense. The wise store up Knowledge, but the mouth of a fool invites ruin. The wealth of the rich is their fortified city, but poverty is the ruin of the poor. The wages of the righteous is life, but the earnings of the wicked are sin and death. Whoever heeds discipline shows the way to life, but whoever ignores correction leads others astray. Whoever conceals hatred with lying lips and spreads slander is a fool. Sin is not ended by multiplying words, but the prudent hold their tongues. The tongue of the righteous is choice silver, but the heart of the wicked is of little value. The lips of the righteous nourish many, but fools die for lack of sense. The blessing of the Lord brings wealth, without painful toil for it. A fool finds pleasure in wicked schemes, but a person of understanding delights in wisdom". (Proverbs 10:11-23).

As you can see, we must be wise and careful about what we say and how we speak in certain situations. We must guard our words whenever we become angry. In the Word of God, it says:

"My dear brothers and sisters, take note of this: Everyone should be quick to listen, slow to speak and slow to become angry, because human anger does not produce the Righteousness that God desires. Therefore, get rid of all moral filth and the evil that is so prevalent and humbly accept the Word planted in you, which can save you. Do not merely listen to the Word, and so deceive yourselves. Do what it says". (James 1:19-22).

Restraining our words shows reverence for God. In the Word of God, it says:

"God is in Heaven and you on earth; therefore let your words be few". (Ecclesiastes 5:2).

When others are grieving, a silent presence can help more than abundant expressions of sympathy. In the Word of God, it says: *"No one spoke a word to him, for they saw that his grief was great". (Job 2:13).* Choosing to speak less allows us to hear more. It says in Proverbs:

"Sin is not ended by multiplying words, but the prudent hold their tongues". (Proverbs 10:19).

Prayer

Dear Heavenly Father, please grant me wisdom to know when to speak and when not to speak, to listen more and speak less, to encourage others and to care for them as You have cared for me.

"Listen to the words, Lord, consider my lament. Hear my cry for help, my King and my God, to you I pray". (Psalm 5:1-2).

"Let all who take refuge in You be glad; let them ever sing for joy. Spread Your protection over them that those who love Your Name may rejoice in You. Surely, Lord, you Bless the righteous; You surround them with Your favor as with a shield". (Psalm 5:11-12).

In the name of Your Glorious Son Jesus's Name, I pray. Amen.

Our Faith is exchanging our weakness for God's Strength. I will always proclaim this promise from God: *"That is why, for Christ's sake, I delight in weaknesses, in insults, in hardships, in persecutions, in difficulties. For when I am weak, He is strong". (2 Corinthians 12:10).*

The Art of Whistling (Listening)

When I was younger, I always wanted to learn to whistle. It just looks so cool when other people whistling a tune while they are strolling along while they are walking in the park. I tried everything to learn, but to no avail; I failed to whistle; it was always just a humming sound. Many people that I came in contact with knew how to whistle, so I would ask them how they learned to whistle. They would tell me, but even then, I failed to whistle out a song. So then, I asked God, why I cannot learn to whistle. He told me that I did not need to learn to whistle. I just need to listen to His Voice whistling my name. He then had me read this Scripture; that at the time I didn't understand. But then, it came to me. You see, in this world, there are many voices that are surfacing through the air trying to block out God's Voice (which by the way is a soft whistling sound). These voices are trying to throw us off track in following Jesus. However, when we have Jesus in our life, He will teach us how to block out those many disturbing voices of doom. Just read this Scripture that explains this: *"My sheep* [us] *listen to My Voice; I know them, and they follow Me. I give them Eternal Life, and they shall never perish; no one will snatch them out of My Hand. My Father, who has given them to Me, is Greater than all; no one can snatch them out of My Father's Hand. I and the Father are one". (John 10:27-30).*

God speaks to me in ways that signal His Presence in my life. Once I hear Him speaking to me, I know that I am to follow His Instructions. These voices of doom that are continually trying to persuade to follow their fleshy ways are just dust in the wind. For the Voice of Truth is who keeps me breathing the Love, Compassion and Grace that keeps me in the Life (Jesus) that God (the Father) created me to live.

The Voice Truth is the soft whistle that guides us to the Narrow Path of the Journey with the Star Team. The call of God can always be heard. Just stop talking for one moment, read the Scripture and keep listening in the silence for that soft whistle that is calling out your name. Get ready to be called by the Whistle of the Voice of Truth. Stay rooted in God's Word and all will be Peaceful.

Mistakes and Failures

In my fifty years of observing, I have seen and made a lot of mistakes and failures. Some that are too shameful to even mention; not even to think about. I will just tell you who and how I got through all the mistakes and failures (oh yeah, even shame).

My Star Team told me that when I make mistakes, it's how I respond and learn from them that matters. I have been making mistakes for as long as I can remember. In fact, I still make them, but I have come to realize that when I make a mistake or fail at a task, I know I have not been communicating with my Star Team. I heard a statement, which reminds me to communicate more with my Star Team and read my Bible. It says this: 'If you are struggling in any way, make God's Word an ongoing Presence in your life'.

Mistakes are of wrong judgment, identifying incorrectly, and making a blunder in choosing. We make mistakes when we are not paying attention to what is around us, and we only hear part of what is happening. Then, when it comes the time of doing what we should do, we seem to fall short of completing the assignment; we start shifting the blame to someone else.

In Genesis 3:12-13, in the Garden of Eden, when Adam blamed Eve and then Eve blamed the serpent. It seems that no one wants to take the blame for their mistake, because they know the consequences for their wrongdoings is discipline (and no one likes to be disciplined). If we do not have discipline, our lives will be filled with making one mistake after another, for the rest of our lives. Discipline helps us turn away from our wrongdoing.

There are times when we say things that we later regret, which is another example of not thinking of the consequences of what we say. When you say something that you later regret, you are giving into Satan's lies and letting him manipulate you into turning and running away from God. This is the worst mistake you can ever make running from God, like Jonah did and he caused a storm to brew from his mistake. However, when Jonah realized what was happening and why it was happening, he turned back to God. Here is what happens, when you are not listening and obeying the commands of God:

Jonah Flees from the Lord

"The Word of the Lord came to Jonah son of Amittai: **'Go to the great city of Nineveh and preach against it, because its wickedness has come up before me'**. *But Jonah ran away from the Lord and headed for Tarshish. He went down to Joppa, where he found a ship bound for that port. After paying the fare, he went aboard and sailed for Tarshish to flee from the Lord. Then the Lord sent a great wind on the sea, and such a violent storm arose that the ship threatened to break up. All the sailors were afraid and each cried out to his own god. And they threw the cargo into the sea to lighten the ship. But Jonah had gone below deck, where he lay down and fell into a deep sleep. The captain went to him and said, "How can you sleep? Get up and call on your god! Maybe he will take notice of us so that we will not perish". Then the sailors said to each other, "Come, and let us cast lots to find out who is responsible for this calamity". They cast lots and the lot fell on Jonah. So they asked him, "Tell us, who is responsible for making all this trouble for us? What kind of work do you do? Where do you come from? What is your country?*

What kind of people are you?" He answered, "I am a Hebrew and I worship the Lord, the God of heaven, who made the sea and the dry land." This terrified them and they asked, "What have you done?" (They knew he was running away from the Lord, because he had already told them so). The sea was getting rougher and rougher. So they asked him, "What should we do to make the sea calm down for us?" "Pick me up and throw me into the sea," he replied, "and it will become calm. I know that it is my fault that this great storm has come upon you." Instead, the men did their best to row back to land. But they could not, for the sea grew even wilder than before. Then they cried out to the Lord, "Please, Lord, do not let us die for taking this man's life. Do not hold us accountable for killing an innocent man, for you, Lord, have done as you pleased." Then they took Jonah and threw him overboard, and the raging sea grew calm. At this, the men greatly feared the Lord, and they offered a sacrifice to the Lord and made vows to him. Now the Lord provided a huge fish to swallow Jonah, and Jonah was in the belly of the fish for three days and three nights. From inside the fish Jonah prayed to the Lord his God. He said:

"In my distress I called to the Lord, and He answered me. From deep in the realm of the dead, I called for help, and you listened to my cry. You hurled me into the depths, into the very heart of the seas, and the currents swirled about me; all your waves and breakers swept over me. I said, 'I have been banished from Your Sight; yet I will look again toward Your Holy Temple'. The engulfing waters threatened me, the deep surrounded me; seaweed was wrapped around my head. To the roots of the mountains I sank down, the earth beneath barred me in forever. But you, Lord my God, brought my life up from the pit. When my life was ebbing away, I remembered you, Lord, and my prayer rose to you, to your holy temple. Those who cling to worthless idols turn away from God's Love for them. But I, with shouts of grateful praise, will sacrifice to you. What I have vowed I will do good. I will say, 'Salvation comes from the Lord'". And the Lord commended the fish, and it vomited Jonah onto dry land". (Jonah 1:1-17 and 2:1-10).

These verses of Scripture really spoke to me. For I had been in a place that Jonah was in. Oh, it was not a great fish's belly, but it was a room of four walls with no windows or doors and people were trampling on me. People, I didn't even know, were trying to stump me out of existence. I cried out to Jesus for help, and He heard me and pulled me out.

This was all because I had started to take the wide path that led to destruction. I also was not focusing on the one thing that can pull me through all the troubles and make me forget the past and move forward to the Glory that lies ahead. As the Word of God says:

"Not that I have already obtained all this, or have already arrived at my goal, but I press on to take hold of that for which Christ Jesus took hold of me. Brothers and sisters, I do not consider myself yet to have taken hold of it. But one thing I do: Forgetting what is behind and straining toward what is ahead, I press

on toward the goal to win the prize for which God has called me heavenward in Christ Jesus".(Philippians 3:12-14).

Making mistakes will definitely lead you to failures, and failures are a lack of success, falling short in one's work. When I am face-to-face with a failure, I turn to God in repentance and trust Him to respond the best way He always does. To get back up again from failing is having hope in God who will get me through the failures I seem to be facing a lot in this world.

The Word of God says:

"For though the righteous fall seven times, they rise again, but the wicked stumble when calamity strikes". (Proverbs 24:16).

"Do not gloat over me, my enemy! Though I have fallen, I will rise. Though I sit in darkness, the Lord will be my light". (Micah 7:8).

"We are hard pressed on every side, but not crushed; perplexed, but not in despair; persecuted, but not abandoned; struck down, but not destroyed". (2 Corinthians 4:8-9).

I often asked God, "How do I keep from failing?" and here is what He revealed to me:

"Be still and know I am God, I will be exalted among the nation. I will be exalted in the earth". *(Psalm 46:10).*

"My flesh and my heart may fail, but God is the strength of my heart and my portion forever". (Psalm 73:26).

"For the word of God is alive and active. Sharper than any double edged sword, it penetrates even to divide soul and spirit, joints and marrow; it judges the thoughts and attitudes of the heart. Nothing in all creation is hidden from God's sight. Everything is uncovered and laid bare before the eyes of Him to whom we must give account". (Hebrews 4:12-13).

"Finally, brothers and sisters, whatever is true, whatever is noble, whatever is right, whatever is pure, whatever is lovely, whatever is admirable, if anything is excellent or praiseworthy, think about such things. Whatever you have learned or received or heard from me, or seen in me, put it into practice. And the God of peace will be you". (Philippians 4:8-9).

Listening to God and His instructions guarantees you wisdom to be able to learn from your failures and move forward to complete the journey that God has you walk on this world.

"Therefore, everyone who hears these words of Mine; and puts them into practice is like a wise man who built his house on the rock"'. (Matthew 7:24).

To avoid failures and mistakes, follow the ways of God and you will never go wrong or fail in anything. Here are some Promises from God on failures in your Life:

"The Lord makes firm the steps of the one who delights in Him; though he stumbles, he will not fall, for the Lord upholds him with His hand". (Psalm 37:23-24).

"For the Lord loves the just, and will not forsake His faithful ones. Wrongdoers will be completely destroyed. The offspring of the wicked will perish. The righteous will inherit the land and dwell in it forever". (Psalm 37:28-29).

"Trust in the Lord forever, for the Lord, the Lord Himself is the Rock eternal. He humbles those who dwell on high—He lays the lofty city low; He levels it to the ground and casts it down to the dust". (Isaiah 26:4-5).

"My soul yearns for you in the night; in the morning my spirit longs for you. When your judgments come upon the earth, the people of the world learn righteousness". (Isaiah 26:9).

To know that God is our Judge (our only Judge), this is what He will do when He judges:

1. Give us what we deserve, for in His sight, He knows what is best.

2. Instruct us on how we should live, for His word is life lived.

3. Rule over us and is our Savior, for He is a judge that is just and perfect.

The Word of God says:

"Look on Zion, the city of our festivals; your eyes will see Jerusalem, a peaceful abode, a tent that will not be moved; its stakes will never be pulled up, nor any of its ropes broken. There, the Lord will be our Mighty One. It will be like a place of broad rivers and streams. No galley with oars will ride them, no mighty ship will sail them. For the Lord is our judge, the Lord is our lawgiver, the Lord is our king; it is He who will save us". (Isaiah 33:21-22).

"For we must all appear before the judgment seat of Christ, so that each of us may receive what is due us for the things done while in the body, whether good or bad". (2 Corinthians 5:10).

When someone betrays you or turns against you, you must not seek revenge, but you must seek God (in prayer—laying the situation before Him). For God knows how to best deal with the situation that you place before Him and then instructs you on what to do. No situation, God cannot solve. All our wounds are healed and tears are dried, and all broken hearts are mended.

This kind of dependence upon our Father God is the best way to show Him that you give Him full control and trust with your life. Then He will deliver you from the harm of the situation that you placed before Him. The Word of God says:

"The Day of the Lord will come like a thief. The Heavens will disappear with a roar, the elements will be destroyed by fire, and the earth and everything done in it will be laid bare. Since everything will be destroyed in this way, what kind of people ought you to be? You ought to live holy and godly lives, as you look forward to the day of God, and speed its coming. That day will bring about the destruction of the heavens by fire, and the elements will melt in the heat. But in keeping with His promise, we are looking forward to a new heaven and a new earth, where righteousness dwells". (2 Peter 3:10-13).

"Therefore, dear friends, since you have been forewarned, be on your guard, so that you may not be carried away by the error of the lawless and fall from your secure position. However, grow in the Grace and Knowledge of our Lord and Savior Jesus Christ. To Him be Glory, both now and forever! Amen". (2 Peter 3:17-18).

Unrepentant sin always brings the discipline of God. This is a serious thing (of unrepentance) with God, just knowing that you sinned against God and not acknowledging it is the sin on top of your sin you have not yet repented of. In the Word of God, it says:

"If we say we have not sinned, we make Him a liar, and His word is not in us". (1 John 1:10).

"If we say we have no sin, we deceive ourselves, and the truth is not in us".

(1 John 1:8).

"Whoever makes a practice of sinning is of the devil, for the devil has been sinning from the beginning. The reason the Son of God appeared was to destroy the works of the devil. No one born of God makes a practice of sinning, for God's seed abides in him, and he cannot keep on sinning, because he has been born of God. By this it is evident who the children of God are, and who are the children of the devil: whoever does not practice righteousness is not of God, nor is the one who does not love his brother". (1 John 3:8-10).

"If we confess our sins, He is faithful and just to forgive us our sins and cleanse us from all unrighteousness". (1 John 1:9).

Therefore, after reading these verses, we must ask ourselves if we have an unrepentant sin that we just might carry around. Because unrepentant sin can weigh you down and make you feel like you are carrying an iron slab. However, the key to being victorious in lifting that iron slab is letting the strength of Jesus (who lives in you) make that iron slab feel as light as a feather. The Word of God tells me:

*"But He said to me, **'My grace is sufficient for you, for my power is made perfect in weakness'.** Therefore, I will boast all the more gladly about my weaknesses, so that Christ's power may rest on me. That is why, for Christ's sake, I delight in weaknesses, in insults, in hardships, in persecutions, in difficulties. For when I am weak, I am strong". (2 Corinthians 12:9-10).*

The Apostle Paul called his trial a "thorn in the flesh." I looked up the word thorn, and it means something that causes distress or irritation, often used in the phrase: 'thorn in one's side'. Having this thorn is not so pleasant. Paul's trial (thorn) must have been ongoing and irritating for a long time, just like my trial (thorn) that keeps repeating itself and irritating me until I learned my lesson from it. God told Paul He will not remove his thorn, because His grace is enough to endure his trial (thorn) that he is facing, and grace is what kept Paul (and me) close to God, always depending on Him at all times.

The grace that God gives me is the reward of my faith in Him, who is with me.

Trusting Jesus in Every Step.

I have been pouring out all my energy in trusting and depending on God for fifty years now. Jesus has been at my side, walking me through all the trials that I have faced, all this time. When the trials seem to be too tiring, Jesus carries me on His shoulders that makes me stronger, and I can see all that is ahead of me. Jesus helps me a lot through all the difficult choices I need to make. By making this one choice, letting Jesus into my life and have full control over my life, I can walk in complete Comfort, Love, and Compassion through this cold and angry world.

The biggest concern that was heavy on my mind was to make sure everyone was pleased and satisfied. However, I would still feel heavy and ugly inside. Until Jesus took over my life, He told me to start concerning myself in pleasing His Father in heaven instead of the people of this world. Pleasing anyone else, then God will hurt us and hinder our walk with Him. I now make sure that God is pleased with me before anyone else and number one, above all else. Doing the will of God brought me the peace and love that I was always looking for. It has been a struggle to conquer the trials that has been before me, but I have the best defense, my Lord and Savior Jesus

Christ. Jesus always had my back, even when the situation looked too dark to endure. I have come across people that can walk through dark situations with ease and no pain at all. However, Jesus told me that they might think that they endured the darkness on their own, but they have not.

Walking this earth without Jesus's Light will only be a temporary victory. For Jesus's light never goes out, and in turn, the darkness can never claim victory. So if we keep focus on Jesus and not on our situation, His Light will lead us through the darkness and right into the Presence of His Father. As the Word of God says:

"Even though I walk through the darkest valley, I will fear no evil, for you are with me; your rod and your staff, they comfort me". (Psalm 23:4).

"Do not judge, or you too will be judged, for in the same way you judge others, you will be judged, and with the measure you use, it will be measured to you". (Matthew 7:1-2).

"Fear of man will prove to be a snare, but whoever trusts in the Lord is kept safe. Many seek an audience with a ruler, but it is from the Lord that man gets justice". (Proverb 29:25-26).

The Word of God—The Weapon to Make Satan Flee.

I get all my advice from the word of God. In the Bible, the word of God is referred to as a sword (a weapon). This Sword (weapon) is part of the Armor of God (the Shield that protects us). As the Word of God says: *"Take the helmet of salvation and the sword of the Spirit, which is the Word of God". (Ephesians 6:17).* And Satan will try to steal away the Word of God, if you are not totally in God's Word (of Knowledge and Strength). As the Word of God tells us:

"The Farmer sows the Word [the seed]. Some people are like seeds along the path, where the Word is sown, as soon as they hear it, and Satan comes and takes away the Word that was sown in them". (Mark 4:14-15).

Satan will use the worries and desires of this world to choke the word of God out of us, making us unfruitful for serving and fulfilling God's will. In the Word of God, it says: *"The worries of this life, the deceitfulness of wealth and the desires for other things, comes in and chokes the word, making it unfruitful". (Mark 4:19).*

Finally, we must be the seed planted in good soil that produces good fruit. Therefore, when you hear the Word of God, accept it, listen to it, and do it, and you will receive a great reward of a hundred times its worth. Be like what it says in the Bible, *"Others are like seed sown on good soil, they hear the word, accept it and produce a crop, thirty, sixty or even a hundred times what was sown". (Mark 4:20).*

The Word of God is the only weapon that can resist all those arrows that Satan throws our way in our daily life. Staying in Word of God and never getting tired of serving Him will make you strong and prepared for all of Satan's burning arrows that he throws your way. I cannot say it enough. Never tire of doing God's work that He gives you to do. The work may seem hard at the times, but with the strength that Jesus provides, we can do anything. As Word of God says:

"I can do all things through Christ who strengthens me". (Philippians 4:13). And don't forget: *"With God nothing is impossible".* (Matthew 19:26). Therefore, you must always remember to Praise God wholeheartedly. Glory and Victory is God's, always and forevermore. Amen.

Going to and Listening to the Star Team.

We must be attuned to God's Voice and be willing to sit with Him and listen to all He has to say. For Jesus went through everything that we are going through (and much worse!). Jesus knows every angle to conquer all situations. Jesus went to the cross for us so that we can have His Father's Protection and Presence when we need a helping hand and a place of refuge.

As long as we confess, repent of our sins, and come to Him, God will listen to us. The only path to the Father is His Son Jesus. Nothing can separate us from God. Jesus said it all when He said on the Cross: *"When He had received the drink, Jesus said, 'It is finished'. With that, He bowed His Head and gave up His Spirit".* (John 19:30). The Curtain of the Temple was torn in two so that we are free to enter His Father's Presence and be face-to-face to talk (and listen) out all that needs to be talked out. Jesus is mine (and yours), a constant companion, when there is no one else around. Someone that understands all of my situations that I face on this earth. All I need to do is to reach out my hand and whisper His Name. In that moment, His Light shines down, and I begin to feel His Love, comforting me in the midst of confusion, while His Hand pulls me ever so closer to His Heart of gold. As the Word of God says:

"The Sovereign Lord has given me a well-instructed tongue, to know the word that sustains the weary. He wakes me morning by morning, wakes my ear to listen like one being instructed. The Lord has opened my ears; I have not been rebellious, I have not turned away, because the Sovereign Lord helps me, and I will not be disgraced. Therefore have I set my face like flint, and I know I will not be put to shame". (Isaiah 50:4-5, 7).

"Listen, listen to Me, and eat what is good and you will delight in the richest fare. Give ear and come to Me; listen, that you may live. I will make an everlasting

covenant with you, my faithful love promised to David. (Isaiah 55:2b-3).

"Seek the Lord while He may be found; call on Him while He is near. Let the wicked forsake their ways and the unrighteous their ways. Let them turn to the Lord, and He will have mercy on them, and to our God, for He will freely pardon. For my thoughts are not your thoughts, neither are your ways my ways", declares the Lord". (Isaiah 55:6-8).

"And when Jesus had cried out in a loud voice, He gave up His spirit. At that moment, the curtain of the temple was torn in two, from top to bottom. The earth shook, the rocks split and the tombs broke open. The bodies of many holy people who had died were raised to life. They came out of the tombs after Jesus' resurrection and went into the holy city and appeared to many people". (Matthew 27:50-53).

When I relax in the everlasting arms of God, all my weaknesses are made strong, giving me energy to continue on the journey that I am on. Therefore, I continually walk gently through these hard days, leaning on Jesus for help and comfort. It is the best way to live life on this angry and cold world. There is nothing on the earth that Jesus cannot fix. The Word of God says: *"The eternal God is your refuge, and underneath are the everlasting arms. He will drive out your enemies before you, saying, 'Destroy them!'". (Deuteronomy 33:27).*

"I remain confident of this: I will see the goodness of the Lord in the land of the living. Wait for the Lord; be strong and take heart and wait for the Lord". (Psalm 27:13-14).

Here are just a few things to do to keep your walk gentle:

<u>One</u>: To give a friendly smile.

<u>Two</u>: Show mercy, kindness, patience and forgiveness toward others.

<u>Three</u>: Utilize God's Wisdom in all situations.

<u>Four</u>: Use loving guidance for those who have gone astray.

<u>Five</u>: Use gentle, healing words of peace. Never use harsh words, for they never solve anything.

Those harsh words will start arguments and rage, which may lead to sinning. Therefore, do what the Word of God says:

"A soft answer turns away wrath, but a harsh word stirs up anger". (Proverbs 15:1).

"Take my yoke upon you, and learn from me, for I am gentle and lowly in heart, and you will find rest for your souls. For my yoke is easy, and my burden is light". (Matthew 11:29-30).

"Let your reasonableness be known to everyone. The Lord is at hand; do not be anxious about anything, but in everything by prayer and supplication with thanksgiving let your requests be made known to God". (Philippians 4:5-6).

"In your hearts, revere Christ the Lord. Always be prepared to give an answer to everyone who asks you to give the reason for the hope that you have. However, do this with gentleness and respect, keeping a clear conscience, so that those who speak maliciously against your good behavior in Christ may be ashamed of their slander. For it is better, if it is God's will, to suffer for doing good than for doing evil. For Christ also suffered once for sins, the righteous for the unrighteous, to bring you to God. He was put to death in the body, but made alive in the Spirit". (1 Peter 3:15-18).

"Remind the people to be subject to rulers and authorities, to be obedient, to be ready to do whatever is good, to slander no one, to be peaceable and considerate, and always to be gentle toward everyone". (Titus 3:1-2).

"For where you have envy and selfish ambition, there you find disorder and every evil practice. However, the wisdom from heaven is first of all pure; then peace-loving, considerate, submissive, full of mercy and good fruit, impartial and sincere. Peacemakers who sow in peace reap a harvest of righteousness". (James 3:16-18).

"Brothers and sisters, if someone is caught in a sin, you who live by the Spirit should restore that person gently. However, watch yourselves, or you also may be tempted. Carry each other's burdens, and in this way you will fulfill the law of Christ". (Galatians 6:1-2).

"Love is patient and kind. It does not envy, it does not boast, it is not proud. It does not dishonor others, it is not self-seeking, it is not easily angered, it keeps no record of wrong. Love does not delight in evil, rejoices with the truth. It always protects, always trusts, always hopes, and always perseveres. Love never fails". (1 Corinthians 13:4-8a).

Trusting God one day at a time keeps us close to Him and Him close to us. As the Bible says: *"Remain in Me, as I also remain in you. No branch can bear fruit unless you remain in Me. I am the Vine; you are the branches. If you remain in Me, and I in you, you will bear much fruit; apart from Me you can do nothing. If you do not remain in Me, you are like a branch that is thrown away and withers; such branches are picked up, thrown into the fire and burned. If you remain in Me and My Words remain in you, ask whatever you wish, and it will be done for you. This is to My Father's Glory, that you bear much fruit, showing yourselves to be my disciples"*. *(John 15:4-8)*.

We must yield to the Holy Spirit's gentle touch that prompts us to live in deep dependence on God. As the Word of God says: "Therefore do not worry about tomorrow, for tomorrow will worry about itself. Each day has trouble of its own" (Matthew 6:34). Our depending on God is what God is asking us to do. Living out God's ways is living a worry free life.

We Live by God's Ways.

To live by God's ways, we can do these three simple things:

<u>One</u>: Give God your full attention. Set aside all distractions and focus only on seeking a closer relationship with Him.

<u>Two</u>: Follow God's Directions when He speaks to you. This is necessary; for it is His Directions to obey all the His Instructions that God reveals to you. Listen to God's Voice and all He speaks to you, and it will bring His Peace to your soul. I know this is true, because I went through a season of not listening to what God told me, and my mind was all in confusion and a place where nothing fits together (and there is no peace). I got it together after I read 1 Peter 3:10-12. It says: *"Whoever desires to love life and see good days, let him keep his tongue from evil and his lips from speaking deceit; let him turn away from evil and do good; let him seek Peace and pursue it. For the Eyes of the Lord are on the righteous, and His Ears are open to their prayer. But the Face of the Lord is against those who do evil."*

<u>Three</u>: Accept God's Provision as a requirement, to base all your actions and decisions on the Truth of God's Word, always depending on Him for

everything and anything.

With these three simple ways to live as God desires us to, it should make our choice easier to proclaim that I have chosen to walk humbly and simply, side by side with Jesus, because this is the best way to live out God's ways and desires. Because God is watching over all and He is watching all time.

Here now are some Scriptures to remind you to live by God's Ways. Meditate on these Scriptures and do what they say. Your mind will be full of Peace and Joy, which is what God offers to those who listen and obey His Word:

"'Whoever acknowledges Me before others, I will also acknowledge before My Father in Heaven. But whoever disowns Me before others, I will disown before My Father in Heaven'".

(Matthew 10:32-33).

"'Whoever finds their life will lose it, and whoever loses their life for my sake will find it. Anyone who welcomes you, welcomes me, and anyone who welcomes Me welcomes the One who sent Me'". *(Matthew 10:39-40).*

"'And whoever welcomes a righteous person as a righteous person will receive a righteous person's reward'". *(Matthew 10:41b).*

With Jesus by my side, I have courage to not fear in times of trouble, courage to trust in all His Promises—the Promises that make Him the God of Power and of Love. I know that *"God is Love". (1 John 4:8)*; it is who He is. I also know that I can trust Him that He will never leave me or fail to finish the work He started with me. I am so full with so much gratitude for my Star Team that I am overwhelmed with Joy and Peace. Nothing compares to this Truth - Jesus lives in me!

How does Jesus's indwelling presence affect me? Well, it affects me a lot. You see, my Lord Jesus came to live within me, at a time in my life when I was unsure of myself and I was slipping into that pit of despair. I am now confident that Jesus will dwell in me as long as I dwell in Him. There is no better companion than my Lord and friend Jesus. Jesus will always be there for me (and you too) whenever I call out for help.

Spiritual transformation and growth can be in reach by submitting to

Jesus and allowing Him to express Himself in us. As I let Jesus express Himself through me, I start to break free from any kind of worry that is lingering in my mind. As the Word of God says:

"Therefore, I tell you, do not worry about your life, what you will eat or drink; or about your body, what you will wear. Isn't life more than food and the body more than clothes? Therefore, do not worry about tomorrow, for tomorrow will worry about itself. Each day has enough trouble of its own". (Matthew 6:25, 34).

When we are followers of Jesus, we need not be anxious, for Jesus takes all our worry away. We do not need to worry when we believe that Jesus will carry our burdens for us. The Word of God says, ***"Come to Me, all you who are weary and burdened, and I will give you rest. Take***

My yoke upon you and learn from Me, for I am Gentle and Humble in heart, and you will find rest for your souls. For My yoke is easy and my burden is Light". *(Matthew 11:28-30).*

A believer has to place his trust in the Lord Jesus, for Salvation and Hope, you then receive Eternal Life. A follower goes beyond what the believer does and seeks to know and obey God.

When you begin your seek through the Word of God (the Bible), Jesus begins to live in you; and you in Him. This action begins the process of avoiding ways of worry. I say process because it does not happen overnight to have a worry-free life. I still battle those arrows of doubt that Satan continually throws my way. However, with my Bible and Jesus by my side helping me, I can shield off Satan's arrows. This is what God looks for in us, for us to trust and believe that His Son Jesus is with us every step. Nothing else can prove to God that we are trustworthy and worry-free than when we walk hand-in-hand with Jesus's His beloved Son.

From the first moment I needed help to today's beautiful sunrise, my Star Team has been with me comforting me, protecting me, helping me, and most of all loving me. I will always be thankful for that first moment that Jesus comforted me and for never leaving me. That first moment in my life, I learned to let go of any kind of worldly possessions that I thought I needed.

That moment, Jesus extended out His hand to me and told me to follow Him, to a life of Peace and Love. I knew then that I would always have Love and Comfort with me; that He so freely gives to those who need it. Jesus will always be holding my hand, even though the fire of this world will always be in front of me; for that fire will never burn me. I love my Star Team and my Star Team loves me. My security (hope) lies in His arms, where He will always welcome me.

Every step I take in God's Light will always shine down on me; to keep me protected from the arrows of temptation that Satan is continually throwing in my direction. The One who will never change or never leave me is the One that will always be holding on to my hand, so I never am lost or hurt.

The Power of Scripture (God's Word).

Read these Scriptures and feel the Power of the Star Team:

"Righteousness and Justice are the Foundation of Your Throne; Love and Faithfulness go before You. Blessed are those who have learned to acclaim You, who walk in the Light of Your Presence, Lord. They rejoice in Your Name all day long; they celebrate Your Righteousness. For you are their Glory and Strength, and by Your favor You exalt our horn. Indeed, our Shield belongs to the Lord, our King to the Holy One of Israel". (Psalm 89:14-18).

"Jesus Christ is the same yesterday and today and forever. Do not be carried away by all kinds of strange teachings. It is good for our hearts to be strengthened by Grace, not by eating ceremonial foods, which is of no benefit to those who do so". (Hebrews 13:8-9).

"For I am the Lord your God who takes hold of your right hand and says to you—Do not fear; I will help you". *(Isaiah 41:13).*

"Therefore, do not grumble, as some of them did—and were killed by the destroying angel". (1 Corinthians 10:10).

"Therefore, since we are receiving a kingdom that cannot be shaken, let us be thankful, and so worship God acceptably with reverence and awe, for our 'God is a consuming fire'". (Hebrews 12:28-29).

"The Wrath of God is being revealed from Heaven against all the godlessness and wickedness of people, who suppress the truth by their wickedness, since what may be known about God is plain to them, because God has made it plain to them. For since the creation of the world God's invisible qualities—His eternal power and divine nature— have been clearly seen, being understood from what has been made, so that people are without excuse". (1 Corinthians 1:18-20).

"Repent, then, and turn to God, so that your sins may be wiped out, that times of refreshing may come from the Lord, and that He may send the Messiah, who has been appointed for you—even Jesus. Heaven must receive Him until the time comes for God to restore everything, as He promised long ago through His holy prophets". (Acts 3:19-21).

"Sow Righteousness for yourselves, reap the Fruit of Unfailing Love, and break up your unplowed ground; for it is time to seek the Lord, until He comes and showers His righteousness on you". (Hosea 10:12).

"Here is a trustworthy saying: If we die with Him, we also live with Him; if we endure, we will also reign with Him. If we disown Him, He will also disown us; if we are faithless, He remains faithful, for He cannot disown Himself". (2 Timothy 2:11-13).

Jesus Christ is the Ultimate servant-leader. We can learn by His example of leadership and how to be a servant to others. As the Bible says:

"The Son is the image of the invisible God, the firstborn over all creation. For in Him all things were created: things in heaven and on earth, visible and invisible, whether thrones or powers or rulers or authorities; all things have been created through Him…. And in Him all things hold together". (Colossians 1:15-17).

God's Message to me is that I am to trust and wait for Him before I do anything. Directing all my attention is on Him and what He will do will give me the patience to wait and trust Him, with every fiber of my heart and soul, the way that God designed me to live. While I am here on this earth, I will be living in deep dependence on God and doing all that He instructs me to do and say. God will keep me safe in His Presence, where I will receive the Joy and Peace He gives me while waiting for Him. Waiting on God is being quiet and listening for His Voice to tell me where He wants me to go and spread His Message of Love, Hope, and Peace. All the things I do are for the Glory of God.

We are never alone in the waiting. Jesus is right beside us, giving us the strength to do His Father's work. Going forward with Jesus is all that we need to do to spread the joy and love that God gives us. In addition, we must be forgiving and let go of all worldly things that hinders our walk with Jesus. In turn, our Heavenly Father will renew our minds, heal our wounded hearts, and strengthen us because as the Word of God says:

"I can do all things through Christ who strengthens me". (Philippians 4:13).

"Do not conform to the pattern of this world, but be transformed by the renewing of your mind. Then you will be able to test and approve what God's will is—His Good, Pleasing and Perfect Will". (Romans 12:2).

"The Lord is close to the brokenhearted and saves those who are crushed in spirit. The righteous person may have many troubles, but the Lord delivers him from them all; He protects all his bones, not one of them will be broken". (Psalm 34:18-20).

"And provide for those who grieve in Zion—to bestow on them a crown of beauty instead of ashes, the oil of joy instead of mourning, and a garment of praise instead of a spirit of despair. They will be called oaks of righteousness, a planting of the Lord for the display of His splendor". (Isaiah 61:3).

"My flesh and my heart may fail, but God is the Strength of my heart and my Portion forever". (Psalm 73:26).

"Be still and know I am God. I will be exalted among the nations. I will be exalted among the earth". (Psalm 46:10).

Intimacy with the Almighty God - Through His Son, Jesus Christ:

The first thing you need to do to have an intimate relationship with God is believe in His Son Jesus and then confess your sins, repenting of them and turning away from them even in times of temptation that arises in this world. Then, fix your eyes on Jesus (at all times) and continually read your Bible, and Jesus will ask His Father to forgive, comfort, and protect you (always) through the fires of this corrupt world. The Word of God says:

"I am the way, and the truth, and the life. No one comes to the Father except through Me'".

(John 14:6).

"And I will do whatever you ask in My Name, so that the Father may be Glorified in the Son. You may ask Me for anything in My Name, and I will do it. If you love Me, keep My Commands'". (John 14:13-15).

This is why we choose the closeness of our Lord Jesus, let Him into our hearts, have full control, and carry us upon His shoulders when we become feeling weak. There are two more reasons to draw closer:

First:

Desire to be known (and to know) by God, which requires intense vulnerability and humility.

Second:

Have a relationship with God (through His Son) and all who He puts in our path, which also requires hard work and humility. The Word of God says, *"With God nothing is impossible". (Matthew 19:26).*

Whatever our Heavenly Father asks us to do, we will be able to do it. Of course, with His help. When our relationship with God is right, then all relationships will come together. You must dust off your Bible and read it to know God. If you do not have one, get one; it will keep your relationship close. There is no other way without opening your Bible that you will find God's Principles of how to live, breathe, and walk with Him. We must fill our minds with godly things and not worldly things. A prayer life is also essential.

These godly things do not just happen; They require effort on our part. That effort starts with prayer and reading God's Word (the Bible). I cannot say it enough, of how important it is to read the Bible. The Bible is where you can hear God speaking to you. The Bible says:

"All Scripture is God-breathed and is useful for teaching, rebuking, correcting

and training in righteousness, so that the servant of God may be thoroughly equipped for every good work". (2 Timothy 3:16-17).

When we live in communication with God, through His Son, Jesus, and reading the Bible, we establish an intimate relationship with Him. When we live the way God intends us to live, we Glorify Him, and He will look down and smile to say; 'Well done, my faithful friend'. We then will receive the Peace of God, and as His Son tells us:

"Peace I leave with you My peace I give you. I do not give to you as the world gives. Do not let your hearts be troubled and do not be afraid"*. (John 14:27).*

This only happens when you spend time in the Word of God and follow the example of His Son Jesus. We are God's children not His enemy, so you must act like His children, living in obedience, to Him and only Him. If you feel that you are falling away from God, just get on your knees, and in the name of Jesus, ask His Father why you feel this way and what you can do to right the wrong (if any), to get closer to Him. This is what reconciles us to our Heavenly Father. We then have the Peace that He Promised to give us. The word Peace translates to be the absence of hostility, strife, and disorder. As the Bible says: *"God is not a God of disorder, but of Peace—as in all the congregations of the Lord's people". (1 Corinthians 14:33).*

When you are one with Jesus, you can walk through difficult times with indescribable tranquility. I found, when facing trials, three Scriptural Truths that can guard my heart and mind:

"And we know that in all things God works for the good of those who love Him, who have been called according to His purpose". (Romans 8:28).

"The Lord has established His throne in heaven, and His kingdom rules over all". (Psalms 103:19).

"This is what the Lord says, He who made the earth, the Lord who formed it and established it, the Lord is His name: 'Call to Me and I will answer you and tell you great and unsearchable things you do not know'". (Jeremiah 33:2-3).

When troubles comes, remember that God is ruling over the situation, and He is greater than the troubles that you may be going through. God is in control. We just need to ask Him for help and depend on Him for everything. This is God's greatest desire, because everything God desires is in His Son Jesus. This is why our relationship with Jesus is very important to fulfill. For He gives us a sense of acceptance, purpose, and direction. A distinguishing characteristic of Jesus's peace is that when you least expect it, Jesus comes to you, and suddenly your troubling circumstances become distant memories.

***Remember, when Jesus told His disciples: *"In Me you may have Peace. In this world you will have tribulation, but take courage; I have overcome the world". (John 16:33).*

There is no limit to Jesus's peace. All you have to do is invite Him into your life and you receive His Unlimited Peace. To show Jesus your love for Him is to show your willingness to obey every command He gives you. You then receive the strength to face every challenge. When our first response is to seek out God's thoughts on the situation and follow all His Instructions, He will respond quickly with His Grace and Comfort that will strengthen us for the challenges.

Four things that will cause people (believers too) to lose God's Peace:

1. Sin. When you live in your sin, your peace evaporates.

2. Unbelief and Doubt. When you doubt God's promises, uncertainty and fear rules your thoughts.

3. Worry. When you have no trust in what Jesus tells, your thoughts start wandering. Remember this Scripture: *"Do not worry about tomorrow; for tomorrow will care for itself. Each day has enough trouble of its own". (Matthew 6:34).*

4. Mistreatment. When people use unkind or false words to hurt you, that brings you down.

If you bring everything to God in prayer and thankfulness, His Peace will surround you and protect you through every situation. Simply look up to God for help and continue reading His Word and watch what He does in your life. Our hearts will be calm enough to endure any circumstance that may want us to be anything but calm.

<u>Prayer</u>

Thank you, Father, for all your protection that you provided in my life. You were with me when I was young, and you are with me now. No place on earth I would rather be than in your comforting arms. In Jesus's name, I pray. Amen.

It is never too late to begin pursuing a deeper relationship with God. The Bible says: *"Forgetting what is ahead, behind and straining toward what is ahead, I press on toward the goal to win the prize for which God has called me heavenward in Christ Jesus". (Philippians 3:13b, 14).*

Here are some steps that you just might want to take to get started moving Heaven-bound. I did, and I will always be grateful that I did. I feel assured that I have a place in God's heart. You can have this assurance too.

<u>Step 1</u>: Read the Scriptures.

God will speak and teach you through His Word. Revealing who He is and what He does and how to live a righteous life in this dark and cold world.

<u>Step 2</u>: Always be willing to spend time alone with God.

That is in prayer, meditation, and worship. This time alone with God is to get to know Him better. The benefits are well worth your time.

<u>Step 3</u>: Put your Trust in God.

The base of any relationship depends on the level of trust. On a scale from 1 to 10, the trust that you should have for God should be a 10. Any less and you will find yourself struggling just getting up in the morning.

<u>Step 4</u>: Obey God.

Stepping out in obedience to Him shows that you trust Him, which leads to receiving the blessing He has for you. In addition, it reveals more of Him in your life.

<u>Step 5</u>: Observe always how Jesus is in your life.

Paying attention to how He works in your life shows Him that His ways are what works to overcome this dark and cold world.

<u>Step 6</u>: Make God your top priority.

You must, I repeat, you must be willing to lay aside anything that competes with your loyalty and devotion to God. Nothing even comes close to the Love of God. Knowing God intimately is attainable. The key is persistence.

Forget past failures and press on. Keep calm, and push back the past. Learn from those past failures, trust in God, and walk confidently with Jesus.

The Ultimate Example

W̶e all need an example to follow to live a righteous and calm life. That example is our Lord and Savior Jesus Christ. In this world, we cannot find one. Some settle with what the world offers; which does not last. What happens to them if they do follow what the world offers? They end up wandering aimlessly, bitter, empty, and alone. We need to live the way Jesus does, with total trust in His Father. Jesus overcame this world, and He knows all the ins and outs of this world. Holding on to Jesus gives you the courage and strength that we all need to overcome this world. We become our true selves when we abide in Jesus as Jesus abides in us.

As the Word of God says: *"For it is God who works in you to will and to act in order to fulfill His good purpose. Do everything without grumbling or arguing, so that you may become blameless and pure". (Philippians 2:13-15a).*

"Have I not commanded you? Be strong and courageous. Do not be afraid; do not be discouraged, for the Lord you God will be with you wherever you go". (Joshua 1:9).

This is the heart of the Gospel, not that Jesus saved us from death, but that He empowers us to live for Him as He lives in and through us.

Always Desiring Jesus in Our Lives:

The Word of God is powerful and life-changing.

The Word of God is awesome and well worth living.

The Word of God gives me reason to seek and desire to know more about my Heavenly Father and my Lord Jesus.

The Word of God is more precious than gold. Every time I open my Bible, I am always encouraged and inspired. Here are some of my favorite

Scriptures (not the only ones) that keep me recharged and inspired:

"All Scripture is God-breathed and is useful for teaching, rebuking, correcting and training in righteousness, so that the man of God may be thoroughly equipped for every good work". (2 Timothy 3:16-17).

"He gives power to the weak and strength to the powerless. Even youths will become weak and tired, and young men will fall into exhaustion. However, those who trust in the Lord will find new strength. They will soar high on wings like eagles. They will run and not grow weary. They will run and not grow weary. They will walk and not faint". (Isaiah 40:29-31).

"Come to Me, all who are weary and burdened, and I will give you rest. Take My yoke upon you and learn from Me, for I am gentle and humble in heart and you will find rest for your souls". (Matthews 11:28-29).

"And this same God who takes care of me will supply all your needs from his glorious riches which have been given to us in Christ Jesus". (Philippians 4:19).

"But whoever listens to Me will live in safety and be at ease, without fear of harm". (Proverbs 1:33).

"For I know the plans I have for you,' says the Lord. 'They are plans for good and not for disaster, to give you a future and a hope'" *(Jeremiah 29:11).*

"And because of His glory and excellence, He has given us great and precious promises. There are promises that enable you to share His divine nature and escape the world's corruption caused by human desires". (1 Peter 1:4).

"If you confess with your mouth that Jesus is Lord and believe in your heart that God raised Him from the dead, you will be saved". (Romans 10:9).

"For the wages of sin is death, but the free gift of God is Eternal Life through Christ Jesus our Lord". (Romans 6:23).

"I am leaving you with a gift, peace of mind and heart. In addition, the Peace I give is a gift the world cannot give. So do not be troubled or afraid". *(John 14:27).*

"My flesh and my heart may fail, but God is the strength of my heart and my portion forever". (Psalm 73:26).

"Be still and know I am God. I will be exalted among the nation. I will be exalted in the earth". (Psalm 46:10).

Three ways that show that we are living in a deep faith:

First: Believe! Second: Believe! Third: Believe!

Yes, that is all it takes. Just believe, and nothing will shake you. No matter the circumstances or how we feel, we must hang on to God's unchanging character: He is good, loving, all-powerful, knows every detail of our life, is in control, will save us, and will intercede when things get too hard for us. God does not change our circumstances. God promises to be with us and walk with us right through those hard circumstances that weigh us down so much.

Remember all the things that God has already done for you and gotten you through and strengthened every day to walk through the shadows of the world and into the gates of His kingdom. The place where you will find all the best treasures is in heaven, waiting for you. For there is nothing in the earth that could please us more than the Love of our Father in Heaven. The Word of God says; "I have not departed from the Commands of God's lips; I have treasured the Words of His mouth more than my daily bread". (Job 23:12).

Jesus says: *"I will never leave you; I will never abandon you"*. *(Hebrews 13:5)*.

Faith and Obedience (A Life Apart)

*M*any times in the Bible I read that Faith and Obedience is the Key to move mountains: The mountains of evil doings, the mountains of difficulties, and the mountains of despair. Both Faith and Obedience must go hand-in-hand to achieve the action of moving the mountains that we come across in this world. Living a Life of Faith and Obedience is a Life apart from living in this world. God rewards those who live, seek His presence, and faithfully obey Him. Enabling them with Courage and Strength that conquers all the troubles of this world. Three important things you must do to live the Life that is apart from this world:

<u>First</u>, we must; seek God, know God, enjoy God, and most of all love God. Let Him guide you through the 'valleys of darkness'. Then you will not fear anything that Satan throws your way to make you stumble.

<u>Second</u>, we must persevere and hold on to Jesus's strength. For we have to struggle through this world for His name's sake, for we all know that Jesus overcame this world and knows exactly what to do to send Satan running away with his tail between his legs.

<u>Third</u>, we must be ready to live apart from this world and live with Jesus in Peace and Love, being ready to obey every Command He says. Spreading God's Love and Joy is much easier than we think.

When we live out His ways, we show the world who God is. God's Compassion shines through us when we walk in Trust and Obedience alongside Jesus Christ our Lord, Savior, and Friend.

"For to us a child is born, to us a Son is given and the government will be on His shoulder. And He will be called; Wonderful Counselor, Mighty God, Everlasting Father, prince of Peace". (Isaiah 9:6).

I know God goes before me. God stands behind me. God is right beside me to guide me all the time. I can walk with confidence and hope of His Protection. What really matters is that the Great I Am is, was, and always will be forever with me, no matter what this dark and angry world throws at me.

From the first day that I opened the door to my Lord, and invited Him into my life, I can depend upon Him to give me His tender loving comfort and friendship, in my time of need; when no one was around. My Star Team is always available for me when I am in need.

There are two key qualities that Jesus Commands for us to do:

"'Love the Lord your God, with all your heart and with all your soul and with all your mind'. This is the first and Greatest Commandment. And the second is like it: 'Love your neighbor as yourself'. All the Law and the Prophets hang on these two Commandments'". (Matthew 22:37-40).

With these two Commands that our Lord gives us makes it quite clear what we are to do and how we are to live. Faith, Obedience and most of all Love, to help us keep these two commands alive.

Five Facts and Scriptures to Help You Understand about Spiritual Maturity:

1. Spiritual Maturity is intentional.

"So, Christ Himself gave the apostles, the prophets, the evangelists, the pastors and teachers, to equip His people for works of service. So that the body of Christ may be built up until we all reach unity in the faith and in the knowledge of the Son of God and become mature, attaining to the whole measure of the fullness of Christ. Then we will no longer be infants, tossed back and forth by the waves, and blown here and there by every wind of teaching and by the cunning and craftiness of people in their deceitful scheming. Instead, speaking the truth in love, we will grow to become in every respect the mature body of Him who is the head, that is, Christ. From Him the whole body, joined and held together by every supporting ligament, grows and builds itself up in love, as each part does its work". (Ephesians 4:11-16).

(Meaning of this Scripture is that through our reading of Word of God and accepting His Son Jesus, we are equipped and ready to go out and spread the good news of the gospel).

2. Spiritual Maturity is a process.

"Therefore, dear friends, since you have been forewarned, be on your guard so that you may not be carried away by the error of the lawless and fall from your secure position. However, grow in the grace and knowledge of our Lord and Savior Jesus Christ. To Him be the glory both now and forever! Amen". (2 Peter 3:17-18).

(Meaning of this Scripture is to always seek first the kingdom of God, and you will have the knowledge and strength to fulfill God's will and purpose).

3. Spiritual Maturity requires discipline.

"Everything God created is good, and nothing is to be rejected if it is received

with thanksgiving, because it is consecrated by the word of God and prayer. If you point these things out to the brothers and sisters, you will be a good minister of Christ Jesus, nourished on the truths of the faith and of the good teaching that you have followed. Have nothing to do with godless myths and old wives' tales; rather, train yourself to be godly. For physical training is of some value, but godliness has value for all things, holding promise for both the present life and the life to come. This is a trustworthy saying that deserves full acceptance. That is why we labor and strive, because we have put our hope in the living God, who is the Savior of all people, and especially of those who believe. Command and teach these things.

Do not let anyone look down on you because you are young, but set an example for the believers in speech, in conduct, in love, in faith and in purity. Until I come, devote yourself to the public reading of Scripture, to preaching and teaching. Do not neglect your gift, which was given you through prophecy, when the body of elders laid their hands on you. Be diligent in these matters; give yourself wholly to them, so that everyone may see your progress. Watch your life and doctrine closely. Persevere in them, because if you do, you will save both yourself and your hearers". (1 Timothy 4:6-15).

(Meaning of these Scripture verses are quite clear. Following the commands of God will give us the knowledge and wisdom we so need to show and teach others who God is and how much He loves us).

4. Spiritual Maturity is about love-based obedience (of listening and doing).

"Do not merely listen to the word, and so deceive yourselves. Do what it says. Anyone who listens to the word but does not do what it says is as if someone who looks at his face in a mirror and, after looking at himself, goes away and immediately forgets what he looks like. But whoever looks intently into the perfect law that gives freedom, and continues in it—not forgetting what they have heard, but doing it—they will be blessed in what they do". (James 1:22-25).

(Meaning—When we just listen to the Word of God and do not immediately put it into action, we forget what we hear, giving Satan his chance to lure us into his wicked world).

Therefore, to me I will thrive to put all I hear and read of God's Word into action, to stay strong and courageous, in Jesus's Name. Amen. Keeping out of Satan's wicked schemes is very impossible for us to do on our own. However, we have Jesus (who overcame Satan) by our side, and so you and I can overcome Satan too. Thank you, Jesus!

5. Spiritual Maturity is about growing closer to Jesus.

"Remain in Me, as I also remain in you. No branch can bear fruit by itself; it must remain in the vine. Neither can you bear fruit unless you remain in me. I am the vine; you are the branches. If you remain in Me and I in you, you will bear much fruit; apart from Me you can do nothing. If you do not remain in Me, you are like a branch that is thrown away and withers; such branches are picked up, thrown into the fire and burned. If you remain in Me and My words remain in you, ask whatever you wish, and it will be done for you. This is to my Father's Glory, that you bear much fruit, showing yourselves to be my disciples". (John 15:4-8).

(Meaning—It is very important to draw close to Jesus and keep that close relationship with Him, ever so fresh, so you can overcome Satan and his evil ways).

Four Truths about the Indwelling of Jesus Christ in Us (with Scripture):

1. Our Lord Jesus is our only source for the seeking of His Father's wisdom, for without continually seeking nourishment from Him, we have no life.

"Jesus said to them, **'Very truly I tell you, unless you eat the flesh of the Son of Man and drink His blood, you have no life in you. Whoever eats My flesh and drinks My blood has Eternal Life, and I will raise them up at the last day. For my flesh is real food and my blood is real drink'".** (John 6:53-55).

"'Just as the living Father sent Me and I live because of the Father, so the one who feeds on Me will live because of Me'". (John 6:58).

2. The wonderful mystery of Christ-living is evidence of a future reality of a completely restored life.

"The mystery that has been kept hidden for ages and generations, but is now disclosed to the Lord's people. To them God has chosen to make known among the Gentiles the glorious riches of this mystery, which is Christ in you, the hope of glory. For He is the one we proclaim, admonishing and teaching everyone with all wisdom, so that we may present everyone fully mature in Christ". (Colossians 1:26-28).

3. Our Spiritual Identity is rooted in Christ's Righteousness.

"You, however, are not in the realm of the flesh but are in the realm of the Spirit, if indeed the Spirit of God lives in you. In addition, if anyone does not have the Spirit of Christ, they do not belong to Christ. However, if Christ is in you, then even though your body is subject to death because of sin, the Spirit gives life because of righteousness. In addition, the Spirit of Him who raised Jesus from the dead is living in you; He who raised Christ from the dead will also give life to your mortal bodies because of His Spirit who lives in you. Therefore, brothers and sisters, we have an obligation—but it is not to the flesh, to live according to it". (Romans 8:9-12).

"For this reason I kneel before the Father, from whom every family in heaven and on earth derives its name. I pray that out of His glorious riches He may strengthen you with power through His Spirit in your inner being, so that Christ may dwell in your hearts through faith. And I pray that you, being rooted and established in love". (Ephesians 3:14-17).

4. Putting your faith in Jesus as you increasingly become your true self. Jesus took the cross for you; your false self was buried along with your sin.

"Since then, you have been raised with Christ, set your hearts on things above, where Christ is seated at the right hand of God. Set your minds on things above, not on earthly things. For you died, and your life is now hidden with Christ in God. When Christ, who is your life, appears, then you also will appear with Him in glory. Put to death, therefore, whatever belongs to your earthly nature: sexual immorality, impurity, lust, evil desires and greed, which is idolatry. Because of these, the Wrath of God is coming". (Colossians 3:1-6).

Taking a Slower Pace

The quiet time you take to dwell in God's presence must be at a slow pace. This time with God is not to be in a hurry, like how the world lives. In this world, our daily lives are so full of appointments of many kinds. We start to "panic" and start worrying if we are going to get everything done by the end of the day. This is why we need quiet time with the Star Team (not being in much anguish). The Bible says:

"*Do not let your heart be troubled; believe in God, believe also in Me*". *(John 14:1).*

*"**Peace I leave with you; My peace I give to you; not as the world gives do I give to you. Do not let your heart be troubled, nor let it be fearful**"*. *(John 14:27).*

"If a ruler's anger rises against you, do not leave your post; calmness can lay great offenses to rest". (Ecclesiastes 10:4).

"Do not fret because of those who are evil or be envious of those who do wrong; for like the grass they will soon wither, like green plants they will soon die away. Trust in the Lord and do good; dwell in the land and enjoy safe pastures. Take delight in the Lord, and He will give you the desires of your heart. Commit your way to the Lord; trust in Him and He will do this: He will make your righteous reward shine like the dawn, your vindication like the noonday sun. Be still before the Lord and wait patiently for Him; do not fret when people succeed in their ways, when they carry out their wicked schemes. Refrain from anger and turn from wrath; do not fret—it leads only to evil. For those who are evil will be destroyed, but those who hope in the Lord will inherit the land. A little while, and the wicked will be no more; though you look for them, they will not be found. But the meek will inherit the land and enjoy Peace and Prosperity". (Psalm 37:1-11).

Therefore, as you dwell in God's Presence, you must do so at a slow pace and spend that precious time alone with Him. There is no one else that can calm you down as only God can. We need to set aside time every day (even if it is just ten minutes of our time) to be comforted by the One who can fill us with His Calmness and to remember the things that brought us to Him.

Here are some of things:

1. God's Creation.

"In the beginning, God created the Heavens and the earth". (Genesis 1:1).

2. Our brokenness.

"If any of you lacks wisdom, you should ask God, who gives generously to all without finding fault, and it will be given to you. However, when you ask, you must believe and not doubt, because the one who doubts is like a wave of the sea, blown and tossed by the wind. That person should not expect to receive anything from the Lord. Such a person is double-minded and unstable in all they do". (James 1:5-8).

3. Through a relationship with His Son Jesus.

*"**All things have been committed to Me by My Father. No one knows the Son except the Father, and no one knows the Father except the Son and those to whom the Son chooses to reveal Him. Come to Me, all you who are weary and burdened, and I will give you rest. Take My Yoke upon you and learn from Me, for I am Gentle and Humble in heart, and you will find rest for your souls. For My Yoke is Easy and My Burden is Light'**". (Matthew 11:27-30).*

"This is the message we have heard from Him and declare to you; God is Light; in Him there is no darkness at all. If we claim to have fellowship with Him and yet walk in the darkness, we lie and do not live out the Truth. But if we walk in the Light as He is in the Light, we have fellowship with one another, and the Blood of Jesus, His Son, purifies us from all sin". (John 1:1-7).

*"**Remain in Me, as I also remain in you. No branch can bear fruit by itself; it must remain in the Vine. Neither can you bear fruit unless you remain in Me. I am the Vine; you are the branches. If you remain in Me and I in you, you will bear much fruit; apart from Me you can do nothing'**". (John 15:4-5).*

"This is Love: not that we loved God, but that He loved us and sent His Son as an atoning sacrifice for our sins. Dear friends, since God so loved us, we also ought to love one another. No one has ever seen God; but if we love one another, God lives in us and His love is made complete in us". (1 John 4:10-12).

"Therefore, get rid of all bitterness, rage and anger, brawling and slander, along with every form of malice. Be kind and compassionate to one another,

forgiving each other, just as in Christ God forgave you". (Ephesians 4:31-32).

4. The need to receive Mercy and Grace.

"The Lord is merciful and gracious; He is slow to get angry and full of unfailing love". (Psalm 103:8).

These moments with God are not for being lazy but to rest, worship, and acknowledge Him. God's Presence is to greatly admire and honor Him, for it is the beginning of the relationship with Him. What follows is priceless, worthy of His Praise. Let us slow down then and rest in God's Presence to be refreshed physically, mentally, and emotionally.

Prayer

Father, Grant us with Your Spiritual and Physical Rest. Help us to take the time to spend with You. Please remove any obstacle that would keep us from having a more balanced Spiritual Life spent with You. Thank you. In Jesus's Name, I pray. Amen.

Having a Conquering Spirit

----

*D*ay after day, we face countless obstacles, which at times we feel like giving up (which we must not). When I feel the urge to give up, I start remembering that Jesus never gave up or gave in to the temptations that Satan was hurling at Him (Jesus was faithful in fulfilling His Father's will). I also picture my journey as a race, with hope in getting to the finish line and hearing God tell me, **'Well done, my faithful servant, you have done a good job'.** This gets me through the dark valleys and rocky paths, which make me stumble on this earth.

To have a Conquering Spirit, we need to work these five things into your life; to assure you are on the Right Path to Glory:

1. Courage:

God delights in empowering us in our weaknesses, so He gets the victory and glory.

"Be strong and of good courage, do not fear nor be afraid of them; for the Lord your God, He is the One who goes with you. He will not leave you nor forsake you". (Deuteronomy 31:6).

2. Confidence:

When we doubt, we stumble. Then we question our ability to do God's Will. So instead of doubting just put your confidence in Jesus, knowing that He will enable you to do His Father's Will with His Strength.

"Therefore, let us draw near with confidence to the throne of grace, so that we may receive mercy and find grace to help in our time of need". (Hebrews 4:16).

3. Commitment:

We must be committed completely and totally to God to carry out His will. For He will guide us and provide for us whatever we need.

"For this is the Will of God, your sanctification; that is, that you abstain from sexual immorality; that each of you know how to possess his own vessel in sanctification and honor, not in lustful passion, like the Gentiles who do not know God". (1 Thessalonians 4:3-7).

4. Persistence:

We have to press on through adversity toward that Eternal Value.

"Let us not become weary in doing good—for at the proper time we will reap a harvest if we do not give up".(Galatians 6:9).

5. Forward Focus:

We must forget what lies behind and stay focused on Jesus and reach forward to that eternal finish line. Those that are holding on to baggage from the past lose sight of their eternal goal. *"Do not be overcome by evil, but overcome evil with good". (Romans 12:21).*

The key to success in this race is a consuming desire for you to reach the Eternal Goal. If we understand what awaits us in Heaven, we will be able to press on through the obstacles of this life. Pray this Psalm, Jesus' Name: *"Teach me, Lord, the Way of Your decrees, that I may follow it to the end. Give me Understanding, so that I may keep Your Law and obey it with all my heart. Direct me in the Path of Your Commands, for there I find delight. Turn my heart toward Your Statutes and not toward selfish gain. Turn my eyes away from worthless things; preserve my life according to Your Word. Fulfill Your Promise to Your servant, so that You may be feared. Take away the disgrace I dread, for Your Laws are Good". (Psalm 119:33-39).*

So walk in that Truth and press on to that finish line. Be ready with a purpose (God's Purpose). He will fill you with all the skills (see Exodus 35:35) you need. Yes, God does supply each one of us with a skill that will help spread His Purpose (the Gospel). We must go to God in prayer, and He will tell us our skill to further His Kingdom. Sometimes God will just tell us; ***"to be still and know I am God"***. *(Psalm 46:10a).* Our response to God should be; *"You are with me, Your Rod and Your Staff, they comfort* *me". (Psalm 23:4).*

God promises to be with us always when He sees us praying and seeking to know Him better. The Bible asks us, *"What other nation is as great as to have their gods near them, the way the Lord our God, is near us, whenever we pray to Him?" (Deuteronomy 4:7).*

There is no other God that is alive to be with us. For our Heavenly Father knows every heart of every person that walks this earth, and He is never far away. *"God is not far from each one of us". (Acts 17:27).* He will never leave us. *"I will not leave you". (Genesis 28:15). "You will go out in joy and be led forth in peace". (Isaiah 55:12).*

I will simply enjoy God's Company and His Peace every time He invites me to lay down my cares and seek to know Him more. I want to be in His Presence of Comfort and Love always.

I cannot do anything without my Star Team (the Father, His Son Jesus, and the Holy Spirit). It was the Holy Spirit that helped me open my heart to let my Lord Jesus live in my heart and walk with me all through the lonely moments;I thought I was alone. It was then that I started my relationship with the Star Team.

When I spend alone time in the Word of God, I feel His Company with me, speaking every Word in His gentle and powerful voice. Having Jesus abiding in me gives me the assurance that I will never be alone. There is no one I would rather have by my side than my Lord and Savior Christ Jesus. I am so thankful to Him. Jesus is, was and always will be my friend.

The Holy Spirit will guide our minds and hearts to seek God with a whole heart. When we open our hearts to God, He will always watch over us. Remember, that God is with us and is always for us. God gives blessings that flow more easily when we are committed to Him with a whole heart.

Here are some Scriptures that you can (like me), be assured of His Presence by your side:

"And I will give you a new heart, and I will put a new spirit in you. I will take out your stony stubborn heart and give you a tender, responsive heart". (Ezekiel 36:26).

"The one who believes and is baptized will be saved, but the one who does not believe will be condemned". (Mark 16:16).

"He leads the humble in what is right and teaches the humble His ways". (Psalm 25:9).

"I will instruct you and teach you in the way you should go; I will counsel you with my eye upon you". (Psalm 32:8).

"Trust in the Lord with all your heart, and do not lean on your own understanding. In all your ways acknowledge Him, and He will make straight your paths". (Proverbs 3:5-6).

"Ask, and it will be given to you; Seek, and you will find; Knock, and it will be opened to you". (Matthew 7:7).

"When the Spirit of Truth comes, He will guide you into all the Truth, for He will not speak on His own authority, but whatever He hears He will speak, and He will declare to you the things that are to come". (John 16:13).

"If we confess our sins, He is faithful and just to forgive us our sins and to cleanse us from all unrighteousness". (1 John 1:9).

Walking this long, hard and dark journey on this earth can be very lonely and frightening. However, I found that we are not alone in this walk. We have someone that is always with us and that will never leave us, helping us when things seem to get too hard for us. That someone is our Lord Jesus Christ.

We have two paths to choose, one that is wide and the other that is narrow. In the Bible, Jesus tells us which path is the best to choose: ***"Enter through the Narrow Gate. For wide is the gate and broad is the road that leads to destruction, and many enter through it. But small is the Gate and Narrow the road that leads to Life and only a few find it"***. *(Matthew 7:13-14).*

As I read this Scripture, I sat back and took in that picture, of a wide road (taken by a large crowd) and of a Narrow road (taken by few). I then thought of my own life, before acknowledging my Savior Jesus into my life. I had walked that wide road, which did lead me to destruction. It was not a big destruction, but it was enough to teach me lessons to not follow that wide path. Some may think that I have not suffered enough to say that I walked in destruction, but I really did. Here are just a few of the destructions that I have walked and learned from:

The first one:

When I was in elementary school; I was the brunt of ridicule and disrespect, names that are not appropriate for any ears to hear. This destruction made my self-esteem very low. And this destruction overflowed into my high school years leaving me to spend most of my time avoiding others, not speaking to anyone; giving me no social life at all.

The second one:

Came through my coworkers, my friends, and even my family, when they ignored me, giving me a sense of insecurity and no comfort or support. I felt like an invisible person.

The third one:

Came when my dad left my mom (after thirty-five years), making me confused, shattering my dreams of having a marriage and family life. This last one, I got over when God gave me my husband that helped me to put together my shattered dreams.

Going through these three destructions made me realize that my Star Team was watching over me all along, defending me when I needed it. The lessons I have learned made me realize that I had turned down the wrong path (the wide one) and fell into that pit of despair. Until I was brought to my knees and opened the door to Jesus, my Savior. As Jesus assured me that:

"My yoke is easy and My burden is Light". *(Matthew 11:30)*. Therefore, I gave everything that was weighing me down to Jesus and continued forward on His Narrow Path, holding on to Him, who has overcome this world of ridicule and disrespect.

Every one of us has to go through seasons that may break us or make us. However, with Jesus walking with us, we can do anything. As the Word of God says:

"I can do all things through Christ who strengthens me". (Philippians 4:13); and *"All things are possible with God". (Matthew 19:26).*

My Lord, My Savior, and My Friend: Jesus Christ.

Facing the impossible of this world is difficult on my own. However, when I call out, 'Help me, Jesus! I need you'; He responds quickly with His Comforting Touch and Words of Encouragement. My Loving Savior says: *"**Do not fear, for I am with you; do not be dismayed, for I am with. I will strengthen you and help you; I will uphold you with My Righteous Right Hand"**. (Isaiah 41:10).*

I then felt unafraid, and a surge of warmth went through my body, making me feel strong enough to face the impossible that I was facing. This was the assurance that I needed, that all the times that I thought I was alone, I never was. My Star Team has been walking with me all this time.

The day I opened the door to my friend Jesus, letting Him into my life and inviting Him to stay in my heart (having total control over everything), was the best choice that I ever made. Before I opened the door, I was always hearing a voice calling my name (no one being in the room). I then went to my Bible for my daily dose of the Word of God. Somehow, I found myself searching in the Book of Revelation. I then heard the Voice again calling out my name. Along with my name, the Voice said these Words:

*"**Here I am! I stand at the door and knock. If anyone hears My Voice and opens the door, I will come in and eat with that person, and they with Me"**. (Revelation 3:20).*

Then a Bright Light then came, and His Hand was reaching out for me. I grabbed hold of His hand, and He has been sitting, talking, listening, and walking with me ever since. To have my Lord sit down with me and want to listen to all that is worrying me was so awesome and comforting.

All my life, I had found it very impossible to find someone that would be willing, and wanting, to listen to me. Once again the Word of God says:

"Ask and it will be given to you; seek and you will find; knock and the door will be opened to you". (Matthew 7:7). "All things are possible with God".

(Matthew 19:26).

Now, I need not to be lonely and ashamed when I need to talk to someone. I just go to my Star Team (who is always with me), and I am then comforted, loved, and encouraged. The words 'Jesus is Lord' (when spoken aloud) will send all evil fleeing from you. This is a true statement. These words have been working for me ever since I opened the door and let Jesus into my life. Read these verses from the Book of John and begin to know about our Lord Jesus Christ:

"Through Him all things were made; without Him nothing was made that has been made. In Him was life, and that life was the light of all humankind. The light shines in the darkness, and the darkness has not overcome it" (John 1:3-5).

"The word became flesh and made His dwelling among us. We have seen His glory, the glory of the one and only Son, who came from the Father, full of Grace and Truth". (John 1:14).

"No one has ever seen God, but the One and only Son, who is Himself God and is in closest relationship with the Father, has madeHim known". (John 1:18).

"For God so loved the world that He gave His one and only Son, that whoever believes in Him shall not perish but have eternal life". (John 3:16).

"For God did not send His Son into the world to condemn the world, but to save the world through Him. Whoever believes in Him is not condemned, but whoever does not believe stands condemned already because they have not believed in the name of God's one and only Son. This is the verdict: Light has come into the world, but people loved darkness instead of light because their deeds were evil". (John 3:17-19).

We need to know all we can about our Lord Jesus for who He is and what He can do for us. Here is a list of who I know and see who my Lord Jesus is:

Jesus is my Savior:

"Because of His words, many more became believers. They said to the woman, We no longer believe just because of what you said; now we have heard

for ourselves, and we know that this man really is the Savior of the world". (John 4:41-42).

"For the Son of Man has come to seek and to save that which was lost" (Luke 19:10).

<u>*Jesus is Lord*</u>:

"God raised Him from the dead, freeing Him from the agony of death, because it was impossible for death to keep its hold on Him. David said about Him: 'I saw the Lord always before me.

Because He is my right hand, I will not be shaken. Therefore, my heart is glad and my tongue rejoices, my body also will rest in hope, because You will not abandon me to the realm of the dead, You will not let your holy one see decay. You have made known to me the paths of life; You will fill me with joy in your presence'". (Acts 2:24- 28).

"Blessed be the Lord, who daily loads us with benefits, the God of our salvation! Selah".

(Psalm 68:19).

<u>*Jesus is my Love*</u>:

"The Lord appeared to us in the past, saying: **'I have loved you with an Everlasting Love; I have drawn you with Unfailing Kindness'**". (Jeremiah 31:3).

"And God demonstrates His love toward us, in that while we were still sinners, Christ died for us". (Romans 5:8).

"God so loved the world that He gave His one and only Son, that whoever believes in Him should not perish, but have everlasting life". (John 3:16).

"Above all, love each other deeply, because love covers over a multitude of sins". (1 Peter 4:8).

<u>*Jesus is my Peace*</u>:

"You will keep him in perfect peace, whose mind stays on You, because he trusts in You". (Isaiah 26:3).

"And let the Peace of God rule in your hearts, to which also you were called *in one body; and be thankful". (Colossians 3:15).*

"I will both lie down in peace, and sleep; for You alone, O Lord, make me dwell in safety". (Psalm 4:8).

Jesus is my Forgiveness:

"I, even I, am He who blots out your transgressions, for My own sake, and remembers your sins no more". *(Isaiah 43:25).*

"For as high as the Heavens are above the earth, so great is His love for those who fear Him; as far as the east is from the west, so far has He removed our transgressions from us". (Psalm 103:11-12).

"For I will forgive their wickedness and will remember their wickedness and will remember their sins no more". *(Hebrews 8:12).*

Jesus is my Righteousness:

"God made Him who had no sin to be sin for us, so that in Him we might become the righteousness of God". (2 Corinthians 5:21).

"This righteousness is given through faith in Jesus Christ to all who believe. There is no difference between Jew and Gentile, for all have sinned and fall short of the glory of God, and all are justified freely by His Grace through the redemption that came by Christ Jesus. God presented Christ as a sacrifice of atonement, through the shedding of His blood; to be received by Faith. He did this to demonstrate His righteousness, because in His forbearance He had left the sins committed beforehand unpunished—He did it to demonstrate His righteousness at the present time, so as to be just and the one who justifies those who have faith in

Jesus". (Romans 3:22-26).

"The fruit of that righteousness will be peace; its effect will be quietness and confidence forever". (Isaiah 32:17).

Jesus is my Deliverer:

"Therefore, there is now no condemnation for those who are in Christ Jesus, because through Christ Jesus the law of Spirit who gives life has set you free from the law of sin and death".(Romans 8:1-2).

"The Spirit of the Lord is on Me, because He has anointed me to proclaim

good news to the poor. He has sent Me to proclaim freedom for the prisoners and recovery of sight for the blind, to set the oppressed free, to proclaim the year of the Lord's favor". (Luke 4:18-19).

"Now the Lord is the Spirit, and where the Spirit of the Lord is, there is freedom. And we all, who with unveiled faces contemplate the Lord's glory, are being transformed into His image with ever-increasing glory, which comes from the Lord, who is the Spirit". (2 Corinthians 3:17-18).

Jesus is my Fellowship:

"Therefore, you do not lack any spiritual gift as you eagerly wait for our Lord Jesus Christ to be revealed. He will also keep you firm to the end, so that you will be blameless on the day of our Lord Jesus Christ. God is faithful, who has called you into fellowship with His Son, Jesus Christ our Lord". (1 Corinthians 17-:9).

Jesus is my Example:

"To this you were called, because Christ suffered for you, leaving you an example that you should follow in Hissteps. He committed no sin, and no deceit was found in His mouth.

When they hurled their insults at Him, He did not retaliate; when He suffered, He made no threats. Instead, He entrusted Himself to Him who judges justly". (1 Peter 2:21-23).

Jesus is my Companion:

"Let your conduct be without covetousness; be content with such things as you have. For He Himself has said, 'I will never leave you nor forsake you'". (Hebrews 13:5).

"When my father and my mother forsake me, then the Lord will take care of me". (Psalm 27:10).

Jesus is my Brother:

"For whoever does the will of my Father in Heaven is my brother and sister and mother". (Matthew 12:50).

Jesus is my Guardian:

"When you pass through the waters, I will be with you; and through

the rivers they shall not overflow you. When you walk through the fire, you shall not be burned, nor shall the flame scorch you'". (Isaiah 43:2).

<u>Jesus is my Security</u>:

"The Lord is Faithful, who will establish you and guard you from the evil one. We have confidence in the Lord that you are doing and will continue to do the things we command. May the Lord directs your hearts into God's love and Christ's perseverance". (2 Thessalonians 3:3-4).

"Who also has sealed us and given us the Spirit in our hearts as a guarantee". (2 Corinthians 1:22).

<u>Jesus is my Sufficiency</u>:

"I can do all things through Christ who strengthens me". (Philippians 4:13).

"If you abide in Me, and My words abide in you, you will ask what you desire, and it shall be done for you". (John 15:7).

<u>Jesus is my Fulfillment</u>:

"Blessed are those who hunger and thirst for righteousness, for they shall be filled". (Matthew 5:6).

<u>Jesus is my Everything</u>:

"If you abide in Me, and my Words abide in you, you will ask what you desire, and it shall be done for you'". (John 15:7).

"And my God shall supply all your needs according to His Riches in Glory by Christ Jesus".

(Philippians 4:19).

<u>Jesus is my Friend</u>:

"Greater love has no one than this that someone lays down His life for His friends". (John 15:13).

"A man who has friends must himself be friendly, but there is a friend who sticks closer than a brother". (Proverbs 18:24).

<u>Jesus is my Light</u>:

*"When Jesus spoke again to the people, He said; **'I am the light of the world. Whoever follows me will never walk in darkness, but will have the light of life'**" (John 8:12).*

<u>*Jesus is my Hope:*</u>

"'Be still and know I am God. I will be exalted among the nations. I will be exalted in the earth'". *(Psalm 46:10).*

Knowing who Jesus is can make this journey much easier to walk. And the more I read the Scriptures to find out more who Jesus is I find out who He is and how much He loves me. Scripture makes me stronger when I see that He is living in everything and everywhere that I am. Acknowledging Jesus in every situation makes His Father in Heaven smile with Joy.

Jesus feels the same emotions that you and I do. We can learn from how Jesus displays His emotions. To experience these emotions is to experience Jesus and live the way Jesus lives. Here are ten emotions that our Lord went through, just as we go through, every day, as we walk this earth. Learning from them can help us overcome the ways of this earth, as Jesus overcame the world. Please take note how Jesus handled these emotions; and He did not sin:

<u>*Fatigue (Tiredness):*</u>

When Jesus felt fatigued and despaired of what His Father wanted Him to do, He would go to the Mount of Olives and pray to His Father, asking for strength to continue on with His assignment that His Father gave Him. Read these passages from the Word of God: *"He [Jesus] withdrew about a stone's throw beyond them [His disciples], knelt down and prayed; **'Father, if You are willing, take this cup from Me; yet not My will, but Yours be done'**. An angel from Heaven appeared to Him and strengthened Him".* *(Luke 22:41-43).*

We can be encouraged to also go to His Father, for strength, when we are weary and tired. This is the Father's Will for us to ask Him for help and strength. With His Son by our side, His Father will lovingly listen and respond right at the moment we call out for help.

Sleep (Weary):

When Jesus felt the need to sleep, He would just go and sleep, because of His Faith and Trust in His Father to protect Him when a storm would come. Check this out from the Word of God: *"Without warning, a furious storm came up on the lake, so that the waves swept over the boat. However, Jesus was sleeping. The disciples went and woke Him, saying; 'Lord, save us! We are going to drown!' He [Jesus] replied, 'You of little faith, why are you so afraid?' Then, He got up and rebuked the winds and the waves, and it was completely calm". (Matthew 8:24-26).*

With this, we learn that Jesus has a lot of Faith in His Father to not let Him perish and to protect Him when He needs the help. As the disciples woke Jesus, all He said to the storm, **'Be quiet'**, and the wind ceased and the sea was calm. Two words spoken from our Lord can send away all evil that comes against us. With this kind of faith and trust, we could move mountains (struggles or roadblocks) with the power of Jesus.

Suffering:

"Because He [Jesus], Himself suffered when He was tempted, He is able to help those who are being tempted". (Hebrews 2:18).

We do not have to search very far for an example of someone who overcame suffering—there is our Lord Jesus. Just speaking His Name makes evil shake with fear. Jesus went through the worst of sufferings, more than we will ever go through.

Compassion:

"I will tell of the kindnesses of the Lord, the deeds for which He is to be praised, according to all the Lord has done for us—yes, the many good things He has done for Israel, according to His

*Compassion and many Kindnesses. He [Jesus] said, **'Surely they are My people, children who will be true to Me'**; and so He became their Savior. In all their distress, He too was distressed, and the angel of His presence saved them. In His love and mercy He redeemed them; He lifted them up and carried them* *all the days of old". (Isaiah 63:7-9).*

Our Lord Jesus did His Father's Will to receive His Father's Compassion so that we can also receive His Father's Compassion through Him. The afflictions that we receive here on this earth are covered by our Heavenly Father's Compassion and overcome by His Son, Jesus. Therefore, we can live the peaceful life that He intended for us to live.

<u>*Weeping:*</u>

The shortest Scripture in the Bible, *"Jesus wept". (John 11:35)*, shows how much compassion He has for His friend Lazarus. In addition, Jesus weeps for us when we do not obey His

Father's Instructions.

<u>Anger and Indignation (Righteous Anger):</u>

"He [Jesus] drove out the sheep and oxen, scattered the money changers' coins and told them, **'Get these things out of here. Don't turn My Father's House into a marketplace!'** *" (John 2:15-17).*

Jesus used indignation (righteous anger), for that is the only kind of anger that is necessary, anger at sin. Any other kind of anger is sin.

<u>*Grief:*</u>

"Then He [Jesus] said to them, 'My soul is overwhelmed with sorrow to the point of death. Stay here and keep watch with me". (Matthew 26:38).

<u>Jesus is Unique and Powerful.</u> Jesus knows how to overcome this dark, cold, and angry world. Take a few minutes and reflect on these truths about our Lord Jesus Christ, the Son of our Heavenly Father: Jesus was born of a virgin, with no human father. By the Holy Spirit of God the Father, He was conceived: *"This is how the birth of Jesus the Messiah came about: His mother Mary was pledged to be married to Joseph, but before they came together, she was found to be pregnant through the Holy Spirit". (Matthew 1:18).*

<u>Jesus was without sin throughout His life here on earth.</u> Even though Jesus was tempted.

As the Word of God says: *"He [Jesus] committed no sin, neither was deceit found in His mouth". (1 Peter 2:22).*

"Everyone who sins breaks the law; in fact, sin is lawlessness. However, you know that He appeared so that He might take away our sins. In addition, in Him there is no sin. No one who lives in Him keeps on sinning. No one who continues to sin has either seen Him or known Him". (1 John 3:4-6).

<u>Jesus was, is, and always will be the Way to His Father's Heart</u>. As the Bible says: *"For we do not have a high priest who is unable to empathize with our weaknesses, but we have One who has been tempted in every way, just as we are—yet He did not sin". (Hebrews 4:15).*

"The Word became flesh and made His dwelling among us. We have seen His glory, the glory of the one and only Son, who came from the Father, full of grace and truth". (John 1:14). "I and the Father are one" (John 10:30).

When walking with Jesus by your side, it gives you confidence in receiving mercy, grace, comfort, and most of all love from His Father in your time of need. Through Jesus, we can enter into His Father's Presence. There is no other way to the Great, Almighty God. There is only one thing we must do, and that is to turn from our sin and become loyal followers of His word and His Ways. Oh, and of course, believe in His Son, Jesus Christ, staying focused on Him, who is the Way, Truth, and the Life. As the Bible says: *"Jesus answered,* **'I am the Way and the Truth and the Life. No one comes to the Father except through Me'".** *(John 14:6).*

<u>Jesus is the Master Teacher</u>. No one can teach like Jesus can (except His Father in heaven). Jesus teaches about His Father and His Kingdom. Jesus learned absolute obedience and love from His Father; and we can learn absolute obedience and love from Jesus to assure us our place as citizens of God's Kingdom. Our conduct of how we live here on earth should reflect the Life that Jesus lives. As the Word of God teaches: *"You are the salt of the earth. However, if the salt loses its saltiness, how can it be made salty again? It is no longer good for anything, except to be thrown out and trampled underfoot. You are the light of the world. A town built on a hill cannot be hidden. Do people either light a lamp and put it under a bowl? Instead, they put it on its stand, and it gives light to everyone in the house. In the same way, let your Light*

shine before others so that they may see your good deeds and glorify your Father in Heaven". (Matthew 5:13-16).

<u>Jesus demonstrates His Power over sickness and disease and overcomes all temptations</u>. With His Father's love and protection, even death could not hold Jesus. The only way we could have that same assurance is to believe and trust that Jesus is the only way to His Father. Also not to be shaken when troubles come our way.

Here are some Truths from the Bible that gives us assurance in God:

"These things I have written to you who believe in the name of the Son of God, so that you may know that you have eternal life". (1 John 5:13).

"Therefore, brothers and sisters, since we have confidence to enter the Most Holy Place by the blood of Jesus, (by a new and living way), opened for us through the curtain. That is, His body, and since we have a Great Priest over the House of God, let us draw near to God, with a sincere heart and with the full assurance that faith brings. Having our hearts sprinkled to cleanse us from a guilty conscience, and having our bodies washed with pure water. Let us hold unswervingly to the hope we profess, for He who promised is faithful". (Hebrews 10:19-23).

"If we confess our sins, He is faithful and just and will forgive us our sins and purify us from all unrighteousness". (1 John 1:9).

"That is why I am suffering as I am. Yet this is no cause for shame, because I know whom I have believed, and I am convinced that He is able to guard what I have entrusted to Him until that day". (2 Timothy 1:12).

"It is written in the Prophets: 'They will all be taught by God'. Everyone who has heard the Father and learned from Him comes to Me. No one has seen the Father except the One who is from God; only He has seen the Father. Very truly, I tell you, the one who believes has eternal life. I am the bread of life". (John 6:45-48).

"My goal is that they may be encouraged in heart and united in Love, so that they may have the full riches of complete understanding, in order that they may know the mystery of God, namely, Christ, in whom are hidden all the treasures of wisdom and knowledge".(Colossians 2:2-3).

"Even though I walk through the darkest valley, I will fear no evil, for You

are with me; Your rod and Your staff they comfort me". (Psalm 23:4).

"Now faith is confidence in what we hope for and assurance about what we do not see. This is what the ancients were commended for". (Hebrews 11:1).

"For God so loved the world that He gave His one and only Son, that whoever believes in Him shall not perish but have eternal life. For God did not send His Son into the world to condemn the world, but to save the world through Him". (John 3:16-17).

"Bring joy to your servant, Lord, for I put my trust in You. You, Lord, are forgiving and good, abounding in love to all who call to You. Hear my prayer, Lord; listen to my cry for mercy. When I am in distress, I call to You, because You answer me". (Psalm 86:4-7).

"According to His eternal purpose that He accomplished in Christ Jesus our Lord. In Him and through Him we may approach God with freedom and confidence". (Ephesians 3:11-12).

"God is not unjust; He will not forget your work and the love you have shown Him, as you have helped His people and continue to help them. We want each of you to show this same diligence to the very end, so that what you hope for may be fully realized". (Hebrews 6:10-11).

"Know that the Lord has set apart His faithful servant for Himself; the Lord hears when I call to Him. Tremble and do not sin; when you are on your beds, search your hearts and be silent. Offer the sacrifices of the righteous and trust in the Lord". (Psalm 4:3-5).

"In peace I will lie down and sleep, for You alone, Lord, make me dwell in safety". (Psalm 4:8).

"I know that my redeemer lives, and that in the end He will stand on the earth". (Job 19:25).

"The Spirit Himself testifies with our spirit that we are God's children". (Romans 8:16).

Now here are seven things that God says about me (and you too) that assure me every time I read them, that He loves me (and you). I call this 'God says'. After each phrase is a Scripture to meditate on.

I am a child of the One True God.

"Yet to all who did receive Him, to those who believed in His name, He gave the right to become children of God". (John 1:12).

I am special, and I am ordained for a purpose.

"We declare God's Wisdom, a mystery that has been hidden, and that God destined for our glory before time began". (1 Corinthians 2:7).

I am created with a special calling.

"I wish that all of you were as I am. But each of you has your own gift from God; one has this gift, another has that". (1 Corinthians 7:7).

I am never alone.

"Have I not commanded you? Be strong and courageous. Do not be frightened, and do not be dismayed, for the Lord your God is with you wherever you go". (Joshua 1:9).

"Teaching them to observe all that I have commanded you. And behold, I am with you always, to the end of the age". (Matthew 28:20).

I am never forgotten.

*"Keep your life free from love of money, and be content with what you have, for He has said, **'I will never leave you nor forsake you'**. Therefore, we can confidently say, **'The Lord is my helper; I will not fear; what can man do to me?'"** (Hebrews 13:5-6).*

I am always loved.

"In all these things we are more than conquerors through Him who loved us. For I am sure that neither death nor life, nor angels, nor rulers, nor things present, nor things to come, nor powers, nor height, nor depth, nor anything else in all creation, will be able to separate us from the love of God in Christ Jesus our Lord". (Romans 8:37-39).

*"**This is to My Father's Glory, that you bear much fruit, showing yourselves to be my disciples. As the Father has loved Me, so have I loved you. Now remain in My Love. If you keep my Commands, you will remain in My Love, just as I have kept My Father's Commands and remain in His Love'".** (John 15:8-10).*

I am a friend:

*"**Greater Love has no one than this: to lay down one's life for one's**

friends. You are My friends if you do what I command. I no longer call you servants, because a servant does not know his master's business. Instead, I have called you friends, for everything that I learned from My Father, I have made known to you. You did not choose me, but I chose you and appointed you so that you might go and bear fruit—fruit that will last—and so that whatever you ask in my name the Father will give you. This is My Command: Love each other'''. (John 15:13-17).

Prayer:

Dear Heavenly Father, I pray that you help us stand strong in you. Moreover, give us endurance to run the race and not give up (even when things look dim). Please, strengthen us for the battle that may knock us down. You are the healer and restorer, and we look to You. Make us whole in You as You created us to be. Thank you. In Jesus's Name, I pray. Amen.

In getting to know and understanding God's will, we must simply follow these two ways and weave them into the way we live our daily lives on this earth. In doing these two simple things, we can walk humbly the way Jesus walks with His Father:

*First, you must open your Bible (God's Word) and read it!

*Second, you must take some moments before starting your day and pray. Take that first fifteen minutes of every morning, and be filled with the Renewing Strength of God's Presence to face the mountains of that day.

When you read the Bible, you will get the sense of God being right there in front of you, speaking the instructions for His will. All the while that you are reading His Word, He is right there to explain anything that you do not understand. Praying and reading the Bible is the foundation that enables you to discover God's Will and Purpose for your life. In addition, the Word of God puts Love in your heart and a smile on God's Face that you are so dependent on Him and Him alone.

The Seasons of Our Life: A Journey-Walk with Jesus

Springtime (Renewal) is a time of refreshing the dull in our life journey, to bring us opportunity to receive the new things that God has in store for you.

Summertime (Labor and Spiritual Growth) is a time of living out all that you learned from God.

Fall (Harvesting) is to separate anything and everything that does not line up with God.

Winter (Withdraw) is to withdraw from an activity that God can only resolve.

Each season is required for us to go through at the right time. So that you can be healthy in your walk with Jesus. When you recognize what season you are in and embrace it, you are able to understand what God is instructing you to do.

The seasons of our lives vary from year to year and person to person. At times God may choose to prolong a season that you are going through because you may have strayed from accomplishing His work. Many times, you might have a lot that needs to die.

The season of winter may seem like it will never end, slowing you down, in moving forward into the next season. Nevertheless, we must believe that God is always in control and continue to cling to Him in trust. His work reveals special things, only for you to accomplish.

Sometimes we need to be reminded of these difficult battles for God to fight. God will equip us for the battles that we need to fight. We must not worry and stress out about how we are to fight the battle in front of us. Leave the worrying to Him. God can win the battle faster than we ever can. We will slow down the victory when we try to fight the battle on our own.

Check out these examples of people in each season:

People in the spring season are exploring new possibilities and feeding on the encouragement they receive.

People in the summer season are hard workers and helping that person who is in despair and needs help.

People in the fall season are harvesting and working on getting rid of all that does not line up with God.

People in the winter season are experiencing a drawing to a close and needing prayer and encouragement.

Did you recognize what season you are in at this moment? You must be able to know what season you are in order to embrace it and wait on God's Instruction of what to do next. The Word of God tells us to: *"Listen carefully to My words; let your ears take in what I say". (Job 13:17).*

The truth is that God does not tell us why bad things happen to us. However, He will let us know how to walk through them, with Faith, Hope, and Patience. We can trust God to give us the answers to any questions we ask Him. Despite our questions, we could still faithfully proclaim,

"Though He slayed me, yet will I hope in Him". (Job 13:15a).

God still controls the world, even a world with unexplainable suffering. The human mind cannot have perfect understanding, but God can be trusted to treat us with Justice and Mercy. God is Sovereign, and He does not owe us an explanation for His actions.

We do not need to carry our burdens that load us down in despair. Burdens are a heavy load to carry and are hard to carry. They are troublesome. However, they do not have to be, for Jesus said it Himself, ***"Take My Yoke upon you and learn from Me, for I am Gentle and Humble in heart, and you will find rest for your souls. For My Yoke is Easy and My Burden is Light"***. *(Matthew 11:29).*

One day I came across this poem that really made me reevaluate my walk. The author is unknown, and I truly thank this person, for putting into words how it feels to go through an addiction and/or a difficult decision that this world is so full of. When you read this poem, you may see yourself in it; as I did. This poem is for everyone who has suffered from an addiction or bad choice.

The Walk…

I walk down the street; there is a deep hole in the sidewalk.
I am lost…I am helpless. It is not my fault. I fell in.
It takes forever to find my way out.
I walk down the street; there is a deep hole in the sidewalk.
I pretend I do not see it. I fell in again.
I cannot believe I am in the same place, but it is not my fault.
It still takes me a long time to get out.
I walk down the street; there is a deep hole in the sidewalk.
I see it there. I still fall in…it is a habit.
My eyes are open. I know where I am.
It is my fault. I get out immediately.
I walk down the same street; there is a deep hole in the sidewalk.
I walk around it. I walk down another street.

When I first read this poem, I did see myself in it. I remembered when I was a smoker and drank alcohol. These habits caused me not to see the true me; it was the worldly me. However, thanks be to God, I walked down the other street (the street of peace and righteousness). I am ever so grateful for God's Compassion that He had for me and taking me under His wings and making me the way He created me to be.

When there was no one to turn to, Jesus was there for me. Thank you, Jesus. Jesus is the friend that never leaves me, and He will never make fun of me; like so many people in my life have. It feels so good to know that I have someone that accepts me for who I am and created to be.

Deliverance from the Pit of Despair

To receive deliverance from God, we must be calm, be true, be quiet, and rest in His Love. God is watching over us, and as He sees us bask in His Joyful Presence, we can be assured that we are

His children. Thankfulness and Joy opens the Gates for Deliverance. This is why we worship and praise God. Being very glad, very happy, and very thankful can bring God's Blessings to us who wait patiently in the manner that pleases Him. Laughter can produce a lot of attention from God quickly. For laughter shows that we are living in His continuous Love and in His Ways no matter what we are facing in this world. In addition, laughter brings praise to Him.

Here are some Scriptures from the Word of God that remind us of the importance of Joy (Jesus): Rejoice in reading these Scriptures. There are more all through the Bible.

"You make known to me the path of life; in Your presence there is the fullness of joy; at your right hand are pleasures forevermore". (Psalm 16:11).

"Then my soul will rejoice in the Lord, exulting in His salvation". (Psalm 35:9).

"Let those who delight in My righteousness shout for joy and be glad and say evermore, 'Great is the Lord, who delights in the welfare of His servant!'" (Psalm 35:27).

"Folly is a joy to him who lacks sense, but a man of understanding walks straight ahead". (Proverbs 15:21).

"When justice is done, it is a joy to the righteous but terror to evildoers". (Proverb 21:15).

"With joy you will draw water from the wells of salvation". (Isaiah 12:3).

"The meek shall obtain fresh joy in the Lord, and the poor among mankind shall exult in the Holy One of Israel". (Isaiah 29:19).

"For you shall go out in joy and be led forth in peace; the mountains and the hills before you shall break forth into singing and all the trees of the field shall clap their hands". (Isaiah 55:12).

"Though the fig tree should not blossom, nor fruit be on the vines, the produce of the olive fail and the fields yield no food, the flock be cut off from the fold and there be no herd in the stalls, yet I will rejoice in Lord; I will take joy in the God of my salvation". (Habakkuk 3:17-18).

"*Rejoice on that day, and leap for joy, for behold, your reward is great in Heaven; for so their fathers did to prophets*". *(Luke 6:23)*.

"*For the kingdom of God is not a matter of eating and drinking but of Righteousness and Peace and Joy in the Holy Spirit*". *(Romans 14:17)*.

"*But the fruit of the Spirit is love, joy, peace, patience, kindness, goodness, gentleness, faithfulness and self-control*" *(Galatians 5:22)*.

"*Rejoice in the Lord always; again I will say, 'Rejoice!'*" *(Philippians 4:4)*.

A Love Offering Prayer Letter:

To my Dear Heavenly Father.

I thank you for being my Lord and Savior. You are a gracious and loving God. I will rest in Your Love, walk in Your Ways, and move steadily forward, toward Your Kingdom. I know You judge not on outward appearances but judge the heart of every person that seeks You to do Your Will. As I seek to know You more, I love You more, and You pour out more Courage and Strength into me so I could love, laugh, rejoice, and shine Your Light, showing others it is not me that lives but You that lives in me.

Thank you for <u>everything</u> that You have done for me. I know that You are the only One who will be there for me, for You love me for who I am. I have nothing if I do not have You. With all the love You give me, I will give it right back to You by loving, living, waiting, and watching for all You are doing.

My love offering is my life to You. Just like Your love offering of your one and only Son, Jesus. I cannot do nothing without Your love. My cup overflows with love for You and Your Son, Jesus. I am in awe of You. Take my life, and make it an instrument to bring more of Your peoples to You.

I love You, always and forever. In Jesus's name, I pray. Amen!

We need to believe, receive, and stop trying to earn our way into God's Heart. The one lesson I learned about thinking that I had to earn my way into God's Heart is that I thought that I had to fix other people's problems to get God to notice me. But all it did was leave me feeling loved for the moment, which did not last. The moment I started feeling unloved again, the Star Team came to my rescue and assured me of how much He loves me and that He will never leave me alone; and His Love will never make me feel unloved again.

God will always assure us of His Presence, as long as we continue to acknowledge and obey His Commands, for He knows that we will need His Comfort in our lonely times. For His Spirit entered within us, the moment we answered His Son's Knock to let Him come in and dine, live, and walk with us. With God, with us, we do not have to fear ever being alone.

Here are some compelling images of how God that reveals His Glory and His Presence:

<u>One</u>: A consuming fire and a cloud. *"To the Israelites the glory of the Lord looked like a consuming fire on top of the mountain. Then Moses entered the cloud as he went on up the mountain. And he stayed on the mountain forty days and forty nights". (Exodus 24:147-18).*

<u>Two</u>: A colorful rainbow. *"And God said,* **'This is the sign of the covenant I am making, between Me and you, and every living creature with you. A covenant for all generations to come: I have set my rainbow in the clouds, and it will be the sign of the covenant between the earth and Me'.** *Therefore, God said to Noah,* **'This is the sign of the covenant I have established between Me and all life on the earth'".** *(Genesis 9:12-13, 17).*

"Like the appearance of a rainbow in the clouds on a rainy day, so was the radiance around Him. This was the appearance of the likeness of the glory of the Lord. When I saw it, I fell facedown, and I heard the Voice of One speaking". (Ezekiel 1:28).

<u>Three</u>: The new self. *"Do not lie to each other, since you have taken off your old self with its practices and have put on the new self, which is being renewed in knowledge, in the image of its Creator". (Colossians 3:9-10).*

"Do you not know that you are God's temple and that God's Spirit dwells in you?" (1 Corinthians 3:16).

These are just some images of the glory of God. The greatest image lives in our hearts and minds. That is our Lord Jesus, who will never leave us. When we speak God's word, we are speaking His Glory, and He is the only One that can fill us with His Glory. For He indwells among us as we invite Him into our hearts and give Him total control of our lives. Our bodies are

His temple as the Apostle Paul says, *"Do you not know that your bodies are temples of the Holy Spirit, who is in you, whom you have received from God? You are not your own; you were bought at a price. Therefore, honor God with your bodies".* (1 Corinthians 6:19).

Here is a statement to help you turn away from your sin and seek out the Holiness of our God:

'Sin drives out Holiness and destroys the relationship with God'.

Remembering this simple statement can keep you walking the Righteous Path, to draw closer to our Heavenly Father and His Grace and Love. There is no room for both sin and God. We must make the choice, and the Best Choice is choosing God. Because our Heavenly Father loves us so much that He will hear the moment you cry out for help and turn you away from the sin that is in your life; and give you rest in His Arms of Comfort and Love. This is His Grace that He freely gives to those who seek Him.

Let us see more of what the Word of God says about choosing to Rest in God's Arms:

"Thanks be to God! He gives us victory through our Lord Jesus Christ. Therefore, my dear brothers and sisters, stand firm. Let nothing move you. Always give yourselves fully to the work of the Lord, because you know that your labor in the Lord is not in vain". (1 Corinthians 15:57-58).

"Be on your guard; stand firm in the faith; be men of courage; be strong. Do everything in love". (1 Corinthians 16:13-14).

God's Presence in Hard Times.

In this life, when we are hurting, we can be sure of two things:

1. God is with us in our troubles. He knows the suffering of this world and the rejections and loss of loved ones. God wants us to be mindful of His constant Presence so we will know that we are never alone.

2. God has a purpose for allowing trials. We may not be going through the trials of this world; however, it is so we can live by faith and believe in His promise that He is in control, even in difficult circumstances and confrontations. The Word of God says:

"Keep your life free from the love of money, and be content with what you

have, for He has said, **'I will never leave you nor forsake you'**. *So, we can confidently say, 'The Lord is my helper; I will not fear; what can man do to me'?"* *(Hebrews 13:5-6).*

There are three lessons that I can learn that the troubles that are confronting me:

One. Those difficulties will always continue in this world until God's purpose is accomplished. That is teaching us key ingredients, which we need for the fulfillment of His Will and Purpose.

Two. To learn from the dark is to reject all temptation with the Light of God and walk upright with His Joy and Peace.

Three. To share with others what we learned from being in the Light of God. Our knowledge from Jesus will help us overcome our trails.

Instead of fearing your hard times, trust God and embrace His Plan for His Glory. For the Great I Am is All-Powerful and All-Knowing, and He has all our problems in His Hands. For when we are too weak to handle these troubles on our own. But with His Strength we can endure these troubles that plague this world. This is why the only way a sinner can be saved is by our Lord Jesus. The Kingdom of God can only be preached by those who have learned the importance of living God's Way.

Remember: Love! Joy! Peace! Hope! God loves you! God knows we are weak, and He will be strong for us; we just have to cry out to Him; and seek Him always.

In pondering the deeper teachings of the Scriptures (God's Word), it is important to start with the Lord's Character and Promises. It is important (critical) that you remember that:

God is Good.

"The Lord is Good to all; He has Compassion on all He has made". *(Psalm 145:9).*

God is Sovereign.

"The Lord has established His Throne in Heaven, and His Kingdom rules over all".

(Psalm 145:9).

God promises believers that He will work all things together for their good.

"And we know that in all things God works for the good of those who love Him, who have been called according to His purpose". (Romans 8:28).

God keeps His Promises.

"For no matter how many promises God has made, they are 'Yes' in Christ. And so through Him the 'Amen' is spoken by us to the glory of God". (2 Corinthians 1:20).

These four facts are just some to help you understand how (and who) God is, in every moment and situation, as we seek to know and love Him better.

Three things that are for your life and always the will of God:

Always acknowledge God in every way.

"In all your ways acknowledge Him and He shall direct your paths".(Proverbs 3:6).

Always live by faith.

"My righteous one will live by Faith. And I take no pleasure in the one who shrinks back".

(Hebrews 10:38).

"For we live by faith, not by sight". (2 Corinthians 5:7).

Always worship God. *"For it is written: 'Worship the Lord your God, and serve Him only".*

(Matthew 4:10b).

If you are not looking in the right direction and focused on Jesus, then you can get yourself into big trouble with your Heavenly Father. This is why you need someone by your side at all times.That someone who knows what you are going through; and will be going through. That someone is our Lord and Savior Jesus Christ. Always remember this:

"Keep your lives free from the love of money and be content with what you

have, because God has said: *'**Never will I leave you, never will I forsake you**'. So we say with confidence, 'The Lord is my helper; I will not be afraid. What can man do to me?'" (Hebrews 13:5-6).*

In addition, remember what God said to Joshua:

*"'**No one will be able to stand up against you all the days of your life. As I was with Moses, so I will be with you, I will never leave you nor forsake you. Be strong and courageous'**". (Joshua 1:5,6a).*

A sure way to know Jesus is walking with you is to always make sure you acknowledge God's awesome love for you and trust Him always. Here are some Scriptures that always acknowledge God:

"I praise you because I am fearfully and wonderfully made; Your Works are wonderful, I know that fully well". (Psalm 139:14).

*"'**For I know the plans I have for you'**, declares the Lord, '**plans to prosper you and not to harm you, plans to give you hope and a future. Then you will call on me and come and pray to me, and I will listen to you'**". (Jeremiah 29:11-12).*

"Do not be carried away by all kinds of strange teachings. It is good for our hearts to be strengthened by Grace, not by eating ceremonial foods, which is of no benefit to those who do so". (Hebrews 13:9). "So that the servant of God may be thoroughly equipped for every good work". (2 Timothy 3:17).

*"The Lord appeared to us in the past, saying: '**I have loved you with an everlasting love; I have drawn you with unfailing kindness. I will build you up again**". (Jeremiah 31:3, 4a).*

I am totally committed to God and His ways; in complete obedience and wholeheartedly. Giving my whole heart to what God wants. For it is said in the Word of God, and it's a Commandment: *"Love the Lord your God with all your heart and with all your soul and with all your strength". (Deuteronomy 6:5).*

Once God had my whole heart, I was never the same. My thoughts were different, my speech was different. I felt stronger and more assured of myself. You too will have God's Strength and Mighty Power anytime you cry out to Him. In addition, you will be able to accomplish all of

His Instructions you are to do for Him. Just make sure you do these four very important things: Acknowledge Him always;in everything, trust Him always; in everything, and keep in communication (praying) with Him. Oh, there is one more very, very, very important thing to do and that is to be thankful in all that He does for you, especially that He gave His Son to you, to walk along this journey on this earth. As Jesus walks along beside me through my day, He shields me from the arrows that Satan is continually throwing at me.

When we walk with Jesus, we are with Him, and He carries the weight of all our burdens. Jesus lifts our fears and confusions from our shoulders and puts them on His shoulders, replacing them with His Strength, Kindness, Compassion and Love. Therefore, we can spread that Kindness, Compassion and Love to all who need it. This is what God waits for, for us to welcome His Son into our lives and continue to depend on Him for all our needs. In the Bible it says: *"Carry each other's burdens, and in this way you will fulfill the law of Christ. If anyone thinks they are something when they are not they deceive themselves. Each one should test their own actions. Then they can take pride in themselves alone, without comparing themselves to someone else, for each one should carry their own load. Nevertheless, the one who receives instruction in the word should share all good things with their instructor".* (Galatians 6:2-6).

Once God puts in your heart His purpose, you must put it into action.

Prayer:

Father, as I focus on you, I see your face in front of mine. I know you are right by my side at all times. Thank you for being my friend and helping me when I cry out to you. I will always put a smile on my face to show you how much I am grateful for your presence. Thank you for carrying my burdens, and I thank you for giving me the strength to keep moving forward, in furthering your kingdom. I pray that all who come to You for help are grateful for your help. Thank you. I am just in awe of you. I love you. In the name of Jesus, I am always yours. Amen.

When facing the giants of this world, you must see and trust that Jesus is walking right beside you, all the way through. Then, nothing can touch you without His permission. Once that God has placed His Shield of Protection around you, nothing can break through and shake or hurt you. Take time out right now and read aloud Psalm 34, and be encouraged and strengthened. See how Jesus is right by your side in every moment and situation. See how He protects and fills you with Love, Joy, Peace, and Hope. See how powerful He is when the enemy tries to bring you down. See how exalting Him can bring so much comfort that will last into eternity.

<u>Psalm 34</u>

"I will extol the Lord at all times; His praise will always be on my lips.
I will glory in the Lord; let the afflicted hear and rejoice.
Glorify the Lord with me; let us exalt His name together.

I sought the Lord, and He answered me; He delivered me from all my fears.
Those who look to Him are radiant; their faces are never covered with shame.
This poor man called, and the Lord heard him; He saved him out of all his troubles.
The angel of the Lord encamps around those who fear Him, and He delivers them.

Taste and see that the Lord is good; blessed is the one who takes refuge in Him.
Fear the Lord, you His holy people, for those who fear Him lack nothing.
The lions may grow weak and hungry, but those who seek the Lord lack no good thing.
Come, My children, listen to Me; I will teach you the fear of the Lord.
Whoever of you loves life and desires to see many good days, keep your tongue from evil and your lips from telling lies.
Turn from evil and do good; seek Peace and pursue it.

The eyes of the Lord are on the righteous, and His ears are attentive to their cry; but the face of the Lord is against those who do evil, to blot out their name from the earth.

The righteous cry out, and the Lord hears them; He delivers them from all their troubles.
The Lord is close to the brokenhearted and saves those who are crushed in spirit.

The righteous person may have many troubles, but the Lord delivers him from them all;
He protects all his bones, not one of them will be broken.

Evil will slay the wicked; the foes of the righteous will be condemned.
The Lord will rescue His servants; no one who takes refuge in Him will be condemned". (Psalm 34:1-22).

As you can see, God knows (and sees) all that is going on in this world, and He will teach you how to live in this chaos. God knows how to make this chaos turn into His good. For He sacrificed His Son Jesus to reveal the truth of His judgment on sin. He makes known that He will turn the chaos of this world into His good. Jesus accomplished this on the cross—our Lord and Savior accomplished this for the entire for all of humanity, just to be in a right-standing relationship with His Father in heaven. Jesus made redemption the foundation of human life. Living off this foundation is why we have to focus on Jesus and His leading. Jesus is the only Way, the Truth, and the Life. Jesus came to die for you and me, and the Cross was Jesus's

Purpose, to take away the sins of this world.

The Cross is not of man but of God, and the Cross should never be fully comprehended through human experience; it is the gateway through which we can enter into oneness with the Father in Heaven.

The Cross is not a gate just to pass through; you need to abide in the Life of Jesus, whom we can find there and whom we invite into our lives and have total control over our lives. God calls you to the Cross, the door of Salvation, to walk through, and to leave behind all that this world has to offer and begin living the Life of Christ Jesus. The heart of Salvation is the Cross of Christ, where the Way of Eternal Life will open up that Free Living that our Lord gives us.

In this world, we lack understanding of the things of God. In this world, we are too distracted with what the enemy throws our way. In this world, without Jesus by our sides, we cannot receive the Things that make us in the right condition for that Free Spiritual Living.

In the Word of God, Jesus said, *"I have much more to say to you, more than you can now bear. However, when He, the Spirit of Truth comes, He will guide you into all the Truth. He will not speak on His own; He will speak only what He hears, and He will tell you what is yet to come. He will glorify Me because it is from Me that He will receive what He will make known to you. All that belongs to the Father is mine. That is why I said the Spirit will receive from Me what He will make known to you"*. *(John 16:12-15).*

We must have oneness with Jesus, before we can be prepared to bear any kind of truth from Him. To know about the oneness with Jesus is in the Word of God (the Bible), which becomes understandable to us, through the Spirit of Truth (the Holy Spirit). God cannot reveal anything to us if we have not received the Holy Spirit; which we receive when we receive Jesus. Once this happens, all worldly thinking will leave your mind, and the thoughts of God are exchanged.

The person you follow determines the person you become. So as for me, I will follow Jesus and become like Him. As I follow and praise God, He gives me Strength, Honor, and Love. As the Bible says: *"Wealth and honor come from You; You are the ruler of all things. In your hands are strength and power, to exalt and give strength to all. Now, our God, we give you thanks, and praise your glorious name"*. *(1 Chronicles 12-13).*

The cross is the Gateway into Jesus's Life. Jesus has the power to convey His life to us, bringing many to the glory of His Father. As the Word of God says: *"In bringing many sons and daughters to glory, it was fitting that God, for whom and through whom everything exists, should make the pioneer of their salvation perfect through what He suffered. Both the One who makes people holy and those who are made holy are of the same family. Therefore, Jesus is not ashamed to call them brothers and sisters. He says, 'I will declare Your Name to my brothers and sisters; in the assembly I will sing Your Praises', and again, 'I will put my trust in Him.' Again, He says, 'Here am I and the children God has given me'". (Hebrews 2:10-13).*

"For we know that our old self was crucified with Him so that the body ruled by sin might be done away with and that we should no longer be slaves to sin— because anyone who has died has been set free from sin. Now if we died with Christ, we believe that we will also live with Him.

For we know that since Christ was raised from the dead, He cannot die again; death no longer has mastery over Him. The death He died, He died to sin once for all; but the life He lives, to God. In the same, count yourselves dead to sin but alive to God in Christ Jesus. Therefore, do not let sin reign in your body so that you obey its evil desires. Do not offer any part of yourself to sin as an instrument of wickedness, but rather offer yourselves to God as those who have been brought from death to life; and offer every part of yourself to Him as an instrument of righteousness. For sin shall no longer be your master, because you are not under the law, but under grace". (Romans 6:6-14).

God shows His Love for us by the death of His Son Jesus on the Cross. The Word of God says: *"God demonstrates His love for us in this: While we were still sinners, Christ died for us". (Romans 5:8).*

In this life, it is not about what we can do for God but what He does in us and through us. God used His one and only Son for His Purpose of bringing us close to Him. Therefore, even though Jesus has finished His Father's Assignment and is sitting at His Father's right hand, He still continues to help us through the hard times. Our Lord is never too busy to lend us His helping hand.

Many times when I was talking with God, I would ask Him, "How do You desire to use me?" The answer I received from Him was to: "Be still and patient and remember that I love you". I told Him that whatever He desires to accomplish through me and in me, I am ready and willing to do all that He wants me to do. Writing this book is just the first of many assignments that He has put His trust in me. With His help, I will accomplish them all. Because like it says in the Word of God: *"With God nothing is impossible". (Matthews 19:25).*

I know and believe that I will not be alone. My strength comes from Him. *"For when I am weak He is strong". (2 Corinthians 12:10b).* Together, Jesus and I can accomplish anything and everything! I will continue to be ready with open ears for any Instructions that God has for me.

As the Word of God says: *"For I know that good itself does not dwell in me, that is, in my sinful nature. For I have the desire to do what is good, but cannot carry it out". (Romans 7:18).*

"Yet those who wait for the Lord will gain new strength; they will mount up with wings like eagles; they will run and not get tired; they will walk and not become weary". (Isaiah 40:31).

"Therefore, my dear friends, as you have always obeyed, not only in my presence, but now much more in my absence, continue to work out your Salvation with fear and trembling, for it is God who works in you, both to will and to act in order to fulfill His good purpose. Do everything without grumbling or arguing, so that you may become blameless and pure, 'children of God, without fault in a warped and crooked generation'. Then you will shine among them like stars in the sky, as you hold firmly to the Word of Life". (Philippians 2:12-16a).

"Behold, I am the Lord, the God of all mankind. Is anything too hard for me?" (Jeremiah 32:27).

"For those God foreknew He also predestined to be conformed to the image of His Son, that He might be the firstborn among many brothers and sisters. And those He predestined, He also called; those He called, He also justified; those He justified, He also glorified". (Romans 8:29-30).

The Gentleness of God

Gentleness is God's Way of announcing His Presence. The weaker you are, the gentler He approaches. It is like this:

God is watching everything that is going on in your life. Suddenly, He sees trouble approaching you; then, He sees you start to crumble with fear. He then starts whispering your name, but you do not hear Him. So then, He taps on your shoulder; you begin to feel that tap and hear someone whispering in your ear, but you do not seem to acknowledge that it is Him. Jesus then starts tapping loudly on the door of your heart and calling your name. Then you fall to your knees and call out His Name; He then reaches out, picks you up then wraps His arms around you and comforts you, and tells you, 'I am here with you. Do not be afraid'. Suddenly, you become full with warmth and comfort, courage and strength, hope and love, strengthening you as the trouble just passes over you; as a dark cloud does on a gloomy day. The next thing you realize, you are in His arms of refuge, feeling better. Your sadness turns into sunshine.

Through the darkness, Jesus's Light will shine through so you can cling to Him and walk in Love, Hope, Protection and at all times! This assures me to have no fear, for my Star Team is always with me, walking me through all the good and bad that approaches me. For the Word of God tells me: *"God is our refuge and strength, an ever-present help in trouble. Therefore, we will not fear, though the earth gives way and the mountains fall into the heart of the sea, though its waters roar and foam and the mountains quake with their surging".* (Psalm 46:1-3).

"Be joyful in hope; patient in affliction; faithful in prayer". (Romans 12:12).

"May the God of hope fill you with all the joy and peace as you trust in Him, so that you may overflow with hope by the power of the Holy Spirit". (Romans 15:13).

Nothing is more satisfying than knowing Jesus is always with me. Priceless is the cost of His love. Jesus is the friend that is always there for me (and you). Jesus appears to those who turn to Him for refuge and strength. We then are brought to our knees and are filled with His Courage, Love, Wisdom, Discernment, Hope, and Peace that will be able to shield off all the arrows of destruction that are flying in the air of this world. In addition, with the Umbrella of Protection that is placed over you and me by Heavenly Father, we can always walk in that Sunshine of His Love.

My Prayer of Thankfulness

Dear Heavenly Father;

Thank you for teaching me Your Ways and for watching over us. I am ready for You to search me for anything that is hindering me to step out and do Your Will. I want to serve You and only You alone. My life is Your Life. There is nothing I want more than to walk by Your side and listen to all You have to say. Remove all that is not of You. I want to thank You for guiding me through the many changes this life can bring. I will continually trust You, even when things do not seem clear of what You are doing in my life. I believe You are my safest place of refuge in this world. Help me move when You move, stay when You stay, Love when You love, speak Your Words of Wisdom when Your Words are needed. Direct my steps into Your promises you have stored up for me. Make me a woman of Faith and Love. In Your Precious Son's Name, I thank you. Amen.

"Not that I have already obtained all this, or have already arrived at my goal, but I press on to take hold of that for which Christ Jesus took hold of me". (Philippians 3:12).

"Commit your way to the Lord; trust in Him and He will do this: He will make your righteous reward shine like the dawn, your vindication like noonday sun. Be still before the Lord and wait patiently for Him; do not fret when people succeed in their ways, when they carry out their wicked schemes. Refrain from anger and turn from wrath; do not fret—it leads only to evil. For those who are evil will be destroyed, but those who hope in the Lord will inherit the land".

(Psalm 37:5-9).

"The Lord makes firm the steps of the one who delights in Him; though he may stumble, he will not fall, for the Lord upholds him with His hand". (Psalm 37:23-24).

<u>Standing in the Faith</u>

Faith believes that God is who He says He is.

Faith believes that He will do what He says He will do.

Faith believes God in His Word.

Faith is whole and having Faith makes you whole.

Faith is hearing your own voice speaking God's Promises.

Faith is responding to the Word you hear.

Jesus is the Author and Finisher of your Faith.

"Consequently, Faith comes from hearing the Message and the Message is heard through the Word about Christ". ((Romans 10:17).

Our responsibility is to feed our Faith with the Word of God and starve our doubts to death. Starving doubt is to live out every Word of God, sending doubt fleeing from the existence around you. In this world, doubt will always be in the air, because doubt is Satan's only weapon that he can use to throw us off the righteous path. As the Word of God says: *"Yet he did not waver through unbelief regarding the promise of God, but was strengthened in his faith and gave glory to God, being fully persuaded that God had power to do what He had promised. This is why it was credited to Him as Righteousness". (Romans 4:20-22).*

"You need to persevere so that when you have done the Will of God, you will receive what He has Promised. For, 'In just a little while, He who is coming will come and will not delay'. And, But righteous one will by faith. And I take no pleasure in the one who shrinks back'. But we do not belong to those who shrink back and are destroyed, but to those who have faith and are saved". (Hebrews 10:36-39).

"Therefore, since we are surrounded by such a great cloud of witnesses, let us throw off everything that hinders and the sin that so easily entangles. In addition, let us run with perseverance the race marked out for us, fixing our eyes on Jesus, the pioneer and perfecter of Faith. For the joy set before Him He endured the cross, scorning its shame, and sat down at the right hand of the Throne of God. Consider Him who endured such opposition from sinners, so that you will not grow weary and lose heart". (Hebrews 12:1-3).

The Holy Spirit

Receiving the Holy Spirit is part of a process. The Holy Spirit enters our bodies when we let our Lord into our hearts. The Holy Spirit starts sweeping and rearranging our personal lives to make us act right before God. The Holy Spirit invades the whole body.

Once He does this, our old selves die and become new, and then our Lord takes charge of everything once we hand everything over to Him. Doing our part of walking in the light of Jesus and obeying all that He teaches to us keeps us right in His Father's eyes and keeps us alive in whom that saved us. The Word of God says:

"In the same way, count yourselves dead to sin but alive to God in Christ

Jesus". (Romans 6:11).

I myself live all the time for Jesus; not for anything in the world. My heart belongs to Jesus, and He lives in me. This eternal life is not a gift from God; it is a gift of God and a precious gift that needs all our love and reverence. When our Heavenly Father sees His Son living in and through you, He will welcome you with open arms, into His glorious presence.

Once you make the decision to identify yourself with Jesus and His life, you will have an ample supply of endless love of His Father. Without His Love, you will stay weak and open to Satan's temptations. As the Word of God says: *"I pray that out of His glorious riches He may strengthen you with power through His Spirit in your inner being, so that Christ may dwell in your hearts through faith. And I pray that you, being rooted and established in love, may have power, together with all the Lord's holy people, to grasp how wide and long and high and deep is the love of Christ, and to know this Love that surpasses knowledge—that you may be filled to the measure of all the fullness of God". (Ephesians 3:16-21).* In addition, the Word of God says: *"Jesus looked at them and said;* **'With man this is impossible, but with God all things are possible'".** *(Matthew 19:26).*

Eternal life has nothing to do with time; it is only a source of life that we can take example of, and you and I have to continually keep letting go of our desires and let God's Desires invade us. For when we are walking with Jesus gives Him complete reign in our lives. Others will take notice of our walking with Jesus, because the Light of Jesus is brighter than any other lights on this earth. Jesus even outshines the sun, moon, and stars. This is why we will never walk in darkness once we let Jesus into our hearts and lives.

Triumph Over Our Failures

We have all walked through the valley of failures. Jesus has told us many times that we would face many failures in this world. The truth is that when we face many failures and shortcomings, they prepare us for serving God. Meaning, our failures bring us closer to God, showing Him that we are ready to be used. When we build walls around our hearts, it lets in our selfishness, stubbornness, and our own desires rule in our lives; deny God's access to turn our wrongful ways into ways of fulfilling His Plan and Purpose in our lives.

Staying focused in God's Word will bring Glory to Him and Blessings to us.

Here is what the Word of God says on triumphing over the failures that we make:

"Many are saying of me, 'God will not deliver him.' However, you, Lord, are a shield around me, my glory, the One who lifts my head high. I call out to the Lord, and He answers me from His Holy Mountain". (Psalm 3:2-4).

"Because of your partnership in the Gospel from the first day until now, being confident of this, that He who began a good work in you will carry it on to completion until the day of Christ Jesus". (Philippians 1:5-6).

"I write these things to you who believe in the name of the Son of God; so that you may know that you have Eternal Life. This is the confidence we have in approaching God: that if we ask anything according to His Will, He hears us. And if we know that He hears us, whatever we ask, we know that we have what we asked of Him". (1 John 5:13-15).

"We know that anyone born of God does not continue to sin; the One who was born of God keeps them safe, and the evil one cannot harm them. We know that we are children of God, and that the whole world is under the control of the evil one. We know also that the Son of God has come and have given us understanding, so that we may know Him who is True. And we are in Him who is true God and eternal life". (1 John 5:18-20).

"The Lord is my light and my salvation—whom shall I fear? The Lord is the stronghold of my life—of whom shall I be afraid?" (Psalm 27:1).

"Then the word of the Lord came to Jeremiah: 'I am the Lord, the God of all mankind. Is anything too hard for me?'" (Jeremiah 32:26-27).

"Be strong and courageous. Do not be afraid or terrified because of them, for the Lord your God goes with you; He will never leave you nor forsake you". (Deuteronomy 31:6).

<u>Kindness—A Quality that Pleases God</u>

All my life I have always had this longing to be kind to others. The Word of God says:

"Let not mercy and truth forsake you; bind them around your neck. Write them on the tablet of your heart". (Proverbs 3:3). This Scripture came true after Jesus showed me mercy, when I needed it most, when I was young. Since then, I have never left His side and His Truth.

I believe, with my whole heart, God Himself who wrote it on my heart. The engraving on my heart makes being unkind just cruel and wrong. I took deliberate responsibility to have compassion for all of God's creatures that need a little bit of kindness in their life. This I now please my because Kindness is who He is and always will be. With the Word of God, it will tell you how Kindness develops in us.

<u>First</u>, you must invite the Holy Spirit to indwell in you; to help you perfect kindness throughout your journey while on this earth. As the Word of God says:

"So, walk by the Spirit, and you will not gratify the desires of the flesh. For the flesh desires what is contrary to the Spirit and the Spirit what is contrary to the flesh. They are in conflict with each other, so that you are not able to do whatever you want. However, if the Spirit leads you, you are not under the law. The acts of the flesh are obvious: sexual immorality, impurity and debauchery; idolatry and witchcraft; hatred, discord, jealousy, fits of rage, selfish ambition, dissensions, factions and envy; drunkenness, orgies, and the like. I warn you, as I did before, that those who live like this will not inherit the kingdom of God. However, the Fruit of the Spirit is Love, Joy, Peace, Patience, Kindness, Goodness, Faithfulness, Gentleness and Self-control. Against such things, there is no law. Those who belong to Christ Jesus have crucified the flesh with its passions and desires. Since we live by the Spirit, let us keep in step with the Spirit. Let us not become conceited, provoking and envying each other". (Galatians 5:16-25).

<u>Second</u>, we must get rid of all that stops us from spreading kindness; and walk away from all unkindness. As believers in Christ Jesus, we are to let kindness flow through us, showing the world the Love of God. Therefore, you must do what the Word of God says: *"Be completely humble and gentle; be patient, bearing with one another in Love. Make every effort to keep the unity of the Spirit through the bond of peace". (Ephesians 4:2-3).*

"Get rid of all bitterness, rage and anger, brawling and slander, along with every form of malice. Be kind and compassionate to one another, forgiving each

other, just as in Christ God forgave you". (Ephesians 4:31-32).

<u>Third</u>, we must focus on the needs of other people. When we focus on ourselves, kindness does not come through. In addition, when focusing on others, we get to know their needs.

"Therefore, as God's chosen people, holy and dearly loved, clothe yourselves with compassion, kindness, humility, gentleness and patience. Bear with each other and forgive one another if any of you has a grievance against someone. Forgive as the Lord forgave you. In addition, over all these virtues put on love, which binds them all together in perfect unity. Let the Peace of Christ rule in your hearts, since as members of one body you were called to peace. And be thankful". (Ephesians 3:12-15).

<u>Fourth</u>, we must ask God to teach us to be kind. We really do not have to go to no one else but God, He but Him is the only One who knows how to express kindness. *"Blessed are the merciful, for they will be shown mercy. Blessed are the pure in heart, for they will see God. Blessed are the peacemakers, for they will be called children of God. Rejoice and be glad, because great is your reward in heaven". (Matthew 5:7-9, 12a).*

<u>Fifth</u>, we must always practice kindness at all times. Always be looking for opportunities to help a person in need. This pleases God.

"Do not be deceived: God cannot be mocked. A man reaps what he sows. Whoever sows to please their flesh, from the flesh will reap destruction; whoever sows to please the Spirit, from the Spirit will reap eternal life. Let us not become weary in doing good—for at the proper time we will reap a harvest if we do not give up. Therefore, as we have opportunity, let us do good to all people, especially to those who belong to the family of believers". (Galatians 6:7-10).

"Therefore, as God's chosen people, holy and dearly loved, clothe yourselves with compassion, kindness, humility, gentleness and patience. Bear with each other and forgive one another if any of you has a grievance against someone. Forgive as the Lord forgave you. And over all these virtues put on love, which binds them all together in perfect unity". (Colossians 1:12-14).

"Get rid of all bitterness, rage and anger, brawling and slander, along with every form of malice. Be kind and compassionate to one another, forgiving each other, just as in Christ God forgave you". (Ephesians 4:31-32).

"This is what the Lord says, 'Let not the wise boast of their wisdom or the

371

strong boast of their strength, or the rich boast of their riches, but let the one who boasts boast about this. That they have the understanding to know Me, that I am the Lord, who exercises kindness, justice and righteousness on earth, for in these I delight,' declares the Lord". (Jeremiah 9:23-24).

"Let love and faithfulness never leave you; bind them around your neck, write them on the tablet of your heart. Then you will win favor and a good name in the sight of God and man. Trust in the Lord with all your heart and lean not on your own understanding; in all your ways submit to Him, and He will make your paths straight. Do not be wise in your own eyes; fear the Lord and shun evil. This will bring health to your body and nourishment to your bones". (Proverb 3:3-8).

The last one is by far least important. It binds all six together to make us delightful in God's eyes.

<u>Sixth</u>, we must speak kind words. I know this is true, because I was always on the receiving end of hurtful words. However, Jesus was there to comfort me; He spoke kind and healing words. From that moment of compassion and kindness from my Lord and Savior, I knew I had a place of refuge.

"Give thanks to the Lord, for He is good; His love endures forever". (Psalm 107:1).

"He heals the brokenhearted and binds up their wounds". (Psalm 147:3).

"Do not be carried away by all kinds of strange teachings. It is good for our hearts to be strengthened by grace, not by ceremonial foods, which is of no benefit to those who do so". (Hebrews 13:9).

"For it is by grace you have been saved, through faith—and this is not from yourselves, it is the gift of God—not by works, so that no one can boast. For we are God's handiwork, created in Christ Jesus to do good works, which God prepared in advance for us to do". (Ephesians 2:8-10).

"May these words of my mouth and this meditation of my heart be pleasing in your sight, Lord, my Rock and my Redeemer". (Psalm 19:14).

Here are some more Scriptures that reflect kind words:

"A gentle answer turns away wrath, but a harsh word stirs up anger. The tongue of the wise adorns knowledge, but the mouth of the fool gushes folly. The

eyes of the Lord are everywhere, keeping watch on the wicked and the good. The soothing tongue is a tree of life, but a perverse tongue crushes the spirit". (Proverbs 15:1-4).

"And the Lord's servant must not be quarrelsome but must be kind to everyone, able to teach, not resentful. Opponents must be gently instructed, in the hope that God will grant them repentance leading them to a knowledge of the truth, and that they will come to their senses and escape from the trap of the devil; who has taken them captive to do his will". (2 Timothy 2:24-26)

Faith vs. Reason

In Hebrews 11:1, it says: *"Now faith is confidence in what we hope for and assurance about what we do not see".* This is what faith is. However, just as we have an enemy (Satan), so does Faith, and that is reason (Satan). Reason (Satan) attempts to override the trust we have in God by reasoning with us to rely on the human mind. This kind of reasoning leads to insecurity and doubt; the two most used weapons of Satan. God will wait patiently for us to acknowledge our need for a savior, and then He responds in Faith.

Faith says: *"With God, all things are possible". (Matthew 19:26).*

Reason says: I don't need God to help me. I can do it myself.

Faith says: *"And my God will supply all your needs according to the riches of His glory in Christ Jesus". (Philippians 4:19).*

Reason says, I can get my own supplies. I don't need anything from God.

Faith says: *"Jesus answered, **'I am the Way and the Truth and the Life. No one comes to the Father except through me. If you really know me, you will know my Father as well. From now on, you do know Him and have seen Him'".** (John 14:6-7).*

Reason says, "There has to be a better way."

As you can see, when you put our faith in God, you live. However, if you start to reason or doubt, you die; slowly and torturous.

Faith wins all the time. As the Word of God says: *"For the Lord you God is the one who goes with you to fight for you against your enemies to give you victory". (Deuteronomy 20:4).*

"No temptation has seized you, except what is common to man. God is Faithful; He will not let you be tempted beyond what you can bear. But when you are tempted, He will also provide a Way out, so that you can stand up under it". (1 Corinthians 10:13).

"Therefore, put on the full Armor of God, so that when the day of evil comes, you may be able to stand your ground, and after you have done everything, to stand. Stand firm then, with the Belt of Truth buckled around your waist, with the Breastplate of Righteousness that comes from the Gospel of Peace". (Ephesians 6:13-15).

"I have told you these things, so that in me you may have peace. In this world, you will have trouble. However, take heart! I have overcome the world". (John 16:33).

Only those belonging to Christ possess Eternal Life. In addition, those who believe that Jesus died for us will always stand firm in faith and let no reason and doubt enter into their minds. Until we deal with our past failures and conquer our sense of inadequacy, we will never be able to handle success. Once we get the negative past out of our heads, and focus on

Jesus. We will be able to move forward toward a meaningful and fulfilling life, we have in Christ. Events, in this world, can cripple our ambitions for doing great things for God. It all starts with letting go of all worldly things and thoughts and rise above the chaos and live for God, not for the enemy (Satan). Staying focused on the things in Heaven makes fear disappear and joy enter in and carry us over the fires of this world. Our Heavenly Father is always watching and walking by our sides, to be the shield that never breaks away. This is God's Will for our lives.

Seeking God's Will is as simple as reading His Word (the Bible), where all the answers to all of the questions that are running through everyone's minds, about the struggles they are facing. That's where I found the answers to these two questions that has been running through my mind:

(1) What is the lesson I am supposed to learn from this current situation?

(2) How can I serve you, Father?

I took these questions in prayer, and through my Lord Jesus, I asked

God for help, and He had me read these Scriptures: ***"For my thoughts are not your thoughts, neither are your ways my ways', declares the Lord. 'As the heavens are higher than the earth, so are my ways higher than your ways and my thoughts than your thoughts'".*** *(Isaiah 55:8-9).*

"To humans belong the plans of the heart, but from the Lord comes the proper answer of the tongue. All a person's ways seem pure to him or her, but the Lord weighs motives. Commit to the Lord whatever you do, and He will establish your plans. The Lord works out everything to its proper end, even the wicked for a day of disaster. The Lord detests all the proud of heart. Be sure of this: They will not go unpunished. Through Love and Faithfulness sin is atoned for; through fear of the Lord evil is avoided". (Proverbs 16:1-6).

"Because of your partnership in the gospel from the first day until now, being confident of this, that He who began a good work in you will carry it on to completion until the day of Christ Jesus". (Philippians 1:5-6).

"In Him we were also chosen, having been predestined according to the plan of Him who works out everything in conformity with the purpose of His will in order that we, who were the first to hope in Christ". (Ephesians 1:11-12).

"Great is the Lord and most worthy of praise, in the city of our God, His holy mountain".

(Psalm 48:1).

"For the Lord is the great God, the great King above all gods….Come let us bow down in worship, let us kneel before the Lord our Maker". (Psalm 95:3, 6).

God weighs our motives, intents, and purposes. As the Word of God says:

"The Lord alone has all the facts. He alone is able to judge the purity of our motives and the reasons for our mind". (1 Corinthians 4:4-5).

"Of the Lord delights in a man's way, He makes his steps firm; though he stumbles, He will not fall for the Lord upholds him with His hand". (Psalm 37:23-24).

Seeking God's will is to know more about Him. The more we know Him, the more we will find His perspective. In addition to finding God's will in His word, we must pray to receive knowledge, wisdom, and insight to walk in the right direction. We do need to seek God at all times and surrender all things that are hindering us in getting a clear knowledge of His will.

I like reading this Scripture from Joshua 1:5-9; it always puts me back into God's Perspective:

"No one will be able to stand against you all the days of your life. As I was with Moses, so I will be with you. I will never leave you nor forsake you. Be strong and courageous…Be strong and very courageous. Do not let the book of the law depart from your mouth; meditate on it day and night, so that you may be careful to do everything written in it. Have I not Commanded you? Be strong and courageous. Do not be terrified; do not be discouraged, for the Lord your God will be with you wherever you go". *(Joshua 1:5-9)*.

Holding on to God's promises is a clear indication of the Hope and Trust that I have in Him. Leading me to a more intimate relationship with Him. Therefore, I recommend just opening the

Book of Psalms and Proverbs to start you off on a search for a closer relationship with God. Let me give you some that started me in the right direction.

"Blessed is the one who does not walk in step with the wicked or stand in the way that sinners take or sit in the company of mockers, but whose delight is in the law of the Lord, and who meditates on His law day and night. That person is like a tree planted by streams of water, which yields its fruit in season and whose leaf does not wither, whatever they do will prosper". *(Psalm 1:1-3)*.

"Do not forget My teaching, but keep My Commands in your heart, for they will prolong your life many years and bring you peace and prosperity. Let Love and Faithfulness never leave you; bind them around your neck, write them on the tablet of your heart. Then you will win favor and a good name in the sight of God and man. Trust in the Lord with all your heart and lean not on your own understanding; in all your ways submit to Him, and He will make your paths straight. Do not be wise in your own eyes; fear the Lord and shun evil. This will bring health to your body and nourishment to your bones". *(Proverb 3:1-8)*.

"*Truly my soul finds rest in God; my salvation comes from Him. Truly He is my rock and my salvation; He is my fortress, I will never be shaken*". (Psalm 62:1-2).

"*Trust in the Lord and do good; dwell in the land and enjoy safe pastures. Take delight in the Lord, and He will give you the desires of your heart. Commit your way to the Lord; trust in Him and He will do this: He will make your righteous reward shine like the dawn, your vindication like the noonday sun. Be still before the Lord and wait patiently for Him; do not fret when people succeed in their ways, when they carry out their wicked schemes. Refrain from anger and turn from wrath; do not fret—it leads only to evil. For those who are evil will be destroyed, but those who hope in the Lord will inherit the land. A little while, and the wicked will be no more; though you look for them, they will not be found. But the meek will inherit the land and enjoy Peace and Prosperity*" (Psalm 37:3-11).

"*The Lord makes firm the steps of the one who delights in Him; though he may stumble, he will not fall, for the Lord upholds him with His hand*". (Psalm 37:23-24).

"*The precepts of the Lord are right, giving joy to the heart. The Commands of the Lord are Radiant, giving Light to the eyes. The fear of the Lord is Pure, enduring forever. The Decrees of the Lord are firm, and all of them are righteous. They are more precious than much pure gold; they are sweeter than honey, than honey from the honeycomb*". (Psalm 19:8-10).

"*The Lord is my shepherd, I lack nothing. He makes me lie down in green pastures, He leads me beside quiet waters, and He refreshes my soul. He guides me along the right paths for His name's sake. Even though I walk through the darkest valley, I will fear no evil, for You are with me;*

Your rod and Your staff, they comfort me". (Psalm 23:1-4).

"***I will instruct you and teach you in the way you should go; I will counsel you with My loving eye on you***'". (Psalm 32:8).

"*The fear of the Lord is the beginning of knowledge, but fools despise wisdom and instruction*". (Proverb 1:7).

"*Whoever listens to Me will live in safety and be at ease, without fear of harm*" (Proverb 1:33).

"To humans belong the plans of the heart, but from the Lord comes the proper answer of the tongue. All a person's ways seem pure to him or her, but the Lord weighs motives. Commit to the Lord whatever you so, and He will establish your plans. The Lord works out everything to its proper end—even the wicked for a day of disaster. The Lord detests all the proud of heart. Be sure of this: They will not go unpunished. Through Love and Faithfulness, sin is atoned; for through the fear of the Lord evil is avoided. When the Lord takes pleasure in anyone's way, He causes their enemies to make peace with them". (Proverbs 16:1-7).

"God is our refuge and strength, an ever-present help in trouble. Therefore, we will not fear, though the earth gives way and the mountains fall into the heart of the sea, though its waters roar and foam and the mountains quake with their surging". (Psalm 46:1-3).

"God says, **'Be still, and know that I am God; I will be exalted among the nations. I will be exalted in the earth. The Lord Almighty is with us; the God of Jacob is our fortress'".** *(Psalm 46:10-11).*

"My flesh and my heart may fail, but God is the strength of my heart and my portion forever. Those who are far from you will perish; you destroy all who are unfaithful to You". (Psalm 73:26-27).

These are just some of the Scripture verses that strengthen my relationship with my Star Team. I am continually getting stronger in the Lord, each time I read His Word. I found out that the more you find yourself struggling in this world, the more you are not making the Word of God an ongoing presence in your life. Just remember this one verse in the Book of Isaiah:

"The Lord will guide you always; He will satisfy your needs in a sun-scorched land and will strengthen your frame. You will be like a well-watered garden, like a spring whose waters never fail". (Isaiah 58:11).

The Will of God is very clear, of how to stay close to Him, just open your Bibles, open your ears to His Voice and listen to Him speaking His Instructions to you to do and which way you should go. In the Word God it says: *"The Lord longs to be Gracious to you; therefore, He will rise up to show you compassion. For the Lord is a God of justice. Blessed are all who wait for Him". (Isaiah 30:18).*

"Although the Lord gives you the bread of adversity and the water of affliction, your teachers will be hidden no more; with your own eyes you will see them.

*Whether you turn to the right or to the left, your ears will hear a Voice behind you, saying, '**This is the way; walk in it**'". (Isaiah 30:20-21).*

Here now is a list of five reasons why you must desire to do the Will of God:

Reason One: To enter the Kingdom of God.

*"'**Not everyone who says to Me; Lord, Lord; shall enter the Kingdom of Heaven, but he who does the Will of My Father in Heaven**'". (Matthew 7:21).*

Reason Two: To avoid living in the lust of the flesh and live for God alone.

"Therefore, since Christ suffered in His body, arm yourselves also with the same attitude, because whoever suffers in the body is done with sin. As a result, they do not live the rest of their earthly lives for evil human desires, but rather for the Will of God". (1 Peter 4:1-2).

Reason Three: To live with God forever.

"The world and its desires pass away, but whoever does the Will of God, lives forever". (1 John 2:17).

Reason Four: To receive the Promise of God.

"You need to persevere so that when you have done the Will of God, you will receive what He has Promised". (Hebrews 10:36).

Reason Five: To avoid unnecessary suffering.

"Dear friends, I urge you, as foreigners and exiles, to abstain from sinful desires, which wage war against your soul". (1 Peter 2:11).

"For it is God's will that by doing good, you should silence the ignorant talk of foolish people. Live as free people, but do not use your freedom as a cover-up for evil; live as servants of God. Show proper respect to everyone, love the family of believers, fear God, and honor the king". (1 Peter 2:15-17).

Now are Scriptures of how to find the Will of God. You must tell, ask, listen, and praise; telling Him you want to live for His Will.

Number One:

"Follow God's Example, therefore, as dearly loved children and walk in the Way of Love, just as Christ loved us and gave Himself up for us as a fragrant offering and sacrifice to His Father". (Ephesians 5:1-2).

Number Two: Ask God for Wisdom to help you understand what His will is.

"Therefore, do not be foolish, but understand what the Lord's will is". (Ephesians 5:17).

"If any of you lacks wisdom, you should ask God, who gives generously to all without finding fault, and it will be given to you. However, when you ask, you must believe and not doubt, because the one who doubts is like a wave of the sea, blown and tossed by the wind. That person should not expect to receive anything from the Lord. Such a person is double-minded and unstable in all they do". (James 1:5-8).

"The fear of the Lord is the beginning of wisdom; all who follow His precepts have good understanding. To Him belongs eternal praise". (Psalm 111:10).

"The fear of the Lord is the beginning of wisdom, and knowledge of the Holy One is understanding". (Proverb 9:10).

"Who is wise and understanding among you? Let them show it by their good life, by deeds dome in the humility that comes from wisdom. However, if you harbor bitter envy and selfish ambition in your hearts, do not boast about it or deny the truth. Such 'wisdom' does not come down from Heaven but is earthly, unspiritual, and demonic. For where you have envy and selfish ambition, there you find disorder and every evil practice. However, the wisdom that comes from heaven is first of all pure; then peace-loving, considerate, submissive, full of mercy and good fruit, impartial and sincere. Peacemakers who sow in Peace reap a Harvest of Righteousness". (James 3:13-18).

"Fools give full vent to their rage, but the wise bring calm in the end". (Proverb 29:11).

<u>Number Three: Ask God to enable you to do His Will.</u>

"Now, may the God of peace, who through the blood of the eternal covenant, brought back from the dead our Lord Jesus, that great Shepherd of the sheep, equip you with everything good, for doing His will, and may He work in us what is pleasing to Him, through Jesus Christ, to whom be glory forever and ever. Amen". (Hebrews 13:20-21).

<u>Number Four: Listen for God's Voice speaking to your heart.</u>

*"Whether you turn right or to the left, your ears will hear a voice behind you, saying, **'This is the way; walk in it'"**. (Isaiah 30:21).*

"My sheep listen to My voice; I know them, and they follow Me. I give them Eternal Life, and they shall never perish; no one will snatch them out of My Hand. My Father, who has given them to Me, is Greater than all; no one can snatch them out of My Father's Hand. I and the Father are one'". *(John 10:27-30).*

"Consequently, faith comes from hearing the message, and the Message is heard through the Word about Christ". (Romans 10:17).

"Call to Me and I will answer you and tell you great and unsearchable things you do not know'". *(Jeremiah 33:3).*

"Whoever belongs to God hears what God says. The reason you do not hear is that you do not belong to God". (John 8:47).

"For the Word of God is alive and active. Sharper than any double-edged sword, it penetrates even to divide soul and spirit, joints and marrow; it judges the thoughts and attitudes of the heart. Nothing in all creation is hidden from God's Sight. Everything is uncovered and laid bare before the eyes of Him to whom we must give account". (Hebrews 4:12-13).

"My dear brothers and sisters, take note of this: Everyone should be quick to listen, slow to speak and slow to become angry, because human anger does not produce the righteousness that God desires. Therefore, get rid of all moral filth and the evil that is so prevalent and humbly accept the word planted in you, which can save you. Do not merely listen to the Word, and so deceive yourselves. Do what it says". (James 1:19-22).

<u>Number Five: Praise God and give thanks to Him in everything</u>.

"In everything, give thanks in all circumstances; for this is the will of God". (1 Thessalonians 5:18).

"Give thanks to the Lord, for He is good; His love endures forever. Let the redeemed of the Lord tell their story—those He redeemed from the hand of the foe, those He gathered from the lands, from east and west, from north and south". (Psalm 107:1-3).

"Let your gentleness be evident to all. The Lord is near. Do not be anxious about anything, but in every situation, by prayer and petition, with thanksgiving, present your requests to God. In addition, the peace of God, which transcends all understanding, will guard your hearts and your minds in Christ Jesus. Finally, brothers and sisters, whatever is true, whatever is noble, whatever is right, whatever is pure, whatever is lovely, whatever is admirable—if anything is excellent or praiseworthy—think about such things". (Philippians 4:5-8).

"Thanks be to God for His indescribable gift!" (2 Corinthians 9:15).

"Give praise to the Lord, proclaim His name; make known among the nations what He has done. Sing to Him, sing praise to Him; tell of all His wonderful acts". (Psalm 105:1-2).

<u>Number Six: Ask God to work His Will into your life all for His glory</u>.

"Let us fix our eyes on Jesus, the Author and Perfecter of our Faith; who for the Joy set before Him endured the Cross, scorning its shame, and sat down at the Right Hand of the Throne of God. Consider Him who endured such opposition from sinful men, so that you will not grow weary and lose heart". (Hebrews 12:2-3).

We must reflect the Light that is in Jesus. When we reflect that Light, we reflect it into that someone who is sitting in the darkness of this world. To keep that Light shining in us, we need to stay close to the source; who is our Lord Jesus, the only One who has that Glorious Light of the Almighty Father God. The more we let His Light shine through our eyes, the more we become like Him. The Word of God says:

"Whenever anyone turns to the Lord, the veil is taken away. Now the Lord is the Spirit, and where the Spirit of the Lord is, there is freedom. And we all, who with unveiled faces contemplate the Lord's glory, are being transformed into His

image with ever-increasing glory, which comes from the Lord, who is the Spirit". *(2 Corinthians 3:16-18).*

Let us now be keepers of God's Light, ensuring that the Light of His Love burns brightly so that all can see how much He loves His children. There are people who need to absorb just a little of His Light into their hearts; a small beacon of His Light goes a long way to display God's Love. The darkness that most of us hold on to, Jesus will break. God delights when His children take joy in Him and His Son. God never gives up on us, so let us not give up on Him. When we celebrate Him, He celebrates us.

When we invite Jesus into every aspect of our lives, God will exchange our past pain for His Present Comfort. Jesus turns our deep sorrows into divine delight. All our wounds are altered into fresh new wisdom. Our stale, old thoughts are converted into new ideas in creative divine ways to solve problems. Jesus can surely turn a cold, silent stare into a warm conversation. When we draw close to Jesus, we find out the secret that His power can change everything.

Here are some of the most Spiritual needs of people today. Along with Scriptures that explain, each needs to live like Jesus and for His Father in Heaven. Nothing of this world can satisfy us as the Word of God can. Nothing!

To believe that life is meaningful and has purpose:

"For God so loved the world that He gave His one and only Son, that whoever believes in Him shall not perish but have eternal life". (John 3:16).

"When Jesus spoke again to the people, He said, ***'I am the light of the world. Whoever follows Me will never walk in darkness, but will have the Light of Life'".*** *(John 8:12).*

"All Scripture is God-breathed and is useful for teaching, rebuking, correcting and training in righteousness, so that the servant of God may be thoroughly equipped for every good work". (2 Timothy 3:16-17).

"If anyone teaches otherwise and does not agree to the Sound Instruction of our Lord Jesus Christ and to Godly Teaching, they are conceited and understand nothing. They have an unhealthy interest in controversies and quarrels about words that result in envy, strife, malicious talk, evil suspicions and constant

friction between people of corrupt mind, who have been robbed of the Truth and who think that Godliness is a means to financial gain. However, Godliness with contentment is great gain. For we brought nothing into the world, and we can take nothing out of it. But if we have food and clothing, we will be content with that". (1 Timothy 6:3-8).

To have a sense of community and deeper relationships:

"When you heard about Christ and were taught in Him in accordance with the Truth that is in Jesus. You were taught, with regard to your former way of life, to put off your old self (which is being corrupted by its deceitful desires), to be made new in the attitude of your minds; and to put on the new self, created to be like God in true righteousness and holiness. Therefore, each of you must put off falsehood and speak truthfully to your neighbor, for we are all members of one body. In your anger do not sin: Do not let the sun go down while you are still angry, and do not give the devil a foothold. Anyone who has been stealing must steal no longer, but must work, doing something useful with their own hands, that they may have something to share with those in need. Do not let any unwholesome talk come out of your mouths, but only what is helpful for building others up according to their needs, that it may benefit those who listen. In addition, do not grieve the Holy Spirit of God, with whom you were sealed, for the day of redemption. Get rid of all bitterness, rage and anger, brawling and slander, along with every form of malice. Be kind and compassionate to one another, forgiving each other, just as in Christ God forgave you". (Ephesians 4:21-32).

To be appreciated and respected:

"In everything, do to others what you would have them do to you, for this sums up the Law and the Prophets". (Matthew 7:12).

To be listened to:

*"**For I know the plans I have for you**', declares the Lord, '**plans to prosper you and not to harm you, plans to give you hope and a future. Then you will call on Me, and come and pray to Me, and I will listen to you. You will seek Me and find Me when you seek Me with all your heart**'" (Jeremiah 29:11-13).*

"I love the Lord, for He heard my voice; He heard my cry for mercy. Because He turned His ear to me, I will call on Him as long as I live". (Psalm 116:1-2).

To feel they are growing in faith:

"Faith is confidence in what we hope for and assurance about what we do not see". (Hebrews 11:1).

"Grow in the Grace and Knowledge of our Lord and Savior Jesus Christ. To Him be Glory both now and forever! Amen". (2 Peter 3:18).

To get practical help in developing a mature faith:

"As God's chosen people, holy and dearly loved, clothe yourselves with Compassion, Kindness, Humility, Gentleness and Patience. Bear with each other, and forgive one another if you have a grievance against someone. Forgive as the Lord forgave you. In addition, over all these virtues put on Love, which binds them all together in Perfect Unity. Let the Peace of Christ rule in your hearts, since as members of one body you were called to peace. And be thankful. Let the Message of Christ dwell among you richly as you teach and admonish one another with all wisdom through Psalms, Hymns, and Songs from the Spirit, singing to God with gratitude in your hearts. And whatever you do, whether in word or deed, do it all in the Name of the Lord Jesus, giving thanks to God the Father through Him". (Colossians 3:12-17).

We get all these when we accept Jesus into our lives and our hearts. Yes, there may be times that are hard to understand (the hurtful times), but we live in a hurtful world. We know that Jesus overcame this hurtful world, and with Him by our side, we can overcome this hurtful world and live out the Peace of the Almighty God. As Jesus tells us, ***"I have told you these things, so that in Me you may have Peace. In this world, you will have trouble. However, take heart! I have overcome the world"***. *(John 16:33).*

I found a formula to see and understand God's Will in my life, a formula that needs continual working on, where patience comes into play. This world has many things that can keep us from doing the Will of God, so we need to fulfill this Scripture verse: *"Fight the good fight of the Faith. Take hold of the Eternal Life to which you were called when you made your good confession in the presence of many witnesses". (1 Timothy 6:12).*

This formula is easy to maintain. All you need to do is stop what you are doing wrong. Pray to God for forgiveness. Watch for God to answer your prayers. Listen for God's Instructions to stay on the Righteous Path. Solution is to have God's continual Protection, Comfort, and Love is always present in your life. This is just one formula that you can use to maintain a life in Christ Jesus. Our Heavenly Father will reveal many more to you when you go to Him in prayer and ask for help. God breaks us down to make us new. Just take a look at Genesis 32:22-32 when Jacob wrestled with God.

We too will wrestle with God. When we start wondering away from Him, thinking that we can go it alone and we become arrogant and push Him aside and not listening to

His Instructions. God then takes drastic action, wounding us, to stop us from getting too proud until we learn that we need to depend on Him always. This is tough-love, a kind of love that requires discipline and structure. Jacob found himself in this position. Jacob was all alone when God appeared in the form of a man, saw him out, and wrestled with him until daybreak (v. 24). You see God saw that Jacob was heading in a direction that would hurt him, so God wanted to make Jacob into a different person; taking drastic actions. Therefore, *God touched the socket of Jacob's hip, making him walk with a limp the rest of his life (v. 25).*

Many people today would become bitter and get mad at God, turning away from Him. In Jacob's response, he said, *"I will not let go unless you bless me" (v. 26).* Because Jacob knew that he was face-to-face with his God. You are probably thinking how could God wound us when He loves us so much? Simple, that is exactly why He does discipline us. God sent His only Son, Jesus, to the Cross because He loves us: *"God so LOVED the world that He gave us His ONE and ONLY SON, that whoever BELIEVES in Him will never walk in darkness". (John 3:16).*

God breaks our will so we can discover His Will. In addition, God may break our physical strength to know His Strength. Because the Word of God says: *"That is why, for Christ's sake, I delight in weaknesses, in insults, in hardships, in persecutions, and in difficulties. For when I am weak, then I am strong". (2 Corinthians 12:10).* And God says: *"My grace is sufficient for you, for My Power is made Perfect in weakness". (2 Corinthians 12:9).*

These two phrases alone are enough to cling to God until we receive His blessings. It may seem like sometimes we are clinging for a long, long, long time to God, but just when we seem to want to give up, God showers us with a blessing that we never even thought we could have ever deserved. The blessing of His Son Jesus is the proof of His love and blessing that will satisfy us always. No matter what we go through, we could always count on God's Grace to pull us through anything that might be bothering us. Nothing is greater than the Grace of God.

This is our problem today, that we are too anxious, when we go through trials. We focus on our present situation and forget that our Lord Jesus is here to help. In the Word of God, it clearly tells us what to do when the trials of this world are upon us. We should: *"Rejoice in the Lord always. I will say it again: Rejoice! Let your gentleness be evident to all. The Lord is near. Do not be anxious about anything, but in everything, by prayer and petition, with thanksgiving, present your requests to God. In addition, the peace of God, which transcends all understanding, will guard your hearts and your minds in Christ Jesus. Finally, brothers and sisters, whatever is true, whatever is Noble, whatever is Right, whatever is Pure, whatever is Lovely, whatever is Admirable – if anything is Excellent or Praiseworthy; think about such things. Whatever you have learned or received or heard from Me, or seen in Me, put into practice and the God of peace will be with you". (Philippians 4:4-9).*

People who speak words of encouragement and have an attitude of contentment is a delight to God. Being content and trusting God can keep you always speaking words of encouragement. Even when you yourself are facing crisis and pain. When you lift someone up that is in need, it will also help you in your time of need. Speaking the Words of God makes all evil flee. When you show gentleness toward others, it shows that the Lord is with you, and they too will feel the

Joy and Presence of the Lord. We must be content with all that God gives us. Even at times we are walking in the shadows of pain.

Here are some Scriptures to remind us to be content in living God's way:

"Come near to God and He will come near to you. Wash your hands, you sinners, and purify your hearts, you double-minded". (James 4:8).

"God's Divine Power has given us everything we need for a Godly Life through our knowledge of Him who called us by His own Glory and Goodness". (2 Peter 1:3).

"Satisfy us in the morning with your unfailing love that we may sing for joy and be glad all our days". (Psalm 90:14).

"Let them give thanks to the Lord for His Unfailing Love and His Wonderful Deeds for mankind, for He satisfies the thirsty and fills the hungry with Good Things". (Psalm 107:8-9).

"Teach me, Lord, the Way of Your decrees, that I may follow it to the end. Give me understanding, so that I may keep Your Law and obey it with all my heart. Direct me in the path of Your commands, for there I find delight. Turn my heart toward Your statutes and not toward selfish gain. Turn my eyes away from worthless things; preserve my life according to Your word. Fulfill Your promise to Your servant, so that You may be feared. Take away the disgrace I dread, for Your laws are good". (Psalm 119:33-39).

"Blessed are those who act justly, who always do what is right". (Psalm 106:3).

"Blessed are those whose ways are blameless, who walk according to the Law of the Lord. Blessed are those who keep His statutes and seek Him with all their heart; they do no wrong but follow His ways". (Psalm 119:1-3).

"I trust in your unfailing love; my heart rejoices in your salvation. I will sing the Lord's praise, for He has been good to me". (Psalm 13:5-6).

"Praise be to the Lord, for He has heard my cry for mercy. The Lord is my strength and my shield; my heart trusts in Him, and He helps me. My heart leaps for joy, and with my song I praise Him". (Psalm 28:6-7).

*"God says, **'Be still and know I am God; I will be exalted among the nations, I will be exalted in the earth'".** (Psalm 46:10).*

"My flesh and my heart may fail, but God is the strength of my heart and my portion forever. Those who are far from You will perish; You destroy all who are unfaithful to You". (Psalm 73:26-28).

*"Keep your lives free from the love of money and be content with what you have, because God has said, **'Never will I leave you; never will I forsake you'".** (Hebrews 13:5).*

"Though my father and mother forsake me, the Lord will receive me". (Psalm 27:10).

"God is faithful, who has called you into fellowship with His Son, Jesus Christ our Lord". (1 Corinthians 1:9).

"I will not leave you as orphans; I will come to you". (John 14:18).

"For God so loved the world that He gave His one and only Son, that whoever believes in Him shall not perish but have eternal life. For God did not send His Son into the world to condemn the world, but to save the world through Him. Whoever believes in Him is not condemned, but whoever does not believe stands condemned already, because he has not believed in the name of God's only Son". (John 3:16-18).

"Everyone who does evil hates the light, and will not come into the Light for fear that his deeds will be exposed. But whoever lives by the Truth comes into the light, so that it may be seen plainly that what he has done has been done through God". (John 3:20-21).

"Whoever drinks the water I give him will never thirst. Indeed, the water I give him will become in him a spring of water welling up to Eternal Life". (John 4:14).

"I can do all this through Him who gives me strength" (Philippians 4:13).

To be Available (Faithfully) and Obedient:

I will be faithfully available and obedient to my Lord and Master, Father God. Whatever assignment He assigns for me, I will thrive in achieving it, even if it is out of my comfort zone. I love and trust my Lord Jesus enough to follow Him wherever He may lead. Wherever I go, my loyal and faithful friend, Jesus, will always be there.

The process of being obedient is to love God, to serve Him, to listen to Him, to walk with Him, to watch with Him, and to always seek Him. I will do this process all the days of my life as I live here on this earth. I am now passionately in pursuit of Jesus.

How to live out His way, His will, and to love as the Almighty God loves. I will embrace the Cross that shattered all the strongholds that kept me from receiving more of what God wants to give me. I will gaze upon His face, listen to His audible voice, feel His unmistakable touch, and become a witness for His Glory.

Yes! Yes! Yes, Lord, I am available for service. Here I am. Send me wherever you need me to be. All for Your Glory. In the Name of Jesus. Amen.

The Reminders of Walking Humbly Are in the Book Micah 6:1-9

Micah reminds us that God sees the heart. God always knows when we are being genuine with our humble expressions of repentance. In addition, God sees when our sacrifices are for His

Glory. Those sacrifices are to be honest and not just for looking good. We must do it for God, not for man. When we do everything for God, all goes well in our life. Here are some must dos:

First is to act justly, love mercy, and walk humbly:

"God has shown you, O mortal, what is Good. What does the Lord require of you? To act justly and to love mercy and to walk humbly with your God". (Micah 6:8).

Second is to fear God is beginning of Wisdom:

"The fear of the Lord is the beginning of Wisdom, and Knowledge of the Holy One, is understanding". (Proverb 9:10).

Third is to listen to what the Lord says and do it:

"Do not merely listen to the word, and so deceive yourselves. Do what it says". (James 1:22).

Fourth is to give thanks to God daily:

"Give thanks in all circumstances; for this is the will of God in Christ Jesus". (1 Thessalonians 5:18).

Fifth is to take obedience as a joyful word, not a grudging, and dutiful word:

"Have confidence in your leaders and submit to their authority, because they keep watch over you as those who must give an account. Do this so that their work will be a joy, not a burden, for that would be of no benefit to you". (Hebrews 13:17).

<u>Sixth is to call out to God for help with day-to-day battle that is an ongoing thing on this earth</u>: *"Submit yourselves to God. Resist the devil, and he will flee from you".* *(James 4:7).*

Obedience becomes joyful when we stop and respond with abandonment to the One who loves us. Abandonment is to give up completely, to leave, forsake, desert, to yield completely, surrender to one's feelings or impulses, letting oneself go. In other words, obedience to God is to abandon (give up) all what this world has to offer – this is to live with abandonment.

What is in this world will fade away and die. As the Word of God says:

"Guard what has been entrusted to your care. Turn away from godless chatter and the opposing ideas of what is falsely called knowledge". (1 Timothy 6:20).

It may seem hard to do this, for most of this world's chatter is gossip. Gossip is the hurtful words that are being said of another. I myself was not much of a talker. But when I was younger, to most of the people I came in contact with, I was considered retarded (hurtful word). Moreover, just because I did not talk as much, they talked to me as if I was a five year-old. God sees the motives hidden behind every word and action. So stop chattering (gossiping) and making excuses and start listening to the Voice of Truth. Follow the ways of the Lord, and He will show you who He really is. Take His hand and walk humbly by His side, clinging to Him with your whole heart and never letting go.

Be at One with God.

Be at one with me, O Lord!

You hold the universe, and You are holding me.

I set my affections on the things above, not on the things of this earth.

I only think of and desire, the One that will help me, not hinder my Spiritual Walk.

When I think Love, I think God. For God is Love.

Love reflects God. Love surrounds me. Love is in me. Love is all of who I am.

I am one with God. God is one with me.

On a Crowded Day.

On a crowded day, it can feel very chaotic.

However, believing that God is with us, and controlling all, assures Peace.

Be calm! Never fear! Just know He is God.

Keep singing praises unto the Lord, for He is good.

Be glad at all times. Rejoicing exceedingly.

Have joy in God. Rest in Him.

Fear not. Pray always.

Do not get worried. Jesus is your helper.

Rest in His everlasting arms.

Approach each day with the awareness that God is in control.

On a crowded day, just breathe.

Jesus is:

Jesus is my Conqueror.

Jesus is my Rescuer, my Leader, and my Guide.

Jesus is my Joy-bringer.

Jesus is my Hope and my Light of Life.

Jesus is my Comforter in times of sorrow.

Jesus is my Giver of Love and acceptance.

Jesus is my Deliverer.

Jesus is my Refuge and my Strength.

Jesus is everything to me, and I thank you, Jesus.

I thank my Heavenly Father for giving His son Jesus so He can be my
Savior and Friend.

Glory be to God the Father—the Great I Am!

The Status and Commands that our Lord Jesus teaches us is to prepare us of how to live and take back the land that the enemy (Satan) had taken away from us. We must *"observe them carefully; for this will show your wisdom and understanding to the nations". (Deuteronomy 4:6a).*

"*Only be careful, and watch yourselves closely so that you do not forget the things your eyes have seen or let them slip from your heart as long as you live. Teach them to your children and to their children after them". (Deuteronomy 4:9).*

God is our City of Refuge, for in His Presence, no enemy (Satan) can stand; their knees buckle and all their strength leaves them, which leaves them with no power to fight the battle that they think they can win against Him. In addition, in God's Presence, we learn and are able to understand His Commandments. Let us take a look at them:

The Ten Commandments from the Book of Deuteronomy 5:7-21.

Commandment Number 1: "***You shall have no other gods before Me***".

Commandment Number 2: "***You shall not make yourself an idol in the form of anything in Heaven above or on the earth beneath or in the waters below***".

Commandment Number 3: "***You shall not misuse the name of the Lord your God, for the Lord will not hold anyone guiltless who misuses His name***".

Commandment Number 4: "***Observe the Sabbath day by keeping it Holy, as the Lord your God has commanded you***".

Commandment Number 5: "***Honor your father and your mother, as the Lord your God has commanded you, so that you may live long and that it may go well with you in the land the Lord your God is giving you***".

Commandment Number 6: "***You shall not murder***".

Commandment Number 7: "***You shall not commit adultery***".

Commandment Number 8: "***You shall not steal***".

Commandment Number 9: "***You shall not give false testimony against your neighbor***".

Commandment Number 10: "***You shall not covet your neighbor's wife. You shall not set your desire on your neighbor's house or land, his*** *manservant or maidservant, his ox or donkey, or anything that belongs to your neighbor'"*.

As I was reading these Ten Commandments, I was reminded of something I heard about breaking any of the Ten Commandments. If you break one, you break them all. Take for example the first one: *"'You shall have no other gods before Me'"*. You break this one when you break the second commandment: *"'You shall not make yourself an idol in the form of anything'"*. That is because anything can become your god, like money, automobiles, jewelry, clothes, shoes (and yeah, people too). The only one we should be focusing on is our Heavenly Father and our Lord Jesus Christ. Because when they are Number One in our lives, all the pieces of the puzzle start fitting together, and love and peace reign over the world.

To make sure you are right with God, we must all turn away from all the evil of this world and live the life that our Creator designed us to live. This happen only through prayer and walking alongside Jesus. Having a powerful prayer life with Jesus is what works to walk this journey on this earth. When Satan sees us praying and spending our time with Jesus, he leaves us alone, for Satan knows that Jesus defeated him, and he knows that Jesus is too powerful for him to attack anyone who has Jesus in his or her lives.

The truth is God delights in answering our prayers, and He promises to motivate us to talk to Him as we pray in His Presence. This prayer is a conversation with the Heavenly Father, along with His Son Jesus and the Holy Spirit (the Star Team). We pray before we eat, we pray before we sleep, we pray in the morning before we start our day, we pray for help and protection, and most of all we pray to receive God's Love, Mercy, Forgiveness, Joy, Peace, and Salvation. This is what we should be doing all day long.

When I was younger, I never had anyone to tell me how to pray, so I had to learn by reading my Bible and humbling myself to ask for help. I got on my knees (with my Bible in my hand), asked the same question Jesus's disciples asked, 'Teach me to pray'. I was then prompted to turn to the Book of Matthew, to pray like this: *"This, then, is how you should pray, 'Our Father, in heaven, hallowed be Your name, Your kingdom come. Your will be done, on earth as it is in Heaven. Give us today our daily bread. And forgive us our debts, for we also have forgiven our debtors. And lead us not into temptation, and deliver us from the evil one. For if you forgive other people when they sin against you, Your Heavenly Father will also forgive you. But if you do not forgive others their sins, Your Father will not forgive your sins". (Matthew 6:9-15).*

My Star Team also told me these three simple things to make sure I am involved in my life. <u>First</u> is to be myself and not cover up or hide any wrongdoings from God because He sees all that goes on in my life.

<u>Second</u> is to make it a habit to pray and read the Bible, to be able to not fall into the pit of despair and therefore let the enemy (Satan) get his grabby, filthy little self into my life.

<u>Third</u> is to meditate on God's Word the moment that I feel any darkness approaching me, and trusting God to give me the strength to endure all that I face on this earth.

Since I put these three simple things into my life, I have been growing more mature in my walk with my Lord Jesus. I learned to surrender everything I had and commit my heart and soul to God, giving me peace. I learned to fill my life with prayer, praying for everything and everyone, giving me Strength, Love, Hope, Faith, Joy, and Comfort. Most of all I learned to believe that my Heavenly Father speaks and teaches me His love and compassion so I can share it with my family and anyone else that is in need of love and compassion.

Meditate on these Scripture verses, on Prayer, Love, Comfort, and Compassion:

"Sing to Him, sing praise to Him; tell of all His wonderful acts. Glory in His holy name; let the hearts of those who seek the Lord rejoice. Look to the Lord and His strength; seek His face always". (1 Chronicles 16:9-11).

"Answer me when I call to You, my righteous God. Give me relief from my distress; have mercy on me and hear my prayer". (Psalm 4:1).

"The Lord is Gracious and Compassionate; slow to anger and rich in Love. The Lord is good to all; He has Compassion on all He has made. All Your works praise You, Lord; Your faithful people extol You. They tell of the Glory of Your Kingdom and speak of Your Might, so that all people may know of Your Mighty Acts and the Glorious Splendor of Your Kingdom. Your Kingdom is an Everlasting Kingdom, and Your Dominion endures through all generations. The Lord is Trustworthy in all He promises and Faithful in all He does. The Lord

upholds all who fall and lifts up all who are bowed down. The eyes of all look to You, and You give them their food at the proper time. You open Your hand and satisfy the desires of every living thing. The Lord is Righteous in all His Ways and Faithful in all He does. The Lord is near to all who call on Him, to all who call on Him in Truth. He fulfills the desires of those who fear Him; He hears their cry and saves them. The Lord watches over all who love Him, but all the wicked He will destroy". (Psalm 145:8-20).

"The Lord detests the sacrifice of the wicked, but the prayer of the upright pleases Him. The Lord detests the way of the wicked, but He loves those who pursue righteousness. Stern discipline awaits anyone who leaves the path; the one who hates correction will die". (Proverbs 15:8-10).

"The path of life leads upward for the prudent to keep them from going down to the realm of the dead. The Lord tears down the house of the proud, but He sets the widow's boundary stones in place. The Lord detests the thoughts of the wicked, but gracious words are pure in His sight. The greedy bring ruin to their households, but the one who hates bribes will live. The heart of the righteous weighs its answers, but the mouth of the wicked gushes evil. The Lord is far from the wicked, but He hears the prayer of the righteous. Light in a messenger's eyes brings joy to the heart, and good news gives health to the bones. Whoever heeds life giving correction will be at home among the wise. Those who disregard discipline despise themselves, but the one who heeds correction gains understanding. Wisdom's instruction is to fear the Lord, and humility comes before honor". (Proverbs 15:28-33).

"Rejoice always, pray continually, and give thanks in all circumstances; for this is God's will for you in Christ Jesus. Do not quench the Spirit. Do not treat prophecies with contempt, but test them all; hold on to what is good, reject every kind of evil. May God Himself (the God of peace), sanctify you through and through. May your whole spirit, soul, and body be kept blameless at the coming of our Lord Jesus Christ. The One who calls you is faithful, and He will do it". (1 Thessalonians 5:16-23).

"Therefore, confess your sins to each other, and pray for each other, so that you may be healed. The prayers of a righteous person are powerful and effective". (James 5:16).

"Jesus declared, 'I am the bread of life. Whoever comes to Me will never go

hungry, and whoever believes in Me will never be thirsty"". (John 6:35).

"The path of the righteous is like the morning sun, shining ever brighter till the full light of day". (Proverb 4:18).

"Above all else, guard your heart, for everything you do flows from it. Keep your mouth free of perversity; keep corrupt talk far from your lips. Let your eyes look straight ahead; fix your gaze directly before you. Give careful thought to the paths for your feet and be steadfast in all your ways. Do not turn to the right or the left; keep your foot from evil". (Proverb 4:23-27).

"This is the message we have heard from Him and declare to you: God is Light; in Him there is no darkness at all. If we claim to have fellowship with Him and yet walk in darkness, we lie and do not live out the Truth. However, if we walk in the light, as He is in the light, we have fellowship with one another, and the blood of Jesus, His Son, purifies us from all sin. If we claim to be without sin, we deceive ourselves and the Truth is not in us. If we confess our sins, He is Faithful and Just and will forgive us our sins and purify us from all unrighteousness. If we claim we have not sinned, we make Him out to be a liar and His word is not in us". (1 John 1:5-10).

When you pray and seek His face, you must turn from your sin wholeheartedly. The Word of God says: "If my people, who are called by My Name, will humble themselves and pray and seek My Face and turn from their wicked ways, then I will hear from heaven, and I will forgive their sin and will heal their land" (2 Chronicles 7:14). God sees and hears what is in our hearts, and He will respond accordingly.

Prayer begins on our knees, confessing our sin and asking for forgiveness. Then God will cleanse us and strengthen us to walk away from our sins. Living and walking with Jesus is the best way and the only way to live. Doing so, we display the power of God that forgives comforts and most of all loves. We need this connection to God, to receive His Power to flow through us. Therefore, humble yourself, get on your knees (even crawl) into His presence, lift your eyes, look at Him, and become one with Him. He will take you by the hand and place you in His arms of comfort and love. The Word of God says: *"Do not conform any longer to the pattern of this world, but be transformed by the renewing of your mind. Then you will be able to test and approve what God's will is, His good, and pleasing and perfect will. For by the grace given me I say to every one of you: Do not think of yourself more highly than you ought, but rather think of yourself with sober judgment, in accordance with the measure of faith God has given you". (Romans 12:2-3).*

Give yourself to God completely as a living sacrifice. Fully surrender your life to Him, leaving nothing for you to hold on to, except the hand of His Son Jesus. This means everything!

In the Word of God, it says: *"Therefore, I urge you, brothers, in view of God's Mercy, to offer your bodies as living sacrifices, holy and pleasing to God; this is your spiritual worship". (Romans 12:1).*

Always test God's Will to make sure that you hear a 'yes' or a 'no' before you act according to His instructions. There are four ways to know the Will of God:

(1) Seeking the Scriptures.

(2) Listening in your prayer time.

(3) Seeing God working in your circumstance.

(4) Speaking with a wise counselor.

The testing (knowing) of the Will of God this way will benefit you in the end. God will reveal His Will to those who are close to Him and who ask Him to show what His will entails. Being close to God (through His Son) will spark the flame of His mighty power to flow through you, placing all the pieces of your life that were out of place and fitting them into place in great harmony. With God in the driver's seat, you can never go the wrong way and get lost. Only God has the right license to drive your life. So let Jesus do the driving while you sit in the backseat and enjoy the ride. Letting Jesus drive your life is just the first step to spiritual growth.

Here are three more steps to Spiritual Growth:

<u>Discover</u> through reading the Bible and listening to God's Voice and His Heart; by paying attention to His Teaching and by learning about His Ways and Righteousness.

<u>Discern</u> through studying the Bible by praying and seeking to understand all that is to know about Him. Doing all you have learned from your studies.

The biggest step to step up your Spiritual Growth is prayer.

<u>Prayer</u> is nothing more satisfying and powerful to rest in the Presence of

the Almighty God. This comes when you humble yourself and bring all what concerns you to Him, who can make all wrong into right and new. We need not worry about anything when God is in control.

Praying with Confidence:

When you pray with confidence, you live out the verses spoken in the Book of Matthew; it says:

"Ask and it will be given to you; seek and you will find; knock and the door will be opened to you. For everyone who asks receives; the one who seeks finds; and to the one who knocks the door will be opened". (Matthews 7:7-8).

To ask is to request aid, protection, and to be drawn closer to our Heavenly Father.

To seek is the action we take of the result of opening the Bible; for any answers to our questions.

To knock demonstrates that we are willing to go to the Lord in total dependence and humility, for help in our walk to His Father's House.

This all means that as we keep on asking, seeking, knocking, and listening, God will continue to speak His instructions for us to know how to live out His commands that gives us success in this life here on this earth. Above all, stay calm and unshaken. It does not help to be agitated. For being agitated leads to destruction. God sees our heart and knows when we are agitated and will step in and calm us down and strengthen us to get through the shadows that shakes us. This is why we must always spend time in His Presence and His Word.

Throughout the Bible, there are many effective ways to pray to our Heavenly Father. Jesus taught His disciples to pray like this: *"Our Father in Heaven, hallowed be your name, your kingdom come, your will be done, on earth as it is in Heaven. Give us today our daily bread.*

And forgive us our debts, as we also have forgiven our debtors. And lead us not into temptation, but deliver us from the evil one". (Matthew 6:9-13).

"Then Jesus told His disciples a parable to show them that they should always pray and not give up". (Luke 18:1).

God always answers our prayers when we are consistent and persistent. It may not be in the time we want Him to answer, but it will be when He sees we are in right standing with Him and when we submit to Him and only Him. God wants to be our number above everything else.

"This is the confidence we have in approaching God: that if we ask anything according to His will, He hears us. And if we know that He hears us, whatever we ask, we know that we have what we asked of Him". (1 John 5:14-15).

We may not hear His answer at the time of our asking, for God does not work in our time. Because His Time is the best time for us. God's Time makes the answer even greater than we could ever imagine. God's grace is the best gift that we could ever receive from Him. Because in our weakness, we are made stronger. God told the Apostle Paul, after he asked three times to take the thorn that was bothering him away: *"But He said to me, 'My grace is sufficient for you, for My power is made perfect in weakness'. Therefore, I will boast all the more gladly about my weaknesses, so that Christ's power may rest on me". (2 Corinthians 12:9).*

Our prayers must always be accompanied by the willingness to obey and the readiness to move when God says to move. This is what the Word of God says: *"'Not every one that says to Me, 'Lord, Lord', will enter the Kingdom of Heaven, but only the one who does the Will of My Father who is in Heaven'". (Matthew 7:21).*

"Do not merely listen to the word, and so deceive yourselves. Do what it says. Anyone who listens to the word but does not do what it says is as someone who looks at his face in a mirror and, after looking at himself, goes away and immediately forgets what he looks like. But whoever looks into the perfect law that gives freedom, and continues in it; not forgetting what they heard, but doing it, they will be blessed in what they do". (James 1:22-25).

Promise from God.

"The eyes of the Lord watches over those who do right; and His ears are open to hear their prayer". (1 Peter 3:12).

God loves teaching us to see ourselves as He sees us and to make us available vessels. With the gifts and talents that He gives us, we learn we can go out and share all that we learned with the people that need the love of God. God does not set you on the path for achieving (fulfilling) His will and purpose until you can recognize your worth to love yourself (and God) the way God created you to be. Then and only then can we be able to stand strong in the Lord and His mighty power. Here is what the Word of God says about standing strong:

"Finally, be strong in the Lord and in His mighty power. Put on the full armor of God, so that you can take your stand against the devil's schemes. For our struggle is not against flesh and blood, but against the rulers, against the authorities, against the powers of this dark world and against the spiritual forces of evil in the heavenly realms". (Ephesians 6:10-12).

"By standing firm you will gain life". (Luke 21:19).

"But as for you, continue in what you have become convinced of, because you know those from whom you learned it". (2 Timothy 3:14).

"Anyone who receives instruction in the word must share all good things with his instructor. Do not be deceived: God cannot be mocked. A man reaps what he sows. The one who sows to please his sinful nature will reap destruction; the one who sows to please the Spirit, from the Spirit will reap eternal life. Let us not become weary in doing good; for at the proper time we will reap a harvest if we do not give up". (Galatians 6:6-9).

"Therefore, my dear brothers, stand firm. Let nothing move you. Always give yourselves fully to the work of the Lord, because you know that your labor in the Lord is not in vain". (1 Corinthians 15:58).

"Stand firm then, with the Belt of Truth buckled around your waist, with the Breastplate of Righteousness in place, and with your feet fitted with the Readiness that comes from the Gospel of Peace. In addition to all this, take up the Shield of Faith, with which you can extinguish all the flaming arrows of the evil one. Take the Helmet of Salvation and the Sword of the Spirit, which is the Word of God. In addition, pray in the Spirit on all occasions with all kinds of prayers and requests. With this in mind, be alert and always keep on praying for all the Lord's people". (Ephesians 6:14-18).

With the Love of God, we can do everything that we need to do. God will instruct us to do what He has planned, all for His Glory. Nothing satisfies Him more. Obeying God is what makes enduring these trials on this earth a little easier to bear. Nothing on the earth that will strengthen and refresh you as God can. When we live on this earth's ways, we grow weaker and we are making Satan happier, that we please him instead of pleasing our Heavenly Father. I had fallen many times into Satan's trap, pleasing the people of this earth, and it just brought me to a place of dryness and drought in my soul. However, ten years ago, when I gave Jesus control over my life and He took hold of my hand and led me into the light of life, my Lord Jesus told me that it is more important to please His Father in heaven then the people of this earth. Because when ourHeavenly Father is happy, everyone is happy. Yes, I have moments of drought, but the Holy Spirit leads me right to the source of refreshment, the Bible. Reading my Bible, I know I am spending time with my Star Team and receiving the refreshment to handle anything this earth throws at me.

Spiritual Drought.

Drought is a long period of time during which there is very little or no rain, a prolonged or chronic shortage or lack of something expected or desired. Spiritual drought can be just as bad as earthly drought. Spiritual drought means you are lacking the things of God in your life, which brings darkness and despair and a place of dryness. This place of dryness is where I found myself when I did not spend time in God's Word. Therefore, I would pick up my Bible and pray for God to show me ways to get out of my Spiritual drought.

Boy, did He ever show me! Here are just some of what I had to read that He showed me.

For spiritual refreshment: *"The law of the Lord is perfect, refreshing the soul. The statutes of the Lord are trustworthy, making wise the simple". (Psalm 19:7).*

"The Lord is my shepherd, I lack nothing. He makes me lie down in green pastures, He leads me beside quiet waters, and He refreshes my soul. He guides along the right paths for His name's sake. Even though I walk through the darkest valley, I will fear no evil, for You are with me;

Your rod and your staff, they comfort me". (Psalm 23:1-4).

"Repent, then, and turn to God, so that your sins may be wiped out, that times of refreshing may come from the Lord". (Acts 3:19).

"You gave abundant showers, O God; You refreshed Your weary inheritance". *(Psalm 68:9).*

When you feel like dust in your soul: *"Look at me and answer, Lord my God. Give Light to my eyes, or I will sleep in death; my enemy will say, 'I have overcome him', and my foes will rejoice when I fall. But I trust in your Unfailing Love; my heart rejoices in Your salvation. I will sing the Lord's praise, for He has been good to me".* *(Psalm 13:3-6).*

"You, God, are my God, earnestly I seek You; I thirst for You, my whole being longs for You, in a dry and parched land where there is no water. I have seen you in the sanctuary and beheld Your power and Your Glory. Because Your love is better than life, my lips will glorify You. I will praise you as long as I live, and in your name, I will lift up my hands. I will be fully satisfied, as with the richest of foods; with singing lips, my mouth will praise you. On my bed, I remember You; I think of You through the watches of the night. Because You are my help, I sing in the shadow of Your wings. I cling to You; Your right hand upholds me". *(Psalm 63:1-8).*

When you feel parched in your soul: *"As the deer pants for streams of water, so my soul pants for you, O God. My soul thirsts for God, for the living God. When can I go and meet God?"* *(Psalm 42:1-2).*

"Deep calls to deep in the roar of your waterfalls; all your waves and breakers have swept over me. By day the Lord directs His Love, at night His Song is with me—a prayer to the God of my life". *(Psalm 42:7-8).*

By the Grace of God, I had been refreshed, and I feel the Joy of Salvation again. All it took was reading my Bible and resting in the arms of my Heavenly Father. Nothing pleases our Heavenly Father more than when we spend time with Him. Jesus took every chance that He could to have alone time with His Father. The Word of God says: *"At daybreak, Jesus went out to a solitary place. The people were looking for Him and when they came to where He was, they tried to keep Him from leaving them".* *(Luke 4:42).*

"Jesus often withdrew to lonely places and prayed". *(Luke 5:16).*

"Jesus made the disciples get into the boat and go on ahead of Him to the other side, while He dismissed the crowd. After He had dismissed them, He went up on a mountainside by Himself to pray. Later that night, He was there alone, and the boat was already a considerable distance from land, buffeted by the

waves, because the wind was against it". (Matthew 14:22-24).

In this world, there are things that will try to drag you down, drain your strength, and distract you from following Jesus. However, we must remember that Jesus overcame this world with the strength of His Father, all because He spent alone time with Him. When you spend time alone with God, He reveals to you all that you need to know to live and walk with Him. Here are some things my Star Team told me about spiritual drought.

The first thing my Star Team told me what causes spiritual drought is unchecked lust. Unchecked lust is a combination of impure thoughts and intense longing for sexual desires, making it difficult to receive the spiritual joy that God is continually sending to you. Scripture makes it very clear, leaving any kind of lust out of our lives. Here are some to open your eyes to what lust is and how bad it is to you:

"Do not lust in your heart after her beauty or let her captivate you with her eyes". (Proverb 6:25).

"I tell you that anyone who looks at a woman lustfully has already committed adultery with her in his heart". (Matthew 5:28).

"So I say, walk by the Spirit, and you will not gratify the desires of the flesh. For the flesh desires what is contrary to the Spirit and the Spirit what is contrary to the flesh. They are in conflict with each other, so that you are not able to do whatever you want. However, if the Spirit leads you, you are not under the law. The acts of the flesh are obvious: sexual immorality, impurity and debauchery; idolatry and witchcraft, hatred, discord, jealousy, fits of rage, selfish ambition, dissensions, factions and envy; drunkenness, orgies, and the like. I warn you, as I did before, that those who live like this will not inherit the kingdom of God". (Galatians 5:16-21).

"It is God's will that you should be sanctified, that you should avoid sexual immorality; that each of you should learn to control your own body, in a way that is holy and honorable. Not in passionate lust like the pagans, who do not know God and that in this matter no one should wrong or take advantage of a brother or sister. The Lord will punish all those who commit such sins, as we told you and warned you before. For God did not call us to be impure, but to live a Holy Life". (1 Thessalonians 4:3-7).

"Do not love the world or anything in the world. If anyone loves the world,

love for the Father is not in them. For everything in the world (the lust of the flesh, the lust of the eyes, and the pride of life), comes not from the Father but from the world. The world and its desires pass away, but whoever does the Will of God lives forever". (1 John 2:15-17).

"Flee from sexual immorality. All other sins a person commits are outside the body, but whoever sins sexually, sins against their own body. Do you not know that your bodies are temples of the Holy Spirit, who is in you, whom you have received from God? You are not your own; you were bought at a price. Therefore, honor God with your bodies". (1 Corinthians 6:18-20).

"Put to death, therefore, whatever belongs to your earthly nature: Sexual immorality, impurity, lust, evil desires and greed, which is idolatry. Because of these, the wrath of God is coming". (Colossians 3:5-6).

Remedy for unchecked lust is confession, repentance, and the Word of God. The moment a thought of lust enters your mind, immediately, get on your knees and pray this: *"Have mercy on me, O God, according to your unfailing love; according to your great compassion blot out my transgressions. Wash away all my iniquity and cleanse me from my sin". (Psalm 51:1-3). "Restore to me the joy of your salvation and grant me a willing spirit, to sustain me. Amen!". (Psalm 51:12).*

No longer make provisions for the flesh, but *"rather, clothe yourselves with the Lord Jesus Christ, and do not think about how to gratify the desires of the flesh". (Romans 13:14).*

The second thing that my Star Team told me that causes spiritual drought is pride. Pride blocks us from seeing the truth and beauty of God the Father and His Son Jesus. Pride keeps us away from any selfless acts and away from seeking only the Glory of God (not the glory of man). Pride also hinders your walk with God, for God opposes the proud. The Word of God says, *"The Lord Almighty has a day in store for all the proud and lofty, for all that is exalted; and they will be humbled". (Isaiah 2:12).*

"He gives us more grace. That is why Scripture says, 'God opposes the proud, but shows favor to the humble'". (James 4:6).

"Humble yourselves before the Lord, and He will lift you up". (James 4:10).

"This is what the Lord says, 'Let not the wise boast of their wisdom, or the strong boast of their strength, or the rich boast of their riches, but let the one who

boasts, boast about this; that they have the understanding to know Me. That I am the Lord, who exercises kindness, justice and righteousness on earth, for in these I delight,' declares the Lord". (Jeremiah 9:23-24).

"Do nothing out of selfish ambition or vain conceit. Rather, in humility value others above yourselves, not looking to your own interests but each of you to the interests of the others". (Philippians 2:3-4).

"To fear the Lord is to hate evil; I hate pride and arrogance, evil behavior and perverse speech". (Proverb 8:13).

"When pride comes, then comes disgrace, but with humility comes Wisdom". (Proverb 11:2).

"Where there is strife, there is pride, but wisdom is found in those who take advice". (Proverb 13:10).

"The Lord detests all the proud of heart. Be sure of this: They will not go unpunished". (Proverb 16:5).

"Pride goes before destruction, a haughty spirit before a fall. Better to be lowly in spirit along with the oppressed than to share plunder with the proud". (Proverbs 16:18-19).

"Before a downfall the heart is haughty, but humility comes before honor". (Proverb 18:12).

"Haughty eyes and a proud heart—the unplowed field of the wicked—produce sin". (Proverb 21:4).

"The proud and arrogant person—'Mocker' is his name—behaves with insolent fury". (Proverb 21:24).

"In his pride the wicked man does not seek Him; in all his thoughts there is no room for God". (Psalm 10:4).

The third thing that my Star Team told me that causes spiritual drought is love of money.

The things of this earth are temporary, and you must not think of them as treasures. For our lasting treasure is in heaven awaiting us. When you fix your eyes on the things not of God, our bodies fill up with the darkness of this earth and the glory of God is far off in the distance.

The solution is simple; it is to believe in the Son of God, pray continually, and love only the things of God. The Word of God says: *"Do not store up for yourselves treasures on earth, where moth and rust destroy, and where thieves break in and steal. However, store up for yourselves, treasures in Heaven, where moth and rust do not destroy, and where thieves do not break in and steal. For where your treasure is, there your heart will be also. The eye is the lamp of the body. If your eyes are good, your whole body will be full of light. However, if your eyes are bad, your whole body will be full of darkness. If then the light within you is darkness, how great is that darkness! No one can serve two masters. Either he will hate the one and love the other, or he will be devoted to the one and despise the other. You cannot serve both God and money". (Matthew 6:19-24).*

These three things that my Star Team told me all come down to, for you and me, to fit into our lives the Word of God. When you neglect reading the Bible, you miss spending time with the One who speaks to you and nourishes your heart and soul.

It is impossible for us to thrive without God; for *"with man all things are impossible, but with God all things are possible". (Matthew 19:26).*

We also lack physical exercise that weighs us down our soul and brings us into darkness. Where we are a prime target for Satan to enter into your life. You also miss the works of God's hands refreshing you each day that you live. As the Word of God says:

"Let perseverance finish its work so that you may be mature and complete, not lacking anything. If any of you lacks wisdom, you should ask God, who gives generously to all without finding fault, and it will be given to you. However, when you ask, you must believe and not doubt, because the one who doubts is like a wave of the sea, blown and tossed by the wind. That person should not expect to receive anything from the Lord. Such a person is double-minded and unstable in all they do". (James 1:4-8).

"The Heavens declare the glory of God; the skies proclaim the work of His hands". (Psalm 19:1).

Scriptures you can get Wisdom and Knowledge from to walk on the Path of Righteousness:

"Until we all reach unity in the faith and in the knowledge of the Son of God and become mature, attaining to the whole measure of the fullness of Christ.

Then we will no longer be infants, tossed back and forth by the waves, and blown here and there by every wind of teaching and by the cunning and craftiness of people in their deceitful scheming. Instead, speaking the truth in love, we will grow to become in every respect the mature body of Him who is the head, that is, Christ. From Him the whole body, joined and held together by every supporting ligament, grows and builds itself up in love, as each part does its work. So, I tell you this, and insist on it in the Lord, that you must no longer live as the Gentiles do (in the futility of their thinking), They are darkened in their understanding and separated from the life of God, because of the ignorance that is in them due to the hardening of their hearts. Having lost all sensitivity, they have given themselves over to sensuality so as to indulge in every kind of impurity, and they are full of greed". (Ephesians 4:13-19).

"Therefore each of you must put off falsehood and speak truthfully to your neighbor, for we are all members of one body. In your anger do not sin: Do not let the sun go down while you are still angry, and do not give the devil a foothold. Anyone who has been stealing must steal no longer, but must work, doing something useful with their own hands, that they may have something to share with those in need. Do not let any unwholesome talk come out of your mouths, but only what is helpful for building others up according to their needs, that it may benefit those who listen. In addition, do not grieve the Holy Spirit of God, with whom you were sealed for the day of redemption. Get rid of all bitterness, rage and anger, brawling and slander, along with every form of malice. Be kind and compassionate to one another, forgiving each other, just as in Christ

God forgave you". (Ephesians 4:25-32).

"So whether you eat or drink or whatever you do, do it all for the Glory of God. Do not cause anyone to stumble, whether Jews, Greeks or the Church of God—even as I try to please everyone in every way. For I am not seeking my own good but the good of many, so that they may be saved". (1 Corinthians 10:31-33).

The Beatitudes.

"Jesus says: **'Blessed are the poor in spirit, for theirs is the Kingdom of Heaven. Blessed are those who mourn, for they will be comforted. Blessed are the meek, for they will inherit the earth. Blessed are those who hunger and thirst for righteousness, for they will be filled. Blessed**

are the merciful, for they will be shown mercy. Blessed are the pure in heart, for they will see God. Blessed are the peacemakers, for they will be called children of God. Blessed are those who are persecuted because of righteousness, for theirs is the Kingdom of Heaven. Blessed are you when people insult you, persecute you and falsely say all kinds of evil against you because of Me. Rejoice and be glad, because Great is your reward in Heaven, for in the same way they persecuted the prophets who were before you". *(Matthew 5:3-12).*

Salt and Light.

"'You are the salt of the earth. However, if the salt loses its saltiness, how can it be made salty again? It is no longer good for anything, except to be thrown out and trampled underfoot. You are the light of the world. A town built on a hill cannot be hidden. Neither do people light a lamp and put it under a bowl. Instead, they put it on its stand, and it gives light to everyone in the house. In the same way, let your Light shine before others, that they may see your good deeds and glorify your Father in Heaven". *(Matthew 5:13-16).*

"Therefore, in order to keep me from becoming conceited, I was given a thorn in my flesh, a messenger of Satan, to torment me. Three times, I pleaded with the Lord to take it away from me. However, He said to me, **'My grace is sufficient for you, for My power is made perfect in weakness.' Therefore, I will boast all the more gladly about my weaknesses, so that Christ's power may rest on me. That is why, for Christ's sake, I delight in weaknesses, in insults, in hardships, in persecutions, in difficulties. For when I am weak. Then I am strong"**. *(2 Corinthians 12:7b-10).*

The Eyes of God Are Watching.

"Humble yourselves, therefore, under God's Mighty Hand, that He may lift you up in due time. Cast all your anxiety on Him because He cares for you. Be alert and of a sober mind. Your enemy the devil prowls around like a roaring lion looking for someone to devour. Resist him, standing firm in the faith, because you know that the family of believers throughout the world is undergoing the same kind of sufferings. In addition, the God of all grace, who called you to His

eternal glory in Christ, after you suffered a little while, will Himself restore you and make you strong, firm and steadfast. To Him be the power forever and ever. Amen". (1 Peter 5:6-11).

"For your ways are in full view of the Lord, and He examines all your paths. The evil deeds of the wicked ensnare them; the cords of their sins hold them fast. For lack of discipline they will die, led astray by their own great folly". (Proverbs 5:21-23).

"One whose heart is corrupt does not prosper; one whose tongue is perverse falls into trouble". (Proverb 17:20).

"A cheerful heart is good medicine, but a crushed spirit dries up the bones". (Proverb 17:22).

"A discerning person keeps wisdom in view, but a fool's eyes wander to the ends of the earth". (Proverbs 17:24).

"Search me, God, and know my heart; test me and know my anxious thoughts. See if there is any offensive way in me, and lead me in the way everlasting". (Psalm 139:23-24).

"Be kind and compassionate to one another, forgiving each other, just as in Christ God forgave you". (Ephesians 4:32).

Here are some more to assure you that God is for us, speaking His Instructions for us to fulfill.

"Do everything without grumbling or arguing". (Philippians 2:14).

"Do nothing out of selfish ambition or vain conceit, but in humility, consider others better than yourselves. Each of you should look not only to your own interests, but also to the interests of others. Your attitude should be the same as that of Christ Jesus". (Philippians 2:3-5).

"At the name of Jesus, every knee should bow, in heaven and on earth and under the earth, and every tongue confesses that Jesus Christ is Lord, to the glory of God the Father". (Philippians 2:10-11).

"For it is God who works in you to will and to act according to His Good Purpose". (Philippians 2:13).

"And they have conquered him by the blood of the Lamb and by the Word of their testimony". (Revelation 12:11)

"Better is one day in your courts than a thousand elsewhere; I would rather be a doorkeeper in the house of my God than dwell in the tents of the wicked. For the Lord God is a sun and shield; the Lord bestows favor and honor; no good thing does He withhold from those whose walk is blameless. Lord Almighty, blessed is the one who trusts in you". (Psalm 84:10-12).

Seven Ways to Develop a Humble Spirit.

1. Die to self.

     Is to refuse to put yourselves first over the Almighty God.

2. Be devoted to helping others.

     Because God made us to be the vessels of His Truth.

3. Delight in helping others and never grow weary of doing so.

     Because when we help others with a delightful heart, God will Bless them and you with Compassion, Grace, and Love.

4. Depend always on God..

     Because relying on Him in every circumstance is what brings on humility and storing up good treasures in Heaven.

5. Direct all your thoughts on God.

     Then you will walk in confidence and Goodness and Grace and you will grow in Him and find His Peace.

6. Distance yourselves from the appeal of this world.

     Such as pride, love of money, approval from man, idols, and addictions.

7. Be determined to obey God's Instructions.

     No matter what is happening in your present circumstance.

When you humble yourself before God, you will receive His Eternal Light shining down on you; then, you will never walk in darkness again. As the Word of God reminds us:

"The Lord is my Light and my Salvation; whom shall I fear? The Lord is the Stronghold of my life; of whom shall I be afraid?" (Psalm 27:1).

"Your word is a lamp to my feet and a light for my path". (Psalm 119:105).

"When Jesus spoke again to the people, He said; 'I am the light of the world. Whoever follows me will never walk in darkness, but will have the light of life'". (John 8:12).

Scriptures to live by always:

"I will always obey your law, forever and ever. I will walk about in freedom, for I have sought out Your precepts. I will speak of your statutes before kings and will not be put to shame, for I delight in your commands because I love them. I reach out for Your commands, which I love, that I may meditate on Your decrees". (Psalm 119:44-48).

"My comfort in my suffering is this: Your promise preserves my life". (Psalm 119:50).

"You are my portion, O Lord; I have promised to obey Your words". (Psalm 119:57).

"My flesh and my heart may fail, but God is the strength of my heart and my portion forever". (Psalm 73:26).

"The earth is filled with Your love, Lord; teach me our decrees". (Psalm 119:64).

"Teach me knowledge and good judgment, for I believe in Your Commands" (Psalm 119:66).

"You are good and what you do is good; teach me Your decrees. Though the arrogant have smeared me with lies, I keep your precepts with all my heart". (Psalm 119:68-69).

"Let Your Compassion come to me so that I may live, for Your Law is my delight". (Psalm 119:77).

"Your Word, Lord, is Eternal; it stands firm in the Heavens. Your Faithfulness continues through all generations; You established the earth and it endures" (Psalms 119:89-90).

"Your commands make me wiser than my enemies, for they are ever with me". (Psalm 119:98).

"I have kept my feet from every evil path so that I might obey Your Word". (Psalm 119:101).

"I have suffered much; preserve my life, Lord, according to Your Word.

Accept, Lord, the willing praise of my mouth and teach me Your Laws". (Psalm 119:107-108).

"My heart is set on keeping Your decrees to the very end". (Psalm 119:112).

Six Essential Things for knowing (Discerning) God and His Will

----

*T*he most important thing that you can do in your pursuit of purity is to get to know the Living God. The One and only Creator of everything. There are six essential things about knowing (discerning) God and His Will. And the one place that I found to discern the Will of God; and that place is in the Word of God. The Scriptures have never failed me.

Here are the Scriptures that tell the six essential things of who God is:

1. Perfect - Being entirely without fault or defect: Flawless.

    "Be perfect, therefore, as your Heavenly Father is Perfect". (Matthew 5:48).

    "Every Word of God is Flawless; He is a Shield to those who take refuge in Him. Do not add to His Words, or He will rebuke you and prove you a liar". (Proverbs 30:5-6).

    "As for God, His Way is Perfect: The Lord's Word is Flawless; He shields all who take refuge in Him. For who is God besides the Lord? And who is the Rock except our God?". (Psalm 18:30-31).

2. Transcendent - Exceeding usual limits: Surpassing.

    "'For My Thoughts are not your thoughts, neither are your ways My Ways', declares the Lord. 'As the Heavens are higher than the earth, so are My Ways higher than your ways and My Thoughts than your thoughts'". (Isaiah 55:8-9).

    "The Lord is exalted over all the nations, His Glory above the Heavens. Who is like the Lord our God, the One who sits enthroned on high, who stoops down to look on the Heavens and the earth?". (Psalm 113:4-6).

    "In the Beginning God created the Heavens and the earth. Now the earth was formless and empty, darkness was over the surface of the deep, and the

Spirit of God was hovering over the waters". (Genesis 1:1-2).

Also the Son of God: *"In the Beginning was the Word, and the Word was with God, and the Word was God. He was with God in the Beginning". (John 1:1-2).*

3.   Omniscient - Knowing everything. Having infinite awareness, understanding, and insight.

"You know when I sit and when I rise; You perceive my thoughts from afar. You discern my going out and my lying down; You are familiar with all my ways. Before a word is on my tongue You, Lord, know it completely". (Psalm 139: 2-4).

"If our hearts condemn us, we know that God is Greater than our hearts, and He knows everything". (1 John 3:20).

"Great is our Lord and mighty in Power; His Understanding has no limit. The Lord sustains the humble but casts the wicked to the ground". (Psalm 147:5-6).

4.   Omnipresent - (of God) Present everywhere at the same time.

*"**'Who can hide in secret places so that I cannot see them?'** declares the Lord. **'Do not I fill Heaven and earth?'** declares the Lord". (Jeremiah 23:24).*

"The Eyes of the Lord are everywhere, keeping watch on the wicked and the good".

(Proverbs 15:3).

"The God who made the world and everything in it is the Lord of Heaven and earth and does not live in temples built by human hands. And He is not served by human hands, as if He needed anything. Rather, He Himself gives everyone Life and Breath and everything else". (Acts 17:24-25).

"He is before all things, and in Him all things hold together". (Colossians 1:17).

5.   All-loving - Infinitely Good, usually in reference to a deity or supernatural being; unable to withhold forgiveness from His people.

"This is how God showed His Love among us: He sent His One and only Son into the world that we might live through Him. This is Love: not that we loved God, but that He loved us and sent His Son as an Atoning Sacrifice

for our sins. Dear friends, since God so loved us, we also ought to love one another. No one has ever seen God; but if we love one another, God lives in us and His Love is made complete in us". (1 John 4:9-12).

"Because Your Love is better than life, my lips will glorify You. I will praise You as long as I live, and in Your Name I will lift up my hands". (Psalm 63:3).

"A new Command I give you: Love one another. As I have loved you, so you must love one another. By this everyone will know that you are My disciples, if you love one another". (John 13:34-35).

"Therefore, keep yourselves in God's Love as you wait for the Mercy of our Lord Jesus Christ to bring you to Eternal Life. Be merciful to those who doubt". (Jude 1:21-22).

"Know therefore, that the Lord your God is God; He is the Faithful God, keeping His covenant of Love to a thousand generations of those who love Him and keep His Commandments". (Deuteronomy 7:9).

6. All-merciful - Full of Mercy: Compassionate.

"The Lord is Gracious and Compassionate, slow to anger and rich in Love". (Psalm 145:8-9).

"Because of the Lord's Great Love we are not consumed, for His Compassions never fail". (Lamentations 3:22-23).

*"**Though the mountains be shaken and the hills be removed, yet My Unfailing Love for you will not be shaken nor My Covenant of Peace be removed**", says the Lord, who has Compassion on you". (Isaiah 54:10).*

"You, Lord, are a Compassionate and Gracious God, slow to anger, abounding in Love and Faithfulness". (Psalm 86:15).

"The Lord your God is with you, the Mighty Warrior who saves. He will take great delight in you; in His Love He will no longer rebuke you, but will rejoice over you with singing". (Zephaniah 3:17).

"All the Ways of the Lord are loving and Faithful toward those who keep the demands of His Covenant". (Psalm 25:10).

"Righteousness and Justice are the Foundation of Your Throne; Love and Faithfulness go before You". (Psalm 89:14).

"For God so loved the world that He gave His One and only Son, that whoever

believes in Him shall not perish but have Eternal Life. For God did not send His Son into the world to condemn the world, but to save the world through Him". (John 3:16-17).

To Knowing God's Word:

"All Scripture is God-breathed and is useful for teaching, rebuking, correcting and training in righteousness, so that the servant of God may be thoroughly equipped for every good work". (2 Timothy 3:16-17).

"Keep this Book of the Law always on your lips; meditate on it day and night, so that you may be careful to do everything written in it. Then you will be prosperous and successful". (Joshua 1:8).

"In the beginning was the Word, and the Word was with God, and the Word was God. He was with God in the beginning. Through Him, all things were made; without Him nothing was made that has been made. In Him was life, and that life was the light of all mankind. The light shines in the darkness, and the darkness has not overcome it". (John 1:1-5).

"For everything that was written in the past was written to teach us, so that through the endurance taught in the Scriptures and the encouragement they provide we might have hope. May the God who gives endurance and encouragement give you the same attitude of mind toward each other that Christ Jesus had, so that with one mind and voice you may glorify the God and Father of our Lord Jesus Christ". (Romans 15:4-6).

"For the Word of God is alive and active. Sharper than any double-edged sword, it penetrates even to divide soul and spirit, joints and marrow; it judges the thoughts and attitudes of the heart. Nothing in all creation is hidden from God's sight. Everything is uncovered and laid bare before the eyes of Him to whom we must give account". (Hebrews 4:12-13).

"Jesus answered, **'It is written: "Man shall not live on bread alone, but on every word that comes from the mouth of God'".** *(Matthew 4:4).*

"Command and teach these things. Do not let anyone look down on you because you are young, but set an example for the believers in speech, in conduct, in love, in faith and in purity. Until I come, devote yourself to the public reading of Scripture, to preaching and to teaching. Do not neglect your gift, which was given you through prophecy when the body of elders laid their hands on you. Be

diligent in these matters; give yourself wholly to them, so that everyone may see your progress. Watch your life and doctrine closely. Persevere in them, because if you do, you will save both yourself and your hearers". (1 Timothy 4:11-16).

"By living according to Your word. I seek You with all my heart; do not let me stray from Your commands. I have hidden Your word in my heart that I might not sin against You. Praise be to You, Lord; teach me Your decrees. With my lips I recount all the laws that come from Your mouth". (Psalm 119:9b-13).

"Blessed is the one who does not walk in step with the wicked or stand in the way that sinners take or sit in the company of mockers, but whose delight is in the law of the Lord, and who meditates on His law day and night. That person is like a tree planted by streams of water, which yields its fruit in season and whose leaf does not wither—whatever they do prospers" (Psalm 1:1-3).

"Do your best to present yourself to God as one approved, a worker who does not need to be ashamed and who correctly handles the Word of Truth. Avoid godless chatter, because those who indulge in it will become more and more ungodly". (2 Timothy 2:15-16).

To Knowing God's Desire:

"'Remain in Me, as I also remain in you. No branch can bear fruit by itself; it must remain in the Vine. Neither can you bear fruit unless you remain in Me. I am the Vine; you are the branches. If you remain in Me and I in you, you will bear much fruit; apart from Me you can do nothing. If you do not remain in Me, you're like a branch that is thrown away and withers; such branches are picked up, thrown into the fire and burned. If you remain in Me and My Words remain in you, ask whatever you wish, and it will be done for you. This is to My Father's Glory, that you bear much fruit, showing yourselves to be My disciples'". (John 15:4-8).

"My feet have closely followed His steps; I have kept to His way without turning aside. I have not departed from the commands of His lips; I have treasured the words of His mouth more than my daily bread. However, He stands alone, and who can oppose Him? He does whatever He pleases". (Job 23:11-13).

"When I am afraid, I put my trust in you. In God, whose word I praise—in God I trust and am not afraid. What can mere mortals do to me?" (Psalm 56:3-

4).

"*Finally, be strong in the Lord and in His mighty power. Put on the full armor of God, so that you can take your stand against the devil's schemes. For our struggle is not against flesh and blood, but against the rulers, against the authorities, against the powers of this dark world and against the spiritual forces of evil in the heavenly realms. Therefore, put on the full armor of God, so that when the day of evil comes, you may be able to stand your ground, and after you have done everything, to stand. Stand firm then, with the belt of truth buckled around your waist, with the Breastplate of Righteousness in place, and with your feet fitted with the Readiness that comes from the Gospel of Peace. In addition to all this, take up the Shield of Faith, with which you can extinguish all the flaming arrows of the evil one. Take the Helmet of Salvation and the Sword of the Spirit, which is the Word of God*". *(Ephesians 6:10-17).*

"**Have I not commanded you? Be strong and courageous. Do not be afraid; do not be discouraged, for the Lord your God will be with you wherever you go**"*. (Joshua 1:9).*

"*Every word of God is flawless; He is a shield to those who take refuge in Him. Do not add to His words, or He will rebuke you and prove you a liar*". *(Proverbs 30:5).*

"*My son, pay attention to what I say; turn your ear to my words. Do not let them out of your sight; keep them within your heart, for they are life to those who find them and health to one's whole body. Above all else, guard your heart for everything you do flows from it. Keep your mouth free of perversity; keep corrupt talk far from your lips. Let your eyes look straight ahead; fix your gaze directly before you. Give careful thought to the paths for your feet and be steadfast in all your ways. Do not turn to the right or the left; keep your foot from evil*". *(Proverbs 4:20-27).*

"*Do not fret because of those who are evil or be envious of those who do wrong; for like the grass they will soon wither, like green plants they will soon die away. Trust in the Lord and do good; dwell in the land and enjoy safe pastures. Take delight in the Lord, and He will give you the desires of your heart. Commit your way to the Lord; trust in Him and He will do this: He will make your righteous reward shine like the dawn, your vindication like the noonday sun. Be still before the Lord and wait patiently for Him; do not fret when people succeed in their ways, when they carry out their wicked schemes. Refrain from anger and turn from wrath; do not fret—it leads only to evil. For those who are evil will be destroyed, but those who hope in the Lord will inherit the land". (Psalm 37:1-9).*

*"In the beginning God created the heavens and the earth. Now the earth was formless and empty, darkness was over the surface of the deep, and the Spirit of God was hovering over the waters. And God said, '**Let there be light**', and there was light. God saw that the light was good".(Genesis 1:1-4a).*

To Knowing Timing of God:

*"I will stand at my watch and station myself on the ramparts; I will look to see what He will say to me, and what answer I am to give to this complaint. Then the Lord replied, '**Write down the revelation and make it plain on tablets so that a herald may run with it. For the revelation awaits an appointed time; it speaks of the end and will not prove false. Though it will linger, wait for it; it will certainly come and will not delay'**". (Habakkuk 2:1-3).*

"Do you not know? Have you not heard? The Lord is the everlasting God, the Creator of the ends of the earth. He will not grow tired or weary, and His understanding no one can fathom. He gives strength to the weary and increases the power of the weak. Even youths grow tired and weary, and young men stumble and fall; but those who hope in the Lord will renew their strength. They will soar on wings like eagles; they will run and not grow weary, they will walk and not be faint". (Isaiah 40:28-31).

"I remain confident of this: I will see the goodness of the Lord in the land of the living. Wait for the Lord; be strong and take heart and wait for the Lord". (Psalm 27:13-14).

"But do not forget this one thing, dear friends: With the Lord a day is like a thousand years, and a thousand years are like a day. The Lord is not slow in keeping His promise, as some understand slowness. Instead, He is patient with you, not wanting anyone to perish, but everyone to come to repentance. However, the day of the Lord will come like a thief. The heavens will disappear with a roar; the elements will be destroyed by fire, and the earth and everything in it will be laid bare". (2 Peter 3:8-10).

"Do not forget My Teaching, but keep My Commands in your heart, for they will prolong your life many years and bring you Peace and Prosperity. Let

Love and Faithfulness never leave you; bind them around your neck, write them on the tablet of your heart. Then you will favor and a good name in the sight of God and man. Trust in the Lord with all your heart and lean not on your own understanding; in all your ways submit to Him, and He will make your paths straight. Do not be wise in your own eyes; fear the Lord and shun evil. This will bring health to your body and nourishment to your bones". (Proverbs 3:1-8).

"Be still, and know that I am God; I will be exalted among the nations, I will be exalted in the earth. The Lord Almighty is with us; the God of Jacob is our fortress". (Psalm 46:10-11).

"You, Lord, are forgiving and good, abounding in love to all who call to you. Hear my prayer, Lord; listen to my cry for mercy. When I am in distress, I call out to you, because you answer me". (Psalm 86:5-7).

"Therefore, since we have been justified through Faith, we have Peace with God through our Lord Jesus Christ, through whom we have gained access by Faith in this Grace in which we now stand". (Romans 5:1-2).

To Knowing Counsel of God:

"Listen to me, you descendants of Jacob, all the remnants of the people of Israel, you whom I have upheld since your birth, and have carried since you were born. Even to your old age and gray hairs I am He, I am He who will sustain you. I have made you and I will carry you; I will sustain you and I will rescue you. Remember this, keep it in mind, take it to heart, you rebels. Remember the former things, those of long ago; I am God, and there is no other; I am God, and there is none like me. I make known the end from the beginning, from ancient times what is still to come. I say, 'My purpose will stand, and I will do all that I please'. From the east, I summon a bird of prey; from a far-off land, a man to fulfill my purpose. What I have said, that I will bring about; what I have planned, that I will do". (Isaiah 46:3-4, 8-11).

"Trust in the Lord from this time forward, the Lord Himself, is the Rock eternal. He humbles those who dwell on high; He lays the lofty city low; He levels it to the ground and casts it down to the dust. Feet trample it down—the feet of the oppressed, the footsteps of the poor. The path of the righteous is level; you, The Upright One, make the way of the righteous smooth. Yes, Lord, walking in the way of your laws, we wait for you; your name and renown are the desire of

our hearts. My soul yearns for you in the night; in the morning, my spirit longs for you. When your judgments come upon the earth, the people of the world learn righteousness. But when grace is shown to the wicked, they do not learn righteousness; even in a land of uprightness they go on doing evil and do not regard the majesty of the Lord". (Isaiah 26:4-10).

This is what the wicked are like: *"In his arrogance the wicked man hunts down the weak, who are caught in the schemes he devises. He boasts about the cravings of his heart; he blesses the greedy and reviles the Lord. In his pride, the wicked man does not seek Him; in all his thoughts, there is no room for God. His ways are always prosperous; Your laws are rejected by him; he sneers at all his enemies. He says to himself, 'Nothing will ever shake me'. He swears, 'No one will ever do me harm'. His mouth is full of lies and threats; trouble and evil are under his tongue. He lies in wait near the villages; from ambush, he murders the innocent. His eyes watch in secret for his victims; like a lion in cover he lies in wait. He lies in wait to catch the helpless; he catches the helpless and drags them off in his net. His victims are crushed, they collapse; they fall under his strength. He says to himself, 'God will never notice; He covers His face and never sees'". (Psalm 10:2-11).*

"The Lord looks down from heaven on all mankind to see if there are any who understand, and who seek God. All have turned away, all have become corrupt; there is no one who does good, not even one. Do all these evildoers know nothing? They devour my people as though eating bread; they never call on the Lord. However, there they are, overwhelmed with dread, for God is present in the company of the righteous. You evildoers frustrate the plans of the poor, but the Lord is their refuge". (Psalms 14:2-6).

"You, God, are my God, earnestly I seek you; I thirst for you, my whole being longs for you, in a dry and parched land where there is no water…Because your love is better than life, my lips will glorify you. I will praise you as long as I live, and in your name, I will lift up my hands. I will be fully satisfied, as with the richest of foods, with singing lips, my mouth will praise you. On my bed, I remember you; I think of you through the watches of the night. Because you are my help, I sing in the shadow of your wings. I cling to you; your right hand upholds me". (Psalms 63:1, 3-8).

"Seek first His kingdom and His righteousness, and all these things will be

given to you as well. Therefore, do not worry about tomorrow, for tomorrow will worry about itself. Each day has enough trouble of its own". (Matthew 6:33-34).

ALWAYS: *"First, seek the counsel of the Lord". (1 Kings 22:5b).*

"When my heart was grieved and my spirit embittered...Yet, I am always with you; you hold me by my right hand. You guide me with your counsel, and afterward you will take me into glory. Whom have I in Heaven but you? In addition, the earth has nothing I desire besides you. My flesh and my heart may fail, but God is the strength of my heart and my portion forever. Those who are far from you will perish; you destroy all who are unfaithful to you. However, as for me, it is good to be near God. I have made the Sovereign Lord my refuge; I will tell of all your deeds". (Psalm 73:21, 23-28).

To Knowing to Fear God Is the Beginning of Knowledge:

"The fear of the Lord is the beginning of knowledge, but fools despise wisdom and instruction". (Proverbs 1:7).

"The fear of the Lord is the beginning of wisdom, and knowledge of the Holy One, understands. For through wisdom your days will be many, and years will be added to your life. If you are wise, your wisdom will reward you; if you are a mocker, you alone will suffer". (Proverbs 9:10-12).

"For the word of the Lord is right and true; He is faithful in all He does. The Lord loves righteousness and justice; the earth is full of His Unfailing Love. By the Word of the Lord the Heavens were made, their starry host by the breath of His mouth. He gathers the waters of the sea into jars; He puts the deep into storehouses. Let all the earth fear the Lord; let all the people of the world revere Him. For He spoke, and it came to be; He commanded, and it stood firm. The Lord foils the plans of the nations; He thwarts the purposes of the peoples. But the plans of the Lord stand firm forever, the purposes of His heart through all generations" (Psalm 33:4-11).

"Teach me your way, Lord, that I may rely on your faithfulness; give me an undivided heart, that I may fear your name. I will praise you, Lord my God, with all my heart; I will glorify your name forever. For great is your love toward me; you have delivered me from the depths, from the realm of the dead" (Psalm 86:11-13).

"Praise the Lord. Blessed are those who fear the Lord, who find great delight

in His Commands". (Psalms 112:1).

"Charm is deceptive, and beauty is fleeting; but a woman who fears the Lord is to be praised". (Proverbs 31:30).

"In God, whose word I praise, in the Lord, whose word I praise—in God I trust and am not afraid. What can man do to me? I am under vows to you, my God; I will present my thank offerings to you. For you have delivered me from death and my feet from stumbling, that I may walk before God in the light of life". (Psalms 56:10-13).

"The faithless will be fully repaid for their ways, and the good rewarded for theirs. The simple believe anything, but the prudent give thought to their steps. The wise fear the Lord and shun evil, but a fool is hotheaded and yet feels secure. A quick-tempered person does foolish things, and the one who devises evil schemes is hated. The simple inherit folly, but the prudent are crowned with knowledge. Evildoers will bow down in the presence of the good and the wicked at the gates of the righteous". (Proverbs 14:14-19).

"Commit to the Lord whatever you do, and He will establish your plans". (Proverbs 16:3).

"He [the Lord] did this so that all the peoples of the earth might know that the hand of the Lord is powerful and so that you might always fear the Lord your God". (Joshua 4:24).

Sin—What Is It?

Sin is anything that goes against God. By which we humans rebel and miss the Purpose of God, which He has for our lives. Sin is Satan's only weapon that he has to weaken us and cause us to be separated from God. Sin is the root of every problem that we encounter, to steer us off the Path of Righteous living.

Holding on to sin gives way for it to mutate in your heart, crowding out the Love of God, and when His Love is crowded out, all that is left is an empty, dark, and cold heart; where Satan loves to live. This is why it is important to continually feed your heart and mind the Word of God, warding off the coldness and darkness of Satan. Many times in my life, I have slipped into that darkness that Satan continually displays before me. However, since Jesus started walking by my side, pulling me away from the darkness that was trying to get a hold of me; giving me assurance and strength to walk out of the darkness and continue to walk in His Light of Life.

Still today, I slip, and still today, Jesus is right at my side, pulling me away from the darkness and keeping me in His Light, where I am sheltered in the safety of His Loving Embrace.This is why I treasure only the Word of God to Light my way before me (and within me), so I never, ever walk in the darkness of Satan. I will always proclaim this verse from the Book of Psalms:

"Your Word is a Lamp to my feet and a Light for my path". (Psalm 119:105).

This is just one verse that says it all about how Jesus has been with me all this time. Living God's Way is the only way to have His Light shine down on my path and in my life. I will never be alone. Therefore, I tell you this, give all your cares to Jesus and the darkness of Satan will fade away into the sunset. The Word of God also says:

"Therefore I tell you, do not worry about your life, what you will eat or drink; or what you will wear. Is not life more than food and the body more than clothes? Look at the birds of the air; they do not sow, reap, or store away in barns, and yet your Heavenly Father feeds them. Are you not much more valuable than they? Can any one of you by worrying add a single hour to your life?" (Matthew 6:25-27).

"For the pagans run after all these things, and your Heavenly Father knows that you need them. However, seek His Kingdom and His Righteousness, and all these things will be given to you as well. Therefore, do not worry about tomorrow, for tomorrow will worry about itself.

Each day has enough trouble of its own". (Matthew 6:32-34).

"Let your gentleness be evident to all. The Lord is near. Do not be anxious about anything, but in every situation, by prayer and petition, with thanksgiving, present your requests to God. And the peace of God, which transcends all understanding, will guard your hearts and your minds in Christ Jesus". (Philippians 4:5-7).

"Come to Me, all who are weary and burdened, and I will give you rest. Take my Yoke upon you and learn from Me, for I am Gentle and Humble in heart, and you will find rest for your souls. For My Yoke is easy and My burden is Light". *(Matthew 11:28-30).*

"Peace I leave with you; My Peace I give you. I do not give to you as the world gives. Do not let your hearts be troubled and do not be afraid". *(John 14:27)*.

"Let the peace of Christ rule in your hearts, since as members of one body you were called to peace. In addition, be thankful. Let the Message of Christ dwell among you richly as you teach and admonish one another with all wisdom through psalms, hymns, and songs from the Spirit, singing to God with gratitude in your hearts. And whatever you do, whether in word or deed, do it all in the name of the Lord Jesus, giving thanks to God the Father through Him". (Colossians 3:15-17).

"Now, may the Lord of peace, Himself give you peace at all times and in every way. The Lord be with all of you". (2 Thessalonians 3:16).

"Cast your cares on the Lord and He will sustain you; He will never let the righteous be shaken. However, you, God, will bring down the wicked into the pit of decay; the bloodthirsty and deceitful will not live out half their days. But as for me, I trust in you". (Psalm 55:22-23).

"In the same way, you who are younger, submit yourselves to your elders. All of you clothe yourselves with humility toward one another, because, 'God opposes the proud but shows favor to the humble'. Humble yourselves, therefore, under God's mighty hand, that He may lift you in due time. Cast all your anxiety on Him because He cares for you. Be alert and of a sober mind. Your enemy the devil prowls around like a roaring lion looking for someone to devour. Resist him, standing firm in the faith, because you know that the family of believers throughout the world is undergoing the same kind of sufferings". (1 Peter 5:5-9).

"Even though I walk through the darkest valley, I will fear no evil, for you are with me; your rod and your staff, they comfort me". (Psalm 23:4).

"When I am afraid, I put my trust in you". (Psalms 56:3).

"Have I not commanded you? Be strong and courageous. Do not be afraid; do not be discouraged, for the Lord your God will be with you wherever you go". (Joshua 1:9).

"Keep your lives free from the love of money and be content with what you have, because God has said; 'Never will I leave you; never will I forsake you'. So we say with confidence, 'The Lord is my helper; I will not be afraid. What can mere mortals do to me?". (Hebrews 13:5-6).

"For I am convinced that neither death nor life, neither angels nor demons, neither the present nor the future, nor any powers, neither height nor depth, nor anything else in all creation, will be able to separate us from the love of God that is in Christ Jesus our Lord". (Romans 8:38-39).

Living God's way is the only way to a worry-free living. There is no better companion than Jesus, our Lord and Savior. Jesus is the best friend that took the punishment for our sins so you could live with Him in His Father's house. When we finally walk through the Gates of the Kingdom of God that is when we will understand all the Ways of our Heavenly Father and His Son Jesus, which is a step into the Glorious Winner's Circle of the Peace and Love of God.

What opens the door to the Treasures of our Heavenly Father is to believe in His Son Jesus and turn away from the ways of this world. Then (and only then), you can enter into God's Presence. Being thankful will also affirm to the Father that you know the Truth that Jesus is the Light and that He shines away the darkness that is so present in this world. As in the Word of God it says: *"Through Him all things were made; without Him nothing was made that has been made. In Him was the Life of all mankind. The Light shines in the darkness, and the darkness has not overcome it". (John 1:3-5).*

"This is the Message we have heard from Him and declare to you: GOD IS LIGHT! In Him, there is no darkness at all. If we claim to have fellowship with Him and yet walk in the darkness, we lie and do not live out the Truth. However, if we walk in the Light, as He is in the Light, we have fellowship with one another, and the blood of Jesus, His Son, purifies us from all sin". (1 John 1:5-7).

Jesus, our Savior and Lord, is the security and assurance of the Goodness of His Father (who meets all basic needs) to live in an unsecure world that is always subjected to sin (anger, lust, and greed). You can rest in the knowledge of the only One (who controls your life) and trust that He will provide everything that you need.

Nothing you need more than the Love and Light of God our Father. As the Word of God says: *"He who dwells in the Shelter of the Most High will rest in the Shadow of the Almighty. I will say of the Lord, 'He is my Refuge and my Fortress, my God, in whom I trust'". (Psalm 91:1-2).*

"It is good to praise the Lord and make music to Your Name, O Most High,

to proclaim your Love in the morning and Your Faithfulness at night, to the music of the ten-stringed lyre and the melody of the harp. For you make me glad by Your Deeds, O Lord; I sing for joy at the works of Your Hands. How great are your works, O Lord, how profound Your Thoughts!" (Psalm 92:1-5).

"Come, let us sing for joy to the Lord; let us shout aloud to the Rock of our Salvation. Let us come before Him with thanksgiving and extol Him with music and song. For the Lord is the great God, the Great King above all gods. In His hand are the depths of the earth, and the mountain peaks belong to Him. The sea is His, for He made it, and His hands formed the dry land". (Psalm 95:1-5).

"This is the message we have heard from Him and declare to you: God is Light; in Him there is no darkness at all". (1 John 1:5).

You do not need to search for security when you have the Assurance (Security) in our Lord Jesus, who is also the Anchor that will keep you calm so that you can relax in the Peace of God and accomplish the goal that you need to finish the Journey to the Father's House. It is harder to try to do things on your own; you only become frustrated and confused. Just do what you have to do, and keep focus on God's Light and continue to stay connected with Him, through His Son, and you cannot go wrong. The Word of God says: *"You will keep in perfect peace him whose mind is steadfast, because he trusts in you. Trust in the Lord forever, for the Lord, the Lord, is the Rock Eternal. He humbles those who dwell on High; He lays the lofty city low; He levels it to the ground and casts it down to the dust". (Isaiah 26:3-5).*

"For our light and momentary troubles are achieving for us an Eternal Glory that far outweighs them all. So we fix our eyes not on what is seen, but on what is unseen, since what is seen is temporary, but what is unseen is Eternal". (2 Corinthians 4:17-18).

Let God choose which way you should go and always think with your heart of Jesus, not the heart of the world. Worship God in spite of what is going on around you, for God makes everything and all things for our good. It says in the Bible, *"Therefore, if anyone is in*

Christ, the new creation has come: The old has gone, the new is here!" (2 Corinthians 5:17).

*"He who was seated on the throne said, 'I am making everything new!' Then He said, **'Write this down, for these words are trustworthy and true'".***

(Revelation 21:5).

Fix your eyes on Jesus. Keep the door of your heart open for Jesus, and always delight in Jesus, for He will delight in you. The Word of God says:

"Take delight in the Lord, and He will give you the desires of your heart". (Psalm 37:4).

"The Lord your God is with you, the Mighty Warrior who saves. He will take great delight in You; in His Love He will no longer rebuke you, but will rejoice over you with singing". (Zephaniah 3:17).

Empty your mind of all the worldly trash and fill it with all of who God is:

"Set your minds on things above, not on earthly things". (Colossians 3:2).

"Rather, clothe yourselves with the Lord Jesus Christ, and do not think about how to gratify the desires of the flesh". (Romans 13:14).

"Do not be anxious about anything, but in everything—by prayer and petition—with thanksgiving, present your requests to God. In addition, the peace of God, which transcends all understanding, will guard your hearts and your minds in Christ Jesus. Finally, brothers (and sisters), whatever is True, whatever is Noble, whatever is Right, whatever is Pure, whatever is Lovely, whatever is Admirable—think about such things. Whatever you have learned or received or heard from me, or seen in me—put into practice. And the God of peace will be with you". (Philippians 4:6-9).

Leave all choices to God (having no regrets or doubts). The Journey is long and weary, so let God carry you through these days here on this earth. God will always give you rest and never will He turn you away in your time of need. All because He loves you, and He will never leave you. Always remember this Scripture: *"For God so loved the world that He gave His only begotten one and only Son, that whoever believes in Him shall not perish but have eternal life" (John 3:16).* This Scripture had gotten me through many times of abandonment and feelings of being unloved. I need not worry of those feelings of abandonment and being unloved, for my Lord Jesus is always with me and will never fail me.

God has many times told me not to worry about tomorrow, because each day has its own troubles, and He will be right at my side all the way, clearing any obstacles. God created each day with enough grace to handle the troubles. I know that I (we) cannot handle the troubles of each day on my own. When I tried, I failed very badly. I reached out for Jesus, and he took my hand and led me to safety. That is what it takes to humble yourself in complete trust that He is right there (an arm reach away) to rescue you from the troubles of this world. The moment you give God that trust, all worries and troubles start melting away and you are stronger in Him.

This is what the Bible says, *"Therefore, do not worry about tomorrow, for tomorrow will worry about itself. Each day has enough trouble of its own"*. *(Matthew 6:34).*

*"But He said to me; **'My grace is sufficient for you, for My power is made perfect in weakness'**. Therefore, I will boast all the more gladly about my weaknesses, so that Christ's Power may rest on me"*. *(2 Corinthians 12:9).*

"Trust in Him at all times, you people; pour out your hearts to Him, for God is our refuge". *(Psalm 62:8).*

I trust God that He will strengthen me in my times of weaknesses. I will hold on to His hand all the days of my journey here on this earth. God's grace is like a waterfall raining down on you when you trust in Him. There is no greater place to rest than in the compassionate arms of our Almighty God. Here are two Psalms that will help you step up to a committed relationship with our Almighty God the Father and our Lord Jesus Christ. These two are of many that sealed my commitment to my Star Team.

"As the deer pants for streams of water,
so my soul pants for you, my God.
My soul thirsts for God, for the living God.
When can I go and meet with God?
My tears have been my food day and night,
while people say to me all day long, 'Where is your God?'
These things I remember as I pour out my soul:
how I used to go to the house of God under the protection of the
Mighty One

with shouts of joy and praise among the festive throng.
Why, my soul, are you downcast?
Why so disturbed within me?
Put your hope in God, for I will yet praise Him, my Savior and my
God.
My soul is downcast within me;
therefore, I will remember you from the land of the Jordan,
the heights of Hermon—from Mount Mizar.
Deep calls to deep
in the roar of your waterfalls,
all your waves and breakers
have swept over me.
"By day, the Lord directs His love,
at night His song is with me—
a prayer to the God of my life.
I say to God my Rock, '
Why have you forgotten me?
Why must I go about mourning, oppressed by the enemy?'
My bones suffer mortal agony
as my foes taunt me, saying to me all day long, 'Where is your God?'
Why, my soul, are you downcast?
Why so disturbed within me?
Put your hope in God,
for I will yet praise Him,
my Savior and my God".
(Psalm 42:1-11).

"You, God, are my God, earnestly I seek you;
I thirst for you, my whole being longs for you, in a dry and parched
land where there is no water.

I have seen you in the sanctuary and beheld you power and your glory.

Because your love is better than life, my lips will glorify you.

I will praise you as long as I live, and in your name, I will lift up my hands.

I will be fully satisfied, as with the richest of foods, with singing lips, my mouth will praise you. On my bed, I remember you; I think of you through the watches of the night.

Because you are my help, I sing in the shadow of your wings.

I cling to you; your right hand upholds me.

Those who want to kill me will be destroyed; they will go down to the depths of the earth.

They will be given over to the sword, and become food for jackals.

But the king will rejoice in God; all who swear by God will glory in Him, while the mouths of liars will be silenced".

(Psalm 63:1-11).

As we live in this world that is filled with so many choices (temptations) that would bring death to our souls, we can need not worry, for we have the assurance of the one and only choice to deflect all of the weapons that Satan uses to bring down and make us feel unwanted and unloved. That choice is our Lord Jesus Christ, which is the only way we could secure our place in His Father's heart.

When we continue walking with Jesus and fixing our eyes always on Him, it will always crowd out the ways of Satan. This happens when we obey and commit to ways and commands of God, which will bring us life everlasting and the enemy (and his tactics) out of our lives. The Word of God tells us: *"For I command you today to love the Lord your God, to walk in obedience to Him, and to keep His Commands, Decrees and Laws; then you will live and increase, and the Lord you God will bless you in the land you are entering to possess. However, if your heart turns away and you are not obedient, and if you are drawn away to bow down to other gods and worship them, I declare to you this day that you will certainly be destroyed. You will not live long in the land you are crossing the Jordan to enter and possess. This day I call the heavens and the earth as witnesses against you that I have set before you, life and death, blessings and curses. Now choose life, so that you and your children may live and that you may love the Lord you God, listen to His voice, and hold fast to Him. For the Lord is your life, and He will give you many years in the land He swore to give to you fathers, Abraham, Isaac and Jacob". (Deuteronomy 30:16-20).*

These words that the Lord is speaking to us are very clear of what choice to make, between life and death. We all know that Life is being a committed and obedient follower of Jesus, and death is being a follower of Satan. Many of the things of this world are weapons that Satan uses to distract us, leading us to the death pit. However, if we continue to think of the things in Heaven, walk with Jesus, and keep our eyes fixed on Him, we will be able to stand strong, in obeying every command and instruction. Then Satan (and his ways) will fade out of sight and mind. There is no other defender than our Lord Jesus to help us to walk through this journey on this corrupted earth. Jesus tells us Himself in the Word of God:

"I am the Way, the Truth and the Life. No one gets to the Father, except through Me". *(John 14:6).*

"I am the Light of the world. Whoever follows Me will never walk in darkness, but will have the Light of Life". *(John 8:12).*

Along with these two Verses, I put into practice this verse: *"Rejoice in the Lord always. I will say it again: Rejoice! Let your gentleness be evident to all. The Lord is near. Do not be anxious about anything, but in every situation, by prayer and petition, with thanksgiving, present your requests to God. In addition, the peace of God, which transcends all understanding, will guard your hearts and your minds in Christ Jesus. Finally, brothers and sisters, whatever is True, whatever is Noble, whatever is Right, whatever is Pure, whatever is Lovely, whatever is Admirable, (if anything is Excellent or Praiseworthy), think about such things. Whatever you have learned or received or heard from me, or seen in me—put it into practice. And the God of Peace will be with you". (Philippians 4:4-9).*

The words I capitalized are all of who our Heavenly Father, His Son Jesus, and the Holy Spirit are. Thinking of them gives me (and you too) such joy in my heart that I could face anything that Satan hurls at me. I know now that God is Greater than any misfortune that is on this earth. I know that the day of the Lord is very, very, very near, and I am doing everything I can to be ready for Him. This is why I let go of all negative and unwholesome thoughts and things of this world, which made me boring in the sight of man. However, I will always remember who I am in God's Sight. Here what I tell myself and read in the Word of God:

I am > A child of His.

"Yet to all who did receive Him, to those who believed in His name, He gave the right to become children of God". (John 1:12).

I am > Chosen by Him.

"You are a chosen people, a royal priesthood, a holy nation, God's special possession that you may declare the praises of Him who called you out of darkness into His wonderful Light". (1 Peter 2:9).

I am > Loved by Him.

"For He chose us in Him before the creation of the world to be holy and blameless in His sight. In love He predestined us for adoption to sonship through Jesus Christ, in accordance with His pleasure and will—to the praise of His glorious grace, which He has freely given us in the One He loves". (Ephesians 1:4-6).

I am > Strengthened by Him.

"I can do all this through Him who gives me strength". (Philippians 4:13).

I am > Forgiven by Him.

"If we confess our sins, He is faithful and just and will forgive us our sins and purify us from all unrighteousness". (1 John 1:9).

I am > Filled with His Holy Spirit by Him.

"And hope does not put us to shame, because God's love has been poured out into our hearts through the Holy Spirit, who has been given to us". (Romans 5:5).

I am > At peace with Him through His Son.

"Therefore, since we have been justified through faith, we have peace with God through our Lord Jesus Christ". (Romans 5:1).

I am > Never alone.

"If you love me, keep my commands. And I will ask the Father, and He will give you another advocate to help you and be with you forever—the Spirit of Truth". (John 14:15-17a).

*"Keep your lives free from the love of money and be content with what you have, because God has said, **'Never will I leave you; never will I forsake you'".** (Hebrews 13:5).*

Negative thoughts were a real struggle for me. I never knew how to handle them. I did not have anyone to teach me how to reject the negative thoughts from my mind until I started reading my Bible. When I find myself bombarded with all the negative things that the enemy is throwing at me, I go to my Bible. With my Bible, I have Someone with me all the time, Someone that knows what I am going through and knows how to overcome these nasty, negative thoughts.

I now use the Bible as my Shield to repel those negative thoughts from my life. Oh yeah, those thoughts do try to come back to my mind at times of my weakness, but I am stronger now and I have my Star Team to help send those negative thoughts fleeing from my sight.

Satan may think he is clever, but he is weak when it comes to the Word of God; it really makes him slither away. This is why in the Bible, God is speaking these phrases many times: **'do not worry'** and **'do not be afraid'** and **'be of good courage'** and most often **'I will be with you and never leave you'.** These phrases have pulled me out of many despairs, so I could keep moving forward on my walk with my Lord Jesus. The struggles of this world seem minor when I know that my Star Team has my back at all times. Therefore, I tell you, to be sure not to worry about the things here on this earth and walk with comfort and trust that you will make it to that reward that our Heavenly Father has for us when we finally make it home to Him.

When David was fighting Goliath (see 1 Samuel 17:1-58), he defeated Goliath, because he had the Lord with him, and he trusted Him to help him fight this giant named Goliath. This is how I feel about my Star Team. David had a sling and a stone to knock Goliath down. My sling and stone is my Star Team. (The sling being the Father, His Son, and the Holy Spirit, and the stone being the Bible, the Word of God). Once I spoke aloud a Scripture to my giant (Satan), he would stop in his tracks and turn and flee from my sight. Because, Satan knows the Power in the Word of God, and Satan has no weapon against the power of God.

In this world, many people worry so much that it makes them ill. I know that this is true, because I used to be one of those people. I would continually worry about why people were always making fun of me and telling me that I was not smart enough to make it in this world.

However, back then, I did not read the Bible, and I did not pray as much as I do now. I did not know my Heavenly Father was seeing all that was going on and He took me out of the situation as soon as the time was right. I also knew people that died that worried too much.

The Bible talks about that worrying is a sin, and that it leads to death; both physical and spiritual. So I make sure that I am always in good with God and do everything He tells me to do and leave the worrying and struggles to Him; who knows how best to handle them.

Here, now, are some of the many verses that helps me, that will help you, to reject Satan's many arrows of negativity and keep you walking confidently with Jesus, right on through the struggles of this world. You need not memorize them; just reading them aloud is comforting and powerful enough. In addition, you will get to know all about my Star Team better and live how we are designed to live and breathe.

"Love is patient, love is kind. It does envy, it does not boast, it is not proud. It does not dishonor others, it is not self-seeking, it is not easily angered, and it keeps no record of wrongs. Love does not delight in evil but rejoices with the truth. It always protects, always trusts, always hopes, and always perseveres. However, where there are prophecies, they will cease; where there are tongues, they will be stilled; where there is knowledge, it will pass away. For we know in part and we prophesy in part, but when completeness comes, what is in part disappears. When I was a child, I talked like a child; I thought like a child, I reasoned like a child. When I became a man, I put the ways of childhood behind me. For now, we see only a reflection as in a mirror; then we shall see face-to-face. Now I know in part; then I shall know fully, even as I am fully known". (1 Corinthians 13:4-13).

"We know that we have come to know Him if we keep His commands. Whoever says, 'I know Him,' but does not do what He commands is a liar, and the Truth is not in that person. However, if anyone obeys His Word, love for God is truly made complete in them. This is how we know we are in Him: Whoever claims to live in Him must live as Jesus did". (1 John 2:3-6).

"Anyone who claims to be in the light but hates a brother or sister is still in the darkness. Anyone who loves their brother and sister lives in the light, and there is nothing in them to make them stumble. However, anyone who hates a brother or sister is in the darkness and walks around in the darkness. They do not know where they are going, because the darkness has blinded them". (1 John 2:9-11).

"A new Command I give you: Love one another. As I have loved you, so you must love one another. By this everyone will know that you are My disciples, if you love one another". *(John 13:34-35).*

"Follow God's example, therefore, as dearly loved children and walk in the way of love, just as Christ loved us and gave Himself up for us as a fragrant offering and sacrifice to God". (Ephesians 5:1-2).

"Keep your lives free from the love of money and be content with what you have, because God has said, 'Never will I leave you; never will I forsake you.' So we say with confidence; 'The Lord is my helper; I will not be afraid. What can mere mortals do to me?' (Hebrews 13:5-6).

"Submit yourselves, then, to God. Resist the devil, and he will flee from you. Come near to God and He will come near to you. Wash your hands, you sinners, and purify your hearts, you double-minded". (James 4:7-8).

"The Lord is my Light and my Salvation—whom shall I fear? The Lord is the stronghold of my Life—of whom shall I be afraid? When the wicked advance against me to devour me, it is my enemies and my foes who will stumble and fall. Though an army besiege me, my heart will not fear; though war breaks out against me, even then I will be confident. One thing I ask from the Lord, this is the only thing I seek: that I may dwell in the house of the Lord all the days of my life, to gaze on the beauty of the Lord and to seek Him in His temple. For in the day of trouble He will keep me safe in His dwelling; He will hide me in the shelter of His sacred tent and set me high upon a rock". (Psalm 27:1-5).

"Though my father and mother forsake me, the Lord will receive me. Teach me your way, Lord; lead me in a straight path because of my oppressors". (Psalm

27:10-11).

"I remain confident of this: I will see the goodness of the Lord in the land of the living. Wait for the Lord; be strong and take heart and wait for the Lord". (Psalm 27:13-14).

"In Christ Jesus you are all children of God through faith, for all of you who were baptized into Christ have clothed yourselves with Christ. There is neither Jew nor Gentile, neither slave nor free, nor is there male and female, for you are all one in Christ Jesus. If you belong to Christ, then you are Abraham's seed and heirs according to the promise". (Galatians 3:26-29).

"For the eyes of the Lord range throughout the earth to strengthen those whose hearts are fully committed to Him". (2 Chronicles 16:9a).

*"I say to you, **'Do not be terrified; do not be afraid of them. The Lord your God, who is going before you, will fight for you, as He did for you in Egypt, before your very eyes, and in the wilderness. There you saw how the Lord your God carried you, as a father carries his son, all the way you went until you reached this place'".** (Deuteronomy 1:30-31).*

"Finally, all of you, be like-minded, be sympathetic, love one another, and be compassionate and humble. Do not repay evil with evil or insult with insult. On the contrary, repay evil with blessing, because to this you were called so that you may inherit a blessing. For, whoever would love life and see good days must keep their tongue from evil and their lips from deceitful speech. They must turn from evil and do good; they must seek peace and pursue it. For the eyes of the Lord are on the righteous and His ears are attentive to their prayer, but the face of the Lord is against those who do evil. Who is going to harm you if you are eager to do good?" (1 Peter 3:8-13).

"The Lord your God is with you, the Mighty Warrior who saves. He will take great delight in you; in His love He will no longer rebuke you, but will rejoice over you with singing". (Zephaniah 3:17).

"The Lord is my shepherd, I lack nothing. He makes me lie down in green pastures, He leads me beside quiet waters, He refreshes my soul. He guides me along the right paths for His Name's sake. Even though I walk through the darkest valley, I will fear no evil, for You are with me; Your Rod and Your Staff, they comfort me. You prepare a table before me in the presence of my enemies. You anoint my head with oil; my cup overflows. Surely your goodness and love

will follow me all the days of my life, and I will dwell in the house of the Lord forever". (Psalm 23:1-6).

"Jesus said to them, **'Very truly I tell you, it is not Moses who has given you the bread from Heaven, but it is My Father who gives you the true bread from Heaven. For the Bread of God is the Bread that comes down from Heaven and gives life to the world'.** *'Sir,' they said, 'always give us this bread'. Then Jesus declared,* **'I am the Bread of life. Whoever comes to Me will never go hungry, and whoever believes in Me will never be thirsty. But, as I told you, you have seen Me and still you do not believe. All those the Father gives Me will come to Me, and whoever comes to Me I will never drive away. For I have come down from Heaven not to do My will but to do the will of Him who sent Me. In addition, this is the will of Him who sent Me; that I shall lose none of all those He has given Me, but raise them up at the last day. For My Father's will is that everyone who looks to the Son and believes in Him shall have Eternal Life, and I will raise them up at the last day'".** *(John 6:32-40).*

"In the same way, you who are younger, submit yourselves to your elders. All of you, clothe yourselves with humility toward one another, because; 'God opposes the proud but shows favor to the humble'. Humble yourselves, therefore, under God's mighty hand that He may lift you up in due time. Cast all your anxiety on Him because He cares for you. Be alert and of sober mind. Your enemy the devil prowls around like a roaring lion looking for someone to devour. Resist him, standing firm in the faith, because you know that the family of believers throughout the world is undergoing the same kind of sufferings. And the God of all Grace, who called you to His Eternal Glory in Christ—after you have suffered a little while—will Himself restore you and make you strong, firm and steadfast. To Him be the power forever and ever. Amen". (1 Peter 5:5-11).

"Do not let your hearts be troubled. You believe in God; believe also in Me. My Father's house has many rooms; if that were not so, would I have told you that I am going there to prepare a place for you? And if I go and prepare a place for you, I will come back and take you to be with Me so that you also may be where I am. You know the way to the place where I am going'. *Thomas said to Him, 'Lord, we do not know where You are going, so how can we know the way? Jesus answered,* **'I am the way and the truth**

and the life. No one comes to the Father except through Me. If you really know Me, you will know my Father as well. From now on, you do know Him and have seen Him'". (John 14:1-7).

"*Rejoice in the Lord always. I will say it again: Rejoice! Let your gentleness be evident to all. The Lord is near. Do not be anxious about anything, but in every situation, by prayer and petition, with thanksgiving, present your requests to God; and the peace of God, which transcends all understanding, will guard your hearts and your minds in Christ Jesus. Finally, brothers and sisters, whatever is True, whatever is Noble, whatever is Right, whatever is Pure, whatever is Lovely, whatever is Admirable (if anything is Excellent or Praiseworthy), think about such things. Whatever you have learned or received or heard from Me, or seen in Me, put it into practice. And the God of Peace will be with you". (Philippians 4:4-9).*

"*Let the Peace of Christ rule in your hearts, since as members of one body you were called to Peace. Be thankful. Let the Message of Christ dwell among you richly as you teach and admonish one another with all wisdom through psalms, hymns, and songs from the Spirit, singing to God with gratitude in your hearts. And whatever you do, whether in word or deed, do it all in the Name of the Lord Jesus, giving thanks to God the Father through Him". (Colossians 3:15-17).*

"*Open the gates that the righteous nation may enter, the nation that keeps faith. You will keep in perfect peace those whose minds are steadfast, because they trust in You. Trust in the Lord forever, for the Lord, the Lord Himself, is the Rock eternal". (Isaiah 26:2-4).*

"*And my God will meet all your needs according to the riches of His Glory in Christ Jesus. To our God and Father be Glory forever and ever. Amen". (Philippians 4:19-20).*

"*Therefore, I tell you, do not worry about your life, what you will eat or drink; or about your body, what you will wear. Is not life more than food and the body more than clothes? Look at the birds of the air; they do not sow, reap, or store away in barns, and yet your Heavenly Father feeds them. Are you not much more valuable than they are? Can any one of you by worrying add a single hour to your life?" (Matthew 6:25-27).*

"*So, do not worry, saying; 'What shall we eat?' or 'What shall we drink?' or 'What shall we wear?' For the pagans run after all these things, and you Heavenly*

Father knows that you need them. However, seek first His kingdom and His righteousness, and all these things will be given to you as well. Therefore, do not worry about tomorrow, for tomorrow will worry about itself. Each day has enough trouble of its own". (Matthew 6:31-34).

"Those who live according to the flesh have their minds set on what the flesh desires; but those who live in accordance with the Spirit have their minds set on what the Spirit desires. The mind governed by the flesh is death, but the mind governed by the Spirit is life and peace. The mind governed by the flesh is hostile to God; it does not submit to God's law, nor can it do so. Those who are in the realm of the flesh cannot please God". (Romans 8:5-7).

"My son, do not let wisdom and understanding out of your sight, preserve sound judgment and discretion; they will be life for you, an ornament to grace your neck. Then you will go on your way safely, and your foot will not stumble. When you lie down, you will not be afraid; when you lie down, your sleep will be sweet. Have no fear of sudden disaster or of the ruin that overtakes the wicked, for the Lord will be at your side and will keep your foot from being snared". (Proverbs 3:21-26).

"Whoever dwells in the Most High will rest in the shadow of the Almighty. I will say of the Lord, 'He is my refuge and my fortress, my God, in whom I trust. Surely, He will save you from the fowler's snare and from the deadly pestilence. He will cover you with His feathers, and under His wings, you will find refuge; His faithfulness will be your shield and rampart. You will not fear the terror of night, nor the arrow that flies by day, nor the pestilence that stalks in the darkness, nor the plague that destroys at midday. A thousand may fall at your side, ten thousand at your right hand, but it will not come near you. You will only observe with your eyes and see the punishment of the wicked. If you say, 'The Lord is my refuge,' and you make the Most High your dwelling, no harm will overtake you, no disaster will come near your tent". (Psalm 91:1-10).

"Peace I leave with you; My peace I give you. I do not give to you as the world gives. Do not let your hearts be troubled and do not be afraid". *(John 14:27).*

"Therefore, go and make disciples of all nations, baptizing them in the Name of the Father and of the Son and the Holy Spirit, and teaching them to obey everything I have commanded you. And surely I am with you always, to the very

end of the age". (Matthew 28:19-20).

"For the sake of His Great Name the Lord will not reject His people, because the Lord was pleased to make you His own. As for me, far be it from me that I should sin against the Lord, by failing to pray for you. And I will teach you the way that is good and right, but be sure to fear the

Lord and serve Him faithfully with all your heart; consider what great things He has done for you. Yet, if you persist in doing evil, both you and your king will perish". (1 Samuel 12:22-25).

"So, do not fear, for I am with you; do not be dismayed, for I am your God. I will strengthen you and help you; I will uphold you with my righteous right hand. All who rage against you will surely be ashamed and disgraced; those who oppose you will have nothing and perish. Though you search for your enemies, you will not find them. Those who wage war against you will be nothing at all. For I am the Lord your God who takes hold of your right hand and says to you, 'Do not fear; I will help you'". (Isaiah 41:10-13).

"Do you not know? Have you not heard? The Lord is the everlasting God, the Creator of the ends of the earth. He will not grow tired or weary, and His understanding no one can fathom. He gives strength to the weary and increases the power of the weak. Even youths grow tired and weary, and young men stumble and fall; but those who hope in the Lord will renew their strength. They will soar on wings like eagles; they will run and not grow weary, they will walk and not be faint". (Isaiah 40:28-31).

"I will not leave you as orphans; I will come to you" *(John 14:18).*

"Be strong and courageous. Do not be afraid or terrified because of them, for the Lord your God goes with you; He will never leave you nor forsake you'". (Deuteronomy 31:6).

***"Though the mountain be shaken and the hills be removed, yet my 'unfailing love for you will not be shaken nor my covenant of peace be removed'"*,** *says the Lord, who has compassion on you". (Isaiah 54:10).*

"My flesh and my heart may fail, but God is the strength of my heart and my portion forever. Those who are far from you will perish; you destroy all who

are unfaithful to you. But as for me, it is good to be near God. I have made the Sovereign Lord my refuge; I will tell of all your deeds". (Psalm 73:26-28).

"God is our refuge and strength, an ever-present help in trouble. Therefore, we will not fear, though the earth gives way and the mountains fall into the heart of the sea, though its waters roar and foam and the mountains quake with their surging" (Psalm 46:1-3).

"God says: **'Be still and know I am God; I will be exalted among the nations, I will be exalted in the earth'".** (Psalm 46:10).

"For the Spirit God gave us, does not make us timid, but gives us power, love and self-discipline. So, do not be ashamed of the testimony about our Lord or of me His prisoner. Rather, join with me in suffering for the gospel, by the power of God. He has saved us and called us to a holy life, not because of anything we have done, but because of His own purpose and grace. This grace was given us in Christ Jesus before the beginning of time, but it has now been revealed through the appearance of our Savior, Christ Jesus, who has destroyed death and has brought life and immortality to light through the gospel". (2 Timothy 1:7-10).

"The Spirit you received does not make you slaves, so that you live in fear again; rather, the Spirit you received brought about your adoption to son-ship. And by Him we cry, 'Abba, Father.' The Spirit Himself testifies with our spirit that we are God's children. Now if we are children, then we are heirs—heirs of God and co-heirs with Christ, if indeed we share in His sufferings in order that we may also share in His glory". (Romans 8:15-17).

"Whoever dwells in the shelter of the Most High will rest in the shadow of the Almighty. I will say of the Lord, 'He is my refuge and my Fortress, my God, in whom I trust. Surely, He will save you from the deadly pestilence. He will cover you with His feathers, and under His wings, you will find refuge; His faithfulness will be your shield and rampart. You will not fear the terror of night, nor the arrow that flies by day, nor the pestilence that stalks in the darkness, nor the plague that destroys at midday. A thousand may fall at your side, ten thousand at your right hand, but it will not come near you. You will only observe with your eyes and see the punishment of the wicked'". (Psalm 91:1-8).

"If you say; 'The Lord is my refuge,' and you make the Most High your dwelling, no harm will overtake you, no disaster will come near Your tent. For He will command His angels concerning you to guard you in all Your Ways; they* *will lift you up in their hands, so that you will not strike your foot against a stone"* (Psalm 91:9-12).

"My son, do not let wisdom and understanding out of your sight, preserve sound judgment and discretion; they will be life for you, an ornament to Grace your neck. Then you will go on your way safely, and your foot will not stumble. When you lie down, you will not be afraid; when you lie down, your sleep will be sweet. Have no fear of sudden disaster or of the ruin that overtakes the wicked, for the Lord will be at your side and will keep your foot from being snared". (Proverbs 3:21-26).

"When I am afraid, I put my trust in you. In God, whose word I praise—in God I trust and am not afraid. What can mere mortals do to me? (Psalm 56:3-4).

"In God, whose word I praise, in the Lord, whose word I praise—in God I trust and am not afraid. What can man do to me? I am under vows to you, my God; I will present my thank offerings to you. For you have delivered me from death and my feet from stumbling that I may walk before God in the light of life". (Psalm 56:10-13)).

"Love the Lord, all His faithful people! The Lord preserves those who are true to Him, but the proud He pays back in full. Be strong and take heart, all you who hope in the Lord". (Psalm 31:23-24).

"So we say with confidence; 'The Lord is my Helper; I will not be afraid. What can mere mortals do to me?'" (Hebrews 13:6).

"The Eternal God is your refuge, and underneath are the everlasting arms. He will drive out your enemies before you, saying; 'Destroy them!'". (Deuteronomy 33:27).

"For God, who said; 'Let light shine out of darkness', made His light shine in our hearts to give us the light of the knowledge of God's Glory displayed in the face of Christ. However, we have this treasure in jars of clay to show that this all-surpassing power is from God and not from us.

We are hard pressed on every side, but not crushed; perplexed, but not in despair; persecuted, but not abandoned; struck down, but not destroyed". (2 Corinthians 4:6-9).

"And we know that in all things God works for the good of those who love

Him, who have been called according to His purpose". (Romans 8:28).

"*Though I walk in the midst of trouble, you preserve my life. You stretch out Your hand against the anger of my foes; with your right hand, you save me. The Lord will vindicate me; you love, Lord, endures forever—do not abandon the works of your hands". (Psalm 138:7-8).*

"*I lift my eyes to the mountains—where does my help come from? My help comes from the Lord, the Maker of heaven and earth. He will not let your foot slip—He who watches over you will not slumber; indeed, He who watches over Israel will neither slumber nor sleep". (Psalm 121:1-4).*

"*Since then, you have been raised with Christ, set your hearts on things above, where Christ is, seated at the right hand of God. Set your minds on things above, not on earthly things. For you died, and your life is now hidden with Christ in God. When Christ, who is your life, appears, then you also will appear with Him in glory. Put to death, therefore, whatever belongs to your earthly nature: sexual immorality, impurity, lust, evil desires and greed, which is idolatry. Because of these, the Wrath of God is coming". (Colossians 3:1-6).*

"*Guard your steps when you go to the house of God. Go near to listen rather than to offer the sacrifice of fools, who do not know that they do wrong. Do not be quick with your mouth; do not be hasty in your heart to utter anything before God. God is in heaven and you are on earth, so let your words be few. A dream comes when there are many cares, and many words mark the speech of a fool. When you make a vow to God, do not delay to fulfill it. He has no pleasure in fools; fulfill your vow. It is better not to make a vow than to make one and not fulfill it. Do not let your mouth lead you into sin. (Ecclesiastes 5:1-6).*

"*Much dreaming and many words are meaningless. Therefore, fear God". (Ecclesiastes 5:1-7).*

"*Finally, brothers and sisters, whatever is True, whatever is Noble, whatever is Right, whatever is Pure, whatever is Lovely, whatever is Admirable—if anything is Excellent or Praiseworthy—think about such things. Whatever you have learned or received or heard from me, or seen in me—put into practice. And the God of peace will be with you". (Philippians 4:8-9).*

"*Finally, be strong in the Lord and in His Mighty Power. Put on the full Armor of God, so that you take your stand against the devil's schemes. For our struggle is not against flesh and blood, but against the rulers, against the authorities, against the powers of this dark world and against the spiritual forces of evil in the heavenly realms. Therefore, put on the full Armor of God, so that when the day of evil comes, you may be able to stand your ground, and after you have done everything, to stand your ground, and after you have done everything, to stand. Stand firm then, with the Belt of Truth buckled around your waist, with the Breastplate of Righteousness in place, and with your feet fitted with the Readiness that comes from the Gospel of Peace. In addition to all this, take up the Shield of Faith, with which you can extinguish all the flaming arrows of the evil one. Take the Helmet of Salvation and the Sword of the Spirit (which is the Word of God). In addition, pray in the Spirit on all occasions with all kinds of prayers and requests. With this in mind, be alert and always keep praying for all the Lord's people. Pray also for me, that whenever I speak, words may be given me so that I will fearlessly make known the mystery of the Gospel". (Ephesians 6:10-19).*

In this world, we will have concerns that are bidding for our attention. That is why we are to be always to be wearing the Armor of God, to be ready for those concerns and face them with the power of our Lord Jesus (who by the way overcame all the concerns of this world). What better example can we have? The answer is, none. Our Lord Jesus says it best when He says: **'I am the Way, the Truth and the Life. No one comes to the Father except through Me'".** *(John 14:6).*

In addition, He also says: **"'I am the Light of the world. Whoever follows Me will never walk in darkness, but will have the Light of Life'".** *(John 8:12).*

As long as we are here on this earth, we will have worries and concerns. Nevertheless, we just have to remember Jesus overcame this world, and He is with us (always) to help us when we are frazzled. As it says in the Word of God: **"'I have told you these things, so that in Me you may have Peace. In this world, you will have trouble. However, take heart! I have overcome the world'".** *(John 16:33).*

We must always remember that Jesus has gone through everything that we are going through; and He did not sin, He overcame. Acknowledging this every time we go through a trial or get anxious makes the worries and anxieties fade away so that Satan cannot loosen the grip we have to our Lord Jesus, which frees us to do all that our Heavenly Father instructs us to do.

Keep on clinging to Jesus. Once that I started clinging to Jesus, everything I thought was worrisome was not that worrisome, and I could live in the freedom of the Love and Peace of God. In other words, I stopped being a backseat driver; telling Jesus what to do and letting Him do all the driving and thinking. My life is in the Hands of my Star Team. My Heavenly Father knows my heart and mind, and He knows how much I can handle to not get me so frazzled. I will always hold on to these verses from the Book of Joshua: *"Be strong and very courageous. Be careful to obey all the law my servant Moses gave you; do not turn from it to the right or to the left that you may be successful where you go. Keep this Book of the Law always on your lips; meditate on it day and night, so that you may be careful to do everything written in it. Then you will be prosperous and successful. Have I not Commanded you? Be strong and courageous. Do not be afraid; do not be discouraged, for the Lord your God will be with you wherever you go"*. *(Joshua 1:7-9)*.

In addition to all these Scriptures, God is always telling me: *"Be still and know I am God"* *(Psalm 46:10)*. This is always a reminder that He wants me to read my Bible and listen to what He has to say to me and the Instructions He has me do. The Bible is the only weapon to defeat the ways of Satan, so start today and watch how Satan will go fleeing from you.

This book is to help you get on track to a life of spending time with your Heavenly Father and walking with His Son Jesus through all of the difficult times that this earth has. As you are walking along this Journey, do not be afraid to ask for help from the One that is always with you. That is what He here with you, to be always dependent on Him, who cares and comforts. From the first step, I took with Jesus; I was on my way transforming into a woman of God, seeking and following Him and Him alone. I see only my Star Team, walking every step with me. I know that my Heavenly Father is continually working in my life. So I said "yes" to Him (the One who made me) to teach me, to tell me, and to use me for whatever He wants to do with me. I am fully committed and willing to go that extra mile for my Star Team, the team that will go that extra mile for me helping me through the troubles of this world. Have fun getting to know your Heavenly Father and His Son Jesus Christ. Let us not forget the Holy Spirit, who makes sure you stay on the righteous path and follow in our Lord's steps.

Thank you for taking out the time to listen to what I have to say about my Lord Jesus. Bless you all and have fun walking with Jesus, who is right beside you, reading along with you. God really does love you. Always remember these very important Scriptures; it will keep you in step:

"For God loved the world that He gave His one and only Son that whoever believes in Him shall not perish but have eternal life". (John 3:16).

"Blessed is the one who trusts in the Lord, whose confidence is in Him. They will be like a tree planted by the water that sends out its roots by the stream. It does not fear when heat comes; its leaves are always green. It has no worries in a year of drought and never fails to bear fruit". (Jeremiah 17:7-8).

To trust God is to live in His peace.

To live in the peace of God is to seek who He is.

To seek God is to obey His commands.

To obey God is to love Him.

To love God is to find Wisdom and Knowledge.

To find Wisdom and Knowledge is to receive the Grace of God.

There is no one or nowhere in this world that you will find the satisfaction that God has given us. Therefore, open your Bibles, get on your knees, and learn how our Loving and Compassionate God desires us to live. This is what God is waiting for us to do. Life on this earth will be much easier to handle.

Epilogue

I will end this book with a Psalm that remind you to always walk in the Ways of God:

"Whoever dwells in the Shelter of the Most High

will rest in the Shadow of the Almighty.

I will say of the Lord, 'He is my Refuge and my Fortress,

my God, in whom I trust'.

Surely He will save you from the fowler's snare

and from the deadly pestilence.

He will cover you with His Feathers, and under His Wings you
will find Refuge;

His Faithfulness will be your Shield and Rampart.

You will not fear the terror of night, nor the arrow that flies by
day,

nor the pestilence that stalks in the darkness,

nor the plague that destroys at midday.

A thousand may fall at your side, ten thousand at your right hand,

but it will not come near you.

You will only observe with your eyes and see the punishment of the
wicked.

If you say, 'The Lord is my Refuge', and you make the Most High
your dwelling,

no harm will overtake you, no disaster will come near your tent.

For He will Command His angels concerning you to guard in all
your ways;

they will lift you up in their hands, so that you will not strike your foot against a stone.

You will tread on the lion and the cobra; you will trample the great lion and the serpent.

'Because He loves Me', says the Lord,

'I will rescue him; I will be with him in trouble,

I will deliver him and honor him.

With long life I will satisfy him and show him My Salvation'".

(Psalm 91:1-13).

Therefore, I will all this time follow in the Ways of my Star Team in every situation. I will always love and trust my Star Team to be walking right beside me, giving me the courage and strength to keep moving forward. Thank you, Star Team.

Keep seeking to know, love, and trust God. May the Grace of God be with all of you.

I pray this in Jesus's name. Amen.

www.ingramcontent.com/pod-product-compliance
Lightning Source LLC
Chambersburg PA
CBHW070858120626
46546CB00001B/46